John Elliott Cairnes

Some leading principles of political economy newly expounded

John Elliott Cairnes

Some leading principles of political economy newly expounded

ISBN/EAN: 9783337134662

Printed in Europe, USA, Canada, Australia, Japan

Cover: Foto ©Suzi / pixelio.de

More available books at **www.hansebooks.com**

SOME LEADING PRINCIPLES

OF

POLITICAL ECONOMY

NEWLY EXPOUNDED.

BY

J. E. CAIRNES, M.A.,

EMERITUS PROFESSOR OF POLITICAL ECONOMY IN UNIVERSITY COLLEGE, LONDON.

NEW YORK:
HARPER & BROTHERS, PUBLISHERS,
FRANKLIN SQUARE.

1874.

PREFACE.

THOUGH the following work is an attempt to recast some considerable portion of Political Economy, I should be sorry it were regarded as in any sense antagonistic in its attitude toward the science built up by the labors of Adam Smith, Malthus, Ricardo, and Mill. On the contrary, my hope is that it will—should its reasonings find acceptance—strengthen, in some sensible degree, and add consistence to that fabric. As regards those assumptions respecting human character and the physical conditions of external nature which constitute the ultimate premises of economic science, the position I have taken is identical with that of the four great writers I have named; and I have endeavored also to follow the method of combined deduction and verification by comparison with facts, which was theirs, and which is, as I believe, the only fruitful, or indeed possible method in economic inquiry. Nor do the final conclusions which I have reached differ very widely on any important points from those at which they had arrived. The points on which I have ventured to join issue with them are what, in Bacon's language, may be called the *axiomata media* of the science—those intermediate principles by means of which the detailed results are connected with the higher causes which produce them. If I have not deceived myself, there is in this portion of Political Economy, as at present generally received, no small proportion of faulty material; and the present work may be regarded as an attempt, so far as it goes, to replace this element of weakness with matter better fitted to endure the strain of modern criticism.

The nature of the undertaking has brought me, much oftener than I could have wished, into collision with more than one living writer for whose abilities and acquirements I feel high respect, and with whose practical aims I not unfrequently strongly sympathize; and in particular I have been compelled in several parts of the book to express my strong dissent from some of the views of my friend Mr. W. T. Thornton. Mr. Thornton, in his work on "Labor," has contributed much, for which economists will be grateful, to the elucidation of the relations between labor and capital in this country; but he has also taken up certain theoretic positions which it seems to me are fundamentally erroneous. When my path has lain across these, I have not hesitated to challenge them, using here the same freedom which Mr. Thornton has himself employed when criticising the views of preceding writers. I trust that I have also profited by the example he has set me of courtesy toward opponents.

Though the main purpose of the book is, as I have already intimated, to aid the improvement of economic theory, I have nevertheless embraced every opportunity that offered of bringing theoretic doctrines into comparison with the facts presented by modern industry and commerce. I have in this way been led to examine the power and pretensions of Trades-Unions, the efficacy of Strikes, and other practical questions involved in the relations of labor and capital; and, in the portion of the book devoted to International Trade, I have, with the same view, considered in some detail the present position of the external trade of the United States, as well as the system of Protection which, in defiance alike of theory and experience, that country has so strangely adopted.

I can not conclude these remarks without once again gratefully acknowledging my deep obligations to my friend Professor Nesbitt, who has, both by supervision of the work while in progress, and by correction of the proofs as it passed through the press, very materially contributed to its now at length being brought to a close.

J. E. CAIRNES.

KIDBROOK PARK ROAD, S.E., *March*, 1874.

CONTENTS.

PART I.—VALUE.

CHAPTER I.
PRELIMINARY.

	PAGE
§ 1. Meaning of Value	11
Value and price	12
"A sum of values"	12
When a change in exchanging relations is described as a rise or fall of commodity A, rather than as a fall or rise of commodity B, what is meant?	13
§ 2. Three problems concerning Value	14
I. Conditions essential to the existence of value	14
II. Causes which determine "market values"	14
III. Causes which determine "normal values"	14
§ 3. Problem I.—Conditions essential to the existence of value	14
§ 4. Relation of value to utility.—Professor Jevons's theory examined	16

CHAPTER II.
SUPPLY AND DEMAND.

§ 1. Fundamental truth in connection with Supply and Demand	22
§ 2. Analysis of the phenomena	23
Supply and Demand strictly analogous conceptions	25
Mr. Mill's criticism on this point unfounded	26
§ 3. Demand, as "quantity demanded," occasionally a convenient, but not the proper sense of the term	27
§ 4. Supply and Demand, as aggregates, are strictly interdependent phenomena, and increase or diminish together	30
§ 5. Similarly, Production and Consumption are interdependent phenomena. This doctrine not irreconcilable with the existence of an idle rich class who are consumers merely	31
Case of foreign residents engaged in no industry, but simply expending and consuming	33
§ 6. Supply and Demand, as related to particular commodities	35
In this sense *not* interdependent phenomena: either may increase or diminish irrespective of the other	36
What is meant by the equality or inequality of Supply and Demand?	36
§ 7. The supply of a commodity tends to adapt itself to the demand at the normal price	37
	41

CHAPTER III.
NORMAL VALUE.

§ 1. Nature of Normal Value	43
§ 2. Current theories, which confine normal value to exchanges governed by cost of production, too narrow	45
Mr. Mill's doctrine of Cost of Production	46
§ 3. Criticism of the received theory	48
§ 4. Examples of practical errors resulting from the received view	54

CONTENTS.

§ 5. Statement of the theory of Cost of Production as governing normal value 57
    Effective competition an indispensable condition in order to the action of the principle of cost 58
    Extent to which effective competition is actually realized in industrial communities 60
    Non-competing industrial groups 66
    Complication of results 69
    Nature of the law of "cost" 72
§ 6. Analysis and characterization of the constituents of "cost" 73
    The labor element of "cost" 75
    Relation of skill to "cost" and to "value" 76
    Nature of "abstinence" 80
    How far does "abstinence" stand in need of reward? 81
    The sacrifices involved in cost of production not necessarily undergone by distinct persons 83
    In computing cost of production, it is the average sacrifice that is to be taken account of 85
§ 7. Normal value as determined by Reciprocal Demand 87
    Nature of Reciprocal Demand as between nations and non-competing industrial groups 91
    Difference in the modes of action of Cost of Production and of Reciprocal Demand 93
    Probable effect of improved popular education on Reciprocal Demand, and, through Reciprocal Demand, on normal values, in this country. 95

CHAPTER IV.
MARKET VALUE

§ 1. Market Value, amenable to law 97
§ 2. Adam Smith's doctrine of Market Price 98
§ 3. Mr. Mill's doctrine 101
§ 4. Proposed theory of Market Price in wholesale markets 104
    Play of forces in the market 106
    "Proper market price" 107
    Function of Speculators 109
    Subordinate importance of the theory 110
§ 5. Prices in retail markets 112
    Capital in retail trade excessive 114
    Co-operative competition 115

CHAPTER V.
ON SOME DERIVATIVE LAWS OF VALUE.

§ 1. Character of the industry of new communities 117
    Action of the law of "diminishing productiveness" 118
§ 2. Course of price in meat and timber 119
§ 3. Course of price in the staple food 123
§ 4. Reciprocal movements in tillage and pasture 127
    Effects on the progress of rent 127
§ 5. Course of price in accessory products 128
§ 6. Adam Smith's insight 130
§ 7. Course of price in mineral products 131
§ 8. " " in manufactures 132
    " " in coarse and refined manufactures 135
§ 9. Derivative laws in fluctuations of the market 135
§ 10. Laws of fluctuation as affecting manufactures 137
§ 11. " " as affecting raw products 141
    " " as affecting the staple food of a people 142
§ 12. Market fluctuations differ in intensity and in duration 143
    In vegetable products more intense 143
    In animal products of longer duration 144
    Fish and game 145

PART II.—LABOR AND CAPITAL.

CHAPTER I.
THE RATE OF WAGES.

	PAGE
§ 1. The problem of relative wages solved by the theory of value, but not that of positive wages.	149
§ 2. Reasons for treating apart labor and commodities as subjects of exchange value.	150
§ 3. Are we justified in speaking of a "general" rate of wages? Mr. Longe's objection considered.	154
§ 4. Present state of the controversy.	157
§ 5. The Wages-fund theory.	159
§ 6. Positions taken by the disputants on either side.	161
§ 7. Mr. Longe's doctrine that "the demand for commodities determines the quantity of wealth spent in the wages of laborers" considered.	162
§ 8. Exposition of the Wages-fund theory.	167
Causes determining the amount of investment.	168
Three leading constituents of capital—Fixed Capital, Raw Material, and Wages-fund. Causes determining the proportions in which they combine.	170
Mode in which the supply of labor affects the amount of the Wages-fund	173
§ 9. Law of the growth of of the Wages-fund.	174
Social consequences.	177
§ 10. Industrial crises—effects on the Wages-fund.	178
§ 11. Mr. Thornton's objections to the Wages-fund doctrine considered.	180

CHAPTER II.
DEMAND FOR COMMODITIES.

§ 1. Two conditions of Demand for Commodities.	189
1. Where, aggregate expenditure remaining the same, a change takes place in the direction of demand.	189
2. Where aggregate expenditure, and therefore the aggregate demand for commodities, undergoes increase.	189
§ 2. Action on the Wages-fund of changes in the direction of the demand for commodities.	190
Where competition is effective.	190
Where competition is not effective.	191
International effects produced by changes in the direction of demand.	193
§ 3. Action on the Wages-fund of an increase in the aggregate demand for commodities.	194
§ 4. Summary of results.	199
§ 5. Wages and prices.	200
Incomplete theories.	201
§ 6. Statement of the relation between wages and prices.	203
Corresponding movements.	204
§ 7. I. Case of an increase in wages from a growth of capital more rapid than of population, while the productiveness of industry remains unaltered.	205
§ 8. II. Case of an increase of wages due to improved industrial processes, or to an extension of trade.	206
§ 9. III. Case of an increase of wages due to an enlarged supply of money.	207
Principle connecting wages and prices.	209
§ 10. Monetary paradox.	210

CHAPTER III.

TRADES-UNIONISM.—NO. I.

§ 1. Question of the limitation of the Wages-fund fundamental in Trades-Union controversy.. 214
§ 2. Economic limits of the Wages-fund.................................... 215
    Law of the tendency of profits to a minimum....................... 216
    Bearing of this on the question of limitation....................... 217
§ 3. The character of the limitation not such as to exclude Trades-Union action 219
    Proper province for this action....................................... 224
    Practical utility of strikes depends upon the ability of leaders to discriminate states of the market.. 225
    How far is this ability likely to be acquired....................... 226
§ 4. The foregoing conclusions applicable to countries in which profits are above the minimum; for example, the United States............... 230
§ 5. Recent advance in wages, how far due to Trades-Union action......... 231
§ 6. Power of capitalists by combination to control the labor market...... 233
§ 7. Relation of wages to profits... 235
    Mr. Brassey's doctrine as to the uniform cost of labor examined... 238

CHAPTER IV.

TRADES-UNIONISM.—NO. II.

§ 1. Three methods by which Trades-Unions may operate on the rate of wages 242
§ 2. Their mode of acting on the supply of labor......................... 243
    Effectual for its immediate purpose; but incapable of being made a means for the social advancement of laborers....................... 244
§ 3. Mode of acting on the rate of wages by "making work"............. 249
    Theoretical grounds of this mode of action plausible, but fallacious... 249
    Mr. Thornton's view stated and examined.......................... 249
    Notion that work and wages are convertible expressions............ 254
    Practical refutation... 255
    Notion that the quantity of work to be done at any given time is fixed 256
    Social work indefinite.. 257
    True and only limit to the employment of labor.................... 257
§ 4. Examples of Trades-Union rules for "making work"................ 258
    Analysis and characterization of such rules........................ 260
    Principle of this policy not confined to Trades-Unions............ 261

CHAPTER V.

PRACTICAL DEDUCTIONS FROM THE FOREGOING PRINCIPLES.

§ 1. Socialistic objections to distribution determined by economic principles. 263
§ 2. Maxims of distributive justice... 263
    "To each according to his wants".................................... 264
    "To each according to his works".................................... 264
    "To each according to his sacrifice"................................. 264
§ 3. Examination of their applicability to actual problems............... 266
§ 4. Distribution of wealth under the action of economic laws, how far coincident with the principles of abstract justice................... 268
§ 5. Our present system of industry defensible on utilitarian grounds..... 270
    Need of a large accumulated capital................................. 271
    Failure of socialist schemes to provide for this.................... 272
§ 6. Prospects offered to the laboring classes under the present *régime* of industry.. 273
    Productiveness of industry, how related to profits and wages...... 275
    Coincidence of a slight increase in the rates of wages and profits with a greatly increased productiveness of general industry explained.... 277
    The phenomenon, in what way related to rent...................... 279
    Discouraging result of this aspect of the case....................... 280

	PAGE
§ 7. No considerable improvement in the laborer's condition possible while he remains a mere recipient of wages......................................	284
Recognition of this truth by socialistic writers; but their expedients for meeting the difficulty indefensible.............................	285
§ 8. Practical problem: To attain the socialistic end by means compatible with existing institutions..	287
Difficulties moral and intellectual, not physical............	287
§ 9. Co-operation offers the sole escape from a hopeless position............	289
Present prospects of co-operation	290
§ 10. An objection answered...	291

PART III.—INTERNATIONAL TRADE.

CHAPTER I.

DOCTRINE OF COMPARATIVE COST.

§ 1. Are there grounds for a separate theory of *International* trade?..........	297
Rationale of trade in general...	298
Special province of International trade.................................	300
Impediments to the movement of capital and labor between nations...	302
§ 2. Character and relative importance of such impediments	305
§ 3. Development of the doctrine of comparative cost of production..........	307
"Comparative cost" to be understood as measured by the sacrifices undergone, *not* by the wages and profits received, by producers	310
Costs compared are the respective costs in each country of the exchanged commodities, *not* the costs of the same commodity in the exchanging countries...	312
Examples of the practical working of the principle in the trade of the world...	312
Verification of abstract theory in the occurrences following the gold discoveries...	315
Trade between New York and Barbados..............................	316
Character of a large portion of International trade obscured by erroneous conceptions of cost...	317

CHAPTER II.

INTERNATIONAL TRADE IN ITS RELATION TO THE RATE OF WAGES.

§ 1. Theory of International trade as expounded by Ricardo and Mill, not invulnerable.......................................	319
The proximate conditions of trade are prices, not cost..................	319
"Every transaction in commerce is an independent transaction ".....	320
Reply from Ricardo's stand-point.......................................	321
Criticism of this reply...	322
§ 2. Proposed modification of the theory of International trade..............	323
§ 3. Prevalent opinion as to the connection between wages and International trade..	324
In conflict with the received economic doctrine as expounded by Ricardo	325
Grounds of the popular view, superficial and untenable...............	326
§ 4. Illustrative examples showing the effects of *partial* movements in wages on International trade..	327
Sugar cultivation in Queensland....................................	329
Effects on the external trade of England of a fall of wages in some leading branch of manufacture, discussed...............................	330
§ 5. Nature of the connection between *general* wages and foreign trade......	334
Illustration offered by Australian experience...........................	335
Hypothetical illustration showing the nature of the connection as it would be developed in given circumstances in England.............	337
General wages and foreign trade connected as co-ordinate effects of a common cause..	339

CHAPTER III.

INTERNATIONAL VALUES.

§ 1. Statement of the problem 342
§ 2. Doctrine of international values as set forth in the received text-books, not reconcilable with that of Cost of Production, to be found in the same authorities 343
But reconcilable with the view of cost here contended for 344
§ 3. Practical criterion showing the relation of exchange value to cost 345
Application of this criterion to the circumstances of the leading commercial countries 347
§ 4. Functions respectively of Reciprocal Demand and of Cost of Production in relation to International values 348
Varieties of industrial monopoly in International trade—strict and qualified, one-sided and reciprocal 349
§ 5. Conditions of commercial equilibrium 353
§ 6. Effects of international lending and borrowing on the commercial equilibrium 359
§ 7. The foregoing principles illustrated by the course of the United States external trade since 1860 364
§ 8. Present state and immediate prospects of that trade 367

CHAPTER IV.

FREE-TRADE AND PROTECTION.

§ 1. Present state of the controversy 375
§ 2. Protection, an outgrowth of the Balance of Trade system 376
Either system, consistently carried out, fatal to International trade 377
§ 3. M. Alby's statement of the protectionist theory 379
Criticism of M. Alby's statement 380
§ 4. Practical issue taken in the United States—the cost of production of commodities 382
The criterion proves too much 383
And, rightly understood, refutes the protectionist argument 384
§ 5. Alleged inability of the United States to compete with the cheap labor of Europe examined 386
§ 6. Examination of a ten years' experiment of Protection in the United States 388
Difficulty of interpreting an industrial experiment 388
Complication of results only to be unraveled by the deductive method 389
Mr. Wells's contributions to the investigation 391
Lesson of the experiment 395
§ 7. Political argument in favor of Protection, as favoring variety in industry 395
Unfounded in the domain of "extractive industry" 397
And not better founded in that of manufactures 399
Demoralizing effects of a protective *régime* 402

CHAPTER V.

ON SOME MINOR TOPICS.

§ 1. Nature of a country's interest in the scale of its general prices 407
Maxim that "gold is of the same value all the world over" examined . 408
A nation is interested not in having its prices high, but in having its gold cheap 410
§ 2. Attempts to measure the gain on foreign trade 415
The problem insoluble 418

PART I.

VALUE.

SOME LEADING PRINCIPLES

OF

POLITICAL ECONOMY.

PART I.

VALUE.

CHAPTER I.

PRELIMINARY.

§ 1. THE sense proper to value in economic discussion may, I think, be said to be universally agreed upon by economists, and I may, therefore, at once define it as expressing the ratio in which commodities in open market are exchanged against each other. This, as every one is aware, is not the only or perhaps the most common meaning borne by "value" in general discourse, and hence occurs a source of ambiguity which some writers have proposed to avoid by eliminating the term altogether from the nomenclature of Political Economy. Professor Jevons, for example, would substitute for "value" the expression of "ratio of exchange." Something, it is possible, might be gained in point of clearness by the substitution; but, on the other hand, the term "value" has become far too deeply rooted in the ordinary modes of economic thought to be easily displaced; nor, for my part, do I think this extreme course needed; for, though no doubt there is the danger—associated as the word is with other meanings, and more particularly with the idea of "utility"—of sliding in argumentative discussion from the scientific into some other sense, this may, to a very great extent, if not entirely, be precluded by the simple contrivance of qualifying the term, in all doubtful contexts, with the prefix "exchange." "Exchange value" involves little departure from ordinary usage, and can hardly fail to remind the reader, where this is necessary, of the special and limited sense in which the word is employed.

Value expressing a ratio or proportion existing between the commodities exchanged, it follows, of course, as is explained in all treatises, that a general rise or a general fall of values is an impossibility, or, rather, a contradiction in terms. If A rise in relation to B, B must fall in relation to A. A and B can not both rise or both fall at the same time in relation to each other; and what is true of two commodities is true of any number, and of all commodities. But though commodities in general can not rise or fall simultaneously in relation to each other, they may rise or fall in relation to any selected one among the number; and if gold or silver be the one selected, commodities in general may rise or fall in relation to gold or silver. The value of other commodities in relation to a commodity thus selected is called "price." It is plain, then, that while a general rise or a general fall of values is a contradiction in terms, a general rise or a general fall of prices is a perfectly possible, as indeed it is a not uncommon, event.

At the same time, although "value" expresses a relation, I apprehend we may use without impropriety such expressions as "a sum of values," or "an increase or diminution in the aggregate amount of values." Where, *e. g.*, the quantity of valuable things possessed by a community has been increased, the conditions of production remaining the same; or where, the quantity remaining the same, the conditions of producing commodities have been so altered as to cause a given quantity to exchange for a larger quantity than before of commodities of which the conditions of production have remained constant—in either of these cases, it seems to me, we may not improperly say that the sum of values, or the aggregate amount of values, has increased in that community. The usage may be illustrated and justified by analogous expressions employed with reference to power. Power, like value, expresses a relation; and a general increase of the power of individuals or of nations in relation to each other is, of course, an impossibility. But this does not prevent us from saying that the aggregate power of any given number of individuals or nations has increased; meaning thereby, not that their relative position has been altered, but that the elements which go to support power in them have been multiplied. We should thus say that the power of European nations has greatly increased within the last century. In a precisely similar sense we may speak—and it will often be convenient to speak—of an increase or diminution of aggregate values; value being only another name for purchasing power.

One word more of explanation may be given. If value expresses simply a relation, what is meant when the question is raised whether, in the case of two commodities of which the proportions in exchanging have undergone a change, the change is to be attributed to a fall in the value of the one, or to a rise in that of the other? Suppose, for example, we ask whether the advance in the price of butcher's meat is due to meat having risen or to money having fallen in value, what do we mean? Value expressing simply the relation of the commodities in exchange, the price being given, that relation is determined. Obviously there is a tacit reference to the causes on which value depends; and the question really raised is not strictly as to the change in the exchange value of meat and money, but as to the cause or causes which have produced the change. If we believe that the change is traceable to a cause primarily affecting meat, we say that meat has risen, not that money has fallen, in value; while in the opposite case, we should attribute the change to the reduced value of money.

§ 2. So much being premised as to the meaning and use of the term "value" in Political Economy, let us now endeavor to set before our minds as distinctly as may be the precise problems respecting value which the science proposes to solve. These are comprised under the following heads:

I. We may inquire as to the circumstances which confer on a commodity the power of commanding other things in exchange—in other words, as to the conditions *essential* to the existence of value.

II. We may inquire as to the circumstances on which depend the particular proportions in which commodities exchange; in other words, as to the conditions which *determine* value—an inquiry which resolves itself into two distinct issues. For, first, we may consider value as manifested in a given act of exchange, and inquire into the causes which determine it at a given time and place; which is the problem of "market values." Or, secondly, we may regard value as the average proportion resulting from a series of exchanges numerous enough to allow of the neutralization of exceptional influences; and this is the problem of "normal values." The general problem of value, accordingly, embraces these three distinct inquiries: 1, as to the conditions essential to the existence of value; 2, as to the conditions determining market values; and, 3, as to the conditions determining normal values.

§ 3. The two latter inquiries will be the subject of future consideration; but we may at once endeavor to dispose of the first of the three problems. And here it is obvious that one of the circumstances essential to the existence of value is a capacity of satisfying some human desire. Plainly, if an object be unable to fulfill this condition, there can be no motive for seeking to obtain it, still less for parting with something we possess in exchange for it: such an object would, therefore, be incapable of exchange value. The capacity, therefore, of satisfying a desire—in other words, the possession of utility, is the first condition essential to the existence of value.

The mere circumstance, however, that a commodity is capable of satisfying a human desire will not necessarily confer upon it the power of commanding other things in exchange. Human beings will not, in pursuit of the satisfaction of their desires, incur sacrifice—such a sacrifice, for example, as is implied in parting with something they possess—if the end can be attained without submitting to this condition; and therefore, in order that a commodity should have the power of commanding other commodities in exchange, not only must it be capable of satisfying a desire, it must also be unattainable except on the condition of undergoing a sacrifice of some sort. No one living in a healthy locality, for example, will give any thing in exchange for atmospheric air; nor, where water is abundant and also universally accessible, will water fetch a price. But if atmospheric air be required to supply a diving-bell, or if water can only be had by going some distance to fetch it, water and atmospheric air will both acquire exchange value. It results, then, that the necessity of undergoing sacrifice of some kind as a condition of obtaining the commodity, or, let us say, "difficulty of attainment," must concur with utility in order to the existence of exchange value. And it is plain also that we must add, as a further condition, the possibility of transferring the possession of the articles which are the subject of the exchange.

These three circumstances then—utility, difficulty of attainment, and transferableness—are the conditions essential to the existence of value. Where they are combined in a commodity, that commodity has the power of commanding other things in exchange: where any one of them is absent, exchange value can have no place.

§ 4. This point being settled, it will be convenient here to enter so far into the larger problems of our subject as to discuss a question much debated some half-century ago, and which has lately been revived: Does utility alone give the law of exchange value? in other words, are commodities exchanged for each other simply in proportion as they are useful? To put the question in a concrete form—supposing gold and silver to exchange for each other in the proportion of 1 to 15; silver and copper to exchange in the proportion of 1 to 30; and copper and iron to exchange in the proportion of 1 to 3; are these ratios due to the fact that gold is fifteen times more useful than silver; that silver is thirty times more useful than copper; and that copper is three times more useful than iron? Do the proportions of exchange invariably correspond to the relative utilities of those metals? And does this rule hold in all cases of exchange? Unsophisticated readers would, I should think, have no difficulty in answering this question in the negative; and, in truth, this is the sense in which it has in general been answered by political economists. Widely as writers have differed respecting the law governing value, they have generally at least agreed in the negative conclusion that it does not 'simply follow the utility of the commodity. In a passage which will be familiar to most readers, Adam Smith says: "The things which have the greatest value in use have frequently little or no value in exchange; and, on the contrary, those which have the greatest value in exchange have frequently little or no value in use. Nothing is more useful than water; but it will purchase scarce any thing; scarce any thing can be had in exchange for it. A diamond, on the contrary, has scarce any value in use, but a very great quantity of other goods may frequently be had in exchange for it." To the same effect Ricardo writes: "When I give 2000 times more cloth for a pound of gold than I do for a pound of iron, does it prove that I attach 2000 times more utility to the gold than I do to the iron? Certainly not. . . . If utility were the measure of value, I should probably give more for the iron." Again, "If I give one shilling for a loaf, and twenty-one shillings for a guinea, it is no proof that this, in my estimation, is the comparative measure of their utility."

In this view the English school of Political Economy have, I think, very generally acquiesced. The principal dissentients, and they have not been numerous, have been in France; and of these the most eminent, perhaps, has been M. Say, who in his celebrated *Traité* takes the position that utility is not only essential to value, but also constitutes the exclusive condition determining in all cases the proportions of exchange. The arguments by which M. Say supported this position will be found in his treatise. They were answered by Ricardo in a later edition of his great work; and I have, for my part, been accustomed to regard the controversy as settled by that reply; nor should I have thought it necessary here to refer to the question as an open one, but that the view of M. Say has quite lately been revived by Professor Jevons, in his ingenious work on the "Theory of Political Economy." Following M. Say, Professor Jevons maintains that "value depends entirely upon utility;" and propounds a theorem which recognizes the degree of utility possessed by a commodity as the exclusive condition determining its exchange value. Under these circumstances, it will be proper to consider briefly the precise significance and importance of this view of the law of value.

And here I may say at once—what indeed, with the passages which I have quoted from Adam Smith and Ricardo before him, will already be evident to the reader—that the question raised by Professor Jevons, and which had previously been raised by M. Say, is primarily a question of words—a question as to what is the proper meaning of "utility." This, I say, is evident, because, accepting utility in the sense in which it is used in those passages, the statements advanced are really not open to controversy. Nor can there be much doubt or difficulty as to what that sense is. Manifestly by utility Adam Smith and Ricardo, and those who have followed their doctrine on this point, have understood the quality of being suitable to human purposes—this quality purely and simply, and irrespective of extraneous considerations; while they would doubtless have regarded the degree of utility as measured by the importance of the purposes to which the useful commodity ministered. In this sense it is true beyond controversy that water is useful, even though it fetched nothing in the market, and more useful than many articles—*e. g.*, alcohol — that sell for more. The world could manifestly get on better without alcohol than without water. Similarly, it is true to say that a diamond is less useful than, *e. g.*, coal, and that gold is less useful than iron; or, at all events, that the degree of utility of these several products—the importance of the services which they render in the economy of human society—is not represented by the proportions in which they exchange for each other. These propositions, I say, are indisputable in the sense in which they are laid down; and, accordingly, in taking the position that value depends entirely upon utility, and is measured by the degree of utility, Mr. Jevons must be understood to employ the term, as M. Say formerly employed it, in a different sense from that in which it is understood by those who maintain the ordinary view. In point of fact this is so. Professor Jevons means by utility, not what Adam Smith and Ricardo meant, but their idea *plus* something more. If we ask what that something more is, we find it to consist of all circumstances and considerations whatever which, in any given act of exchange, exert an influence on those taking part in it. Thus the fact that water is capable of ministering to important human purposes would not, as I understand the doctrine, entitle water to be considered, in economic estimation, a useful commodity. Before pronouncing on the point, we must know the circumstances under which any given dealings in the commodity take place. If they take place in London, where water can not be procured in the quantity required by the population without expense, and where it consequently bears a price, water is a useful commodity. But if the scene be changed to a country village, where water is abundant beyond the needs of the inhabitants, and consequently fetches nothing in exchange, water suddenly becomes useless. Consistently with this view, the degree of utility is measured, not by the importance of the purposes which the article subserves, but by the effect produced by all the considerations aforesaid in deciding what it shall sell for. A woolen coat sells for less now than it did a century ago; therefore it is less useful now than then. It sells for more in Australia than in England; therefore it is more useful in Australia than in England. According to the same standard of utility, every improvement in production, just in proportion as it cheapens a commodity, diminishes its utility; while every thing that raises the cost enhances the utility. If, then, I have correctly interpreted Mr. Jevons's doctrine (and I have certainly taken every pains to understand it), the term "utility" stands with him for an entirely different conception from that which it expresses in the language of Adam Smith, and of most political economists. In attempting, therefore, to estimate his view, we have to consider two points—first, a question of nomenclature, as to the convenience of this particular use of the term; and, secondly, one of scientific theory, as to the light thrown by the doctrine—utility being understood in the sense explained—on the phenomena of exchange value.

As regards the question of nomenclature, it will scarcely, I think, be denied that Mr. Jevons's use of the term "utility" is wide of the common signification, and on this ground open to serious objection. A use of language according to which water is only useful where it is paid for, and in proportion as it is paid for; according to which atmospheric air is only useful in diving-bells, mines, and other places whither it is costly to carry it; according to which meat and corn are less useful commodities in the United States than in England, and clothing and cutlery less useful in England than in the United States; according to which diamonds are more useful than coal, and iron is the least useful of the metals—such a use of language, it will be admitted, requires strong reasons for its justification. No doubt, in framing a scientific nomenclature, it is often necessary to depart from the ordinary use of words. Political Economy draws its technical terms from popular language; and the mere circumstance that it is obliged to assign a precise meaning to these terms, and to adhere strictly to this meaning once assigned—this circumstance alone constantly compels a deviation from the more or less vague and fluctuating sense which attaches to all words in extensive popular use. So much must be admitted. But at least the necessity for deviation should be made out. If a new sense be given to a term in order to convey a novel doctrine, it should at least be shown that the innovation is needed for the due appreciation of the phenomena, and that the idea is best expressed by the term. In other words, it should be shown that the theory, for the sake of which the term is employed in the unusual way, can justify itself by the only test by which a theory is justified, namely, by explaining facts, and, if it be a new theory, by explaining facts not explicable, or not so simply explicable, by received theories. Now I must frankly say, I have failed to find in Mr. Jevons's volume any such justification of his doctrine.

I must go farther. The current theories respecting value, though, as will be seen, I am far from thinking them perfect, nevertheless do succeed in explaining a large proportion of the facts actually presented in the dealings of commerce. But I am wholly unable to conceive how any thing amounting to a real explanation can be extracted from the theory we are now considering. What does it really amount to? In my apprehension to this, and no more—that value depends upon utility, and that utility is whatever affects value. In other words, the name "utility" is given to the aggregate of unknown conditions which determine the phenomenon, and then the phenomenon is stated to depend upon what this name stands for. Suppose, instead of "utility," we call the unknown conditions x, we might then say that value was determined by x; and the proposition would be precisely as true, and, so far as I can see, as instructive, as Mr. Jevons's doctrine. In either case the information conveyed would be that value was determined by the conditions which determine it—an announcement, the importance of which, even though presented under the form of abstruse mathematical symbols, I must own myself unable to discern.*

There seems, therefore, no reason for departing from the hitherto commonly received sense of utility; and it is accordingly in this sense—already defined—that I shall henceforth employ the term. Thus understood, utility, however essential to the existence of value, does not alone and exclusively give the law of the phenomenon. That law, or rather (for, as I have already observed, the phenomenon is twofold) those laws, we have yet to find.

---

* I should be sorry if my dissent from Mr. Jevons on this point should convey an impression that I undervalue the work in which the doctrine I have combated is advanced. Though my ignorance of mathematics disqualifies me for entering into many of the discussions, I am far from being insensible to the lucid statements of economic doctrine, and to the numerous original and suggestive remarks, with which the volume abounds.

CHAPTER II.

SUPPLY AND DEMAND.

§ 1. BEFORE proceeding to deal with the more specific problems of value, it will be convenient to devote a brief space to a consideration of the agencies of Supply and Demand. If we were to judge by the careless freedom with which these terms are tossed to and fro in popular discussion, we should be apt to conclude that there was no portion of economic science which the general public had more completely at its fingers' ends. "The law of Supply and Demand" is commonly supposed to be a principle capable of explaining all or nearly all the phenomena of wealth, and which at the same time reveals itself by its own light. No one is imagined so ignorant as not to know what it means, or so dull as not to perceive its marvelous efficacy as a solvent of problems. Indeed, with a large number of people, Supply and Demand would seem to be not so much conditions to be taken account of in solving problems, as conjuring terms, by pronouncing which difficulties may be exorcised, and obstacles of all sorts removed from our path. In point of fact, I believe there is no doctrine of Political Economy more generally misunderstood, or, to speak plainly, respecting which a more complete absence of all clear understanding of any kind prevails, than this very doctrine. The terms are used and the supposed "law" is appealed to, for the most part, without any distinct ideas being attached to the phrases employed. Nay, even among not a few of the professed cultivators of economic science there seems to be, in respect to this doctrine, if I may venture to say so, a want of thoroughness and clearness of view singularly prejudicial to sound reasoning, and which has not a little tended to throw a haze over some important problems of the science.

The fundamental truth to be seized in connection with Supply and Demand—the failure to seize which is the source of most of the loose reasoning and fallacious inference of which those terms are made the vehicle—is that, conceived as aggregates, as each comprising all the facts of that kind occurring in a given community, Supply and Demand are not independent phenomena, of which either may indefinitely increase or diminish irrespective of the other, but phenomena strictly connected and mutually dependent; so strictly connected and interdependent that (excluding temporary effects, and contemplating them as permanent and normal facts) neither can increase nor diminish without necessitating and implying a corresponding increase or diminution of the other. Aggregate demand can not increase or diminish without entailing a corresponding increase or diminution of aggregate supply; nor can aggregate supply undergo a change without involving a corresponding change in aggregate demand. These propositions seem to me to be quite fundamental, and indeed elementary—expressing, as they do, consequences which arise directly from the nature of an industrial economy founded on the principle of separation of employments. Fundamental and elementary, however, as they are, and much as has been written on the subject, they stand in need of all the aid that clear exposition and apt illustration can give them.

§ 2. In attempting something, however inconsiderable, toward this much-needed elucidation, I would ask the reader, in the first place, to set before his mind the phenomena in their most elementary form, and to observe their essential character and place in the economy of industry. Supply and Demand are evidently facts incident to the exchange of the products of industry, which again is a consequence of the separation of employments. So soon as people engage in productive industry upon the principle of separation of employments, the need arises of exchanging the results of their work; each becomes a supplier of what he has produced, a demander of what he seeks to consume. Let us suppose a *régime* of barter: under such circumstances Supply would consist in the commodities offered in exchange for other commodities. In what would Demand in such a case consist? We can only give the same reply: in the commodities offered in exchange for other commodities. In other words, under the simplest and most elementary form of exchange, Demand and Supply, as general phenomena, as aggregates, could not be discriminated. Each commodity would be in turn Supply and Demand —Supply in reference to the person seeking to obtain it, Demand in reference to the person who used it as the means of obtaining something else. It would be possible indeed, even in this state of things, to use the terms with a distinct meaning, so long as we referred the acts to individuals or to particular products. A. B. would be a demander of certain articles, a supplier of others; and the demand for meat or for corn would be a perfectly distinct circumstance from the supply of meat or of corn. But, so soon as the point of view was shifted from the particular to the general—so soon as we attempted to conceive Supply or Demand as proceeding from the community at large—the phenomena would be confounded, or rather would converge into one. This, I say, would be the character of Supply and Demand under a *régime* of barter. Let us now observe how this simple character is modified by the introduction of a medium of exchange. A medium of exchange represents general purchasing power; and, all transactions being conducted through this medium, it becomes possible to distinguish Demand and Supply, not merely in reference to particular persons and products, but as general ideas. Every act of exchange may now be regarded either from the point of view of him who offers general purchasing power, or from that of him who offers specific commodities; all acts of the former class may be considered together, and apart from all acts of the latter: and we thus arrive at distinct general ideas of Demand and Supply. Accordingly, under our actual *régime* we speak of Demand and Supply, not merely as of this or of that person, but as of a whole community, and not merely with reference to this or that product, but with reference to all products: aggregate Demand or aggregate Supply thus become possible ideas. I would, therefore, define the terms as follows: Demand, as the desire for commodities or services, seeking its end by an offer of general purchasing power; and Supply, as the desire for general purchasing power, seeking its end by an offer of specific commodities or services.

The reader will not fail to observe that, as I have developed the ideas in question, Demand and Supply are strictly analogous conceptions. There is on each side a mental element, a desire, and on each a material element, specific commodities and services* in one case, and that particular commodity which is taken as the representative of general purchasing power in the other; and as in each case the desire may be regarded as indefinite and practically unlimited, so in each case the complex phenomenon is limited by its material element— Supply by the quantity of specific commodities offered for sale, and Demand by the quantity of purchasing power offered

---

* It will be said, perhaps, that a "service" is not a material condition. But conceding this—though in truth the most numerous class of services really consist in their material effects—still conceding this, the capacity to render a service is always embodied in a material form. The supply of services, therefore, will be measured by the number of human beings able and willing to render services. The supply of any given kind of labor, *e. g.*, will be measured by the number of laborers able and willing to perform this kind of labor.

for their purchase.* The two conceptions are thus strictly analogous—a point on which I feel it the more necessary to insist, inasmuch as the contrary view is countenanced, in one portion of his work on "Political Economy," by the high authority of Mr. Mill. Criticising the expression "a ratio between Demand and Supply," Mr. Mill asks, "What ratio can there be between a quantity and a desire, or even a desire combined with a power?" The criticism has been accepted as decisive, as far as I have observed, by all later writers: nevertheless, I feel bound to demur to it; and further, I must contend that the perception of the strict analogy between the ideas in question is a point of very great importance. "What ratio can there be between a quantity and a desire combined with a power?" But surely it is not correct to describe Supply simply as a quantity. A mere quantity of goods does not constitute Supply until it is offered for sale, that is to say, until the quantity is connected with a mental feeling; and though it is true, as I have just pointed out, that the phenomenon is measured by the quantity and not by the feeling, it is not the less true that Demand is also measured by its material element. The two conceptions are thus essentially analogous; and the recognition of this seems to be indispensable to the correct apprehension of their true relation. Accept the notion that Demand and Supply are facts of a different order, incapable of comparison and measurement, and you can hardly refuse to acknowledge that they are independent facts which may increase or diminish irrespective of each other. But this is precisely the idea that is at the bottom of most of the prevalent fallacies connected with those terms.

---

* I say *quantity* of purchasing power, because ultimately all purchasing power is resolvable into quantity—under our system into weights of gold; under others into weights of silver, or of gold and silver; under inconvertible currencies into numbers of bits of paper printed in a certain way.

§ 3. Mr. Mill, indeed, fully recognizes—no one more fully—the importance of keeping in view the strict analogy of Demand and Supply; and it is apparently, at least in part, with a view to this end that he gives the peculiar definition of "demand" which is to be found in the chapter from which I have quoted. Demand, as there defined, is to be understood as measured, not, as my definition would require, by the quantity of purchasing power offered in support of the desire for commodities, but by the quantity of commodities for which such purchasing power is offered. There is no doubt that, as thus conceived, that is to say, as quantity demanded and quantity supplied, Demand and Supply are perfectly analogous facts; but, as I think I have shown, this way of regarding them is by no means necessary in order to render them analogous, while it seems to me that the idea of "demand" as quantity demanded, though not foreign to economic discussion, is very far from being adequate to the general purposes of the science.

In offering a few remarks in justification of this opinion, let me here say that, while contending for the idea of "demand," as set forth above, as the proper meaning of the term, I have no desire to restrict the term exclusively and invariably to that meaning. I quite admit that it may be convenient occasionally to employ "demand" in other senses; and though the employment of the same economic term in different senses is not free from objection, it is an expedient to which the economist must, in the dearth of language, occasionally have recourse; nor will much harm result, if we only bear in mind that the senses *are* distinct, and do not confound them in argument. Moreover, I am willing to allow that the meaning given to "demand" by Mr. Mill in the passage in question expresses a sense in which it is sometimes convenient, perhaps necessary, to use the word. But, while conceding this much, I must still contend for the correctness of my own definition, as expressing the principal and proper sense of the term in economic science—meaning by this a sense more important and fundamental than any other to which the term in that science is applied—a sense indispensable to economic exposition, and which "demand" easily and naturally expresses.

The importance and fundamental character of a scientific idea must, I apprehend, be judged by the place which it occupies in the theories of a science. Now I have no need to go beyond Mr. Mill's work to show that the sense assigned to "demand" in my definition may be justified by this criterion. I take three capital theories of the science—wages, money, and foreign trade. In each of these Supply and Demand form the pivots of the doctrine, the two poles on which the exposition turns. But when we come to consider in what sense "demand" is used in those theories, we find that in every instance it is regarded as represented and measured by the purchasing power offered, not by the quantity of commodities or services demanded. It is fundamental in Mr. Mill's doctrine of wages,* as in every sound exposition of that subject, that demand for labor should be understood as measured by the quantity of capital and other wealth offered in exchange for labor. When the economist speaks of an increased demand for labor as tending to raise wages, he does not mean a demand for a larger number of laborers — a condition which would have no such tendency, unless accompanied by an increase of purchasing power, in this instance of capital offered; and, this condition being present, the increased demand would tend to raise wages, whether the numbers actually responding to the call were larger or not; and so of the other conclusions affecting wages deduced from the law of Demand and Supply: the sense which I have assigned to the term is the only sense in which they will hold good for a moment. Similarly, in his theory of money Mr. Mill considers the demand for money as measured

---

* "Principles of Political Economy," sixth edition, book ii., chap. xi., § 1.

by the quantity of goods of all sorts offered in exchange for money, not by the quantity of money demanded.* And again, in his theory of foreign trade,† we find "demand" steadily employed, as it seems to me, in the same sense. As the imports of each country represent in relation to it the measure of foreign supply, so its exports represent the force of its demand for foreign products. Thus, if England spent more largely on such products, that expenditure would be carried into effect through an increase of exports; and that increase of exports would indicate an increase of international demand on the part of England, whatever might be the quantity of commodities imported. The exports of each country are thus the measure of its international demand; and, as when we extend our view from a particular country to the commercial world, the same commodities are in turn exports and imports, Supply and Demand become (as Mr. Mill is careful to point out) "Reciprocal Demand." It is only by thus understanding the term that I am able to assign any meaning to the very important principle, as I regard it, developed by Mr. Mill in the chapter to which I am referring, and which he designates "the Equation of International Demand."‡

---

* "Principles of Political Economy," book iii., chap. viii., § 2.
† Ibid., book iii., chap. xviii., § 4.
‡ Mr. Mill indeed states that "the Equation of International Demand is but an extension of the more general law of value, which we called the Equation of Supply and Demand," and refers to his chapter on the latter subject; but I must confess myself unable to follow his reasoning in this remark. On the contrary, the two doctrines appear to me to be perfectly distinct. The equation of Supply and Demand, in the chapter on that subject, refers, as I understand it, to an equality (realized, it is alleged, in every market) between the *quantity* of a commodity demanded and the *quantity* of the *same* commodity supplied. The equality asserted, therefore, has reference to quantity, and to quantity embodied in a single commodity, that which is the subject-matter of exchange. The doctrine, in truth, as I shall hereafter have occasion more particularly to point out, amounts to an assertion that what is bought is equal to what is sold, that a given quantity of a given com-

§ 4. I conceive, therefore, that I am justified by Mr. Mill's practice, if not by his precept, in understanding Demand and Supply in the sense in which I have defined them; and what I wish now to establish is, that, as thus understood, Demand and Supply, in their general character, and excluding temporary effects, are not independent phenomena, but fundamentally the same phenomena regarded from different points of view— different faces of the same facts; and that consequently neither can increase nor diminish without a corresponding increase or diminution of the other.

If the reader will recall the description which I gave a few pages back of what would be the nature of Supply and Demand under a system of barter, he will have no difficulty, I think, in admitting the essential soundness of this position, though he may not find it easy at once to reconcile it with some facts that we witness under our actual industrial economy. It was then pointed out that Demand and Supply, on the supposition of exchange being carried on by barter, though distinct conceptions so long as we refer them to particular individuals or products, become incapable of discrimination, so soon as we pass from the particular to the general point of view and regard them as aggregates. The total demand of a community would under such circumstances be represented by all the commodities and services there offered in exchange for other commodities and services; and these would also constitute the total supply in that community. Now the essential character of exchange is not altered by the employment of a circulating medium, however the increased complexity of the

---

modity is equal to itself. But the equality asserted in "the Equation of International Demand," as I understand it, is far from being of this nature: it refers not to quantity but to *value*, the value, namely, of the imports and exports of each commercial country; nor is it realized in a single commodity, but in two distinct groups of commodities, namely, those issuing from and those entering such countries.

facts may tend to conceal its true nature. The process is facilitated, but what happens is in effect the same. It is still an exchange of commodities and services against commodities and services: and the relation between Demand and Supply remains what it was in the simpler case. It is true, where we have a medium of exchange, we can form the conception of general Demand as distinct from general Supply—a distinction which disappears under a barter *régime*—because we can separate *in our thoughts* general purchasing power from specific commodities. But in point of truth and fact the two things are not separable. Purchasing power, in the last resort, owes its existence to the production of a commodity, and, the conditions of industry being given, can only be increased by increasing the quantity of commodities offered for sale; that is to say, Demand can only be increased by increasing Supply. The purchasing power of England is represented by the aggregate of all her products; and as it can not increase except through an increase of these, so an increase of her products (if adapted and duly proportioned to the requirements of human beings), will, other things being the same, carry with it a corresponding increase of her purchasing power. It follows, therefore, that the relation of general Demand and general Supply to each other is not affected by the employment of a circulating medium, but continues essentially the same under a monetary, as under a barter, *régime*. In neither case are they independent facts, but essentially the same facts presenting themselves under different aspects. Demand, as a general phenomenon, can not exist without Supply, and can not increase except in proportion as Supply increases. This, I repeat, is fundamental in the theory of exchange; and all assumptions to the contrary must be regarded as baseless and absurd.

§ 5. The illusion which I am combating, that Demand and Supply are independent economic forces, sometimes assumes another form in the notion that producers and consumers are distinct classes, and that production and consumption are acts which may go on irrespective of each other. It is true, indeed, there are consumers who are not producers (and the bearing of this fact on the theory just expounded I shall presently consider); but in the main the relation of consumers and producers in an industrial community may be thus illustrated. A certain number of people, A, B, C, D, E, F, etc., are engaged in industrial occupations—A produces for B, C, D, E, F; B for A, C, D, E, F; C for A, B, D, E, F, and so on. In each case the producer and the consumers are distinct, and hence, by a very natural fallacy, it is concluded that the whole body of consumers is distinct from the whole body of producers; whereas they consist of precisely the same persons. Producers are identified with Supply; consumers with Demand; and thus the belief in the independence of those agencies seems to find confirmation. The prevalence of this notion was brought into view very prominently in the discussion which took place a year or two back on the nine hours' movement. By several of those who took part in that discussion, and among these by some who wrote with not a little parade of economic knowledge, it was assumed almost as axiomatic, that the result of the movement, supposing it to be extended to the whole circle of industry, would be a general increase of Demand beyond Supply, issuing in a general advance of prices. The producers, it was seen (unless their industry gained in efficiency what it lost in duration), would on the whole produce less; and therefore Supply would diminish; but, not perceiving any connection between Supply and Demand, the disputants took it for granted that Demand would go on as before. It will be scarcely necessary now, I trust, to point out the gross fallacy of the assumption. The producers are also consumers; and if, on the whole, less is produced, there would, on the whole, be fewer commodities to be exchanged. But why should this affect the proportions in which they are exchanged? or why should it affect the relations between commodities in general and money? If a given group of laborers and capitalists produce less (however they may divide the produce among themselves), they have, as an aggregate, less to offer for sale; and, as all other groups of laborers and capitalists, including those who are the means, direct or indirect, of bringing gold and silver into the country, would also have less to offer for sale, the relative position of each to the community would not be disturbed; and the diminution of general Supply would be exactly balanced by a corresponding diminution of general Demand. The absurdity of the supposition might indeed be more easily shown by simply adverting to the principles governing the value of money, and by showing the impossibility of its being altered by such a cause as the movement in question; but the error, in truth, goes deeper, and can only be adequately exposed by reference to the fundamental character of industrial exchange as determined by the separation of employments.

But a formidable obstacle to the doctrine of the mutual interdependence and fundamental identity of Demand and Supply is supposed to exist in the presence in all wealthy communities of a large body of persons who are consumers merely, the idle rich, *nati consumere fruges*—people, it will be urged, who takes a large and effective part in consumption and Demand, but who produce nothing, and contribute nothing to Supply. How, it will be asked, is the existence of this class to be reconciled with the doctrine for which I am contending? It must at once be admitted that the existence of an idle rich class shows that the classes of producers and consumers are not necessarily and always conterminous; but this is not the issue I have raised, but the dependence of consumptive power upon production, and of Demand upon Supply. Let me here explain that by "consumptive power" I mean, as I apprehend those who employ it in this controversy mean, not the mere physical capacity to consume, but the economic conditions which minister to the physical capacity. Understanding it in this sense, then, I contend that in the case of the idle rich, as in all other cases, consumptive power is limited and measured by production, and Demand by Supply. To perceive this, we have, in truth, only to dip just below the surface. Whence is their purchasing power derived? It does not descend to them from the skies; nor is it obtained by submarine telegraph direct from California or Australia; nor is its existence exhaustively accounted for by the presence of certain figures on the credit side of their accounts in their bankers' books. Let us suppose the class in question to be represented by certain landlords, mortgagees, and fund-holders. In the first two cases their purchasing power, that is to say, their rents and interest, would, of course, be derived from the sale of certain agricultural products; in the last, also from the sale of products—the products, namely of those who pay the taxes—in all cases from production and supply. The phenomenon is merely one of a transfer of purchasing power from one set of people to another, who in virtue of contracts are entitled to receive it. If the idle landlords, mortgagees, and fund-holders were to vanish into space, would the demand of the community diminish? Certainly not, so long as production and supply continued as before. The only difference would be that different persons would now consume and determine the direction of demand. It was formerly certain idle landlords, mortgagees, and fund-holders: it would now be certain producers and tax-payers, who, finding themselves in possession of an enlarged purchasing power, would, I think we may assume, know how to use it. That useful function, therefore, which some profound writers fancy they discover in the abundant expenditure of the idle rich, turns out to be a sheer illusion. Political Economy furnishes no such palliation of unmitigated selfishness. Not that I would breathe a word against the sacredness of contracts. But I think it is important, on moral no less than on economic grounds, to insist upon this, that no public benefit of any kind arises from the existence of an idle rich class. The wealth accumulated by their ancestors or others on their behalf, where it is employed as capital, no doubt helps to sustain industry; but what they consume in luxury and idleness is not capital, and helps to sustain nothing but their own unprofitable lives. By all means they must have their rents and interest, as it is written in the bond; but let them take their proper place as drones in the hive, gorging at a feast to which they have contributed nothing.

One more illustration of the same fallacy will not perhaps be superfluous. A colony of rich persons establish themselves in a foreign country, where they practice no useful industry or art, but simply expend and consume. We may take as our example the English and other foreign residents at such resorts as Pau, Nice, and Rome. Whether such residents confer benefit of any sort on the people among whom they settle is a point which I do not now raise: I may possibly find occasion to consider it farther on. But what I wish now to make clear is, that, if any benefit does arise from the expenditure of such people, it is no instance of a good accruing to a community from Demand as distinct from and independent of Supply. The demand of those foreign residents owes its efficacy (whatever that may amount to) to the supply by which it is supported, as certainly as if they each and all rented farms and lived upon the direct produce of their own exertions; for how is their purchasing power conveyed to them? They receive it most probably in circular notes or bills, which are perhaps cashed in coin; but how are these instruments finally liquidated? Simply in commodities sent from England or the other countries from which the residents in question come. In other words, every increase in the demand of English people residing in France for French goods is accompanied and rendered possible by an increase in the supply of English commodities to the French people. There is no other way in which in the long run it can be supported—a fact, by-the-way, which throws a curious light on the absurdities of Protection. None are so anxious to encourage such idle residents from foreign countries as protectionists; but while eager to accomplish this object, they do all in their power to render it impossible. They would have English visitors swarming in their capitals, and spending there their money on French products; but they would at the same time put under interdict the only possible means by which in the long run Englishmen can meet their expenses. The protective system is thus an attempt to sever Demand and Supply, and to render them independent of each other—a feat which will be performed when the circle is squared.

§ 6. I have so far spoken of Demand and Supply as general facts, as related not to particular commodities or services, but to commodities and services in general. I proceed now to consider them as they stand related to particular commodities and services. And here we must in the first place note that that fundamental identity and mutual interdependence which have been found to characterize the phenomena in the light in which we have hitherto regarded them, are no longer observable when they are considered with reference to particular commodities. Thus, as I have shown, it is impossible for the general demand of a community to increase or diminish save through a corresponding increase or diminution of the general supply of commodities in that community; but it is perfectly possible that the demand for a particular commodity or service should increase or diminish, the supply undergoing no corresponding change; and, as every one will recognize, such failure of correspondence between Supply and Demand is the most common of all occurrences. In truth, it but rarely happens that the supply of any commodity remains for any length of time in perfect accordance with the demand for it. What we find is a pretty constant state of fluctuation; the demand sometimes in excess of the supply; the supply sometimes in excess of the demand; and the alterations in the relation indicated by parallel alterations in the prices of the commodity so affected.

I have spoken of supply corresponding with, or being greater or less than, demand in the case of a given commodity. There is no expression in more frequent use in commercial and economic discussion; and it is probable that most people will think that it stands in need of no elucidation. But the slightest reflection will show that its meaning is by no means so clear as it might at first sight be considered. What is meant by the supply of a given commodity being equal to the demand for it? The demand varies with the price; and so does the supply. It is evident, therefore, that, to give meaning to our assertion, it must be understood as made with reference to some assumed price; but what price? This is a point which is not at once apparent.

Again, supposing this difficulty got over, and that we have settled at what price Demand and Supply are to be taken, demand at a given price may be measured either by the quantity of purchasing power offered, or by the quantity of the commodity demanded. Which standard are we to adopt? I have already stated my view as to the proper sense of "demand;" nor do I see any necessity for departing in this context from the meaning I have contended for. According to that view, as Supply would be measured by the quantity of the commodity offered, so Demand would be measured by the quantity of purchasing power offered; and the "correspondence" (which I think would be a better word than "equality") of Supply with Demand at a given price would mean such a state of Demand and Supply as would result, on the one hand, in the absorption of the purchasing power forth-coming at this price by the supply at the same price; and, on the other hand, in the absorption of the supply by the purchasing power; while the non-correspondence of Supply and Demand would mean the existence of an unsatisfied residuum on either side. This, I confess, is the sense of the phrase which I should myself, on scientific grounds, prefer. I have admitted, however, that there are occasions in which "demand" may conveniently be employed in other senses; and this perhaps is one of them. At all events it is certain that, understanding Demand in this context as measured by the quantity demanded, the result will not be affected by the change of standard. When Supply corresponds with Demand in the one sense, it will correspond with it in the other; and as the latter, that is to say Demand, as measured by quantity demanded, is perhaps the more familiar conception where the problem has to do with particular commodities, it will on the whole, perhaps, be more convenient to adopt this sense for the purposes of this particular discussion. I shall therefore understand equality or correspondence of Demand and Supply at a given price, when particular commodities are in question, as meaning equality or correspondence of quantity demanded with quantity supplied at that price.

But we have got to determine what is the price assumed or contemplated in statements regarding the equality or inequality of Supply and Demand. To resolve this point, two sorts of such statements must be considered. We may assert the equality or inequality of Demand and Supply either with reference to a particular occasion, or with reference to a continuing state of things. We may say, for example, that the demand for wheat exceeded the supply in a particular market; or we may say that the demand for meat has for some time exceeded, and is likely for some time longer to exceed, the supply of that article. In the former case, it seems to me, the price assumed, so far as people speak with distinct meaning, would always be the price current in the particular market; and the statement would mean that there were people in that market who at the current price would have purchased more wheat had it been at that price obtainable. I am aware that, in assuming the possibility of such an occurrence as a market price which does not equalize Supply and Demand, I am putting myself in conflict with a celebrated theory. I hope, however, afterward to justify this boldness. For the moment I assume that the price current in the particular market is the price with reference to which statements of the kind we are considering are made; and common language certainly presupposes the possibility of a divergence of Demand and Supply at this price. But how with regard to assertions of the other kind indicated, where we declare that, as a continuing state of things, the demand for a commodity is in excess of the supply of it—shall we say, following the analogy of the explanation just given, that the price here assumed is the price current during the period to which the remark applies; and that the meaning is that the demand at that price has been and is likely to be in excess of the supply? If we attempt to deal with any actual case we shall find that this explanation will not serve us. For example, most persons acquainted with the present state of the iron trade would say that the demand for iron at the present time—meaning, not in this or that market, but in the country generally and over a period of some duration—is greatly in excess of the supply, and would point to the advance in price as evidence of this. Now it is certain that, in the opinion of those most competent to form an opinion, in the opinion of dealers and speculators in the article, the demand for iron in the country at the present time is not in excess of the supply of it *at existing prices;* for did they think so, they would at once by purchases raise the price beyond its present level. In truth, the precise function which such persons perform is that of adapting demand to supply by acting on price; and, however the adaptation may fail in particular markets, it is impossible that, as a phenomenon of some duration, the demand at existing prices should remain, and be known to be, in excess of the supply. How, then, are we to deal with the assertion which undoubtedly would be made by those very persons? It is perhaps not improbable that most of those who make it have not very clearly defined their meaning. Still it would be unreasonable to assume that, where so many people, experts in the matter in hand, concur in making the same statement, their assertion is absolutely without meaning. I shall certainly not presume to find a meaning for any one, but I venture to lay down this proposition, that, in order to render such statements as those of which I have given examples at once significant and true, demand must be understood as existing at some price other than that actually prevailing in the markets; and if I am asked to say what that price is, I answer, the "normal price"—the price which, in the absence of disturbing causes, people consider would be the price of the commodity. Accordingly, the sense in which I understand statements of the kind under consideration, which apply not to particular markets but to a state of things for some time in existence, is as expressing the result of a comparison between demand taken *as it would exist* at the normal price, and supply either such as it would be at that same price, or such as it actually is. Thus understood, such statements become significant; and, if founded on knowledge of the facts in question, convey information of a really important kind. The result, then, of this verbal but necessary discussion may be thus summed up:

1st. Supply and Demand, when spoken of with reference to particular commodities, must, if our statements are to be significant, be understood to mean Supply and Demand at a given price; the comparison of Supply and Demand at that price, being made by comparing the quantity of the commodity supplied with the amount of purchasing power offered, or with the quantity of the commodity demanded. For considerations of practical convenience, the latter measure of Demand is employed in this particular discussion.

2d. Where statements respecting the supply and demand of particular commodities have reference to particular markets, the price assumed as that at which Demand and Supply are compared is the price current in that market.

3d. Where such statements have reference to the country at large and to a continuing state of things, then the price assumed as that at which Demand is measured is the normal price of the commodity, while Supply is considered as measured either at this or at the actual price. The comparison instituted is thus between Demand at the normal price, and Supply either at the normal or at actual prices.

§ 7. The meaning of this part of our phraseology being thus ascertained, I proceed to lay down what seems to me the fundamental law of Demand and Supply considered in connection with particular commodities. It is as follows: The supply of a commodity always tends to adapt itself to the demand at the normal price. I may here say briefly, that by the normal price of a commodity I mean that price which suffices, and no more than suffices, to yield to the producers what is considered to be the average and usual remuneration on such sacrifices as they undergo; and the statement is that the supply of each commodity tends to adapt itself to the demand at this price. That it does so is the direct consequence of the motives which induce people to engage in productive industry, and which attract them, so far as circumstances permit, toward those occupations which offer the largest rewards in proportion to the sacrifices undergone. It follows from this that, where the price of a commodity is above the normal level, and where consequently the producers are reaping more than average rewards, more producers will be drawn to that employment, and the supply of the commodity will be increased. But the increase of supply, by the competition for sales, will tend to lower price, and thus to bring it down toward the normal level. If the increase of supply is not sufficient to reduce the market price quite to the normal level, then, under the influence of the same industrial motives, supply will be further increased; and the process will go on till this result is accomplished. On the other hand, if the stimulus to production carry the movement too far and price fall below the normal level, motives of the opposite kind will at once come into play to curtail production, and the price will rise till the normal level be once more reached. Such is the law of Supply and Demand in relation to particular commodities: it is described by Adam Smith under the figure of a gravitation of market toward natural price; but, however described, it is fundamental in this part of our subject, and is the constant assumption running through all reasonings which have to do with value and price. It is not, however, necessary to advert to its bearings further at present; these will sufficiently appear in the course of the following discussions.

I recapitulate briefly the results of the present chapter:

I. Demand and Supply, considered as general facts, are not independent phenomena, but essentially the same phenomena regarded from different points of view; consequently general Demand can not increase or diminish, except in constant relation with general Supply. All notions and doctrines therefore that proceed upon the contrary assumption are unfounded and fallacious.

II. Demand and Supply, considered with reference to particular commodities, may increase or diminish (in the sense explained) in relation to each other; but in all their mutations they obey this law: Supply always tends to adapt itself to Demand at the normal price of the commodity.

CHAPTER III.

NORMAL VALUE.

§ 1. THE attribute of normal or usual value implies systematic and continuous production. We can not predicate normal value of a commodity of which the supply is limited and can not be increased—for example, of a picture of Turner's; because, although it would be possible from a number of sales of such pictures to strike an average, this average would merely represent the mean of fluctuations uncontrolled by any presiding principle, and so, as having no tendency to keep themselves within any certain bounds, incapable of being made the ground of expectation as to the course of future prices. But when a commodity is systematically and continuously produced, the existence of a normal value soon reveals itself. It is perceived that, however greatly the price may vary from time to time, the variations do not occur at random, but obey a hidden principle, and tend to conform to a certain rule. The price of wheat may be unusually high one year, but this at once calls into action forces which control the advance, and ultimately bring back the price to its usual level; or the price may be exceptionally low, and then the same forces are ranged on the opposite side, and the price rises. In this way the fluctuations of the market are kept within certain, not perhaps precisely determinable, but still real, limits, with a constant tendency to approach a central point—the point of " normal value " of which we are in quest.

I have remarked that an average of the actual sales effected of a commodity, that is to say, of its market prices, does not necessarily represent its normal price or value, because the commodity may exist under conditions which do not supply any controlling principle to its fluctuations, and consequently do not develop any tendency in these to revolve round a central point. But it is still true that, where the conditions for evolving a normal value do exist, that is to say, where a commodity is systematically and continuously produced, the normal value will generally be coincident with the average of actual sales, if only the number of instances taken be sufficient to eliminate the effects of what we may call disturbing causes— causes, that is to say, which interfere with the adaptation of supply to demand.* The number of instances necessary to effect such elimination will vary greatly with the nature of the commodity. It will in general be least in articles of ordinary manufacture, much greater in those of raw produce, and greatest of all in products of the animal kingdom. These, however, are points which will be more conveniently elucidated in connection with the subject of market values.

One word more of explanation. Normal values, though, in contrast with market values, they may not improperly be described as average or permanent values, must not be supposed to represent any thing absolutely fixed or constant in the exchange relation of commodities. There is no such fixedness or constancy to be found in that relation. All that we can properly understand by the permanency predicated of such values is that they remain the same so long as the conditions of production remain the same. In point of fact, the conditions of production of all commodities undergo change, and those of most commodities frequent and extensive change. In general, however, these changes, where they are of much importance, occur at intervals of some duration, and in the intervening

---

* For the precise sense in which these words are used the reader is referred to *ante* pp. 10, 41.

periods the normal price remains constant. The centre about which market prices oscillate is thus not a fixed, but a movable centre; moving, however (as will be fully set forth in a subsequent chapter*), for the most part in constant directions, determined by the character of the commodity and the circumstances under which it is produced. Thus in most manufactured goods the course of normal prices in this country has for some centuries been steadily downward; while on the other hand, the normal prices of raw produce, and more particularly of produce of the animal kingdom, have pretty constantly risen.

So far as to the character of the phenomenon which now claims our attention. It remains to consider the conditions which determine it.

§ 2. The current theories of value connect normal value (called by Adam Smith and Ricardo "natural value," and by Mr. Mill "necessary value," but best expressed, it seems to me, by the term which I have used†) with one set of conditions only, those, namely, comprised under the phrase "cost of production;" and some writers would, under this notion, distinguish such values as "cost values." But this, it seems to me, is to take a much too limited view of the range of this phenomenon. The essence lies in the tendency of the exchanges of the market to gravitate toward a central point; wherever that tendency is observable, we can predicate of the commodities which exhibit it the possession of a central, usual, or normal value. Now, to go no farther at present, such a tendency exists in the relative values of the commodities exchanged by different nations, or, as they are called, "interna-

---

* See chap. v. of this Part.
† I have adopted the term from M. Cherbuliez's excellent work, "Précis de la Science Économique."

tional values." In other words, trading countries exchange their productions in certain proportions, which, in any given state of industry, manifest the condition of normality. Deviations may, and do occur, but forces are in existence which tend constantly to bring back the proportions to the normal line. International values, however, are admittedly—or at all events are demonstrably—not governed by cost of production, and we have thus normal values which are not connected with cost, but come under the influence of some other principle. And I shall afterward have occasion to show that, even in domestic exchanges, cost of production is by no means co-extensive with the range of this phenomenon.

Cost of production, however, is undoubtedly the principal and most important of the conditions on which normal value depends. Not only, as will be shown, does it absolutely determine that relation over a very wide field of exchange transactions, but over perhaps a still wider it exercises, not a decisive, but a powerful influence, and within certain limits controls the results. It is therefore necessary, at the outset of our discussion, to ascertain the true nature of Cost of Production, a clear perception of which, I may observe, quite irrespective of the theory of value, is indispensable for the solution of most of the problems of production and distribution.

The following is the analysis of Cost of Production given by Mr. Mill, and which, so far as I know, has been acquiesced in, either expressly or implicitly, by economists alike in this and in other countries:

"The component elements of Cost of Production have been set forth in the first part of this inquiry. The principle of them, and so much the principle as to be nearly the sole, we found to be Labor. What the production of a thing costs to its producer, or its series of producers, is the labor expended in producing it. If we consider as the producer the capitalist who makes the advances, the word 'labor' may be replaced by the word 'wages:' what the produce costs to him, is the wages which he has had to pay. At the first glance, indeed, this seems to be only a part of his outlay, since he has not only paid wages to laborers, but has likewise provided them with tools, materials, and perhaps buildings. These tools, materials, and buildings, however, were produced by labor and capital; and their value, like that of the article to the production of which they are subservient, depends on cost of production, which again is resolvable into labor. The cost of production of broadcloth does not wholly consist in the wages of weavers; which alone are directly paid by the cloth manufacturer. It consists also of the wages of spinners and wool-combers, and, it may be added, of shepherds, all of which the clothier has paid for in the price of yarn. It consists, too, of the wages of builders and brick-makers, which he has reimbursed in the contract price of erecting his factory. It partly consists of the wages of machine-makers, iron-founders, and miners. And to these must be added the wages of the carriers who transported any of the means and appliances of the production to the place where they were to be used, and the product itself to the place where it is to be sold." .... "Thus far of labor, or wages, as an element in cost of production. But in our analysis, in the First Book, of the requisites of production we found that there is another necessary element in it besides labor. There is also capital; and this being the result of abstinence, the produce, or its value, must be sufficient to remunerate, not only all the labor required, but the abstinence of all the persons by whom the remuneration of the different classes of laborers was advanced. The return for abstinence is Profit. And profit, we have also seen, is not exclusively the surplus remaining to the capitalist after he has been compensated for his outlay, but forms, in most cases, no unimportant part of the outlay itself. The flax-spinner, part of whose expenses consists of the purchase of flax and of machinery, has had to pay, in their price, not only the wages of the labor by which the flax was grown and the machinery made, but the profits of the grower, the flax-dresser, the miner, the iron-founder, and the machine-maker. All these profits, together with those of the spinner himself, were again advanced by the weaver, in the price of his material—linen yarn; and along with them the profits of a fresh set of machine-makers, and of the miners and iron-workers who supplied them with their metallic material. All these advances form part of the cost of production of linen. Profits, therefore, as well as wages, enter into the cost of production which determines the value of the produce." ....

"Profits, however, may enter more largely into the conditions of production of one commodity than of another, even though there be no difference in the *rate* of profit between the two employments. The one commodity may be called upon to yield profit during a longer period of time than the other. The example by which this case is usually illustrated is that of wine. Suppose a quantity of wine and a quantity of cloth made by equal amounts of labor, and that labor paid at the same rate. The cloth does not improve by keeping; the wine does. Suppose that, to attain the desired quality, the wine requires to be kept five years. The producer or dealer will not keep it, unless at the end of five years he can sell it for as much more than the cloth as amounts to five years' profit accumulated at compound interest. The wine and the cloth were made by the same original outlay. Here, then, is a case in which the natural values, relatively to one another, of two commodities, do not conform to their cost of production alone, but to their cost of production *plus* something else. Unless, indeed, for the sake of generality in the expression, we include the profit which the wine-merchant foregoes during the five years in the cost of production of the wine: looking upon it as a kind of additional outlay, over and above his other advances, for which outlay he must be indemnified at last."*

And finally he thus sums up:

"Cost of Production consists of several elements, some of which are constant and universal, others occasional. The universal elements of cost of production are the wages of the labor and the profits of the capital. The occasional elements are taxes, and any extra cost occasioned by a scarcity value of some of the requisites."†

§ 3. Such is the view of Cost of Production which must be considered as now generally accepted by economists. But in spite of the great authority properly attaching to any doctrine propounded by Mr. Mill, and enhanced as this is in the present instance by the general concurrence of economists, I am compelled to dissent from it. It seems to me that the conception of cost which it suggests is radically unsound, confound-

---

* "Principles of Political Economy," book iii., chap. iv., § 1, 4, 5.
† Ibid., book iii., chap. vi., § 1.

ing things in their own nature distinct and even antithetical, and setting in an essentially false light the incidents of production and exchange; further, I think it will appear that it leads to practical errors of a serious kind, not merely with regard to value, but also with regard to some other important doctrines of the science.

Of all ideas within the range of economic speculation, the two most profoundly opposed to each other are cost and the reward of cost—the sacrifice incurred by man in productive industry, and the return made by nature to man upon that sacrifice. All industrial progress consists in altering the proportion between these two things; in increasing the remuneration in relation to the cost, or in diminishing the cost in relation to the remuneration. Cost and remuneration are thus economic antitheses of each other; so completely so, that a small cost and a large remuneration are exactly equivalent expressions. Now, in the analysis of cost of production which I have quoted, these two opposites are identified; and cost, which is sacrifice, cost, which is what man pays to nature for her industrial rewards, is said to consist of wages and profits, that is to say, of what nature yields to man in return for his industrial sacrifices. The theory thus in its simple statement confounds opposite facts and ideas, and further examination will show that it involves conclusions no less perplexed, and in conflict with doctrines the most received.

For, first, if the analysis in question be accepted, and wages and profits be taken as the constituents of cost of production, this conclusion follows: that the cost of producing commodities, taking industry as a whole, is a constant condition, incapable, however great or universal the progress of industrial improvement, of undergoing change. Suppose, for example, the general productiveness of industry were increased: this would mean that the aggregate results of industry in return for a given exertion of labor and abstinence were increased:

in other words, that the fund from which wages and profits were paid had increased in relation to the labor and abstinence expended. Wages and profits, therefore, as an aggregate would rise exactly in proportion as industry had become more productive; and the cost of producing a given commodity, measured in wages and profits, would thus remain precisely as before. There would be less labor and abstinence exerted, but this smaller exertion being more highly remunerated, the cost, measured in the remuneration, would suffer no change. I may mention that this is no fanciful deduction of mine, but has in effect been applied by at least two writers to the solution of a practical question. In a paper read some years ago before the Dublin Statistical Society, it was argued by Dr. Hancock that the cost of producing gold had not been reduced by the gold discoveries; and what was Dr. Hancock's proof of this assertion? Simply this, that the wages and profits of the producers of gold had increased as much as the labor and abstinence required for the production of a given quantity of gold had diminished, leaving thus, he said, the cost of production unchanged. The facts were undoubtedly as the argument assumed, and the inference was strictly in accordance with the accepted view of cost of production. But the inevitable conclusion (which Dr. Hancock did *not* draw) would be that the depreciation of gold is impossible.*

Take another example of the consequences involved in this doctrine. If it be true that the wages and profits received by the producers of a commodity are the measure of its cost of production, then it follows that all commodities whatever, it matters not under what circumstances produced, whether of competition or of monopoly, exchange, and can not but exchange, in proportion to their costs of production. This re-

---

* The same argument, in principle, will be found in the sixth volume of Tooke and Newmarch's "History of Prices," part vii., § 14.

sults at once from the consideration that the value of a commodity, where it is continuously produced, constitutes for the producers the fund from which wages and profits are paid. Accordingly, such as the value is, such will be the wages and profits of the producers; but such as are the wages and profits of producers, such, according to the theory, is the cost of production. When, therefore, two commodities exchange for each other, or, varying the expression, when their values or prices are the same, their costs of production, according to the view we are considering, will necessarily be the same. It is evident that this argument applies to every case of value and price, and is wholly irrespective of the circumstances, whether of freedom or monopoly, under which commodities are produced. In truth, the principle that "cost of production determines value" becomes, when thus understood, little more than the assertion of an identical proposition, since it merely amounts to saying that values are in proportion to the aggregate of the elements of which they are made up.

That a doctrine open to objections so fundamental should have obtained the currency and prestige which this has acquired may seem scarcely credible; and I am in some dread lest I should be suspected of misrepresenting the view I am combating. But that I have not done so will be admitted on consideration of the following sentences occurring in the passage quoted above, in which Mr. Mill discloses with perfect clearness the line of thought by which the view in question has been reached: "What the production of a thing costs to its producer, or its series of producers, is the labor expended in producing it. *If we consider as the producer the capitalist who makes the advances, the word labor may be replaced by wages: what the produce costs to him* is the wages which he has had to pay." In other words, the point of view is shifted from the ground of human interests to the partial and limited standpoint of the capitalist employer; and the cost of producing an article, which really consists in the sacrifices required of human beings for its production, is only considered so far forth as it is "cost to him," that much more important portion of the cost which is cost to the laborer being put altogether out of sight. This point of view being once taken, the rest follows simply and naturally. What is cost to the capitalist, that is to say, his advances, consisting of the profits of previous producers as well as of the wages of laborers, profits as well as wages, must evidently be included in cost; and not only the profits of previous producers, but, in order to meet the case of different periods of advancing capital, the profits of the producer of the particular commodity whose cost is considered—an extension of the theory which involves this curious consequence, that among the elements of the cost of producing a commodity is counted the profit obtained on that commodity by the producer, a profit which I need scarcely say is not realized till *after* the commodity is produced. Such is the line of thought by which the view in question has been reached; and it is not difficult to see why, once adopted, it should find easy and general acceptance. The vocabulary of commerce is, for obvious reasons, framed almost wholly from the capitalist's stand-point; and Political Economy is for the most part compelled to draw its nomenclature from the vocabulary of commerce. A doctrine, therefore, of cost of production which resolved all cost into capitalist's cost would easily fall in at once with the general phraseology of economic science, and with the preconceptions and prepossessions generated by commercial modes of thought.

That the laborer's share in the industrial sacrifice is by the current doctrine excluded from the conception of cost of production does not appear to have been seen, or, if seen, to have been adequately appreciated by its adherents. Mr. Mill's language seems to imply that the wages advanced by the capitalist—though he admits they only represent "the cost of producing *to him*," may yet in some way be taken to represent the cost to the laborer also, for, having dealt with this portion of the case, he leads on to the next with the words: "Thus far of labor *or wages*, as an element of cost of production..... There is also capital," etc. But I must absolutely deny that wages can in any sense be taken to represent the labor element in cost of production. Wages, as Mr. Mill observed in the passage already quoted, may be regarded as cost to the capitalist who advances them; though perhaps it would be more correct to say that, so far as they go, they *measure* his cost, which really *consists* in the deprivation of immediate enjoyment implied in the fact of the advance. But to the laborer wages are reward, not cost; nor can it be said that they stand in any constant relation to that which really constitutes cost to him. If they did, wages in all occupations, in all countries, and in all times, would be in proportion to the severity of the toil which they recompensed; whereas the proportion fails, not only in different occupations and in different countries, but whenever a general advance or decline takes place in the conditions of productive industry in the same occupations and in the same countries. That it fails in different occupations in the same country Mr. Mill himself allows; rather, let me say, he has been the first economist strongly to insist upon the importance of this fact; that it fails on a comparison of the condition of labor in different countries is too obvious to need proof; and that it fails in the same country and in the same occupations on the occurrence of important changes in the conditions of productive industry we may satisfy ourselves by simply observing the events now passing before our eyes. The remuneration of labor has for some years been pretty steadily advancing in the majority of occupations in this country—advancing not merely in its money amount, but in the real reward it procures for the laborer. And wherever this has happened without a corresponding increase in the severity of the toil undergone (and in general it has been accompanied rather by a reduction than an extension of working time), the proportion between sacrifice and reward has been altered. I repeat, therefore, that not only do wages not constitute the laborer's share in the cost of production, but they can not be taken in any sense to represent that cost. Where they are advanced by the capitalist they measure, so far as they go, the capitalist's sacrifice, and the capitalist's alone; and an analysis of cost of production, therefore, which takes no account of any sacrifices but those represented by wages, simply omits altogether the most important element of the case.

§ 4. The point for which I am contending will possibly appear to some persons to involve a purely theoretical issue. A theoretical issue no doubt is at stake, but I believe a better example could not easily be found of the intimate connection between theory and practice, and of the way in which an unsound theory can invert for people the true relation of phenomena and mislead in the practical business of life, than is furnished by this doctrine. The truth of this statement will only fully appear in the later chapters of this work; but even here I may give an example or two. What, for instance, is now the grand argument with the people of the United States for the maintenance of protection? Why, the high cost of production in that country. And what is the evidence of this high cost of production? Simply the high rates of wages which prevail. How, they ask, can we, with our high-priced labor, compete with the pauper labor of Europe? I must frankly own that, accepting the point of view of the current theory of cost, I can find no satisfactory reply to this question, and I am quite sure that Mr. Wells, who implicitly adopts this point of view, has wholly failed to furnish one. But to pursue the argument further here would be to anticipate what will come more naturally under review at a later stage of our investigation.

Nor are our commercial writers here entitled to plume themselves on the superiority of their economic notions to those of American protectionists, at least as regards this question of cost of production. In dealing with the labor question, the arguments of our capitalists do not differ in principle from that which I have just criticised. Consider, for example, the significance of such passages as this which I find in the work of so well-informed and thoughtful a writer as Mr. Brassey, and which fairly represents the economic doctrine that pervades it:

"It is the opinion of Mr. Lothian Bell, one of our highest authorities, that, after all the efforts of our iron-masters to contend with the difficulty of high-priced labor by the improvement of machinery, labor costs fifteen per cent. more in England than on the Continent, and this disadvantage, in his opinion, entirely neutralizes the advantages we derive from our great facilities in the proximity of our iron-mines to our coal-beds. Our workmen are not sufficiently alive to the necessity for the exercise of the utmost efforts of ingenuity, in order to enable capital invested in England to hold its own in the industrial campaign."*

Now, I ask, what inversion of the true relations of things can be more complete than to represent high-priced labor as an obstacle to production in the same sense in which the proximity of our coal-beds to our iron-mines constitutes a facility? Dear labor neutralizing the advantages of our coal-beds and iron-mines! As well speak of the large fees reaped by a successful barrister as neutralizing the advantage of his skill; for not more certainly are the large fees the consequence of the barrister's legal skill, than the high wages of our artisans are the consequence of the industrial advantages under which they work. Now what is the explanation of this singular confusion of thought and perversion of facts? Obviously this—the whole problem of industry is looked at exclusively from the capitalist's

---

* See "Work and Wages," p. 19.

point of view. "The advantages *we* derive" from our coal-beds and iron-mines are the advantages which capitalists derive from them. "British trade" means capitalists' profits; and, as the only cost taken account of in production is the capitalists' cost, so naturally the capitalists' remuneration is the only remuneration thought worth attending to. Hence high wages are represented as "neutralizing" industrial advantages, as if nothing were gain which did not come to the capitalist's maw; and the liberal remuneration of the working-people is deplored as a national calamity because it sets limits to the capitalist's share in the produce of their joint exertions. "Dear labor," says Mr. Brassey (p. 142), summing up the argument of a chapter, "is now the great obstacle to the extension of British trade."* It does not occur to him that high profits are an obstacle in precisely the same sense. If British laborers and capitalists will only consent to accept a lower scale of remuneration for their services they may have the satisfaction of indefinitely extending British trade and achieving the great goal of commercial ambition by underselling all the nations of the earth. Each, however, halts, and would prefer that the other should take

---

* I can not resist quoting the sentence which follows: "But we see how cheap labor at the command of our competitors [continental capitalist employers] seems to exercise the same enervating influence as the delights of Capua on the soldiers of Hannibal" (p. 142). To which this, from the *Times's* money article, may serve as a pendant: "It must be borne in mind that no discovery of fresh supplies [of coal], either in Europe or America, would cause any decisive benefit, because the present difficulty in those parts of the world is not from want of coal, but from want of labor. . . . . The East is the only quarter *where labor is untrammeled;* and it would be interesting to the English public to learn, as far as the coal question is concerned, why, in a British settlement, where labor and material are both in abundance, nothing can be accomplished to mitigate an evil which promises to become one of the most serious ever inflicted upon the industry of civilized nations." It is not clear whether the evil deprecated is the scarcity of coal or the high price of British labor; but, from the point of view both of the *Times* and of Mr. Brassey, these would both be evils of the same order.

the initiative in the patriotic sacrifice, desiring, like the French soldiers at the battle of Fontenoy, to give to his opponent the honor of firing first.

§ 5. It seems to me that a sufficient case has now been made out to justify an attempt at a fresh exposition of the doctrine of Cost of Production. I therefore proceed to submit to the reader that view of it which such reflection as I have been able to give to the subject has led me to form.

And here I must, in the first place, insist that cost means sacrifice, and can not, without risk of hopelessly confusing ideas, be identified with any thing that is not sacrifice. It represents what man parts with in the barter between him and nature, which must be kept eternally distinct from the return made by nature on that payment. This is the essential nature of cost; and the problem of cost of production as bearing on the theory of value is to ascertain how far and in what way the payment thus made by man to nature in productive industry determines or otherwise influences the exchange value of the products which result. To find an answer to this question we need not go beyond that fundamental principle of conduct which leads men to seek their ends by the easiest and shortest means. The end of engaging in industry is the acquisition of wealth; and the means, self-denial, toil, forethought, vigilance. The problem of industry is, therefore, to attain wealth at the least expenditure of those bodily and mental exertions—or, as we may say, at the least sacrifice or cost. And the law of cost of production, as governing value, is merely the practical consequence and outcome of the pursuit of wealth under this condition.

In order to perceive this, it is only necessary to keep steadily in view the two following facts: First, that under the influence of the motive just indicated, men, in selecting their occupations, whether as laborers or as capitalists, will, *so far as they have the power of choice,* select those which, in return for a given sacrifice, yield, or promise to yield, the largest rewards; and secondly, the fact that, under a system of separation of employments, industrial rewards consist for each producer, or, more properly, for each group of producers, employed on a given work, in the value of the commodities which result from their exertions. I say in the *value* of the commodities, not in the commodities themselves; for it is not always that the man who is engaged in industry needs the particular commodity on which his own exertions are bestowed, and it is seldom that he needs more than at most an insignificant quantity of what he produces; consequently his remuneration must come, not from the direct but from the indirect results of his labors—from those things, whatever they are, which the commodity he produces enables him by sale and purchase to command—in other words, from its value. Given the productiveness of a man's industry, this alone will not enable us to determine the amount of his remuneration. In order to this, we must further know the proportions in which what he produces will exchange for what he wants—that is to say, for the articles of his consumption. The value of the product resulting from industry forms thus the source from which, under the actual state of things, industry is remunerated. Nor is this conclusion invalidated by the fact that, under the industrial organization prevailing in this and other civilized countries, the laborer commonly receives his reward in the form of wages advanced by the capitalist before the product is completed; since what he receives is subsequently recouped to the capitalist, the sum being drawn from the value of the product; so that it is still *the value of the product* from which the remuneration of all concerned in the creation of that product ultimately comes. Wages and profits in each branch of industry are thus derived from the value of the commodities proceeding from that branch of industry, and, as (with the exception of the case where rent is also an element in the value of commodities—a case which, those acquainted with the economic theory of rent will perceive, does not affect the general argument) wages and profits also absorb the whole of that value, it follows that, other things being the same, the aggregate of wages and profits received by any given group of producers will always vary with the value of the aggregate of commodities which they produce. Where wages and profits, therefore, in different occupations are in proportion to the sacrifices undergone, the value of the commodities proceeding from those occupations will also be in proportion to the same sacrifices, that is to say, the commodities will exchange in proportion to their costs of production. Now wages and profits will be in proportion to the sacrifices undergone wherever, and only so far as, competition prevails among producers — wherever, and so far only as, laborers and capitalists have an effective choice in selecting among the various occupations presented to them in the industrial field. Give them this effective choice, and the correspondence of remuneration to sacrifice, not indeed in every act of production, but as a permanent and continuing state of things, is secured by the most active and constant of human motives. Each competitor, aiming at the largest reward in return for his sacrifices, will be drawn toward the occupations which happen at the time to be the best remunerated; while he will equally be repelled from those in which the remuneration is below the average level. The supply of products proceeding from the better paid employments will thus be increased, and that from the less remunerative reduced, until supply, acting on price, corrects the inequality, and brings remuneration into proportion with the sacrifices undergone. Competition, therefore, is at once the security for the correspondence of industrial remuneration with sacrifice, and also, and because it is so, the security for the correspondence of the values of commodities with the costs of their production.

The indispensable condition to the action of cost of production as the regulator of normal values is thus the existence of an effective competition among those engaged in industrial pursuits; and the point to which we have now to turn our attention is the extent to which such effective competition is actually realized in industrial communities. Confining our attention for the present to England, we find competition here active and widely prevalent. In trade, as distinguished from industry, I mean in the buying and selling of commodities as distinguished from their production, it may be said to be universal and unlimited. Every one is at liberty, and not only at liberty, but in general has the practical power, to sell his commodity,* whatever it may be, in any market in the country. Again, every one, speaking broadly, is free, so far as the law is concerned, to engage in any industrial pursuit he pleases, from hedging and ditching up to the learned professions. But for the present purpose something more than this is necessary. Not only must there be for dealers the right and power of selling the commodity where they please, and for workmen the legal right of admission to whatever occupation each prefers, but there must be, for laborers and capitalists respectively, the practical power of employing their labor and capital in whatever direction each may please—in a word, an effective choice in deciding on the destination of the instrument of which they have each to dispose. It matters not what the obstacle may be to the effectiveness of the choice, whether law, ignorance, or poverty—if there be an obstacle, if the producer can not pass freely from the less to the more lucrative occupation, competition is defeated, so far as regards the requirements of the law of cost, since there can be no security

---

* I say his "commodity," not his "service." The grounds for not including labor and commodities in the same category, in an exposition of the theory of value, will be found stated further on (part ii., chap. i.).

under such circumstances that remuneration shall be brought into correspondence with sacrifice. This is the sort of competition through which cost of production, as a regulator of value, works; and the question is, How far does competition in this sense prevail in this and other industrial communities?

There is a school of reasoners who will not hesitate to answer this question by flatly denying the existence of competition at all in the sense defined. I shall be told that the assumption so readily made by economists, that capital and labor may be shifted about from one occupation to another in search of the highest remuneration, is a mere figment of the economical brain, without foundation in fact. Once embodied in a form suited to actual work, capital, it will be urged, is for the most part incapable of being turned to other uses. The buildings, plant, and material required for one kind of manufacture can rarely be adapted to any other, and, even where the conversion is possible, the process will only be accomplished at great expense and loss. The difficulty of transferring labor, it will be contended, is even greater, since we are here in contact with mental as well as physical obstacles. Industrial skill is not a thing to be acquired in a moment, and that which a man possesses is the result, in general, of considerable time and outlay devoted to its acquisition. Is it likely that, having spent his time and money in acquiring this skill and fitting himself for a particular occupation, a workman will desert the line of life he has chosen on the first sign of an advance in remuneration elsewhere? We are reminded how long the hand-loom weavers persisted in their unprofitable labors after power-looms were in general use; and we can imagine how extreme the case would be which would cause a carpenter to become a smith, or a smith a carpenter, still more, which would cause either to take to hair-dressing or tailoring. On such grounds, it has been contended that competition, such as I have defined it as necessary to the action of the principle of cost, has no real existence, and that consequently all theories assuming its existence fall to the ground. Alike with regard to capital and labor, it is held that either, once embarked in a particular employment, is practically committed to that employment, and may therefore be regarded as taken out of the field of competition with agents of the same kind engaged in other branches of industry. I am anxious to do the fullest justice to the quantum of truth contained in this argument, and I admit at once that the facts alleged are substantially true. But I think it will not be difficult to show that they by no means sustain the practical conclusion they are adduced to support, and that, taking account of other conditions of the case which the argument overlooks, they are perfectly compatible with the existence of an effective industrial competition.

In the first place, it may be remarked that, in order to secure an effective industrial competition—such a competition as shall bring rewards into correspondence with sacrifices—it is not necessary that every portion of capital, or that every laborer, should be at all times capable of being turned to any selected occupation. It is enough that a certain quantity of each agent —varying according to circumstances—should be thus disposable. Suppose some branch of industry to be specially flourishing and to be realizing exceptional gains, there is no need that the whole industry of the country should be disturbed to correct the inequality. A small diversion of capital and labor— small, I mean, in comparison with the aggregate embarked in any important industry—will in general suffice for the purpose. Even on extraordinary occasions, when unlooked-for events in the political or commercial world disturb ordinary calculations and give an enormous advantage to particular industries—such occasions, for example, as occurred in the early years of railway enterprise, or again in the linen trade on the breaking out of the American civil war—even on such occasions, the equilibrium of remuneration and cost can always be restored, not indeed in a moment, but after no long delay, through the action of labor and capital still uncommitted to actual industrial employment, and without any sensible encroachment on the stock already actively employed. All that is necessary, therefore, with a view to an effective industrial competition, is the presence in a community of a certain quantity of those instruments of production existing in disposable form, ready to be turned toward the more lucrative pursuits, and sufficiently large to correct inequalities as they arise. Now, it will not be difficult to show that this condition is fulfilled in many industrial communities, completely in the case of capital, and less perfectly, but still within certain limits really and effectually, in the case of labor also.

The existence of a large amount of capital in commercial countries in disposable form—or, to speak less equivocally, in the form of money or other purchasing power, capable of being turned to any purpose required—is a patent and undeniable fact. Nor is it less certain that this capital is constantly seeking the best investments, and rapidly moves toward any branch of industry that happens at the moment to offer special attractions.* It is plain, too, that the capital thus disposable is suffi-

---

* "Political economists say that capital sets toward the most profitable trades, and that it rapidly leaves the less profitable and non-paying trades. But in ordinary countries this is a slow process, and some persons, who want to have ocular demonstration of abstract truths, have been inclined to doubt it because they could not see it. In England, however, the process would be visible enough if you could only see the books of the bill-brokers and the bankers. Their bill-cases, as a rule, are full of the bills drawn in the most profitable trades, and *cæteris paribus* and in comparison empty of those drawn in the less profitable. If the iron trade ceases to be as profitable as usual, less iron is sold; the fewer the sales the fewer the bills; and in consequence the number of iron bills in Lombard Street is diminished. On the other hand, if in consequence of a bad harvest the corn trade becomes on a sudden profitable, immediately 'corn bills' are created in great numbers, and if good, are discounted in Lombard Street. Thus English capital runs as surely and instantly where it is most wanted, and where there is most to be made of it, as water runs to find its level."—"Lombard Street," p. 13, by WALTER BAGEHOT.

cient for the purpose we have here in view, namely, to render competition effective among the various industries; since we find a portion of it constantly moving abroad for foreign investment—a destination it would scarcely receive while there was a prospect of reaping exceptionally high returns from investment within the country. We have, therefore, in the existence of this fund all that is required for a practically effective competition, so far as *one* instrument of production is concerned, and this without necessitating any serious encroachment on the capital actually engaged in productive operations. But is the corresponding condition satisfied in the case of labor? A little consideration will show that, within certain limits and subject to certain qualifications, it is fulfilled in this as well.

For here also we have a disposable fund, capable of being turned, as remuneration may tempt, in various directions. Granted that labor, once engaged in a particular occupation, is practically committed to that species of occupation; all labor is not thus engaged and committed. A young generation is constantly coming forward, whose capabilities may be regarded as still in disposable form, fulfilling the same function in relation to the general labor force of the country which capital, while yet existing as purchasing power, discharges in relation to its general capital. The young persons composing this body, or others interested in their welfare, are eagerly watching the prospects of industry in its several branches, and will not be slow to turn toward the pursuits that promise the largest rewards. Individual tastes, no doubt, will go for something in the decision, but varieties of tastes, taken over a large area, may be assumed pretty well to balance each other; and there will remain a steady gravitation of disposable labor toward the more remunerative callings. On the other hand, while fresh labor is coming on the scene, worn-out labor is passing off; and the departments of industry, in which remuneration has from any causes fallen below the average level, ceasing to be recruited, the numbers of those employed in them will quickly decline, until supply is brought within the limits of demand, and remuneration is restored to its just proportions. In this way, then, in the case of labor as in that of capital, the conditions for an effective competition exist, notwithstanding the practical difficulties in the way of transferring labor, once trained to a particular occupation, to new pursuits. But, as I have already intimated, the conditions are in this case realized only in an imperfect manner, and this involves, as a consequence, certain limitations on the action of competition in the labor market, and certain corresponding effects on the values of commodities. What the nature of those limitations are I shall now proceed to point out.

I remarked just now that the youthful labor constantly coming forward to recruit the labor market might be compared to the capital still existing in the form of purchasing power, and ready to be applied to any occupation, according as the prospect of profit might determine. In one important respect, however, the analogy fails. Of the capital existing in this disposable form any portion may be applied to any industrial purpose. But of the disposable labor each element—that is to say, each individual laborer—can only choose his employment within certain tolerably well-defined limits. These limits are the limits set by the qualifications required for each branch of trade and the amount of preparation necessary for their acquisition. Take an individual workman whose occupation is still undetermined, he will, according to circumstances, have a narrower or wider field of choice; but in no case will this be co-extensive with the entire range of domestic industry. If he belongs to the class of agricultural laborers, all forms of mere unskilled labor are open to him, but beyond this he is practically shut out from competition. The barrier is his social position and circumstances, which render his education defective, while his means are too narrow to allow of his repairing the defect, or of deferring the return upon his industry till he has qualified himself for a skilled occupation. Mounting a step higher in the industrial scale,— to the artisan class, including with them the class of small dealers whose pecuniary position is much upon a par with artisans, here also within certain limits there is complete freedom of choice, but beyond a certain range practical exclusion. The man who is brought up to be an ordinary carpenter, mason, or smith, may go to any of these callings, or a hundred more, according as his taste prompts, or the prospect of remuneration attracts him; but practically he has no power to compete in those higher departments of skilled labor for which a more elaborate education and larger training are necessary, for example, mechanical engineering. Ascend a step higher still, and we find ourselves again in presence of similar limitations: we encounter persons competent to take part in any of the higher skilled industries, but practically excluded from the professions. It is true, indeed, that in none of these cases is the exclusion absolute. The limits imposed are not such as may not be overcome by extraordinary energy, self-denial, and enterprise; and by virtue of these qualities individuals in all classes are escaping every day from the bounds of their original position, and forcing their way into the ranks of those who stand above them. All this, no doubt, is true. But such exceptional phenomena do not affect the substantial truth of our position. What we find, in effect, is, not a whole population competing indiscriminately for all occupations, but a series of industrial layers, superposed on one another, within each of which the various candidates for employment possess a real and effective power of selection, while those occupying the several strata are, for all purposes of effective competition, practically isolated from each other. We may perhaps venture to arrange them in some such order as this: first, at the bottom of the scale there would be the large group of unskilled or nearly unskilled laborers, comprising agricultural laborers, laborers engaged in miscellaneous occupations in towns, or acting in attendance on skilled labor. Secondly, there would be the artisan group, comprising skilled laborers of the secondary order — carpenters, joiners, smiths, masons, shoe-makers, tailors, hatters, etc., etc., with whom might be included the very large class of small retail dealers, whose means and position place them within the reach of the same industrial opportunities as the class of artisans. The third layer would contain producers and dealers of a higher order, whose work would demand qualifications only obtainable by persons of substantial means and fair educational opportunities — for example, civil and mechanical engineers, chemists, opticians, watch-makers, and others of the same industrial grade, in which might also find a place the superior class of retail tradesmen; while above these there would be a fourth, comprising persons still more favorably circumstanced, whose ampler means would give them a still wider choice. This last group would contain members of the learned professions, as well as persons engaged in the various careers of science and art, and in the higher branches of mercantile business. The reader will not understand me as offering here an exhaustive classification of the industrial population. I attempt nothing of the kind; but merely seek to exhibit in rough outline the form which industrial organization, under the actual conditions of modern life, tends to assume; my object being, by putting the fact in a concrete shape, to furnish help toward a more distinct apprehension of the limitations imposed by social circumstances on the free competition of labor than would be obtained from more general statements. As I have already said, I am far from contending for the existence of any hard lines of demarkation between any categories of persons in this country. No doubt the various ranks and classes fade into each other by imperceptible gradations, and individuals from all classes are constantly passing up or dropping down; but while this is so, it is nevertheless true that the average workman, from whatever rank he be taken, finds his power of competition limited for practical purposes to a certain range of occupations, so that, however high the rates of remuneration in those which lie beyond may rise, he is excluded from sharing them. We are thus compelled to recognize the existence of non-competing industrial groups as a feature of our social economy; and this is the fact which I desire here to insist upon. It remains to be considered how this organization of industry is calculated to modify the action of the principle of cost of production.

The reader will remember that there are two distinct sacrifices undergone in the business of production—the sacrifice of the capitalist, and the sacrifice of the laborer. As regards the former, the competition of capital being, as we have seen, effective over the entire industry of each commercial country, it follows that so much of the value of commodities as goes to remunerate the capitalist's sacrifice, and which may be regarded as the "profit fund," will correspond throughout the range of domestic industry with that portion of the cost which falls to the capitalist. The defalcation from the principle of cost occurs not here, but in that other and larger element in the value of commodities which goes to remunerate the laborer. The nature of the failure may be thus described: The exchange of all commodities produced by laborers belonging to the same industrial group, or competing circle, will be governed by the principle of cost—this results necessarily from the fact that competition *is* effective within such groups or circles; but the exchange of commodities produced by laborers belonging to different groups or competing circles will, for the opposite reason, not be governed by this principle. Thus all the products of unskilled labor will exchange for each other in proportion to their costs; as will also all the products of ordinary artisan labor *as among themselves*. But the latter products will not exchange against the former in proportion to their costs, nor will the products of artisan labor, or of unskilled labor, exchange in proportion to their costs against those of the higher industrial groups. The price of a deal table and the price of a common lock will be found to correspond to the sacrifices actually undergone by their producers; or again, the price of a barometer and the price of a watch will be found to correspond to the same conditions; but if we compare the price of either of the latter commodities with that of either of the former, we shall find that the correspondence fails; the prices of the barometer and of the watch will bear a far larger proportion to their respective costs than those of the deal table, or of the common lock, to theirs. If any one questions the fact, the evidence is to be found in the relative remuneration of the producers of the several articles. That remuneration, as I have shown, comes from the price of the commodity in each case; but, while it is in proportion to the relative sacrifices of production in the case of the workmen who are in competition with each other, it is not in proportion to those sacrifices where the workmen are excluded from mutual competition. The result, then, is that the principle of cost of production controls exchange value in the transactions taking place within certain limited industrial areas; while, in the reciprocal dealings of those several areas with one another, its operation fails.

This is the principal modification suffered by cost of production in consequence of the circumstance we are considering. In reality, however, the effects of that state of things are a good deal more complex than would appear from the statement just made; for in that statement account was not taken of the fact that the same commodity is very frequently the product of labor belonging to different industrial circles. For example, a house is mainly produced by masons, brick-layers, carpenters, plasterers, and others, who would all rank in the class of artisans; but a considerable quantity of purely unskilled labor is also employed in attendance upon these, as labor of a higher degree of skill than that of the ordinary artisan is employed in the finishing and decoration of the house. Now suppose a commodity of this kind, the joint production of workmen of different orders, to be exchanged against one produced by workmen belonging to some one industrial group, or to several groups, but in proportions different from those obtaining in the other case, what principle would here govern exchange value, or—to express the conception in a more familiar form—the relative prices of the commodities? Manifestly more than one principle will be engaged in determining the result. So far as the two commodities are the products of workmen in competition with each other, their values will be governed by cost of production, but so far as they proceed from workmen not in mutual competition, they will be governed by that other principle, yet to be ascertained, which governs normal value in the absence of competition. Supposing the commodity with which a house is compared were produced exclusively by the artisan class, the cost principle would be mainly operative in determining the exchange relation; but it would not be entirely so, since a portion, though a small portion, of the house has been produced by workmen not in competition with the producers of the other article. On the other hand, if the comparison were made between a house and a commodity produced either wholly by unskilled labor, or wholly by labor of a degree of skill superior to that of ordinary artisan labor, the relative values would follow. but in a slight degree, the rule of cost of production, being mainly controlled by the principle prevailing in the absence of the conditions which secure the action of cost. This example will serve to show the great complication that arises in the relative values of commodities under the actual conditions of their production. And if we bear in mind that all manufactured commodities are produced from raw materials which are very frequently the product of workmen not in competition with those who perform the manufacturing process, we shall see how widely the range of this sort of complication extends. Still we must not exaggerate its importance. What mainly happens is, that the bulk of the value of each commodity follows one law—say the law of cost, or what we shall afterward find to be the law of reciprocal demand, while a small remaining element is governed by a different principle. Thus, reverting for a moment to a previous illustration, a barometer and a watch are in very large proportion the products of workmen of a high order of skill, and in industrial competition with each other; in a very insignificant degree, of workmen of an inferior order: as, on the other hand, a deal table and a common lock are mainly the products of ordinary artisan labor, though, it may be in some small degree, also of labor not in competition with the labor of artisans. In so far, however, as any portion of the labor employed on the barometer is out of competition with some portion of that employed on the watch, and in so far as the same is true of the labor employed on the other compared articles, to that extent we were not justified in asserting that the commodities in question exchanged, either pair of them, in proportion to their costs of production. Nevertheless, it is certain that our statement was substantially true, since the chief portion, and so much the chief portion as to be nearly the whole, of the labor employed on each pair fulfilled the required condition; and this would govern a corresponding proportion of their values. A similar qualification would be needed in the case of most assertions of a like nature. In strictness, we can seldom say that the values of two commodities are in their whole extent governed by their costs of production: we can only say that they are so mainly, and in their chief elements. In effect the point in question is of little more than theoretic importance. As a point of theory it is proper to notice it, but the circumstance it deals with has little sensible effect upon the facts of exchange.

The mode in which the cost of producing commodities operates in regulating their values has now, I trust, been made tolerably clear. It will probably have been observed, that as I have departed from the current doctrine in my view of the elements of cost, so also have I departed from it in my manner of representing the operation of the law. That law is ordinarily regarded as a principle governing value *universally* wherever it affects value at all—governing, that is to say, the value of certain classes of commodities *in all exchanges;* so that, the conditions of their production being known, the law of their value is supposed to be known, whatever may be the nature or the conditions of production of the commodities against which they are exchanged. For example, the price of calico would commonly be said to be governed by its cost of production, and this would be laid down without any limitation as to the article which might form the other member in the exchange. If, however, the exposition contained in the foregoing pages be sound, this conception of the law can not be correct. For what has there appeared is a tendency in commodities to exchange in proportion to their costs of production *only so far as there exists free competition among their producers.* The exchange, therefore, in proportion to cost would only take place within the limits of the field of free competition; and a commodity produced within this field, but exchanged against one produced by workmen from beyond it, would not in such case exchange in proportion to its cost of production. Supposing, for example, A, B, C, D, E, F, to be commodities, the producers of which are all in free competition with each other, such commodities would exchange among themselves in proportion to their costs. Again, supposing X, Y, Z, to be commodities produced by workmen also in free competition with each other, but excluded from competing with those who had produced A, B, C, D, etc.; here again the values of X, Y, Z, in the exchanges of these commodities against each other would be governed by the principle of cost. But now suppose the exchange to be made of a commodity belonging to the former category against one belonging to the latter—value would in this case be no longer governed by cost of production, inasmuch as there was no longer free competition among those who had produced the commodities exchanged. Now if the reader will recall the description that has been given of the various non-competing groups of which our industrial system is made up, he will perceive that the case last supposed represents no inconsiderable proportion of all the exchanges which take place within such a country as this; and that, therefore, the action of cost of production in regulating value is by no means as extensively prevalent, even within the limits of the same country, as the current theory would lead us to suppose. The same commodity follows the law of cost of production in some exchanges and does not follow it in others; nor is it true that the value of any commodity conforms to the principle of cost in all exchanges. In order that this should happen, effective competition should be established among producers over the entire field of industry—a condition which, I need hardly say, is very far yet from being anywhere fulfilled. The true conception of the law of cost is thus, not of a law governing universally the values of any class of commodities, but that of one governing the values of certain commodities in certain exchanges.

§ 6. In what has gone before, cost of production has been discussed without more than a passing reference to the nature of the elements which compose it. There was no need to discriminate those elements with particularity while we were occupied in establishing the general principle, but the evidence for that principle having now been set forth, it will be desirable to attempt some analysis and characterization of the constituents of cost.

There can not be much difficulty in determining the principal elements of cost of production, once we have firmly seized the fact that, as cost means sacrifice and not reward, so cost of production means the sacrifice involved in production—in the act or acts of rendering certain objects supplied by nature fitted for human purposes, not the beneficial result or return upon such acts. This sacrifice, so soon as industry has passed its most primitive stage, assumes two distinct forms—first, that involved in the physical or mental exertion incident to taking part personally in the work of production, which we may call briefly the sacrifice of "labor;" and, secondly, that involved in supplying the prerequisites of productive operations, or capital—a form of sacrifice which is conveniently expressed by the term "abstinence." These are the principal kinds of sacrifices involved in productive industry; but there is also a third, the liability, namely, of producers to certain evils over and above the usual and calculable sacrifices incident to their work, which we may call "risk." There is no reason in the nature of things that these several sacrifices should not be undergone by the same person, that is to say, that the same person should not be at once laborer and capitalist, and also incur all the risk of the industrial operation; and in point of fact this arrangement has place more or less in every country, and in some countries, especially those in which peasant proprietorship prevails, to a great extent. In England, however, and in all the non-agricultural industry of most civilized countries, the sacrifices of labor and abstinence are, for the most part, undergone by distinct classes, who are named, accordingly, laborers and capitalists. The sacrifice of risk, on the other hand, falls on both classes of producers alike, though the nature of the risk differs according as it affects one or the other. Affecting the capitalist, it is risk to his property; affecting the laborer, it is risk to his bodily and mental faculties or life, but in either case it is an element of cost; being a real sacrifice incurred by a producer, and demanding consequently a corresponding compensation in the value of the product.*

Our analysis, then, of cost of production resolves it into three principal elements, which, I may remark, are also *ultimate* elements†—Labor, Abstinence, and Risk; the first, under the prevailing industrial arrangements of this and other civilized countries, borne by the laborer, in that enlarged sense of the term in which "laborer" includes all who take a personal part in the business of production; the second by the capitalist; the third falling upon laborer and capitalist alike. A few remarks on each of these elements will suffice for my present purpose.

Considering labor as an element of cost of production, the principal remark that seems called for is that, in estimating it in this character, three circumstances, and three circumstances only, must be taken account of—namely, the duration of the exertion, the degree of its severity or irksomeness, and the risk or liability to injury of any kind attending it. As commodities differ greatly more in the duration of the exertion, or the quantity of the labor required for their production, than in the severity of this labor or the risk attending it, the former is obviously the most important circumstance in the case, and it was to it alone that Ricardo, in his analysis of cost, had re-

---

* In the usual exposition of the doctrine of cost of production the only risk taken account of is that incurred by the capitalist; but this is merely a consequence of that habit of contemplating the work of production exclusively from the capitalist's stand-point, of which I have already spoken.

† As I understand the word, "an ultimate element" in the subject-matter of any science is either an element which in the actual state of knowledge does not admit of being farther resolved, or one the resolution of which belongs to some other department of knowledge. In this sense labor, abstinence, and risk are ultimate elements in Political Economy, since, though they all admit of being traced to prior conditions and so "explained," the task of performing this process falls within the province of other sciences. In what sense profits and wages can, in any case, be considered *ultimate* elements of cost I am at a loss to understand.

gard ; but manifestly his exposition was in this respect defective. The labor employed in producing different commodities differs in severity and in liability to accident as well as in mere quantity, and, in proportion as it is more severe or more liable to accident, implies, other things being the same, a greater sacrifice, and therefore a larger cost. This greater sacrifice will require corresponding compensation, which, as in other cases, can only be furnished from the value of the product. Commodities, accordingly, will exchange—if we confine our attention to the labor element of cost—not simply in proportion to the quantity of labor employed in their production, but in proportion to this multiplied by the severity of the labor or the risk attending it. When, however, we have taken account of quantity, irksomeness, and risk, we have taken account of every incident in virtue of which labor is an element of cost of production, and affects through this principle the value of commodities.

It will be observed that in the brief analysis just given I have not taken any account of skill as an incident of labor entering into the cost of production. In making this omission, I have no doubt I shall be considered by many to have omitted a principal element of the case. Nevertheless, I must maintain that skill, as skill, is no part of the cost of production, and I add, that no article is dearer than another simply in virtue of the skill bestowed upon it. Let me explain. Skill, I say, is no element of cost, but it may be, and generally is, an indication of that which is an element of cost—namely, the sacrifice, whether in the form of labor or abstinence, undergone in acquiring the skill. Now, so far as skill is the product of such sacrifice, it undoubtedly represents an element of the cost of production; but the point to be attended to is, that the addition thus made to the cost of production is in proportion, not to the skill, but to the sacrifice necessary to the acquisition of the skill. As a matter of fact, the products of most kinds of skilled labor exchange against those of unskilled in a proportion much more favorable to the former than cost of production, as I have defined the doctrine, would prescribe. But this does not prove that skill is an element of cost; because it will be found that, where the products of skilled labor command these high terms of exchange, the conditions of production are not those in which cost of production would govern value; in other words, the result in question only occurs where skilled labor represents a monopoly. If we desire evidence of the powerlessness of skill, as such, to affect the value of commodities, we have only to consider the very low prices which many works of the highest literary and scientific excellence fetch, as compared with products of a far lower degree of skill. The eminent skill embodied in such works does not prevent their selling at a price far below their cost of production, as measured by the prices of commodities representing skill of a different order; and if in other instances the products of skill command prices far above what the law of cost would prescribe, no more is this elevated value due to the skill which such products represent, but to the circumstances which limit the possession of this skill to a small number of persons as compared with the demand for their services.*

* The reader will observe that the doctrine here laid down as to the relation of skill to the value of commodities and, as depending on this, to the relative remuneration of services, relates to skill of different kinds as existing in the different departments of industry. *Within the limits of the same trade or profession* differences of skill will, in general, under free competition, be accompanied with corresponding differences of remuneration. What the capitalist employing labor looks to is not the labor, but the result; and, consequently, where two inferior workmen only produce the same result as one of superior skill, it will be worth his while to pay the latter double what he could afford to pay either of the former. Relative wages, therefore, *within the same occupation*, will, where competition prevails, be, in general, pretty accurately adjusted to the different degrees of skill: *in different occupations*—and it is only with these, as furnishing the occasion of exchange, that a theory of value has to do—they will be affected by skill only in the manner pointed out in the text.

The true relation between skill and value may be expressed in the following propositions:

First, skill, as skill, produces no effect upon value; in other words, commodities do not under any circumstances exchange for each other in proportion to the degree of skill bestowed upon them. Secondly, skill, though in itself inoperative on value, nevertheless affects it indirectly in two distinct ways: first, where competition is effective among producers, through the cost which must be undergone in acquiring the skill—in such cases the value of skilled products will, *cæteris paribus*, exceed that of unskilled by the amount of the normal returns upon this cost; and, secondly, in the absence of effective competition, through the principle of monopoly, by limiting the number of competitors in skilled occupations, and so acting on the supply of skilled products. In either of these ways skill may raise value; but, as skill, that is to say, in virtue of its own excellence, whether measured by the standard of utility or of artistic merit, it is powerless for this result.

There is, indeed, a mode of speaking sanctioned by the language of some economists, and much in favor with those who seek to justify in all things existing industrial arrangements, which implies that skill, as such, is a source of value, and that high or low wages and prices are to be explained by reference simply to the results of the skill which services or commodities embody. For example, we constantly hear it said, in reply to complaints of wages being unduly low in certain industries, that this must be so, inasmuch as the services remunerated by these low wages are of little worth, while the higher wages obtained in others are explained by reference to the high worth of the services rendered by the workmen employed. Employers, we are told, can not afford to pay any class of workmen more than their services are worth. Now, what is the standard of "worth" here adopted? There would seem to be but two standards possible; first that furnished by the exchange itself: in other words, the "worth" of a service may be measured by the money it commands. According to this conception of "worth," the statement that wages are low because the services they remunerate are of little worth, and high because the worth of the services is high, merely means that wages are high or low because they are high or low, which does not much elucidate the problem; while, in the assertion that employers can not pay their workmen more than their services are worth, the point at issue is formally begged, since — the standard of worth being the actual terms of the exchange—it amounts to saying that employers can not afford to pay their workmen more than they actually do pay them, which is just what the complainants deny. In truth, however, though this is the standard of worth upon which those who use the argument I am considering would, if pushed, probably rely, their language really suggests something more than this—the idea, namely, that industrial "worth" is something varying with the utility embodied in the services, or, what comes nearly to the same thing, with the skill which is productive of this utility. Some such sense as this must be assigned to their words if they are not to be taken as expressing barren truisms; but in any such sense, the statements in question are wholly unfounded. No such connection between wages (it will be understood that I speak now of *comparative* wages) and the utility or skillfulness of the services rendered exists as the language assumes, any more than a similar connection can be made out between these qualities and the prices of commodities. The true connection is not with either utility or skill, but, where competition is effective, with cost of production, and in the absence of effective competition, with monopoly, more or less qualified, and acting through supply and demand. To return from this partial digression, we find labor, as an element of cost of production, measurable by reference to three of its incidents, and to three of its incidents only—1st, the duration of the exertion, or the quantity of labor; 2d, its severity or irksomeness; and 3d, the risk attending it. In whatever other qualities various sorts of labor may differ, unless so far as these are indications of onerous effort expended, they are no portion of the labor element of cost, and must be regarded as irrelevant to the question now in hand.

The term "abstinence" is the name given to the sacrifice involved in the advance of capital. As to the nature of this sacrifice, it is mainly of a negative kind; consisting chiefly in the deprivation or postponement of enjoyment, implied in the fact of parting with our wealth so far at least as concerns our present power of commanding it. The term, indeed, would imply that the sacrifice is wholly negative; but I am inclined to include in it a certain small positive element, namely, that low degree of risk which is never absent from the advance of capital. That some degree of risk always accompanies the act in question is evident from the nature of the case, since it implies either the trusting of one's wealth to other persons, or, where it is employed by the owner himself in productive industry, the putting of it, with a view to future results, into forms not capable of being directly converted to his uses. It will be more convenient, I think, to consider this slight and inevitable risk, which is always present where abstinence is exercised for economic ends, as an incident of that sacrifice, than as a substantive element of cost to be associated with "risk" as I have defined it in that character. I shall, therefore, so understand it, and shall accordingly define "abstinence" as the act of abstaining from the personal use of wealth with a view to employing it in productive industry, combined with that low degree of risk inevitably attaching to every such act.

This being the nature of abstinence, the question will suggest itself how far it may be properly considered as an industrial sacrifice needing a stimulus to its exercise in the form of specific reward, and to be co-ordinated with labor in an analysis of the sacrifices of production. It must be admitted that its connection with production is not so intimate as that of labor, since capital, however it may augment the efficiency of industry, is not absolutely indispensable to it. What we have to deal with, however, is not industry, as it may exist among savages or in very primitive communities, but industry as it exists in civilized countries; and to industry in this sense, to industry as it must be carried on if the populations now inhabiting civilized countries are to continue to exist, capital is absolutely indispensable. But, if so, then abstinence, the act by which capital comes into existence, must be regarded as a necessary condition toward the efficacious prosecution of industrial pursuits.

But is it properly a sacrifice? a sacrifice which needs, in order that it be undergone, the prospect of a specific reward? To put the question in another form, are profits to be placed on the same line with wages in an analysis of the economy of production? As to the economic foundation of wages, the case is very clear. Wages are necessary, first, to support the laborer, and, secondly, in a free community, to induce him to work. Capital has no need to be fed and clothed, but, in order to its existence, there must be an adequate motive offered to the owners of wealth to induce them to employ it in this way. At present this inducement is found in profit; and the question to be considered is, whether, consistently with the maintenance of capital, this inducement can be dispensed with. There are those who think it may, who hold that capital may be maintained without any deduction in favor of the capitalist from the value of the product which results from its use, and which they would assign in its entirety to those who take a personal, not to say a manual, part in the business of production.* Assuming that those who take this view understand

---

* The language of some of the manifestoes of the International justifies this representation; but I argue the question throughout as if it was only proposed to deprive the capitalist of his profit.

the process by which capital exists and grows, we must suppose them to regard the act of abstaining from present enjoyment as in itself agreeable, and, coupled with the risk which always attends abstinence when practiced for industrial purposes, as constituting in some inscrutable way, irrespective of the gains which flow from it, its own reward; so that, the present inducement being removed, the accumulation and increase of capital would go on with unabated force. It is scarcely necessary to remark on the perfect gratuitousness, not to say preposterousness, of such a notion. It is true, indeed, that abstinence may be for the rich, with whom its exercise rarely implies any sensible encroachment on customary comforts and luxuries, and still less on necessaries, but a trifling sacrifice: but even in their case, when practiced with a view to industrial investment, it means, as we know, risk also; which is certainly a sacrifice great enough not to be undergone without the clear prospect of adequate compensation. And even if we grant that a reservation of a portion of their wealth from immediate consumption would still be practiced by prudent and well-to-do people, even though the specific reward which now attends it were taken away (since there would still be the desire to provide for the future), it does not follow that what was thus reserved would necessarily go to assist productive industry; nay, it is pretty certain that this would not be its destination, since it might with much less risk be converted into gold or silver, and hoarded. Even for those, therefore, with whom the sacrifice of abstinence would be slightest, a specific reward would be needed to secure its exercise. But with those who are not included among the rich, with that great class of dealers and producers, from the ranks of unskilled labor upward, whose aggregate savings form the main support of the capital of civilized states, abstinence, far from being a slight, is always a serious, and often a very severe sacrifice. The mere act of resisting the temptation to present enjoyment, and of repressing the urgent requirements of the moment, often constitutes in itself a severe discipline, and demands for its accomplishment no little strength of character; and to this has to be added the inevitable risk incident to industrial investment. Even as matters stand at present, the inducement is found for many to be all too weak; but take away this inducement, exclude the prospect of future gain as the compensation for present trials, and what reason have we to suppose that such trials will be undergone?

I seem to be laboring to prove a truism; and, indeed, I am inclined to attribute the opinion I am combating rather to blank ignorance, or, at the least, profound mystification, on the part of those who hold it, respecting the nature and source of capital, than to deliberate acceptance of the premises on which alone it can logically rest. That the conversion of wealth to the purposes of productive industry, in other words, the creation of capital,* involves self-denial, is what probably has never crossed their imaginations: much more likely, if they have speculated on its origin at all, it would be connected in their minds with the issue of paper money and other operations of banking. But, however unsettled for them be the question as to the origin of capital, on one point they have no hesitation or doubt. Governments, it is a fixed article in their economic creed, have an unlimited command over capital, and may possess themselves of it at all times, in any quantity required. Where such notions respecting capital prevail, it is natural enough that profits and interest should appear superfluous institutions. Unfortunately for the speculations in question, capital is not the creation of Banks, nor has Government

---

* "Parsimony, and not industry, is the immediate cause of the increase of capital. Industry, indeed, provides the subject which parsimony accumulates. But whatever industry might acquire, if parsimony did not save and store up, the capital would never be the greater."— *Wealth of Nations.* McCulloch's edition, p. 149.

any means of obtaining it, except through the crude expedient of taking it from those to whom it belongs. Unfortunately, again, the process by which capital is brought into existence, maintained, and increased, is, for the great mass of those who take part in the work, a really painful one. Under such circumstances compensation and reward for those who perform this function is plainly an indispensable condition to the effectual prosecution of industry—a consideration which justifies us in co-ordinating abstinence with labor among the elements of cost of production, as we co-ordinate profits with wages in relation to the value of the product.

Perhaps it may be well here to guard against a possible misapprehension of the doctrine just laid down. It has been assumed in the argument that capital is indispensable to the prosecution of systematic industry; and the act, creative of capital, saving, parsimony, or abstinence, has been characterized as a sacrifice distinct from labor. It must not be supposed from this that there is any economic necessity, or any economic reason whatever, at least derivable from the arguments just used, that capitalists should form a distinct class from laborers. The distinctness of the sacrifices constitutes no ground for assigning them to different sets of persons. The same person may both labor and abstain, and, performing the double sacrifice, become entitled to the double reward. So far, indeed, am I from thinking that there is any thing in this combination of the parts of capitalist and laborer in one person which militates against the true economy of productive industry, that it is precisely in this direction that, for my part, I am disposed to look for an escape from the growing embarrassments and difficulties that now beset the relations of capital and labor. But this is a point the consideration of which will more properly fall within another part of this work.

Another possible ambiguity it may be well here to clear up. As was intimated just now, the sacrifice involved in a given act of abstinence is very different in the case of different persons. A rich man abstains from the consumption of his superfluous wealth, and is scarcely conscious, perhaps quite unconscious, of having suffered any deprivation whatever: his surplus income goes to his capital account, which continues to grow, while his expenditure remains precisely as before. On the other hand, the same or a much smaller amount of wealth reserved from personal consumption by an artisan or a small tradesman will frequently demand the most rigorous self-denial. The same individual, too, feels very differently the pains of abstinence at different stages of his career — in the struggling outset and at the successful close. And it is similar with labor. The laborious effort fitted to produce a given result does not represent the same sacrifice for different people: it is one thing for the strong, another for the weak; one for the trained workman, another for the raw beginner. This being so, the question arises—How are such differences to be dealt with in computing the cost of production? Are we to take account of what is personal and peculiar to the actual producers, and regard the cost of the commodity as higher or lower according as it has been produced by a weak or a strong workman, or by capital the result of painful or of painless saving? The answer must be in the negative. The sacrifices to be taken account of, and which govern exchange value, are, not those undergone by A, B, or C, but the average sacrifices undergone by the class of laborers or capitalists to which the producers of the commodity belong. A few remarks will enable us to make this clear.

What at bottom maintains the connection between value and cost of production is, it must always be remembered, the power of choice residing in laborers and capitalists to decide between different occupations. Now what is it determines the choice? No doubt the prospects of the pursuit, the remuneration being compared with the sacrifice. But what sacrifice? Plainly the sacrifice about to be undergone by the particular workman or capitalist who has to make the choice. Each takes account of the incidents of the course proposed as it bears upon himself, and considers how it stands in the comparison with others equally open to him. The conclusion he arrives at on this point determines his decision. Through a process of this kind every laborer and capitalist, either personally himself, or vicariously through a parent or other adviser, passes. Carried on over any given field of industrial competition, it is evident the result of this proceeding must be, not to bring the remuneration of each of the individuals comprised within it into conformity with the sacrifice which each undergoes, but to establish this conformity among the aggregates of those engaged in the several competing occupations; so that the total remuneration falling to each branch of industry shall bear the same proportion to the total sacrifices undergone in that branch as the total remuneration falling to any other within the same field bears to the sacrifices undergone in that other. The total remuneration falling to any branch of industry, however, consists of the total value of the commodities proceeding from it. This value, therefore, will bear the same proportion to the sacrifices undergone in producing it, as the value proceeding from any other industry within the same field of competition bears to the sacrifices of which it is the result. It follows that the relation which competition establishes between cost and value is one, not between the value of particular commodities and the sacrifices of the individual or individuals who have produced each such commodity, but one between commodities taken as sorts and their cost of production. We can not, for example, assert that a particular pair of shoes will exchange against a particular coat in proportion to the sacrifices undergone respectively by the shoe-maker and the tailor in the actual case; but we may assert that, within a given field of competition, shoes, as one sort of commodity, will exchange against coats as another in this proportion. The costs, therefore, to which the values of particular commodities correspond are not the particular sacrifices undergone in producing each commodity, but the average sacrifice undergone in producing each sort of commodity. We may, therefore, state broadly, that differences in the sacrifices incident to production, whether of labor or of abstinence, which are due to peculiarities either in the physical, mental, or social circumstances of individuals, are to be excluded from consideration in estimating cost of production. What we have to do with is, not individual sacrifice, but the average sacrifice of each industrial class.

This point being cleared up, we can have no difficulty in seeing how cost in its principal elements is to be computed. In the case of labor, the cost of producing a given commodity will be represented by the number of average laborers employed in its production—regard at the same time being had to the severity of the work and the degree of risk it involves—multiplied by the duration of their labors. In that of abstinence, the principle is analogous: the sacrifice will be measured by the quantity of wealth abstained from, taken in connection with the risk incurred, and multiplied by the duration of the abstinence.

§ 7. We have now treated the subject of normal value, so far as it is regulated by the principle of cost of production. But, as I stated in the opening of this chapter, the phenomenon in question is by no means confined to cases in which the conditions necessary to the action of cost of production exist. The essence of normal value, as I then remarked, is a tendency in the exchanging proportions of commodities to gravitate toward a central point, and this tendency is observable in departments of exchange where effective competition among exchanging producers has no place. The most important example of this kind is furnished by international trade. As between the producers in different nations, whether laborers or capitalists, there is no effective competition, nothing, therefore, to secure that industrial rewards in different countries shall be brought into correspondence with industrial sacrifices; nor, consequently, that international values shall correspond with cost of production. Nevertheless international values, or, let us say, the relative prices of the products of different nations, do not vary at random irrespective of rule or measure, but exhibit precisely the same tendency to gravitate toward a central point as is manifested in those exchanges which are governed by cost of production. A less striking and hitherto, so far as I know, unnoticed, example of the same kind meets us in domestic trade. As I have pointed out, cost of production does not control value universally even within the limits of a single country: in respect to a considerable class of exchanges—all those, namely, which take place between what I have called non-competing industrial groups—its action fails. Yet not the less we observe here, as in international trade, the phenomenon of normal value. The exchanges between the non-competing groups—or, let us say, the relative prices of the products of such non-competing groups—though unamenable to the law of cost, are not without a controlling force which restrains their fluctuations and guides them toward a normal result. This is the phenomenon with which we have now to deal; and the question to be considered is the nature of the force or forces which, in such cases, come into play.

Fortunately the problem has already, in principle at least, been solved for us by Mr. Mill. Mr. Mill has not, indeed, carried his solution beyond the case of international values; but his doctrine is manifestly applicable to all cases in which groups of producers, excluded from reciprocal industrial competition, exchange their products. Such cases, as I have shown, occur in domestic trade in the exchanges between those non-competing industrial groups of which I have spoken. The principle, therefore, which operates in international trade must operate here; and little more needs to be done, to complete the theory of this part of our subject, than to point the application of Mr. Mill's doctrine to this strictly parallel case.

That doctrine may be thus briefly stated: International values are governed by the reciprocal demand of commercial countries for each other's productions, or, more precisely, by the demand of each country for the productions of all other countries as against the demand of all other countries for what it produces; the result of this play of forces being that, on the whole, the exports of each country discharge its liabilities (of which the principal are on account of its imports) toward all other countries.* Whatever be the exchanging proportions—or, let us say, whatever be the state of relative prices—in different countries which is requisite to secure this result, those exchanging proportions, that state of relative prices, will become normal—will furnish the central point toward which the fluctuations of international prices will gravitate, the rule to which in the long run they will conform. Such is the law governing international values, called by Mr. Mill "the Equation of International Demand." What we have now to consider is the mode in which this principle operates in the case of the non-competing groups of domestic trade.

And first, in what sense are we to understand "reciprocal demand" as applied to non-competing industrial groups? Manifestly, in conformity with the analogy of the international case, as the demand of each group for the products of all other groups compared with the demand of all other groups for what this group produces. How, again, are we to measure

---

* As the doctrine is ordinarily stated, the exports of each country are said to balance its imports, but, as I shall hereafter show, this mode of stating it is not accurate. See *post*, part iii., chap. iii.

such demand? Again I say, in conformity with the same analogy, by the quantity of the products of each group available for the purchase of the products of other groups; while the products of other groups available for the purchase of the products of any given group will measure their demand for the products of that group. Lastly, how are we to understand the "Equation of Demand," as applied to non-competing groups? Still following the international analogy, I reply, as such a state of exchanging proportions among the products of the various groups—or, let us say, as such a state of relative prices among such products as shall enable that portion of the products of each group which is applied to the purchase of the products of all other groups to discharge its liabilities toward those other groups. The two cases thus run strictly on all-fours, and the play of the forces in action is in all respects the same. As in international trade an increased demand for the products of other countries will, other things being equal, affect international values—or, let us say, affect the relative prices of the products of different countries—unfavorably for the country whose demand is increased; and as, again, the converse of this condition, an increased demand by other countries for the products of a given country, will operate in the contrary direction; so it will be in the exchanges which take place between non-competing domestic groups. Whatever increases the demand of a given group for the products of outside, that is to say non-competing, industries, or (what comes to the same thing) whatever increases the supply of its products available for the purchase of the products of such industries, will, other things being the same, depress the prices of its products in relation to the prices of the products of the industries against which they are exchanged, and *vice versa;* while whatever increases the demand of the outside industries for the products of a given group will have the contrary effect, and will raise the level of its prices in relation to those of the non-competing groups with which it trades, and *vice versa*. The relative position, commercially considered, of each group may thus be affected either by an increase or diminution of its own products not consumed within the group, or by an increase or diminution of the products of other groups, so far as those products are disposable for the purchase of the products of the group in question. Such is the nature of "reciprocal demand," and of its mode of action as between the non-competing groups of domestic industry. As the reader will observe, it is simply "supply and demand" taken twice over, first in the sale and then in the purchase, or, rather, we may describe it as Supply and Demand contemplated at once from both sides of a completed exchange.

But it may not be at once apparent how a principle of this character is fitted to accomplish the result ascribed to it—that of determining *normal*, as distinguished from temporary or market, value. As I have remarked, Reciprocal Demand is merely duplicate Supply and Demand regarded in its full significance; but Supply and Demand, as we are most familiar with their action, are, in their relation to prices, merely proximate agencies, governing indeed the fluctuations of the market, but themselves controlled by forces lying deeper in the economy of production. How then does it happen that, in the cases under consideration, those agencies are capable of doing more than this—capable of determining, not simply the fluctuations of the market, but the rule to which, in the long run, the fluctuations of the market conform?

The answer to this question is to be found in the circumstances which give stability to Reciprocal Demand in the class of exchanges we are now considering. Reciprocal Demand, or, if the reader prefers it, Supply and Demand, in relation to a particular commodity, or even to a considerable number of commodities, may, as we know, vary in almost any conceivable degree, and with great rapidity. But when we consider them as affecting aggregates of transactions carried on between limited bodies of producers—for example, between independent nations, or between non-competing industrial groups—the case is very different; and the limits within which variation is possible are in fact pretty strictly determined; for in this case the measure of the aggregate demand of each trading body will be the total of its productions, and the measure of its demand for the productions of the bodies with which it trades will be the proportion of its total production which it desires to apply to the purchase of the productions of those bodies. Now, in the absence of any great changes in the conditions of productive industry, and of legislation specially contrived for this purpose, neither the aggregate production of a community nor the proportion of its means employed in interchanges with other communities can easily undergo on a sudden serious variation. The total production will depend on the nature and extent of its resources; and the proportion employed in external trading on the comparative character of those resources as they stand related to those of the communities with which it trades. These, indeed, are not circumstances which can be regarded as absolutely fixed. On the contrary, the conditions of productive industry over the best portion of the industrial world are and have for long been pretty steadily progressive. But the progress, though steady, has in general been slow. Sudden changes, at least on a scale large enough to effect great aggregates of transactions, but rarely occur; and further, what is pertinent to our purpose, where important improvements in productive industry do happen, they are seldom confined to a single community, but, after an interval more or less brief, are in general shared by other communities, so that the relative positions of the various trading bodies are in the end but slightly affected. It follows that the demand of such bodies, however it may vary in respect to particular commodities, can not easily as an aggregate undergo any great or sudden change; while their reciprocal demand for each other's productions, which expresses their relative industrial condition, will be still less liable to serious or abrupt disturbance. Here, then, we find the conditions fitted to produce that stability of exchanging relations which is implied in the term "normal value." While the prices of particular commodities may fluctuate indefinitely in international as in other trade, the same possibility does not exist for the prices of aggregates of commodities exchanged by definite groups of producers, such as independent nations, or the non-competing sections in domestic industry. The limits to such fluctuations are set in the limited purchasing power, incident to the limited productive power, at any given time possessed by such trading groups. It is in this way that a normal relation arises in the terms of the transactions carried on, and that a central point is furnished toward which the fluctuations of the market gravitate, performing in such trade the same function discharged under a *régime* of competition by the principle of cost.

Cost of Production and Reciprocal Demand in the sense explained, it thus appears, perform in certain circumstances similar economic offices. It remains now to point out an important difference in their modes of action and in the character of the results which flow from them. They each, as I have said, furnish a centre about which market values gravitate; but there is this difference between the two cases: The centre furnished by Cost of Production stands related to the fluctuations of the individual commodity; that supplied by Reciprocal Demand to the average fluctuations of considerable aggregates of commodities. A reduction in the cost of producing a hat will lower its price, but will have no tendency to affect the price of any other thing. But an alteration in the reciprocal demand of two trading nations will act upon the price, not of any commodity in particular, but of every commodity which enters into the trade. What such an alteration necessitates is a change in the *average* terms on which the trade is carried on; but it decides nothing as to the details by which the required average shall be attained and maintained. This is determined, not by international demand, but by those circumstances in the internal industries of each country which regulate in each the relative prices of its products. And similarly in the interchanges of non-competing domestic groups, what the reciprocal demand of the groups determines is the average relative level of prices within each group; the distribution of price among the individual products being regulated by the cause which governs value within it, namely cost of production.

The net result would seem to be this: Reciprocal International Demand determines the average level of prices throughout the entire trade of each commercial country in relation to that prevailing in other countries in commercial connection with it. Reciprocal Domestic Demand determines certain minor relative averages extending over classes of articles, the products of non-competing industrial groups; while Cost of Production acts upon particular commodities, and, in each case, within the range of industrial competition, determines their relative prices. The actual price, therefore, of any given commodity will, it is evident, be the composite result of the combined action of these several agencies.

Another distinction needs to be noticed between Reciprocal Demand and Cost of Production in their operation upon normal value. The former is, on the whole, far more steady and equable in its action than the latter. The reason is plain. Changes in cost of production depend mainly on the progress of the industrial arts, and this has for some time been and, we may perhaps assume, is likely for a long time to continue to be, remarkably rapid. Thus we find in the course of the present century an immense reduction in the costs of producing a large number of articles of general consumption, accompanied by a corresponding reduction in their value. On the other hand, changes in reciprocal demand are chiefly due to moral, social, and political causes, operating on a scale large enough to affect the relative positions of considerable bodies of men. Such changes are necessarily of slow accomplishment; and consequently the variations in value which result from them are rarely of a striking character, and in general proceed so slowly that they can seldom be perceived unless the comparison be made between prices taken at periods separated by considerable intervals of time. Still such changes do occur, and international values, as well as the corresponding class of values in domestic trade, respond to them. For example, I think we may assume that the adoption of free trade by England has improved her international position in the trade of the world. I do not refer to the extension of her trade, which, as all the world knows, has been enormous, but to the terms on which it is carried on. A given exertion of English industry will now command in the exchange with foreign countries the product of a larger exertion of foreign industry than formerly. In the domestic sphere, probably the most potent agency affecting reciprocal demand is the progress of popular education. Supposing, for example, that the system of primary education now being established in this country proves as successful as the friends of education desire; and supposing again, and more particularly, that effective provision is made in it for facilitating the ascent of promising boys from the lower to the higher educational levels, I think we may with some confidence predict that the movement will issue in a considerable change in the relative prices of certain classes of commodities in this country; nor can we have much difficulty in perceiving what will be the general direction of the change. Plainly the effect will be to augment the number of skilled workmen in relation to the unskilled, and of highly skilled workmen in relation to workmen possessing skill of the more common sorts. The social wall of partition which now divides the non-competing groups will to a large extent be broken down, and many of those occupying the lower levels will take advantage of the breach to press into those above them. The result will be a change in the reciprocal demand of the several groups. The demand of the groups representing the higher sorts of industrial skill will increase relatively to that of the groups representing the lower; or, to put the same point in a different form, the supply of the products of the former groups will increase relatively to that of the products of the latter. The inevitable consequence must be a change in relative prices unfavorable to the higher, and in a corresponding degree favorable to the lower sorts, of skilled industry. In a word, the qualified monopolies resting upon social conditions which now exist will be still further qualified: the range of competition will be enlarged; and, just in proportion as these results are attained, relative prices, and with them relative wages, will be made to approximate, more closely than at present, to the rule of cost. We may illustrate the case by the state of things in new colonies. There, owing to causes precisely similar to those which the educational movement is tending to develop here—owing, that is to say, to the great equality of conditions prevailing among the industrial population—the coarser kinds of labor and the lower sorts of skill are not merely positively, but comparatively, in relation to the finer and higher sorts, far more highly remunerated than they are at present with us. The explanation is that which has just been given: competition has there a wider range; and wherever this is so, prices and remuneration will represent more truly the actual sacrifices undergone by producers.

CHAPTER IV.

MARKET VALUE.

§ 1. THE nature of Normal Value has been discussed in the preceding chapter. As was there pointed out, the proportion which it represents is not necessarily that which is realized in any actual sale, but that to which all sales, in the case of commodities which possess normal value, tend to conform. The problem which we have now to consider is that presented by actual sales. What are the conditions which determine the proportions in which commodities exchange for each other on any given occasion in any given market? More briefly, what is the explanation of market prices? This question, after having been discussed by economists from Turgôt and Adam Smith to Mill, was at length supposed to have received its definitive solution in the chapter on "Demand and Supply" in the Principles of Political Economy by the latter authority. That solution, however, has lately been challenged by Mr. Thornton, I must own it seems to me, so far as the negative portion of his criticism is concerned, with success. As regards, however, the explanation he has offered in lieu of that which he has displaced, I fail to discover in it what can be considered a satisfactory account of the phenomenon under discussion. According to Mr. Thornton, market prices depend upon "competition;" while of competition he tells us that, "if it can properly be said to depend on any thing, it depends partly on individual necessity, partly on individual discretion; and as for the first of these there is proverbially, and for the other manifestly, no law, so likewise is there no law of competition. Neither, if there be no law of competition, and if competition be, as it has been shown to be, the determining cause of price, can there be any law of price." As I do not admit that there is "no law" for "individual necessity" any more than I admit that there is "no law" for "individual discretion"—understanding "law" in the scientific sense of the word, which alone is that with which Political Economy is concerned—I should be unable to accept Mr. Thornton's conclusion, even though his analysis of "competition" were much more satisfactory than it seems to me to be. For my part, I believe that, whether we are able to discover it or not, there is a law of market price, as there is a law of normal price, as there is a law of wages, of profits, of rent, as there are laws of the winds and tides and seasons, and of the phenomena of external nature—a law in the only sense in which law can be predicated of natural objects; namely, as consisting in the constancy of the relation between facts and the conditions which produce them.

§ 2. Market price — I speak now exclusively of price in wholesale markets—has from the first been seen to be connected with the agencies of Supply and Demand; it has always been very obvious that an increase of supply tends to lower price, and an increase of demand to raise it; but beyond this rather crude generalization economic speculation did not for some time pass. To furnish what deserves to be called a law of the phenomenon, it is evidently necessary to determine with some degree of precision the elements that enter into Supply and Demand when acting upon the prices of the market, and the mode in which these two agencies co-operate to produce the actual result. In other words, Demand and Supply must be defined, and the manner of their influence ascertained. The following was Adam Smith's contribution toward the solution of this problem: "The market price of every particular commodity is regulated by the proportion between the quantity which is actually brought to market and the demand of those who are willing to pay the natural price of the commodity, or the whole value of the rent, labor, and profit which must be paid in order to bring it thither."* According to this, "Supply" is to be understood as the quantity of a commodity actually brought to market, and "Demand" as the desire to purchase felt by those who are willing to pay the natural, or (as I have phrased it) the normal, price; the terms of the exchange in the particular market being regulated by the "proportion" between these two things. Every economist knows the criticism passed by Mr. Mill on this doctrine.

"These phrases," he says, "fail to satisfy any one who requires clear ideas and a perfectly precise expression of them. Some confusion must always attach to a phrase so inappropriate as that of a *ratio* between things not of the same denomination. What ratio can there be between a quantity and a desire, or even a desire combined with a power?"† This criticism has been generally acquiesced in; but I have endeavored in a former chapter‡ to show that it is not conclusive; that in truth Supply (in the sense in which it affects price) is not simply a quantity, but a quantity accompanied by a mental feeling, as Demand is not simply a mental feeling, but a mental feeling accompanied by a quantity, the quantity, namely, of purchasing power offered by the demander; in short, that Supply and Demand are things essentially of the same order, of the same denomination, and such therefore as may properly be regarded as bearing a ratio to each other. But though not open, as it seems to me, to Mr. Mill's criticism, Adam Smith's

---

* "Wealth of Nations," book i., chap. vii.
† "Principles of Political Economy," vol. i., p. 549.
‡ See *ante*, pp. 25, 26.

doctrine can less easily be defended against objections of another kind. It is not quite clear from the passage in what sense he uses the word "market," whether as a sort of abstract term to comprise all places where things are bought and sold, or as signifying some one particular or given place of this kind. I am, for my part, disposed to understand him in the latter sense; indeed the former would hardly have satisfied the requirements of the problem he had to consider; and taking the word in this sense, his statement is that the price of a commodity in any particular market is regulated by the "proportion" which the quantity of it in that market bears to the demand for it (in the sense defined) there existing. Now it will be seen on reflection that this statement is, as a matter of fact, untrue. The price of corn, for example, in a given market does not depend (other things there being supposed constant) on the quantity of corn brought to that market, understanding by this all that the dealers are then and there prepared to sell. For example, it often happens that intelligence received during the holding of a market respecting supply in some remote quarter of the world affects price, though no change has been made in the quantity of the commodity immediately available in the particular market. And occasions have occurred when a sudden change of weather in some critical period of the year, from the effect it is supposed likely to produce on the harvest, has led to a similar result. It is evident, therefore, that the supply which constitutes one factor in the determination of market price is not simply the quantity of a commodity present in a particular market. A similar criticism may be passed upon Adam Smith's definition of "demand." It is not true that the demand which constitutes the other factor in the case is always, or necessarily, "the demand for the commodity at its natural price." Suppose the selling price at a particular time and place to be above the natural price, so much of the demand as refuses to rise beyond the natural price ceases to affect the result; while, on the other hand, on the supposition that the selling price were lower than the natural price, the result would be affected by a demand at a lower than the natural price, namely, by any demand which is content to give the selling price, or any price above that. Lastly, even though the definitions of "supply" and "demand" given by Adam Smith could be shown to satisfy the conditions of the case, which we have seen they do not, the statement that market price is regulated by the "proportion" between them, while we are left uninformed as to the nature of this proportion, can not but be regarded as too vague to fulfill the requirements of a scientific theory.

§ 3. I turn now to Mr. Mill's doctrine of Market Price. As I have just said, that doctrine has been challenged by Mr. Thornton, and, in my opinion, successfully; but I prefer to state my objection to it in my own way. According to Mr. Mill, demand is measured, not by the purchasing power offered in support of the desire to purchase, but by the quantity of the commodity demanded at the selling price in a given market; and similarly the measure of supply is the quantity offered at the selling price. Understanding Demand and Supply in these senses, he laid it down that the actual price ruling in any given market is the price which equalizes demand and supply. As a matter of fact, however, it may be pointed out, and has been pointed out by Mr. Thornton, that the demand in the market at the selling price may be greater than the supply forthcoming in that market can satisfy; as, on the other hand, the supply at the selling price may be in excess of what the actual demand at that price will take off. In either of these cases (and one or other of them is the case of almost all markets) Supply and Demand are not equalized. In all such instances, therefore, Mr. Mill's theory fails to explain the phenomenon of market price. To this objection Mr. Mill has replied by saying that "reserving a price is to all intents and purposes withdrawing supply"—in other words, so much of the supply as is not sold, either because the owner is dissatisfied with the current price, or can not find sufficient purchasers at that price, is not to be counted as supply.

"When no more than forty shillings a head can be obtained for sheep, all sheep whose owners are determined not to sell them for less than fifty shillings are out of the market, *and form no part at all of the supply which is now determining price*. They may have been offered for sale, but they have been withdrawn..... In the mean while, the price has been determined without any reference to his [the owner's] withheld stock, and determined in such a manner that the demand at that price shall (if possible) be equal to the supply which the dealers are willing to part with at that price. The economists who say that market price is determined by demand and supply do not mean that it is determined by the whole supply which would be forthcoming at an unattainable price, any more than by the whole demand that would be called forth if the article could be had for an old song. They mean that, whatever the price turns out to be, it will be such that the demand at that price, and the supply at that price, will be equal to one another."*

It is evident that the same reasons which require that Supply should be limited to so much of the commodity as is disposed of in actual sale, would make it necessary that Demand should be limited to so much of the desire to purchase as finds satisfaction in actual purchase; since otherwise there would be no security that it might not exceed Supply. So explained, it can not be denied that Mr. Mill's position is logically impregnable. Unfortunately, however, the same limitations which render it logically impregnable make it also not worth defending; for, understood in the sense in which the terms have now been defined, the doctrine of the equality of Demand and Supply as the condition of market price becomes a mere identical

---

* *Fortnightly Review*, May, 1869, Mr. Mill's review of Mr. Thornton's "Labor," pp. 512, 513.

proposition. The quantity demanded and the quantity supplied at the market price are necessarily equal when the quantity demanded is only another name for the quantity bought, and the quantity supplied another name for the quantity sold. They are necessarily equal, since they are one and the same quantity. Mr. Mill's doctrine, then, limited as he has limited it, is undeniably true; but the question remains, what light does it throw upon the phenomenon it undertakes to explain? —how far can it be considered as stating the law of market prices? We desire to know the circumstances which determine price; and we are told that the selling price is always such that the quantity of a commodity purchased in a given market is equal to the quantity sold in that market. The statement is incontrovertible, but I fail to perceive how it helps us to understand the facts. Further, the limitation by which the doctrine is rescued is itself open to serious objection. In the passage I have quoted it is stated that the portion of the supply which is reserved for future sale "forms no part of the supply which is now determining price." Here I join issue on a question of fact. I contend that, in coming to a decision on the actual price, the dealers in a market take account, not merely of the quantity of the commodity that is there actually sold, but of all the commodity in the market; and not merely of this, but of the supply obtainable from other quarters. On this point I can only appeal to facts. It appears to me certain that the supply which determines price is quite as much the supply that is not sold as the supply that is sold; and the demand quite as much the demand that is not satisfied as the demand that is satisfied. In other words, supply and demand outside the market are among the conditions which determine price within the market. But if so, Mr. Mill's doctrine not merely fails to solve the problem of market price, but pointedly excludes from consideration conditions which are essential to the solution of that problem. Under these circumstances I shall perhaps be pardoned for attempting some more precise statement of the facts governing the phenomenon than is furnished by the current doctrine.

§ 4. In order to bring the terms of our theory into conformity with the facts of the case, it appears to me that we must give to the words "supply" and "demand" a much more extended signification than is given to them in the formulas either of Adam Smith or of Mill. By "supply," as affecting market price, I would understand not merely the quantity of a commodity sold, offered for sale, or present in a given market, but the quantity intended for sale wherever it exists which the dealers in the particular market know or believe to be available, to meet, within certain limits of time, the demand which falls within the range of their dealing; and by "demand," a strictly analogous conception, namely, the desire, so far as accompanied by purchasing power anywhere existing for the commodity, which, in the opinion of the dealers in the market, admits of being satisfied within certain limits of time by the attainable supply; the "certain limits of time" in each case being the period intervening between the time of sale and that at which fresh supplies can be brought forward from the ordinary sources of production. I am far from thinking that these definitions are free from flaw, or that cases of supply and demand affecting market price may not be found which will not easily fall within their scope, but I believe they comprise the most important conditions determining the result, and I am sure that no less extensive definitions would be even approximately adequate.

Understanding, then, Demand and Supply in the senses defined, as the factors which conjointly produce the phenomenon, we have next to consider the manner of their operation. This, it is evident, can only be indirect, since price expresses a contract between human beings, whose wills, therefore, must form the primary link in the causal chain. As we have seen, the notion of Adam Smith was, and this is probably still the prevailing idea, that the result is regulated by the "proportion" between demand and supply—this proportion, as we must suppose, producing its effect through the minds of those who take part in the exchange. I have already stated my reasons for regarding Demand and Supply as ideas of the same order, between which, therefore, a proportion may properly be assumed to exist. But to render Adam Smith's doctrine effectual for its purpose, we must not only suppose a proportion existing between demand and supply, but also that between this proportion and the market price there is some constancy of relation, such that, knowing the relation in any given case, we should be able to predict what the price would be in the event of a change in the conditions of the market. Now this is what I believe it would be quite impossible to establish. At all events, it may be shown that the formula, if it were possible to evolve one, would need to be different for every different kind of commodity, and to be altered with every change in either the amount or the distribution of purchasing power in a community. Thus a change in the supply of a necessary of life is, as has often been pointed out, capable of producing effects on price much greater than in proportion to the extent of the change. A reduction of one-fourth, or one-third, for instance, in the food of a people might easily issue in a twofold or threefold advance of price; while an equal change in the supply of a comfort or convenience, which may easily be dispensed with, but may also by increased cheapness rapidly attract a larger demand, is generally attended with effects on price much less marked. And, as I have said, these results would be further varied by every change in the amount or the distribution of the available purchasing power. For these reasons it appears to me that the idea of a proportion, as furnishing a clue to the connection of demand and supply with market price, must be abandoned, if on no other ground, from the impossibility of determining it; and that, instead of a quantitative formula, we must content ourselves with an approximately accurate description.

Let us consider the circumstances under which the selling price comes to be decided in any wholesale market. We will suppose the commodity dealt in to be corn. An intending purchaser enters the market, having previously obtained by such means as were open to him information respecting the stock of corn in the country, or likely within a certain period to be forth-coming from abroad; and he there finds certain quantities offered for sale. He has also made himself acquainted with the demand for ordinary consumption, so far as it seems likely to come within the range of his dealings. On these data he founds an opinion as to what the price of corn ought to be. The opinion thus formed is not absolutely definitive. He allows it to be modified more or less by the opinions which he finds prevailing in the market. Under the influence of all these considerations he comes to a conclusion as to the price, which—while anxious to procure his commodity as cheaply as he can—he will, rather than go without, be prepared to pay. The seller of corn goes through a similar process, with of course the converse object, availing himself according to his intelligence of similar means of information. Supposing the conclusion he comes to be that the demand, in the sense I have defined it, is capable of taking off the supply, understood also in the sense I have defined it, at a higher price than that which formed the conclusion of the buyer's calculations, under these circumstances there would be no transaction between them; and if their opinions represented respectively the opinions of all the buyers and all the sellers in the market, no transaction would in that market take place. This of course is what rarely or never happens. Buyers and sellers in the same town or district, having mostly the same opportunities of information, will not in general differ very widely in their estimates of demand and supply; and where they differ but slightly, their opinions coming in so limited an area within the sphere of each other's attraction, are apt to issue in agreement; the exact price arrived at always depending in some degree on the firmness and shrewdness of individual men. This is what is called the 'higgling of the market'—the process on which, within the narrow limits of variation set by the deliberate opinions of experts, the final result depends.

The influence of Demand and Supply on the price-current in a given market is thus exercised through the opinions of the dealers in that market; and the problem to which the dealers in forming their opinions address themselves, is to ascertain, having regard to the known conditions of the case, what the price of the commodity ought to be. Let us now endeavor to determine, with as much precision as may be, the nature of the problem thus presented to buyers and sellers in a wholesale market. I grant it is very probable that most of those who speak freely of the price which happens to obtain in a market as "too high" or "too low," or "such as it ought to be," might find it difficult, if challenged, to explain the meaning of their words: nevertheless, I believe that these expressions do at least point to a meaning, perhaps a latent one, in the minds of those who use them. However this may be, it can at all events be shown that there is in every market a price at which it is desirable that the commodity, whatever it may be, should sell at that time and place—desirable ultimately in the interest of consumers, but in a certain sense desirable also in the interest of dealers, taking buyers and sellers together, and which the combined operations of both, so far as they are well informed respecting the conditions of supply and demand, really tend to establish. To satisfy ourselves of this, it is only necessary to consider that, in all states of supply and demand, there is always a certain price beyond which, if the markets rise, consumption is unnecessarily checked, and the stocks in the country pass off more slowly than is needful. In time the error is discovered, and a competition sets in among holders of the commodity, which issues in a fall of price, tending to stimulate consumption as much as it had previously been unduly checked. On the other hand, supposing the market price to be set too low, stocks become exhausted too soon, and the undue fall will need to be compensated by a corresponding advance at a later period. Such oscillations are at variance with the interest of the consumer; and the price, therefore, which renders them unnecessary, which is just sufficient, and no more than sufficient, to carry the existing supply over, with such a surplus as circumstances may render advisable,* to meet the new supplies forth-coming, may, I think, be conveniently designated as the "proper price" of the market.† It is this price which, it seems to me, the deal-

---

* It is necessary to introduce this qualifying clause, since it is not always for the interest of the consumer that consumption should proceed at such a pace as to exhaust existing stocks exactly as the new supplies are coming into the market. It would be so if he could be sure that the new supplies would sell at a price not higher than that which had been previously current; but in the case of raw products, and more especially in that of food (for reasons which will presently be pointed out), he can not be sure of this. It is, therefore, in the interest of consumers, that is to say of the community, that, in the uncertainty as to what may be the degree of abundance or scarcity of forthcoming supplies, a certain surplus should be kept in hand, which should be greater or less according to the prospects of the incoming season, with a view to supplement the possible deficiencies of future supplies; and the market price called for by the interest of consumers would manifestly be that which would be sufficient, not merely to carry existing stocks over to the arrival of new supplies, but to maintain also such a surplus. (See TOOKE's "History of Prices," vol. v., part i., § 22, where the reader will find the subject discussed with Mr. Tooke's usual discrimination.)

† According to Mr. Mill, the *actual market price* is the price which equalizes supply and demand in a given market: as I view the case, the "proper market price" is the price which equalizes supply and demand, *not* as existing in the particular market, but in the larger sense which I have assigned to the terms.

ers in the market have dimly in view when by implication they refer to a standard by which they pronounce the actual price to be "too high," or "too low," or "what it ought to be." I would define it as the price which suffices to adjust in the most advantageous way the existing supply to the existing demand pending the coming forward of fresh supplies from the sources of production.

I have now, I hope, made it plain that in a given state of demand and supply there is a certain market price which is identified with the consumer's interest; and, in doing so, I have observed incidentally that the price satisfies no less the true interest of dealers. It remains to show somewhat more explicitly how it comes within the range of the latter's speculations, so as to become the point toward which the operations converge; since it is only in proportion as this is the case that the action of the wholesale market has any tendency to evolve what I have called the "proper price." The buyer, as we know, seeks to buy as cheaply as he can; the seller to sell as dearly as he can; but, with all this, it is the interest of both to know the price beyond which, in one direction the buyer, in the other the seller, can not pass without loss; and this is precisely the price which stands identified with the consumer's interest. For, as we have seen, if the price rises beyond this point, consumption is checked, stocks accumulate, and a fall of price is necessitated, *to the loss of all dealers who have purchased above the depressed rate;* while, on the other hand, if the price falls below it, the result is an advance at a future time, *to the loss of all who had sold while the lower price prevailed.* It is evident, therefore, that dealers are interested in knowing the "proper price" of the market, and further, it is evident that it is toward this point that the combined efforts of buyer

---

To this price the *actual market price* will, according to my view, approximate, in proportion to the intelligence and knowledge of the dealers.

and seller, in proportion as they are well informed respecting the conditions of supply and demand, really converge. Dealers thus, while simply pursuing their own interests, are unconsciously performing for the community a service of first-rate importance — a service which has been well compared by Archbishop Whately to that rendered by the captain of a ship, who, taking account of the stock of provisions at his disposal, and the length of his intended voyage, adjusts to these conditions the rations of his crew. Such is the tendency of the speculation of the market, and the end is attained in proportion to the intelligence and the knowledge of those who engage in the pursuit; and such are the grounds on which freedom of commercial speculation may be justified. Of course mistakes are often made, sometimes very serious mistakes; and then we have reaction, oscillation, and perhaps commercial crises. But under all circumstances the price in the market is determined by the opinions of dealers in the market, founded upon their knowledge of demand and supply — of dealers pursuing their interests under circumstances which, in proportion to the intelligence and knowledge at their command, favor the establishment of the "proper market price."

The foregoing is the nearest approximation I can make to a statement of the law of market price. I can well believe how utterly unsatisfactory it will appear to some economists whose views in connection with their science are much more ambitious than my own, and who apparently do not think it hopeless that we should have, ere long, an exposition of economic principles drawn up in quantitative formulas. That such a consummation would be desirable, assuming the exposition to be sound, I should be the last to deny, though I own I do not expect to witness it; and I can not but think that, whatever may be the case in other instances, at least in that of market price the scientific game would scarcely be worth the candle.

In effect, questions respecting market, as distinguished from normal price, are such as do not often meet us in the field of economic or social speculation. The circumstances which govern prices in the latter sense; which regulate the relative proportions in which the various classes of goods *usually* exchange; which cause the prices of some of the most important articles of consumption to be *permanently* higher in some countries than in others — these are topics of very great moment, which have the closest connection with some most important questions of national and class well-being. But the most accurate determination of the conditions which issue in the price-current in a particular market on a particular day, and which rule the fluctuations of the market from day to day—however important such knowledge may be to the practical merchant and speculator—can furnish, so far as I can see, but slight help toward the solution of any question of large or permanent interest.* I do not, therefore, affect to think that the incom-

---

* The announcements of the pending famine in Bengal warn me that it is possible to disparage too much the importance of the doctrine of market prices. In the comments on this subject by the press of this country, much anxiety has been evinced in some quarters lest merchants, by storing supplies, may force up the price of food to a famine rate in certain isolated districts. A slight acquaintance with the doctrine of market price might serve to re-assure such writers. Provided that the merchants in question have not the power to exclude supplies from the isolated districts, any advance in price beyond what the interest of the consumers in the district requires would, as I have shown in the foregoing pages, be at the cost of the speculators whose operations produced it. What is desirable is, that the price should be raised as soon as possible to a point sufficient at once to compel the utmost economy in consumption, and to attract supplies from the largest possible area. As to the action of the Government for the relief of the famine being a "setting aside of the laws of Political Economy," it would be just as reasonable to talk of precautions against a hurricane, or against a high tide, being a setting aside of the laws of physical nature. Will people never understand that a "law" of Political Economy is a "law" in no other sense than the law of gravitation, and that it is *not* an act of Parliament, or a rule prescribed by any one, which governors-general can "set aside?"

pleteness and imperfection which are apparent enough in this portion of economic theory are very much to be deplored. So far as the doctrine of market price is concerned, it seems to me to suffice for the purposes of Social Philosophy, if we are enabled to set forth in a general way the connection between the fluctuations of the market and the more fundamental conditions on which production and exchange depend. And so much, I venture to think, the theory, as I have stated it, taken in connection with the known facts of particular cases, will sufficiently enable us to perform.

§ 5. The foregoing discussion has been confined exclusively to the question of prices in wholesale markets: it remains to consider the case of retail prices; but these need not detain us long. The chief circumstances in which the determination of price in retail dealings differs from its determination in wholesale markets appear to be these two: first, competition in retail markets is conducted under conditions which may be described as of greater friction than those which exist in wholesale trade. In the wholesale market, the sellers and purchasers meet together in the same place, affording thus to each other reciprocally the opportunity of comparing directly and at once the terms on which they are severally disposed to trade. In retail dealing it is otherwise. In each place of sale there is but one seller; and though it is possible to compare his terms with the prices demanded elsewhere by others, this can not always be done on the moment, and may involve much inconvenience and delay. A purchaser frequently finds it, on the whole, better to take the word of the seller for the fairness of the price demanded than to verify his statements by going on the occasion of every purchase to another shop. It is probable, indeed, that if the charge be excessive, the purchaser will in time come to discover this, and may then transfer his custom to a cheaper market. This shows that competition is not inoperative in retail trade, but it shows also the sort of friction under which it works, and helps to explain, what has often been remarked upon, and what, as a matter of fact, it is practically important people should bear in mind, the different prices at which the same commodity is frequently found to sell within a very limited range of retail dealing —almost in what we may call the same market. This is one circumstance that distinguishes retail from wholesale trading. The other lies in the advantage which his superior knowledge gives the buyer over the seller in the transaction taking place between them—a superiority which has no counterpart in the relations of wholesale dealers. In the wholesale market, buyer and seller are upon a strictly equal footing as regards knowledge of all the circumstances calculated to affect the price of the commodity dealt in. It is the business of each to inform himself as to the state of supply and demand, and if he fails to do so, he has no just ground of complaint if the other party to the transaction gains an advantage in the bargain. The advantage so obtained is the natural and proper reward of the greater skill exhibited—skill which, as I have shown, it is for the interest of the community that each should cultivate to the highest degree. The circumstances of retail dealing are here again in contrast with those of the wholesale trade. The transactions do not take place between dealers possessing, or with the opportunities of acquiring, equal knowledge respecting the commodities dealt in, but between experts on one side, and on the other persons in most cases wholly ignorant of the circumstances at the time affecting the market. Between persons so qualified the game of exchange, if the rules be rigorously enforced, is not a fair one; and it has consequently been recognized, universally in England, and very extensively among the better class of retail dealers in continental countries, as a principle of commercial morality, that the dealer should not demand from his customer a higher price for his commodity than the lowest he is prepared to take. Retail buying and selling is thus made to rest upon a moral rather than upon an economic basis, and, there can be no doubt, for the advantage of all parties concerned. The practice, however, of unprofitable higgling, as all travelers know, is still rife in most parts of the Continent, and, in general, everywhere among the class of smaller dealers, involving a great waste of time, by which perhaps the dealer in the end loses as much as he now and then gains by taking advantage of his superiority over his customer in knowledge of the game.

These, it seems to me, are the principal circumstances which distinguish the determination of price in the retail trade from its determination in wholesale markets; and they suffice to account for, what has often been noticed and is indeed a very patent fact, the much greater variety to be found in the prices of the same and similar commodities in the former than in the latter department of business. I do not think that *fluctuations* of price (to be distinguished from *variety*) are greater in the retail than in the wholesale trade. Perhaps, on the whole, they may in this country be somewhat less; as the practice of having a fixed price for all goods would make the prudent retail dealer unwilling to change his price, and so disappoint and harass his customer, with every slight fluctuation of the wholesale market. But though fluctuations of price may be somewhat less, varieties of price are undoubtedly very much greater. Not only in different localities, but often in different shops in the same locality, it is quite usual to find the same articles, and of the same quality, selling at widely different prices at the same time; and this quite in excess of what the special circumstances of particular localities or situations might account for. This is not a satisfactory state of things; but though perhaps in some degree inevitable, because due to what we may regard as essential incidents of retail trading, the evil is, at least in this country, greatly aggravated by a cause which is quite removable, and which, we may hope, is in process of being removed. This is the excessive amount of capital which, from one cause or another, has found its way into the business of mere distribution. The inevitable consequence is that the capital thus in excess, taking it as an aggregate, turns slowly—more slowly than it need turn consistently with the due discharge of its functions; and that those who have embarked in retail business are compelled, in order to obtain average profits on their capital, to charge higher prices for their goods than would be necessary if the total amount of capital in the trade were less. That such a state of things should exist and continue is doubtless due to that excessive friction in the action of competition in retail dealing of which I have spoken. The prices charged in different retail establishments are but rarely compared, and continue consequently to differ widely from each other, as they no doubt differ still more widely from what they might be in a more healthy condition of the trade. The source of the evil is, thus, the sluggish action of competition: and the remedy must be sought in the quickening of this action. This is what the co-operative retail establishments are, in effect, doing. By adopting a lower scale of prices, and taking good means to advertise their terms, they draw a larger amount of custom to their shops in proportion to the capital embarked than other competing establishments. The result is that, turning their capital more rapidly, they succeed in realizing as high profits as their rivals, while charging lower prices. The opposition given to this movement by the ordinary retail establishments, however little ground for it there may be in reason and justice, is perfectly natural, inasmuch as the drift of it unquestionably is toward the extrusion of some of them from the trade. Nothing less than this, it is clear, will satisfy the exigencies of the case. What we have to contemplate as the proper goal of co-operative competition is a general fall of retail prices; but to reconcile this with a realization by the whole trade of an average remuneration on the capital embarked in it, it would be necessary that this capital should be turned over in a given time as often as the capital of the co-operators. In order to this, however, the entire capital employed in the trade would need to be brought into the same proportion with the business to be done as the co-operators' capital bears to their business—that is to say, the total capital now employed in the business of distribution would need to be largely curtailed. The necessity of this is not always perceived; and people argue that, as the co-operative stores have succeeded in turning over their capital rapidly by the expedient of a reduction in price, so the same end may be attained by the retail trade in general through the adoption of the same means. But this is just one of those cases, so common in Political Economy, in which what is true in particular instances ceases to be true when the instances become the rule. How is it that co-operators have accomplished the more rapid turning of their capital? Simply by drawing off custom through the attraction of low prices from other shops. Supposing these latter now to adopt the same policy, we may assume that their custom would flow back to them. The capital of the whole would then turn at the same rate as formerly; but it was just this slow rate of turning that necessitated exorbitant prices in the retail trade; and if prices are to range lower, other things being the same, profits must decline below their former and average level. Other things, indeed, would not, in the case supposed, remain for any long time the same; for a fall in the rate of profit would have the effect of driving capital from the trade, or at all events of preventing the capital now in the trade from being recruited by the accessions that otherwise would flow to it. The definitive result toward which such a process would tend is manifestly a reduction of the existing capital of retail dealing to an amount which would be no more than adequate to perform the services required of it. This point reached, while the public would enjoy the advantage of lowered prices, retail dealers would, as a body, derive from their investments the rate of remuneration current in the country.

CHAPTER V.

ON SOME DERIVATIVE LAWS OF VALUE.

§ 1. I PROPOSE to call attention in this chapter to some examples of value which I think may not improperly be called "derivative laws" of that phenomenon. I refer to those changes in the values of different kinds of commodities which occur when the general laws of value, such as we have found them to be, come into operation under the actual circumstances of progressive societies.

When a colony establishes itself in a new country, the course of its industrial development naturally follows the character of the opportunities offered to industrial enterprise by the environment. These will of course vary a good deal, according to the part of the world in which the new society happens to be placed; but, speaking broadly, they will be such as to draw the bulk of the industrial activity of the new people into some one or more of those branches of industry which have been conveniently designated "extractive." Agriculture, pastoral and mining pursuits, and the cutting of lumber, are among the principal of such industries; and they, together with the rude handicrafts immediately dependent on them, are what we find, in fact, to be the main occupations of all newly-settled communities. Now it is mainly, if not exclusively, to this class of industrial pursuits that that law of Political Economy, or more properly of physical nature, applies, which Mr. Mill has rightly characterized as the most important proposition in economic science—the law, as he phrased it, of "diminishing productiveness." Most of my readers will be familiar with the principle in question, but it may be well to recall it here. It may be thus briefly stated: In any given state of the arts of production, the returns to human industry employed upon natural agents will, up to a certain point, be the maximum which those natural agents, cultivated with the degree of skill brought to bear upon them, are capable of yielding; but after this point has been passed, though an increased application of labor and capital will obtain an increased return, it will not obtain a proportionally increased return: on the contrary, every further increase of outlay—always assuming that the skill employed in applying it continues the same as before—will be attended with a return constantly diminishing. To this principle, in conjunction with the varying quality of different soils, is due, as every economist knows, the phenomenon of agricultural rent; but this has been so fully illustrated in works now in every one's hands, in its application alike to agriculture and to other branches of extractive industry, that I may content myself with merely referring to it here. What I am concerned now to show is the manner in which, with the progress of society, the law in question affects the course of normal values in all commodities coming under its influence.

The case which I am considering, the reader will remember, is that of newly-settled communities, among whom the conditions of social and industrial life are, on the whole, much more equal and uniform than in old countries like this. It results that industrial competition among the several social classes will at this stage of social growth—unless where restrained by laws enacted directly for this purpose—be more general and effective than in this part of the world we are accustomed to find it; and, as a further consequence from the same state of things, it must follow that the principle of cost of production as governing value is more extensively operative in such societies than with us. For the purposes of our present investigation it will be convenient to assume, and the assumption will be sufficiently near the truth, that, in the case of their domestic exchanges, the principle in question is operative universally. This being so, it is evident that an inquiry into the course of normal values in such communities resolves itself into an inquiry into the changes which occur in the costs of producing the several classes of commodities which are there the subject of exchange; these commodities consisting mainly, as we have seen, at least during the earlier stages of their growth, of the products of extractive industry.

From the law of diminishing productiveness just referred to, taken in connection with the circumstance that the settlers in a new country naturally have recourse, in the first instance, to those natural agents which, from their superior fertility or more convenient situation, promise the largest returns to industry, it follows that, as population increases and larger demands are made upon the resources of the country, the cost of producing commodities tends constantly to rise. This tendency may indeed be counteracted by the progress of mechanical and chemical invention, and the improved industrial processes which usually result. But, in point of fact, it has never been found in the history of any country, that such inventions have kept pace with the declining rate of return yielded by natural agents, as their capabilities have been subjected to the increasing demands of a growing community; and it is therefore safe to assume that the tendency to an increase of cost in the class of commodities under consideration would in any actual case be realized. The degree, however, in which this result occurred would be very different in different kinds of "extractive" products, and this would lead to corresponding differences in the course of their normal values.

§ 2. The class of commodities in the production of which the facilities possessed by new communities, as compared with old, attain their greatest height, are those of which timber and meat may be taken as the type, and comprises such articles as wool, game, furs, hides, horns, pitch, resin, etc. The characteristic of all such products is, that they admit of being raised with little previous outlay, and, therefore, with comparatively little capital, and in general require for their production a large extent of ground. Now capital is the industrial agent which new countries are least able to command, while they commonly possess land in unlimited abundance. There can, therefore, be no difficulty in perceiving that, for the production of the class of commodities mentioned above, newly-settled communities are especially adapted, and that, consequently, the value of all such commodities will be in them exceptionally low.

The circumstance which most powerfully affects the course of values in the products of extractive industry, and in the commodities just referred to among the rest, is the degree in which they admit of being transported from place to place, that is to say, their portableness, depending, as it does, partly on their durability and partly on their bulk. Taking timber and butcher's meat as exemplifying respectively a high and a low degree of portableness, we find that while the values of both range in new countries, where the circumstances are favorable for their production, at a very low point compared with their values in old, the difference is, even at the outset, considerably greater in the case of meat than in that of timber; and further, that while the value of the latter rises in general slowly, and never attains a very great elevation, reckoning from its height at starting, that of the former rises more rapidly, and continues to rise with the growth of the community, the highest point which it is capable of attaining being, in the present state of our knowledge at least, quite indeterminable. The explanation of this contrast lies entirely in the circumstance to which I have adverted—the different portableness of the two commodities. Timber, notwithstanding its bulk, being a very portable commodity, easily finds its way from the forests of new to the markets of old countries. As soon, therefore, as a new community is brought into commercial connection with the more advanced parts of the world, if timber be there an article of production, its price will at once rise to a level lower than that prevailing in old countries only by the cost of transport. This, no doubt, in so bulky a commodity, will represent a considerable proportion of the whole value; but the important point to attend to is that the price thus determined will in future bear a constant relation to the price in old countries;* the difference between the two being always such as the cost of transport will render it. Meat, on the other hand, unsuited as it is, owing to its perishable nature, for a distant traffic, is confined for a market, if not to the immediate locality where it is produced, at least to the bordering countries; and being raised in new countries at very low cost, its value during the early stages of their growth is necessarily low. But as population advances, and agriculture en-

---

* It is not to be supposed from this that the price, as compared with that of other commodities raised within the same district, will cease to be determined by its cost of production. If, for example, the opening afforded by foreign markets had the effect of raising the price of timber above the point prescribed by its cost of production as compared, let us say, with agricultural products, the higher profits of the lumber trade, in the circumstances supposed, would have the effect of drawing off capital and labor from agriculture to lumber cutting. The curtailment of the area of cultivation in agriculture would be attended with a reduction in the cost of its products, involving, *cæteris paribus*, an advance in agricultural profits: while, on the other hand, the extension of the field of production in lumber cutting, necessitating a resort to more distant forests, would be followed by the opposite effect; and this process would manifestly go on till the prices of timber and agricultural products were brought into relation with their respective costs. The normal price of timber, therefore, would still be such as its cost of production prescribed; but this cost of production, as happens with the products of all extractive industry, would tend to rise with the increased demands made upon the natural agent.

croaches on the natural pasture lands originally available for the rearing of cattle, still more as it becomes necessary to cultivate land for the purpose of pasture, the cost of meat constantly rises. It was the opinion of Adam Smith, that, so soon as this last stage was reached, the price of all "extractive" products of whatever kind attained its maximum height, and that no farther advance (unless so far as this might arise from a fall in the value of money) was henceforth to be expected. The only reason he assigns for this opinion is, that if the price rose higher, "more land would soon be turned to that purpose."* I need scarcely point out the entire inadequacy of this reason. More land no doubt would be turned to the production of the article, whatever it might happen to be, the advancing price of which made it profitable to cultivate land for this purpose; but it does not follow, that, as the extension of cultivation went on, the cost of production, and with it the price of the article, would not rise. On the contrary, this is what we know does happen, and has happened in a signal manner in the case of meat. The same cause which depresses the price of meat in the earlier stages of a nation's career—its perishable nature and consequent unfitness for transport—operates to raise the price in the later stages by practically confining each country to what it can itself produce. It is thus led with the increasing demands of a growing population to extend the supply at a constantly increasing cost. The price of meat, accordingly, has, since the time of Adam Smith, though with numerous fluctuations, on the whole steadily advanced; and, notwithstanding the unexampled height which it has now attained in this country, when one considers the peculiar place which meat holds in the dietary of the masses of a people—that it is the article on which, in the event of any improvement in their condition, increased expenditure most

---

* "Wealth of Nations," pp. 101-4, 5.

certainly finds vent—one can not doubt but that its progress must still be upward,* even irrespective of the depreciation of money now going on, which can not fail to accelerate the movement.

§ 3. Next to those products of extractive industry of which meat and timber are the type, and which exhibit in the highest degree the special productive aptitudes of new countries, the commodity which offers greatest scope for their special resources is grain. The course of normal price in this article differs in a very striking way from that of those which we have just considered. Like theirs, indeed, the course is upward; and like that of timber—corn being also an extremely portable commodity—the price is at an early stage brought into relation with the quotations ruling in the great markets of the world; with this difference, however, that the cost of carriage being for corn, in proportion to its value, much less than for timber, its price in the new community approximates more closely to its price in old countries than does that of the latter commodity. But the noteworthy circumstance in the course of price in corn—so far at least as corn forms the staple food of a people—is that advancing, with of course much fluctuation, in the early period of growth, it at length in the progress of industrial development reaches a point beyond which (unless so far as it is affected by changes in the value of money) it manifests no tendency, at least no permanent tendency, to advance farther. I am not aware that this peculiar incident in the price of corn has been pointed out before, and it is

---

* In connection with this subject one perceives the immense national importance of inventions bearing on the preservation of meat, and of the development of a trade in preserved meats, between new countries like Australia and old ones like this. It is satisfactory to find that some progress has been made in this direction; but apparently the art will need great improvement before the preserved meats of Australia can enter largely into our general consumption.

possible it may* be disputed as a matter of fact: nevertheless, I make the assertion with some confidence, inasmuch as I find grounds for it in the economic conditions under which corn is produced, taken in connection with the purposes to which it is applied. Corn is raised at various costs, according to the character of the land and the degree of skill employed in its cultivation; but, as every economist knows, the cost which governs the price of corn is the cost of the most costly portion brought to market. In the early stages of a nation's career, as with the increase of population resort is had to more distant and inferior soils, the cost of this most costly portion steadily rises, and along with it the normal price of corn. But an increase in the cost of corn means a diminished return on the industry employed in producing it; and this diminished return —corn being the principal article of the laborer's consumption —involves for him diminished means of support. It needs but slight reflection to perceive that this circumstance contains within it a necessary limit to the increasing cost of producing corn, and, consequently, to the advance in its price. In the case of what we may call secondary articles of consumption, such as meat and dairy produce, the same consequence does not arise, because an advance in the price of such commodities, entering as they do but sparingly into his consumption, falls, by comparison at least, lightly on the laborer. These articles

---

* Unless Adam Smith's view as to the steadiness of the price of corn, comparing century with century, in contrast with the market fluctuations from year to year, be considered as tantamount to it. Mr. Mill, indeed, has controverted Adam Smith's doctrine, which, he says, "we now know to be an error. Corn tends to rise in cost of production with every increase of population, and to fall with every improvement in agriculture, either in the country itself, or in any foreign country from which it draws a portion of its supplies" ("Principles of Political Economy," vol. ii., p. 104). I venture here to take side with Adam Smith: for though the tendencies pointed out by Mr. Mill do exist and operate, their operation, as I think I have shown in the text, is not inconsistent with the substantial truth of Adam Smith's assertion.

may continue to rise indefinitely, and yet population may continue to live and grow. But an advance in the price of the staple food, after it attains a certain elevation, inevitably reacts on population, and, checking the demand, arrests the extension of cultivation, and by consequence, the advance of normal price. The progress of industrial invention comes no doubt in time to affect the course of agriculture, and then ensues a succession of cyclical movements which may be thus described. The cost of producing corn on the worst soils cultivated is cheapened: the normal price of corn for a time falls: the condition of the laborer improves, and with the improvement in his condition he marries earlier, and brings up a larger family: population increases, and, the demand for food increasing with it, cultivation is extended to soils which, previous to the introduction of the better agricultural processes, could not have been profitably cultivated; at length the "margin of cultivation" attains a range where the inferior quality of the natural agents brought into requisition just neutralizes the gain derived from the advance in agricultural skill. At this point the cost of producing the most costly portion of the nation's food is just where it was before improved processes had been introduced into agriculture; and the normal price of food attains its former elevation. The laborer's condition, unless so far as the standard of comfort has been raised in the interval, returns to its former level; and the high rates of subsistence once more react on and control population. Under the influence of a play of motives of this kind, the normal price of corn has in all long-settled countries been kept, as a permanent state of things, within the limit which it had reached at a comparatively early stage of their career, in this respect strongly contrasting with the course of price in meat, and in most other secondary articles of consumption. M. Cherbuliez,* in connection with this subject.

---

* "Précis de la Science Économique," vol. i., pp. 356, 357.

has remarked that, comparing the present prices of meat and corn in the countries of Western Europe with their prices in former times, it has been found that, in the same period in which the price of corn has risen in the proportion of one to two, the price of meat has risen in the proportion of one to ten. I venture to assert that, at all events since the beginning of the seventeenth century,* the normal price of wheat has not risen in England more than the depreciation of the precious metals since that time will fully account for. According to Adam Smith, the average price of wheat during the first sixty-four years of the eighteenth century ruled at about twenty-eight shillings the quarter, and this price he considered somewhat lower than it would have been had not the period been marked by an unusual number of good harvests. In the last sixty-four years of the preceding century, the price of wheat, according to the same authority, stood somewhat higher. Taking the whole hundred and twenty-eight years, the average price of wheat probably might be taken as ruling between thirty and five-and-thirty shillings. Its price in average years now would, I apprehend, stand at somewhere about fifty shillings the quarter; and the difference is certainly not more than a reference to the diminished value of money would explain. The reader will not understand me as adducing these rough and summary statements *in proof* of the principle to which I am calling attention. I give them merely for the purpose of illustration; but I have little doubt that, if the question were gone into statistically, and due allowance made for changes in the value of money, the results would bear out the conclusion at which, on purely economic grounds, I have arrived.

---

* I have no doubt the date might be put some centuries farther back; but as the question of price in the preceding centuries becomes complicated by the combined effect of the depreciation of money and the deterioration of the standard coin, and as my object is to illustrate my position, not to prove it, I think it better to avoid entering on ground that might be disputed.

§ 4. One or two consequences involved in the state of things I have been describing it may perhaps be worth while here to point out. We have seen that in the early stages of a nation's history the tillage of the soil steadily encroaches upon pasture farming, until the latter becomes at length itself a branch of agriculture. A little later on, the nation, instead of being an exporter of agricultural produce, becomes an importer; and then agricultural industry takes a new turn. Corn can now be imported from abroad, but meat can not; and, whether imported or produced at home, the price of corn, for the reasons I have stated, has no tendency to rise permanently beyond the level it has already attained, whereas the price of meat may advance indefinitely. It follows from these facts that, as the nation increases its numbers and needs augmented supplies of food, it naturally resorts to foreign countries to supplement the deficiency in its corn supply, while the additions needed to its supply of meat are obtained by extending the area under pasture at home. The constant tendency, accordingly, of tillage to encroach upon pasture, which up to this time had been the law of industrial progress, is now reversed; and from this point the area of pasture tends steadily to increase, that of tillage to diminish. The stage in question had been reached by England just about the time that Adam Smith wrote; and notwithstanding the powerful obstacles offered by wars and corn-laws to the natural course of development, the movement of agriculture has, on the whole, been in the direction I have indicated. At the present time it is decidedly and unequivocally so, and indeed I believe the fact is very generally recognized. Another consequence depending on the same causes is exhibited in the movements of agricultural rent. In the early periods of a nation's history the lands from which the highest rent can be obtained are those which offer the greatest advantages for tillage, while pasture lands, owing to the low price of their produce, yield comparatively low returns in rent.

But so soon as that stage in its advancing career is reached when corn begins to be imported from abroad, and meat is raised by extending the area of pasture, the lands which thenceforward yield the highest rent are those whose special excellence lies in the rearing of cattle. I have no statistics which would enable me to illustrate this point, but the inference from the facts of the case is so plain that I think it may be advanced with little hesitation. There will be lands, no doubt, which may equally well be turned to either purpose; but where lands have special aptitudes for one of the two, those which are fitted in the highest degree for the raising of meat (and with meat we may include dairy produce, hops, and in general those articles which I have called "secondary" in relation to human requirements) are, I venture to think, those from which after the period indicated the highest rent will be obtained.

§ 5. There is a class of commodities which in the industry of newly-settled countries occupies an important place, the course of whose values is affected by rather peculiar conditions. I refer to what are called "accessory products"—commodities which are produced, not separately, but as parts of a common industry, and of which the most obvious examples are mutton and wool, beef, tallow and hides, gas and coke, and the like. As regards the values of such commodities, the general law determining them has been stated by Mr. Mill in his chapter on "Some Peculiar Cases of Value."* It is to the following effect: Cost of production here operates, but in a peculiar manner: it determines, not the price of each of the articles conjointly produced, but the sum of their prices; "their values relatively to each other being those which will create a demand for each in the ratio of the quantities in which they are sent forth by the productive process." The working of

---

* "Principles of Political Economy," vol. ii., book iii., chap. xvi.

this principle, under the changing circumstances of advancing communities, is what I desire now to call attention to.

I have already explained the course of price in one of the most important of those commodities—butcher's meat; and it was then seen how powerfully that course is affected by the difficulty of carriage incident to that article. On the other hand, the facility with which the products accessory to the production of butcher's meat, wool, tallow, and hides, are conveyed, is not less powerful in the opposite sense in affecting the course of their prices. Wool, for example, rises at once in a new country to the price ruling in the great markets of commerce, *minus* only the cost of carriage, which, owing to the great portableness of wool, bears but a small proportion to its total value. In other words, the demand for wool, let us say for wool grown in Australia, is only limited by the demand of the entire commercial world; while the demand for meat raised in the same country is practically confined to the local markets. It is evident that this circumstance must lead, in the industrial development of the colony, to a complete divergence in the courses of price of the two commodities. Indeed, that divergence has already become very sensible; for though it is true an advance has occurred in the price of wool since the early days of Australian settlement (mainly due, as I believe, to a fall in the value of money), the price of meat has advanced in a far greater degree. Nor is it difficult to foresee that it is in the directions thus indicated that the future prices of the two commodities will move. In both cases there will probably be an advance due to the declining value of gold; but the price of meat will be urged upward by other, and independent, causes. The durable character and slight bulkiness of wool, which even in the infancy of the colony sustained its price at a level but little below that of European markets, will, in later times, when the now sparse communities of Australia have grown into nations, confine it within limits not greatly larger than it now commands, by furnishing the same facilities for its importation which they now furnish for its exportation —a result exactly the converse of what we found to be the fate of meat, of which the perishable nature, as it excludes it from exportation when nations are young, so prevents its importation, at least on any great scale, when the increasing demand of the growing community outruns the internal facilities of production.

§ 6. In comparing the state of prices in old and new communities, the circumstance in which they stand perhaps most strikingly contrasted is that which has been brought out in the foregoing discussion—the remarkable difference found to exist in the two cases between the relative prices of corn or other products of prime necessity, on the one hand, and, on the other, those of butcher's meat, dairy produce, and such secondary commodities. The contrast was not unperceived by Adam Smith, and has been commented on at much length in the very interesting chapter in the "Wealth of Nations" which he devotes to this subject. The notion, however, which he had taken up as to a limitation, developed with the progress of society, to the advancing price of the latter class of articles, prevented him from seeing the full significance of the facts to which he drew attention; nor indeed are his inferences, even within the range of what he had perceived, absolutely unexceptionable. Nevertheless, his remarks in summing up the results of his investigation are sufficiently striking, and may fitly be quoted here:

"But though the low money price either of goods in general, or of corn in particular, be no proof of the poverty or barbarism of the times, the low money price of some particular sorts of goods, such as cattle, poultry, game of all kinds, etc., in proportion to that of corn, is a most decisive one. It clearly demonstrates, first, their great abundance in proportion to that of corn, and consequently the great extent of the land which they occupied in proportion to what was occupied by corn; and, secondly, the low value of this land in proportion to that of corn land, and consequently the uncultivated and unimproved state of the far greater part of the lands of the country. It clearly demonstrates that the stock and population of the country did not bear the same proportion to the extent of its territory which they commonly do in civilized countries, and that society was at that time, and in that country, but in its infancy. From the high or low money price either of goods in general, or of corn in particular, we can infer only that the mines which at that time happened to supply the commercial world with gold and silver were fertile or barren, not that the country was rich or poor. But, from the high or low money price of some sorts of goods in proportion to that of others, we can infer, with a degree of probability that approaches almost to certainty, that it was rich or poor, that the greater part of its lands were improved or unimproved, and that it was either in a more or less barbarous state, or in a more or less civilized one."

Strictly interpreted, the line of this inference would lead to the conclusion that Australia and California were poor countries, which would scarcely be considered a tenable position; but, barring this slip, as we may regard it, of substituting "rich and poor" for "old and young," the tenor of the remarks is essentially sound and just, and shows, considering the time when they were written, a remarkable insight into the causes governing industrial development.

§ 7. There is another class of "extractive" commodities which does not fall properly under any of the foregoing heads, on which a few remarks seem called for here. These are mineral products, comprising the coarser and precious metals, coal, and a few other articles. The circumstances in which products of this class differ from those which we have just considered appear to be chiefly these two: In the first place, the sources from which they are obtained are distributed over the earth with very great inequality; some countries being entirely destitute of them, others possessing them in great abundance, and of the most varied degrees of fertility; and, secondly, their production is more mechanical in its nature than that of agricultural or pastoral products, from which it results that their cost of production is more directly dependent, than that of other rude products, on the progress of mechanical and chemical invention. To follow out the consequences involved in these distinctions, more especially in the instance of the precious metals, would take me very far afield indeed; nor do I propose to attempt any such excursion here. I shall content myself, as regards this part of my subject, with observing in a general way, that the circumstances of the case have been conducive in the past history of the world to great variation in the normal prices of mineral products; nor can it be said, in spite of the fact that they come so largely under the influence of scientific invention, that the movements of normal price in their case have, with the progress of communities, been in any constant direction. As regards future movements of price in this class of products, so much depends on the discovery of new mines and coal measures, and this is so much a matter of accident, so large a portion of the world, moreover, still remains unexplored, that I do not think we can be said to possess the data for even a probable conjecture.

§ 8. I turn now from the domain of raw products to that other great industrial division—manufacturing industry. Between these two industrial departments it is not indeed possible to draw a perfectly hard and fast line, nor is it at all necessary that we should do so; it is sufficient that the designations —raw products and manufactured goods—indicate a real and important distinction in things, and one which will be easily and with sufficient correctness apprehended. What I have now to consider is the course which normal prices take with the progress of society in the latter of these two classes.

And here this remark may at once be made: that, as the

course of price in the field of raw products is, on the whole, upward, so in that of manufactured goods the course is, not less strikingly, in the opposite direction. The reasons of this are exceedingly plain. In the first place, division of labor—the first and most powerful of all cheapeners of production, but for which there is in extractive industry but very limited scope—finds in manufacturing industry an almost unbounded range for its application; and, secondly, it is in manufacturing industry also that machinery, the other great cheapener of production, admits of being employed on the largest scale, and has in fact been employed with the most signal success. It follows at once from these facts, taken in connection with the further fact that industrial invention does not take place *per saltum*, but gradually—one invention ever treading on the heels of another—and that its advance seems to be subject to no limitation; it follows, I say, from these considerations, that that portion of the cost of manufactured goods which properly belongs to the manufacturing process must, with the progress of society, undergo constant diminution. We can not, indeed, infer directly from this circumstance that the value of such goods must decline, because the manufacturing process represents but a portion of their cost, which also embraces that involved in raising the raw material out of which they are manufactured: and we have already seen that the cost of this element tends to advance with the progress of society. Whether, therefore, the price of manufactures will advance or decline must depend upon whether the tendency to fall, incident to improvements in the manufacturing process, will, on the whole, prevail over the tendency to advance inherent in the raw material, or be surpassed by the latter force. On this point, however, save in the case of a few very slightly manufactured articles, such, for example, as bread, in which the manufacturing process bears but a small proportion to the value of the raw material, there is no room for a moment's doubt. In all the great branches of manufacturing industry the portion of the cost incurred in the manufacturing process bears in general a large proportion to that represented by the raw material, while the influence of industrial invention, in reducing this portion of the cost, is, as every one knows, great and unintermitting in its action. From all these circumstances it results that the tendency to a reduction of cost in manufactured goods must, at least as the conditions of production stand at present, prevail, and in most cases prevail largely, over the tendency to an increase; and that consequently the course of normal prices in this class of commodities is, with the progress of society, inevitably and, at times, rapidly downward. The illustration of this truth is to be found in the history of all manufacturing countries, and pre-eminently in that of Great Britain. There are few commodities of any importance falling within the domain of manufacture which have not within the last century or two fallen to a small fraction of their former price.

But among manufactured commodities, as among raw products, there is a difference. As has just been stated, the two great cheapeners of production are division of labor and machinery, and the degree in which these admit of being applied to manufacture is mainly dependent upon the scale on which the manufacturing process is carried on. Those manufactures, therefore, that are produced upon a large scale are the sort of manufactures in which we may expect to find the greatest reduction in cost; in which, therefore, the fall in price, with the progress of society, will be most marked. But the manufactures which are produced upon the largest scale are those for which there exists the largest demand—that is to say, are those which enter most extensively into the consumption of the great mass of the people. They are also, I may add, those in which a fall in price is apt to stimulate a great increase of demand. All the common kinds of clothing, furniture, and utensils fall within the scope of this remark; and it is in these, rather than in the commodities consumed exclusively or mainly by the richer classes, that we should, accordingly, expect to find the greatest marvels of cheapening. There is indeed one incident of the case the bearing of which, so far as it goes, would, as between the two classes, rather favor the reduction of the more luxurious products. The manufactured articles which enter into the consumption of the masses are, as a rule, less manufactured than those which enter into the consumption of the rich—in other words, the amount of manufacture bestowed upon them bears a smaller proportion to the raw material than is the case with the more elaborate manufactures. Such coarser manufactures, therefore, would feel the effects of the advancing cost of the raw material more sensibly than the refined sorts. Thus, for example, comparing a piece of Brussels lace with a piece of common calico, it is evident that there would need to be a very great change indeed in the value of the raw material to produce any sensible effect in the price of the former article; whereas, as recent experience has taught us, an advance in the price of the raw material of common calico is capable of causing very serious effects in its price. This circumstance, therefore, so far as it goes, certainly favors in the race for cheapness the more luxurious as against the commoner and less elaborate manufactures. Nevertheless, it can not be supposed to compensate the advantages due to the causes I have pointed out which fall to the share of the commoner sorts. It is in this class of goods that the most remarkable reductions in price have been accomplished in the past; and it is in them probably that we shall witness in the future the greatest results of the same kind.

§ 9. Hitherto I have examined the derivative laws of value in so far only as they are exemplified in the movements of normal prices. It will be interesting now to consider whether it is possible to discover in the movements of market prices any corresponding phenomena; whether, that is to say, the fluctuations of the market, as they occur in the several classes of commodities, conform to any modes of action analogous to those which we have found to obtain in the case of normal price.

And here it may be well to state precisely what is to be understood by a "fluctuation of the market," as distinguished from those changes of normal price which we have been considering. Normal price, as we have seen, is governed, according to the circumstances of the case, by one or other of two causes—cost of production and reciprocal demand (in the sense explained in a former chapter). A change in normal price, therefore, is a change which is the consequence of an alteration in one or other of these conditions. So long as the determining condition—be it cost of production or reciprocal demand—remains constant, the normal price must be considered as remaining constant; but, the normal price remaining constant, the market price (which, as we have seen, depends on the opinion of dealers respecting the state of supply and demand in relation to the particular article) may undergo a change—may deviate, that is to say, either upward or downward from the normal level. Such changes of price, occurring while the permanent conditions of production remain unaffected, can only be temporary, calling into action as they do forces which at once tend to restore the normal state of things: they may, therefore, be properly described as "fluctuations of the market;" and the question now to be considered is how far we can connect such phenomena with the causes which determine them, and, by stating this connection, bring them within the domain of scientific law.

With a view to this inquiry, the first point to be attended to is the condition on which the correspondence of market with normal price depends. It is evident that this condition can be no other than such an adjustment of supply to demand—or, to speak more strictly, such a state of opinion among dealers respecting the adjustment of supply to demand—as shall produce the correspondence in question—a state of things which is realized when the disposable supply is regarded as sufficient, and no more than sufficient, to satisfy the demand for the commodity which exists at the normal level of price, or, as we may say, in Adam Smith's phrase, to satisfy the "effectual demand." Bearing this in mind, it will be seen that the deviation of the market price from the normal standard will be mainly influenced by the difficulties in the way of adapting supply to "effectual demand;" or, what comes to the same thing, that the closeness with which the market follows the normal price will depend upon the facilities available for this adaptation. On what, then, do these facilities depend? Chiefly, it appears to me, on the three following circumstances: first, on the conditions of production as affecting the commodity; secondly, on the nature of the commodity; and thirdly, on the greater or less urgency of human wants in relation to it.

In tracing the derivative laws of normal prices we found that the most fundamental distinction between commodities, with a view to the purpose then in hand, lay in the line of separation between the products of extractive and those of manufacturing industry. For our present purpose the same distinction is equally important; and I shall, therefore, once again adopt it. Regarding, then, commodities as falling under one or other of these two great heads, let us observe how, on the one hand, manufactures, on the other, agricultural and pastoral products, stand affected by each of the three conditions just named.

§ 10. Taking manufactures first, it is evident at once that, as regards conditions of production, the circumstances of the case are such as to secure, in general, great rapidity and also great certainty in bringing commodities to market. A deal table may be made in a few hours, a piece of cloth in a few weeks, a moderate-sized house in a month or little more. Tables, cloth, and houses may be produced with certainty in any quantity required. It results from this, that it is scarcely possible that, under ordinary circumstances, the selling price of a product of manufacture should for any long time much exceed its normal price; for so soon as the excess became palpable, inasmuch as this would imply exceptionally high profits for the producers, production would receive a stimulus; and, the facilities for producing the article being great, the supply would quickly be increased until it overtook the "effectual demand;" whereupon the market price would fall to the normal level. This, I say, is what would happen "under ordinary circumstances;" for in order that the supply should be thus rapidly adjusted to the increase of demand, it would be necessary that the latter should not exceed certain limits. In all the most important branches of manufacture fixed capital, chiefly in the form of machinery, is largely employed; and the limited quantity of such capital existing in a country at any time sets limits for the time being to the possible augmentation of supply. If the demand then exceed what the means of production thus immediately available can satisfy, the market price may rule for some considerable time in advance of the normal price—until, that is to say, time is allowed for erecting buildings and machinery suitable to the increased requirements of the community. Even on such occasions, however, it is rare that the elevation of price which results is very great; for here come into play those other conditions of which I have spoken. The nature of manufactures is, in general, such as to fit them admirably for distant transport. Any considerable elevation of price, therefore, is pretty certain to attract supplies from remote sources. Further, considered in their relation to human needs, I think it may be said of manufactured goods, that either the need for them is not very urgent, or, where it happens to be so, substitutes more or less suitable for the commodity or commodities which happen to be scarce may, in general, easily be found. From all these circumstances it results that an advance in the price of a manufacture, so soon as it becomes at all considerable, either attracts supplies from extraordinary sources, or deters purchasers, or brings substitutes into the field—by one or more of such means setting a limit to deviations, and preventing any great departure from the usual terms of the market.

So far as to deviations from the normal standard *upward*. With regard to movements in the opposite direction, the circumstances under which they occur are commonly of this kind. The adaptation of supply to demand is a tentative process, and when any sudden change in demand happens, it is not easy for producers at once to determine its extent. The result is that mistakes are made. Commodities are produced in excess: nay more, fixed capital is created in excess; and capital once committed to a "fixed" form is rarely capable of being applied to any purpose other than that for which it was intended. Hence, the supply once carried beyond the due limits of the "effectual demand," it becomes difficult to reduce it to its proper proportions. Mills and machinery once set up, it is of two evils often the least to continue production at a moiety, or less, of the ordinary profit, rather than to allow capital to lie absolutely unproductive: one hears besides that production, from motives of humanity to the workmen employed, is sometimes carried on even at a loss. Owing to causes of this kind, the markets for manufactured products sometimes continue for many months, possibly for a year or more, below the level of normal price. Here again, however, the same qualities which, as we saw, keep in check the upward movement, come into play to prevent a very great depression. Manufactures not being in general quickly perishable, it is rarely necessary, in their case, to force a sale, while their great portability gives them access to distant markets. On the whole, then, we find that, having regard alike to the conditions of production, the nature of the commodity, and the degree of urgency of human needs in relation to it, the circumstances of the case are such as to reduce within rather narrow limits the fluctuations of the market in the instance of manufactured goods.* And this is the more noteworthy, inasmuch as it is precisely in this class of commodities that, as we have seen, the changes in normal price, depending as they do on changes in the cost of production, are most frequent and most striking.

The state of things just described, and which exhibits, on the whole, a somewhat limited range of variation for the market (as distinguished from the normal) value of the products of manufacturing industry, might at first sight seem to offer but small scope for the sudden creation by individuals of large fortunes; and yet we know that it is in manufacturing industries that the largest and most rapid fortunes have been made. What is the explanation of this circumstance? I apprehend it will be found to lie mainly in the rapidity with which the circulating portion of manufacturing capital admits of being turned. The same rapidity of production which accelerates the reduction of price facilitates the turning of capital. Accordingly, when such a chance occurs as the sudden opening of a large and unlooked-for market—such an occasion, for example, as was presented by the rapid growth of the markets of California and Australia consequent on the gold discoveries; or again, such as the American civil war produced for the

---

* The chief exception to this is where a fluctuation of the market connects itself with some irregularity in the supply of the raw material, as happened during the cotton famine. But in this case the phenomenon should rather be considered as falling under our next head, which deals with the market fluctuations of raw products.

linen manufacturers, when the failing supply of calico threw a large and unexpected consumption upon linen—when, I say, occasions of this kind occur, those whose capital is already embarked in the trade can generally—such are the facilities for rapidly turning capital over in manufactures—contrive, even at a moderate advance of price, to realize large gains before the re-enforcements of fixed capital rendered necessary by the altered state of trade can be brought into the field. This is one, and the principal, source of the very large fortunes occasionally achieved by individuals in this branch of trade. For the rest I should conjecture that, where exceptional and extraordinary gains have been made, the end has been accomplished, less through manufacturing operations properly so called, than through speculations carried on in the raw material of the industry. This, at least, we know, was notoriously the case with the large fortunes made during the continuance of the American civil war.

§ 11. Turning now to the products of agricultural, pastoral, or, more generally, "extractive" industry, we find the circumstances under which this class of goods is brought to market in all respects extremely different from those which we have just examined, and such as to permit a much wider margin of deviation for the market from the normal price. Here the period of production is longer, the result of the process much more uncertain, the commodity is at once more perishable and less portable, and human requirements in relation to it are mostly of a more urgent kind. The shortest period within which additions can be made to the supply of food and raw material of the vegetable kind is in general a year, and if the commodity be of animal origin, the minimum period is considerably longer. Again, the farmer may decide upon the breadth of ground to be devoted to a particular crop, or upon the number of cattle he will maintain, but the actual returns will vary according to the season, and may prove far in excess or far in defect of his calculations. These circumstances all present obstacles to the adjustment of supply to demand, and consequently tend to produce frequent and extensive deviations of the market from the normal price. Nor are the other conditions of the case such as to neutralize the influence of such disturbing agencies. The nature, indeed, of some of the principal agricultural products fits them sufficiently well for distant transport, and so far tends to correct fluctuations of price. But, on the other hand, the relation of these products to human wants is such as greatly to enhance that tendency to violent fluctuation incident to the conditions of their production. More especially is this the case with the commodity, whatever it may be, which forms the staple food of a people. For observe the peculiar nature of human requirements with reference to such a commodity. They are of this kind, that, given the number of a population, the quantity of the staple food required is nearly a fixed quantity, and this almost irrespective of price: except among the very poorest, increased cheapness will not stimulate a larger consumption, while, on the other hand, all, at any cost within the range of their means, will obtain their usual supply. The consequence is, that, when even a moderate deficiency or excess occurs in the supply of the staple food of a people, in the one case the competition of consumers for their usual quantum of food rapidly forces up the price far out of proportion to the diminution in the supply: in the other, no one being inclined to increase his usual consumption, the competition of sellers, in their eagerness to find a market for the superfluous portion of the supply, is equally powerful to depress it. Those who have studied the history of English prices while England was yet under the *régime* of Protection, are aware of the enormous and sudden fluctuations which from time to time occurred under the influence of causes of this description. Such violent fluctuations will scarcely be witnessed again; but even under the moderating *régime* of free trade, the peculiar character of the staple food in its relation to the requirements of human beings continues from time to time to make its influence felt, and to produce sudden and considerable changes in the quotations of the market. And here I may notice the converse of a phenomenon adverted to just now in connection with the market prices of the products of manufacture. I then pointed out that, while circumstances, on the whole, contributed to steadiness of *market* value in such products, their *normal* values were in an especial degree liable to extensive changes. In the case of agricultural products, but more especially in the case of staple food, this relation is inverted. I ventured to assert, and in doing so I was supported by the authority of Adam Smith, that of all commodities whatever, that which forms the staple food of a people is the commodity of which the normal value in the course of time undergoes the least variation. As I have already said, I believe we should find, if we went into the case, that during the course of some centuries the normal value of wheat (I do not say the normal *price*) has altered very little in the more advanced countries of Europe. On the other hand, for the reasons which have been just set forth, wheat is, of all important commodities, that one which exhibits, in the movements of the market, variation in the most extreme degree. Incidents of this kind, it may be observed in passing, show the absolute necessity, if we desire to elucidate the phenomena of price, of distinguishing between market and normal values in economic discussion. The phenomena are perfectly distinct, and, as the foregoing examination has shown, sometimes follow, even in the instance of the same commodities, opposite laws. What likelihood, then, of getting a correct chart of their movements, if they are treated, as frequently happens in treatises on value, as one and the same manifestation, and confounded together as the subject-matter of a single exposition?

§ 12. It will serve still further to elucidate the fluctuations of market price within the sphere of extractive industry if we regard its deviations from normal price under two aspects: 1, with reference to its intensity; 2, with reference to its duration. A commodity may rise very suddenly and greatly in price, but may quickly return to its usual terms of sale; or, on the other hand, rising slowly and not very greatly above its ordinary level, it may, nevertheless, continue for a long time at the elevation thus attained. If now, bearing this distinction in mind, we compare among the raw products of industry those derived from the vegetable with those derived from the animal kingdom, I think we shall find the following rule in the main to hold true: namely, that vegetable products are for the most part subject to market fluctuations of the former character—the fluctuations, that is to say, are apt to be sudden and considerable, but comparatively short; while the market prices of commodities of animal origin rarely rise rapidly, but, when a sensible advance is established, commonly remain for a long time at the enhanced rate. Thus it has happened, even since the establishment of free trade, that the price of corn has, within the space of a few years, been halved and doubled again, and then in another year or two fallen once more to a medium level:* but no such sharp oscillation has, so far as I am aware, occurred (at least in recent times) in the price of any animal product. Butcher's meat is perhaps, among animal products, that one which has lately exhibited the most marked advance. It would, however, be a mistake to assume that the

---

* The weekly average price of wheat, for example, had risen in 1817 to as high a point as 102s. per quarter: within a year from that time it fell to little more than half that price, and in 1851 to as low as 43s. Within two years more, namely, about the commencement of the Crimean war—having in the interval oscillated slightly about the point of 45s.—it rose very suddenly to 73s.; and in January, 1854, attained its maximum elevation of 84s., from which point it gradually declined. (See Tooke's "History of Prices," vol. v., part 1, § 14.)

great rise which has occurred in this article within the last twenty years represents simply a market fluctuation, because there is reason to believe that, if not the cost of production in the strict sense of the term, at all events the cost of production as measured in money, has during this time very considerably risen. Unless, therefore, the value of gold were, by some extraordinary freak of economic nature, to recover what it has lost, there is not the smallest probability that the price of meat will ever return to the level at which it stood twenty years ago. The present advance, therefore, can not be considered, at all events for the chief portion of its amount, as a mere phenomenon of the market, but rather as a definitive rise of the normal price; and it may be added that the same is, in a greater or less degree, true of most instances of augmented price that have recently occurred. To return to the difference in the incidents of market price between vegetable and animal products, its cause is mainly to be found in the conditions of their production. Commodities drawn from the vegetable kingdom can, in general, be multiplied more rapidly than those taken from the animal; and, therefore, deviations from the normal standard of price require for their correction, in this case, a shorter period of time. On the other hand, the same commodities are subject to much greater uncertainty in the process of production than those of animal origin, the agencies employed being here far less amenable to human control. Animals may, at least, be housed, and, by other artificial expedients, sheltered from the violence of natural agencies, but few such means of mitigation can well be employed when the production of vegetables on a large scale is the business in hand. Hence the defalcations of supply are usually more considerable in their case, and hence the oscillations of market price, though shorter, are also more intense.

The most important exception to the rule just laid down occurs in the case of fish and game, but it is an exception of that kind which proves the rule; for, unlike animal products obtained by domestication and breeding, the supply of fish, and in a less degree of game, is singularly at the mercy of causes uncontrollable by man, while the time requisite for catching them, as compared with the time required for the completion of ordinary industrial processes, is extremely short. The principle, therefore, on which the rule rests, would lead us to expect here violent and brief fluctuations, more especially when we take into account, in connection with the conditions of their production, the extremely perishable nature of the articles in question—a circumstance which compels the dealers, at almost any sacrifice, to find a market for their goods within a strictly limited time.

PART II.
LABOR AND CAPITAL.

PART II.

LABOR AND CAPITAL.

CHAPTER I.

THE RATE OF WAGES.

§ 1. In discussing the laws of value, we have already partially solved the problems of wages and profits. For it has appeared that, where production assumes the character of a continuous operation, producers are in effect remunerated out of the values of their products, and that consequently wages and profits in each branch of production must stand, in the normal state of things and on the average, to wages and profits in every other branch, in the same relation as the values of the products from which they are derived. "Relative wages and profits" thus follow the same laws which govern the exchange value of commodities. In other words, our reasoning has involved this conclusion, that wages and profits, regarded as relative phenomena, are governed by Cost of Production, where the producers are in effective competition with one another, and, where they are not, by Reciprocal Demand. So far we were carried toward the solution of the wages and profits problem in the discussion of that of value; but it is important that we should not overrate the progress that has been effected. Let me repeat: what the doctrine of value reveals to us on this subject is the causes which determine the *relative* remuneration of laborers as among themselves, and that of capitalists as among themselves. It tells us why some classes of workmen and some classes of capitalists receive the same or equivalent remuneration, while in other cases inequality in various degrees prevails; but it tells us nothing as to what determines the positive remuneration which any class of capitalists or of laborers receives, nor as to the causes on which depend the average well-being of all classes. In a word, we have ascertained what produces the ripples on the surface of the industrial stream; but of the source from which the waters are derived, and of the depth and force of the current, nothing has yet been disclosed. Why is the remuneration of industry, as a whole, such as we find it to be in the various countries of the earth? Why is it maintained at one level in England, at another on the continent of Europe, at yet another in Asia, and at another still in the United States? And why again is this level progressive in some countries, stationary in others, declining in a third class? These are questions on which the doctrine of value throws no light, and it is, therefore, to this side of the general problem that we have now to direct our attention.

§ 2. I shall perhaps here be reminded that the question of the rate of wages, as well as that of the rate of profits, under whatever aspect we regard them, are, and can never be other than, problems of value; since they are simply questions of the value respectively of labor and abstinence; and that they should be dealt with in connection with that subject in the general theory of which they are implicated. I am certainly not going to dispute the allegation that wages and profits are, in a certain sense, phenomena of value. "Rate of wages" and "value of labor," "rate of profit" and "value of abstinence," are no doubt equivalent expressions; and for my part I see no objection to regarding the doctrines elucidating these phenomena as constituting branches of the same general theory with that which explains the value of commodities. But I apprehend the objection, embodied in the above remark, points to something more than this. What some students of Political Economy seem to desiderate is a comprehensive formula which shall embrace in a single solution, along with the laws of the exchange relations of commodities, those of the exchange relations of labor and abstinence, and, along with these again, the laws of the exchange relations of land—that is to say, the theory of rent. Some such aim seems to have guided the speculations of Bastiat, whose work on the " Harmonies of Political Economy " is in effect an essay toward the determination of the required formula; but the result of Bastiat's attempt is not encouraging to those who would essay the same path. He produces, indeed, generalizations which seem to satisfy the needed conditions; but, closely examined, they either collapse into mere identical propositions, or are found to contain some flagrant *petitio principii*. Where not open to either of these objections, they will be found to relate to the phenomena of *comparative* remuneration—that is to say, to that portion of the theory of wages and profits which I have admitted and shown may be treated in connection with the general laws of value.

The truth is, the fundamental facts of the two problems are too essentially discrepant to admit of this mode of treatment. Verbal generalizations are of course easy. For example, nothing is easier than to say that the value of labor (I put aside abstinence and profit as not included in my present inquiry), like the value of other things, depends upon supply and demand—we may find the formula in any newspaper we take up; but what light does this throw upon the causes which govern the values either of labor or of commodities? Simply none at all, or next to none at all. What we want to know is, not whether an increase of supply will cheapen a commodity or will cheapen labor, and an increase of demand raise the price of each—every coster-monger will tell you this much—but what it is which governs supply and demand in each case. Now, we can not take a step toward dealing with this question without being brought face to face with the fact that the motives which influence human beings in the production and supply of commodities are not those which influence them in the production and supply of labor; in other words, that the conditions operative in the two cases are essentially distinct. If this is not already apparent to the reader, a brief consideration will suffice to make it so.

First, then, the production of commodities is an onerous act, which will only be undertaken in the prospect of reward; whence it follows that the supply of commodities will only be secured on the condition of this prospect presenting itself. On the other hand, the production of labor, which in other words is the production of human beings, is not an onerous act, but a consequence of complying with one of the strongest instincts of humanity—an instinct which, so far from needing the stimulus of reward, can only be kept under due control by powerful restraints. In the one case, action entails self-denial; in the other, self-denial lies in abstaining from action. Prospective recompense indeed comes into requisition in both cases; but in the one it is needed to stimulate, in the other to control. Exclude the prospect of reward from productive industry, and the supply of commodities will cease; exclude the prospect of the reward which results from providence in reproducing human beings, and the supply of labor will run to excess. Nor shall we have need to modify seriously our conclusion upon this point, if, passing from the primary act of reproducing human beings, we take account of what is necessary in order to fit them, once in existence, for an industrial career. They must be fed and clothed; they must be brought up in a certain state of comfort; and they must receive a certain education — conditions which, unlike the act of originating their existence, call for, in order to their fulfillment, continuous and often arduous effort. Here, we must admit, there is an analogy between the preparation of a human being for industrial work, and the production of a commodity for the market; both processes involve cost. But there still remains this broad distinction, which effectually discriminates the two cases: The cost in the production of a commodity is undergone deliberately, and with a distinct view to industrial ends: in the preparation of human beings for their career in life—I will not say that industrial ends have no place at all in the calculation, but I will assert this, that, except in the case of technical or professional education—a mere bagatelle in the general expense of rearing a laborer—industrial considerations are entirely subordinate to considerations of a wider and altogether different character. A man, whatever be his rank of life, brings up his children—I speak of the common case—as far as he is able, according to the ideas prevailing in that rank of life. He does so mainly because he feels certain obligations of morality and affection toward them, and because it would be shameful to do otherwise. His children once arrived at maturity, no doubt his views and theirs will take a direction more distinctly governed by industrial considerations, or at least considerations bearing upon material success in life; but at this point the supply of labor *has been already determined*. It is now in existence; and the industrial motive, now that it comes into play, operates, not upon the aggregate supply of labor, but merely upon the mode of its distribution. I do not deny, indeed, that, in a certain irregular way, and taking considerable periods of time, the supply of labor as a whole follows the demand for labor; but what I contend is, that it is not connected with demand by the same links which connect the supply of commodities with the demand for them. The adaptation of the supply of commodities to the demand is determined by strictly commercial motives: the adaptation of the supply of labor to the demand is not so determined. Illuman beings, at least out of slave countries, are not produced to meet the requirements of the market, but for entirely different reasons. Now, this being so—the conditions determining the phenomena in the two cases being essentially distinct—what can come of forcing the solutions by dint of verbal refinements into a single formula? Simply this: either our theory will be flagrantly untrue, or it will not go more than word-deep, and our show of explanation will merely serve to obscure the essential facts of the problem.

§ 3. These preliminary points being disposed of, I turn now to the proper subject of this chapter—the causes determining the general or average rate of wages. But here an objection meets me on the threshold. Are we justified in speaking of a "general" rate of wages? Are the facts expressed by wages such as may be usefully embraced in a general conception and reasoned about as an aggregate? A recent writer, Mr. Longe, has denied the existence of any facts which can warrant this expression:

"The notion of all the laborers of a country constituting a body of general laborers capable of competing with each other, and whose "general" or "average" wage depends upon the ratio between their number and the aggregate wage-fund, is just as absurd as the notion of all the different goods existing in a country at any given time—for example, the ships, and the steam-engines, and the cloth, etc.—constituting the stock of general commodities, the general or average price of which is determined by the ratio between the supposed quantity of the whole aggregate stock and the total purchase-fund of the community. . . . . How could the shoe-makers compete with the tailors, or the blacksmiths with the glass-blowers? Or how should the capital which a master-shoe-maker saved by reducing the wages of his journeymen, get into the hands of the master-tailor?"*

To the latter questions I think I have already supplied a

---

* "A Refutation of the Wage-fund Theory of Modern Political Economy," by F. D. Longe, pp. 55, 56.

sufficient answer; but with regard to the objection itself, and the illustration by which it is supported, the reader will observe to what length it goes. The author of the passage just quoted is apparently unable to conceive a general or average rate where the average is not realized in each individual instance; otherwise where is the absurdity of speaking of a "general" or "average" price of commodities? If the notion of a general or average price of commodities is absurd, then what does the writer mean when he speaks of a rise or fall in the value of money? Or is that idea also beyond his conceptive power? A rise or fall in the value of money is only another name for a fall or rise of general or average prices. The idea, in short, which Mr. Longe adduces as an extreme example of absurdity, is simply one of the most familiar in the range of economic speculation. A general rate of wages is neither more nor less easy to conceive, neither more nor less absurd, than general prices. I think I know what I mean when I say that prices and wages in the United States, measured in greenbacks, have risen *generally* as compared with prices and wages, measured in gold; that the average rate is higher in the one case than in the other; and I do not think I should be very wide of the mark if I attributed this difference to the different proportions in which purchasing power measured in gold, and purchasing power measured in greenbacks, stand related to commodities and labor. Yet these familiar notions are what Mr. Longe finds it impossible to conceive.

An expression in the passage quoted would seem to imply that universal competition among laborers is an essential condition to the existence of an average rate of wages. Why it should be so (except on the supposition I have referred to, that an average rate requires that the average be realized in each particular instance) I am quite at a loss to imagine; but Mr. Longe's language seems further to imply that, as a matter of fact, the several departments of industry in this and other countries are so practically isolated from each other, that wages in any of them may rise or fall without producing any effect beyond the particular department. I have already considered the extent to which competition is really effective in our industrial life, and have endeavored to show in what way its existence or non-existence affects relative wages. To what was then said I desire now to add that, even where competition among laborers is not effective, and where consequently wages are not in proportion to sacrifices, it is very far from being true that any such industrial isolation obtains as Mr. Longe's argument would suggest. A rise of wages, let us suppose, occurs in the coal trade: does any one suppose that this could continue without affecting wages, not merely in other mining industries in full competition with coal-mining, but in industries the most remote from coal-mining, industries alike higher and lower in the industrial scale? Most undoubtedly it could not; and if any one questions the assertion, he may have his doubts resolved by what is now going on before our eyes. Nor is the explanation far to seek. Though laborers in certain departments of industry are practically cut off from competition with laborers in other departments, the competition of capitalists, as I have already pointed out, is effective over the whole field. The communication between the different sections of industrial life, which is not kept open by the movements of labor, is effectually maintained by the action of capital constantly moving toward the more profitable employments. In this way our entire industrial organization becomes a connected system, any change occurring in any part of which will extend itself to others and entail complementary changes. Not only, therefore, are we justified in generalizing the various facts of wages into a single conception, and in discussing "general" or "average" wages, but we have grounds for regarding this general or average rate as constituted of elements bound together by a common connection, and forming parts of an integral whole.

§ 4. The problem of the general rate of wages, after being the occasion of perhaps more bitter controversy than any other within the field of social inquiry, seemed some years ago to have received, so far as the essentials of the matter went, its definitive solution. The great stumbling-block to its acceptance had long been the law of population, which, in spite of the overwhelming evidence adduced in its support by Malthus, provoked, as all the world knows, a violent opposition, and led to a controversy which, extending over half a century, has only died out, if indeed it has died out, within a few years. This result may be attributed partly, we may perhaps assume, to the gradual progress of sound reason getting the better of the strongest prepossessions; but it has of late been powerfully helped forward by the influence of Mr. Darwin's great work, in which the obnoxious principle—the tendency of human beings to increase faster than subsistence, which had been denounced as at once demoralizing to man and discreditable to the Author of the Universe—was shown to be merely a particular instance of a law pervading all organic existence. However this may be, in point of fact those attacks upon the economic doctrine of wages which were based upon objections to the Malthusian doctrines—attacks upon what we may call the *supply* side of the wages problem—have for some time come to an end. We may therefore assume that so much of the problem has been solved to the general satisfaction of competent thinkers, and are consequently dispensed from entering on its consideration here.

But the controversy has scarcely been closed on one side when it has been opened on another. The law of the supply of labor is no longer called in question; but several able writers have within a few years, in dissertations directed against what is known as the "Wages-fund" doctrine, challenged the view hitherto received as to the law of its demand. Foremost among these has been Mr. Thornton, who, in his book on "Labor,"* has made the Wages-fund doctrine the object of a special and elaborate attack; nor is it possible to deny the ability and skill with which the assault has been conducted, when we find that he can boast, as among the first-fruits of his argument, no less a result than the conversion of Mr. Mill.

Such an event, it must be frankly conceded, affords an extremely strong presumption in favor of the soundness of Mr. Thornton's view. Mr. Mill had himself been, if not the originator of the Wages-fund doctrine, certainly its most able and effective expositor; and this doctrine, supported by his argument, and implicated in his general theory, he has been led by Mr. Thornton's reasoning to discard. I say, it can not be denied that such a circumstance constitutes a weighty presumption in favor of Mr. Thornton's view; but I must also contend that it amounts to no more than a presumption. In the freedom of science, I claim for myself the right of examining the doctrine on its merits. I must own myself unconvinced by Mr. Thornton's reasonings, strengthened and enforced though these have been by the powerful comments of Mr. Mill.† Not indeed that I am prepared to defend all that has been written on what, for convenience, I may call the orthodox side of this question, but I believe the view maintained by those who have written on that side, and pre-eminently the view maintained by Mr. Mill himself—taking it as set forth in his original work, not as explained in his retractation—to be substantially sound, though needing, as it seems to me, at once fuller development and more accurate determination than it has yet received.

---

* "On Labor: its Wrongful Claims and Rightful Dues," etc., by W. T. Thornton. Second Edition, 1870.

† See *Fortnightly Review* for May 1, 1869.

§ 5. I can not, I think, better open the examination which I propose to make of this subject, than by quoting the following statement from Mr. Mill's "Principles of Political Economy," of the nature of the Wages-fund, and its place in the industrial economy:

"Wages, then, depend mainly upon the demand and supply of labor; or, as it is often expressed, on the proportion between population and capital. By population is here meant the number only of the laboring class, or rather of those who work for hire; and by capital, only circulating capital, and not even the whole of that, but the part which is expended in the direct purchase of labor. To this, however, must be added all funds which, without forming a part of capital, are paid in exchange for labor, such as the wages of soldiers, domestic servants, and all other unproductive laborers. There is unfortunately no mode of expressing by one familiar term the aggregate of what may be called the Wages-fund of a country: and as the wages of productive labor form nearly the whole of that fund, it is usual to overlook the smaller and less important part, and to say that wages depend on population and capital. It will be convenient to employ this expression, remembering, however, to consider it as elliptical, and not as a literal statement of the entire truth."*

As I understand this passage, it embraces the following statements: 1st, "Wages-fund" is a general term, used in the absence of any other more familiar, to express the aggregate of all wages at any given time in possession of the laboring population; 2d, on the proportion of this fund to the number of the laboring population depends at any given time the average rate of wages; 3d, the amount of the fund is determined by the amount of the general wealth which is applied to the direct purchase of labor, whether with a view to productive or to unproductive employment. If the reader will carefully consider these several propositions, I think he will perceive that they do not contain matter which can be properly regarded as

---

* "Principles of Political Economy," book ii., chap. xi.

open to dispute. The first is little more than a definition; at most, it assumes that that exists in the aggregate which is admitted to exist in detail. The second merely amounts to saying that the quotient will be such as the dividend and divisor determine. The third equally contains an indisputable assertion; since, whatever be the remote causes on which the wages of hired labor depend (and the question at present is exclusively of *hired* labor) *the proximate act determining their aggregate amount must in all cases be a direct purchase of its services.* In truth, the demand for labor, thus understood, as measured by the amount of wealth applied to the direct purchase of labor, might more correctly be said to be, than to determine, the Wages-fund. It *is* the Wages-fund in its inchoate stage, differing from it only as wealth just about to pass into the hands of laborers differs from the same wealth when it has got into their hands. Our analysis thus leads us to the result, that the passage quoted from Mr. Mill can not be taken to contain controversial matter. The statements are such as may not be disputed, once their meaning is clearly understood. At the same time it must be freely confessed that it contains no solution of the wages problem: it is not a solution, but a statement of that problem—a statement, as it seems to me, at once clear, comprehensive, and succinct, presenting in clear light the two factors which constitute the phenomenon—the Wages-fund resulting from the direct demand for labor, and the laboring population forming the supply. The solution will consist in connecting these factors with those principles of human nature and facts of the external world which form the premises of economic science.*

---

* "The political economy of the wages question," says Mr. Brassey (p. 251), "is simple enough." Certainly it is, if it consists in showing that every rise or fall of wages is traceable to a change in the relation of supply and demand. But it seems to me that Mr. Brassey has mistaken the statement of the problem for its solution. It needs no proof surely to see that if £10,000,000 be added to the ex-

§ 6. As I have already observed, it is with a portion only of this problem that we have need now to concern ourselves. The causes governing the supply of labor may be taken as sufficiently elucidated. Our business is with the causes governing the demand—governing the amount of wealth applied to the direct purchase of labor, or, as we may equally well express it, governing the Wages-fund.

It is here for the first time that room for controversy really occurs; and though the issue has not always been taken with precision, it is in effect on the point just indicated that the recent controversy turns. By the upholders of the Wages-fund doctrine the view taken is, that the amount of a nation's wealth expended in wages at any given time stands—the character of the national industries and the methods of production employed being given—in a definite relation to its general capital, while the amount of its general capital is determined by certain economic conditions resulting from the character of the people and the nature of their environment.* The Wages-fund, therefore, according to this view, depends, the conditions of production being given, proximately on the amount of a nation's capital, and ultimately on those more remote causes which control the growth of this fund. It is against this view

---

isting capital of a country, and the greater portion applied to the direct purchase of labor (the supply of labor and other things continuing the same), wages must rise; or that the withdrawal of a great sum from the payment of wages, as on the occasion of a commercial collapse, must on the other hand, *cæteris paribus*, involve a fall of wages. To tell us this is not to solve the wages question, but to state it. What we want to know is what determines the relation of supply and demand—of the Wages-fund to the laboring population. Why is that relation such as to yield one rate of wages in the United States, another rate in Great Britain, and a third rate on the continent of Europe? If Mr. Brassey would fairly address himself to this problem, I think he would find that the political economy of the wages question is not quite so " simple " as he supposes.

* As set forth, for example, in Mill's "Principles of Political Economy," book i., chap. xi.

of the connection of facts that the opponents of the impugned doctrine have directed their arguments. According to Mr. Thornton there is no portion of a nation's wealth "determined" toward the payment of wages. The amount which actually reaches the laborer is, I presume he would say, the result of circumstances (which, as not being "determined," must be regarded as accidental) of which the most important are those incidents in the position respectively of employer and employed which favor or restrict the capacity for bargaining. And substantially the same language is held by Mr. Longe. Rather inconsistently, however, while denying the determination of any portion of the general wealth to the payment of wages, Mr. Longe propounds a theory to explain the fact of this determination. The determining cause, he says, is not, as alleged in the Wages-fund theory, the economic conditions affecting the growth of capital, but "the demand for commodities." "The demand for commodities certainly does not directly determine the quantity of labor or number of laborers in a country, nor the quantity of corn or other things available for the maintenance of laborers, but it does determine the quantity of labor employed, and the quantity of wealth spent in the wages of laborers" (p. 46). As he elsewhere puts it, "the demand for commodities which can only be got by labor is as much a demand for labor as a demand for beef is a demand for bullocks."

§ 7. Such are the positions taken in this controversy by the disputants on either side. In proceeding to state the doctrine in question, with a view to meet the objections which have been advanced against it, it will be convenient in the first place to examine the theory put forward by Mr. Longe, and which apparently finds favor with Mr. Thornton also, as to the bearing of the demand for commodities upon the remuneration of labor; I shall then set forth the grounds on which the doctrine of the Wages-fund rests; and having done this, I shall be in a position to consider the arguments advanced by Mr. Thornton against the existence of any "determining" causes in the case.

Mr. Longe has refused to admit the existence of, and has thrown doubt upon the possibility of conceiving, "a general rate of wages." He, however, allows, at least by implication, that we may conceive an aggregate quantity of wealth as spent in wages, or what I call a Wages-fund; for in the passage just quoted he tells us the cause which determines the amount of this fund. It is, he says, "the demand for commodities." I need scarcely remark that the view here expressed is not peculiar to Mr. Longe. It is in truth about the most popular of all popular fallacies. From this root has sprung a whole cluster of maxims, such as that "the extravagance of the rich is the gain of the poor," that "profusion and waste are for the good of trade," and others of like import which have in their time done much to perplex and demoralize mankind, and are still far from being extinct. That there is much plausibility in the view here taken of the economy of industry can not indeed be denied, since otherwise how should it have obtained the almost universal vogue which it enjoys? It will therefore be worth while to sift with some care the grounds of an opinion which has certainly exercised no small amount of evil influence on modes of thinking and acting in economic affairs.

To state in its strongest form the argument for the view which I am combating: What, it may be asked, is the primary consideration that weighs with a capitalist in investing his wealth? Is it not the prospect of finding a sale for his products—in other words, the demand for commodities? And, as this is that which first moves him to action, is it not also that which governs the proportions of his operations after he has entered upon action? Increase the demand for his commodities, and he will increase the amount of his investment: diminish the demand, and he will diminish the investment. But, other things being the same, the greater the investment, the greater will be the amount of his wealth spent in the wages of labor. In proportion, therefore, as the demand for his commodity is large, his expenditure in wages will be large. This is true of every capitalist and of every branch of production. From which the conclusion seems to follow that the quantity of wealth spent in the wages of labor—*i. e.*, the aggregate Wages-fund—is determined by the demand for commodities.

It seems to follow, but it does not follow; for, looking closely into the above reasoning, we find that while the conclusion is an assertion as to quantity, the premises relate to proportion. The existence of a demand, for example, for houses in a given degree of intensity will cause a certain quantity of the national capital to be directed to the building of houses; but it will not and can not determine what that quantity shall be. This will depend, in the first place, upon the amount of the total capital available for investment; and secondly, on the relative force of the demand for houses as compared with the demand for other things. What the demand for houses and for other things determines is merely the proportions in which the available capital of a country shall be distributed over the field of production. Those proportions will adapt themselves to the proportions of the various demands for commodities. Increase the demand for a given commodity, and, other things being the same, a larger proportion of the available capital will be directed toward its production; diminish the demand for it, and a contrary result will ensue: but neither in the one case nor in the other will the demand for the commodity determine how much capital shall be devoted to its production; nor for similar reasons will the demand for commodities in general determine a like result with regard to them. It is as if we argued, that because a man distributes his income in the proportion of his various needs, spending more on those articles to purchase which a larger sum is wanted to satisfy his requirements, therefore, the greater his needs the larger must be his income. Large or small, his income will be distributed in proportion to his needs; and, large or small, the Wages-fund will be distributed over the various industrial occupations in the proportions indicated by the demand for commodities. But this tells us nothing as to what determines either the amount of a man's income, or the amount of the Wages-fund. We are thus brought to Mr. Mill's conclusion, that the demand for commodities determines the direction of investment and production, but not the more or less of what the laborer on an average receives.

But it may be well perhaps to give the argument a more practical direction; and for this purpose I will ask the reader to consider some of the consequences which would follow from this theory of which Mr. Longe has made himself the expositor, in connection with the condition of labor in different countries. Supposing it to be true that the amount of wealth spent in the wages of labor is determined by the demand for commodities, then it will follow that, given the demand for commodities, we are given the amount of wealth spent in the wages of labor. The latter will vary with the former, and the Wages-fund will, on this view, bear a constant proportion to the aggregate demand for commodities. Now, as has been explained in a former chapter of this work,* the aggregate demand for commodities depends on the aggregate production of commodities. Speaking broadly, all commodities produced under a *régime* of division of labor are produced in order to be exchanged. The more each man produces, the more he will have to sell, and the more he will be able to buy. It results, therefore, from the theory we are considering, that the aggregate wealth appropriated to the use of the laboring population must always bear a constant proportion to the gross produce

---

* See *ante*, pp. 23 26.

of the community. Now, how does this accord with the facts of wages as presented, let us say, in England and in the United States? According to computations made by Mr. Wells,* the United States Commissioner, taken in connection with some made by Mr. Dudley Baxter for this country, it would seem that the annual gross produce of the United States per head of the population bears to the annual gross produce of the United Kingdom per head of the population the proportion of $140 to $134. The United Kingdom includes Ireland, which can not but sensibly reduce the average for this country. Omitting Ireland, the annual *per capita* produce of Great Britain and of the United States would, therefore, according to these computations, be as nearly as possible the same. But the annual gross produce would determine the demand for commodities, and the demand for commodities, according to Mr. Longe, determines the quantity of wealth spent in the wages of labor. From which several positions the conclusion follows that the Wages-fund of Great Britain stands to that of the United States in the same proportion as the population of the former country to the population of the latter. Now, taking this to be so, and assuming further that the proportion of the population working for hire is the same in both countries, then the average rate of wages would for both countries be the same. In point of fact, the working population constitutes a smaller fraction of the entire population in Great Britain than in the United States: it would, therefore, according to this view, bear a less proportion to the Wages-fund here than there. In other words, we are led by "the demand for commodities" theory, applied to the results ascertained by English and American statisticians, to this singular conclusion, that the rate of wages in Great Britain should be on an average higher than in the United States!

I have taken for comparison Great Britain and the United

---

* Wells's Report, 1869, p. 13.

States, because the requisite data were here easily obtainable; but any one who has followed the foregoing argument will perceive that, had the comparison been made between Great Britain and some still more recently settled country — for example, some of the Western States of North America, or one of our own Australian colonies — the *reductio ad absurdum* would have been yet more glaring. In effect, statistical details in such a comparison are superfluous. The broad facts of the case are such as can not be missed. It is evident at a glance that in such countries as our Australian colonies, or as Illinois or California, the amount of the entire annual production appropriated to the laboring population bears a far larger proportion to the whole than in old countries like Great Britain or France; that is to say, the Wages-fund in those parts of the world bears a larger proportion to the demand for commodities than in Western Europe. The demand for commodities, therefore, does not determine the Wages-fund. Observation, moreover, of the course of industrial development in such countries exhibits this fact, that, while with the progress of society the amount of wealth which goes to support hired labor pretty constantly increases, the *proportion* which this bears to the total produce of industry nearly as constantly declines — growing smaller as the realization of fortunes enables a larger proportion of the people to retire from active work, and as capital assumes more extensively a fixed form. In a word, the most prominent features in the industrial economy of new, old, and advancing countries absolutely precludes the supposition that the demand for commodities has any such connection with the interests of the laboring population as the doctrine I am now considering assumes.

§ 8. So far as to Mr. Longe's theory of Wages. I proceed now to state the doctrine of the Wages-fund, as at least I myself understand it.

It will be remembered that in the enunciation which I quoted from Mr. Mill of the wages problem, the Wages-fund is stated to consist of two distinct parts—one, the largest and by much the most important, constituting a portion of the general capital of the country: while the other is derived from that part of the nation's wealth which goes to support unproductive labor, of which Mr. Mill gives as an example the wages of soldiers and domestic servants. In proceeding to deal with the wages question, it will be convenient to omit for a time all consideration of the latter part: this will be more easily dealt with when we have ascertained the causes which govern the main phenomenon.

Restricting our view then for the present to that portion of the general Wages-fund which goes to support productive labor, we have, in the first place, to observe that the hiring of labor for productive purposes is an incident of the investment of capital. A capitalist engages and pays a workman from precisely the same motives which lead him to purchase raw material, a factory, or a machine. In searching, therefore, for the causes which govern the amount of wealth spent in the hiring of labor, we must advert to the considerations which weigh with men in devoting their means to productive investment. Why, for example, does A. B. employ his wealth in productive operations? And why does he employ so much and no more in productive operations? An adequate answer to these questions will carry us some way toward the goal we have in view.

It seems to me that the proper answer is as follows: A. B. invests his wealth productively in order to obtain a profit on the portion of his means so employed; and he invests so much and no more, because, his total means being what they are, and regard being had on the one hand to his private requirements and taste for indulgence, on the other to his desire to augment his means, coupled with the opportunities afforded him of doing so by making profit, this is the amount which it is suitable to his disposition, in the circumstances in which he is placed, so to invest. In other words, we find the amount of A. B.'s investment determined by the following circumstances: First, the amount of his total means; secondly, his character and disposition as affected by the temptation to immediate enjoyment on the one hand, and by the prospect of future aggrandizement on the other; thirdly, the opportunities of making profit. Alter any of these conditions—his total means, his character, or his opportunities of making profit, and the effect will be an alteration in the amount of his investment. Increase his means, and, other things being the same, he will invest more largely: again, increase the prospect of profit, and, other things being the same, he will invest more largely: lastly, increase the strength of the accumulative principle in his character in relation to the taste for immediate enjoyment, and once more, other things being the same, he will invest more largely: on the other hand, a change in any of these conditions in the opposite direction would lead to his investment being correspondingly contracted.

Applying these considerations to the case of a community, it seems to me that we are justified in laying down the following proposition: That, the amount of wealth in a country being given, the proportion of this wealth which shall be invested in industrial operations with a view to profit will depend, first, upon the strength of those qualities in the average character of its inhabitants which lead to productive investment—what Mr. Mill calls "the effective desire of accumulation;" and secondly, on the opportunities of industrial investment open to the community offering a rate of profit sufficient to call this principle into activity—in a word, on "the extent of the field for investment."

Such being the conditions determining the investment of capital, it is plain that, if all capital consisted in wages, or if wages bore always the same proportion to a given quantity of capital, the problem with which we are immediately concerned would here be solved; and we might refer the phenomenon in question—we may describe it as we please, the extent of the demand for labor or the amount of the Wages-fund—simply and directly to the conditions which have just been stated, viz., in a given state of the national wealth, to the strength of the effective desire for accumulation, taken in connection with the extent of the field for investment. In point of fact, however, wages constitute but a portion of capital, and, what greatly complicates the inquiry, this portion bears no constant relation to the aggregate amount. It therefore still remains for us to determine the circumstances on which depends the distribution of capital between wages and the other elements of which capital consists.

Those other elements may be summed up under the heads of "Fixed Capital" and "Raw Material." Fixed Capital, Raw Material, and Wages-fund, therefore, form the three constituents of Capital, and the problem to be solved is, What are the causes which, in a given field of industry, determine the proportion in which these three constituents combine?

Let us again suppose an individual A. B. contemplating investment; he has decided how much of his whole means he intends to employ in productive operations, but, this point having been settled, he has yet to consider in what proportions the amount shall be divided between Fixed Capital, Raw Material, and Wages. What is to prescribe the respective quotas? Manifestly, in the first place, the nature of the industry in which he proposes to embark his capital. Suppose, for example, his purpose is to engage in cotton or woolen manufacture, a very large proportion of his whole capital will assume the form of buildings, machinery, and raw wool or cotton; that is to say, of fixed capital and raw material, which would leave a correspondingly small proportion available for the payment of wages. On the other hand, if, with the same capital to invest, he had selected agriculture as the field for its employment, the bulk of his capital would take the form of wages, and fixed capital and raw material would assume a relatively unimportant place in his outlay. It is thus evident that the nature of the industry selected for investment must go a long way in determining the proportions in which the capital shall be distributed among the several instruments of production, and, therefore, must go a long way in determining the proportion which the wages element in that particular capital shall bear to its whole amount. Now the considerations which weigh with an individual capitalist are those which weigh with a community of capitalists; and we are therefore justified in concluding that the main circumstance governing the proportion which the Wages-fund shall bear to the general capital of a nation is the nature of the national industries.

We are justified in concluding that this is the main circumstance; but a close examination will show that other circumstances also enter into the conditions which determine the final result. What the nature of the national industries really determines is the proportion in which *labor* shall be combined with the other instruments of production—fixed capital and raw material—in the general industry of a country; but what we want to know is the place which *wages* shall hold in this combination. Now the consideration of a simple example will show that, the proportion of labor to the other instruments of production being given, the proportion which wages shall bear to the total capital may vary.

Let us suppose a capitalist starting with £10,000. He finds that with £5000 he can buy fixed capital and raw material which will give full employment to 100 competent workmen: and if we suppose the rate of wages for these workmen to average £50 a year, the payment of their wages at this rate would absorb the rest of his capital, viz., £5000. His entire capital would thus be divided into £5000 for fixed capital and raw material, and £5000 for wages. But now suppose the current rate of wages for such labor as he required to have been £40 instead of £50 a year, he would have been able to procure the 100 workmen which his fixed capital and raw material required for £4000: £5000 having as before been invested in fixed capital and raw material, he would thus find himself with £1000 of capital still disposable. This we may suppose he would invest in the same business, and it would accordingly be necessary to bring together the instruments of production purchasable for £1000 in the same proportions as before—that is to say, he would have to distribute the £1000 nearly as follows: Fixed capital and raw material (let us say for the sake of round numbers) £550; wages £450. His whole capital will now be divided thus:

Fixed capital and raw material..........................	£5,550
Wages (110 men at £40).................................	4,450
Total capital..	£10,000

The proportion between labor, fixed capital, and raw material would here be the same as before, but whereas in the first case the Wages-fund represented 50 per cent. of his whole capital, it now represents but 44 per cent. It is of course evident that, had I made the opposite supposition, and taken the current rate of wages at £60 instead of £40, it would have been necessary, in order to maintain the due proportion between labor and the other productive instruments, that the wages element should have been increased at the expense of fixed capital and raw material. The distribution of the total capital would then have stood nearly thus:

Fixed capital and raw material..........................	£4,550
Wages of 90 men at £60 (nearly)........................	5,450
Total capital..	£10,000

In other words, the Wages-fund would now constitute 54 per cent. of the total investment.

These examples show that the nature of the national industries do not determine absolutely the distribution of the national capital among the three leading instruments of production, but that the result is liable to be modified by the rate of wages which happens to be current. Now, so far as this is the case, it will perhaps strike the reader that our reasoning has conducted us into a vicious circle, inasmuch as, while seeking a solution of the rate of wages in the causes determining the Wages-fund, we have been suddenly confronted with the phenomenon itself as one of those causes. A little reflection, however, will show that the circle is apparent merely, and that the grounds of our argument are really independent and distinct. For, whatever be the causes which determine the Wages-fund, the amount of that fund being so determined, the rate of wages is merely the industrial outcome, and I might even say, the concrete expression, of the supply of labor. The modifying circumstance, therefore, in the case, though indicated by the rate of wages, is really the supply of labor; and our analysis accordingly issues in the following conditions as the determining causes of the Wages-fund, viz.: the total capital of the country (determined in the manner already explained); the nature of the national industries; and the supply of labor— facts at once distinct, and entirely independent of the subject of our investigation.

It would seem, then, that the amount of the Wages-fund (which the reader will be careful to distinguish from the *rate* of wages) is to some extent affected by the number of competent laborers offering their services, wherever those laborers are employed in conjunction with fixed capital and raw material. Now it may be worth while to point out the manner in which this influence is exerted. Reverting to our previous illustrations, it appears that, other things being the same, a rise in the current rate of wages issues in an expansion of the Wages-fund, and, contrariwise, a fall in the current rate in its contraction. But, the rate of wages, other things being the same, varying inversely with the supply of labor, this is equivalent to saying that the Wages-fund expands as the supply of labor contracts, and contracts as the supply of labor expands. An unexpected consequence, not, so far as I know, before adverted to, results from this play of economic forces, namely, that an increase or diminution in the supply of labor, where it is of a kind to be employed in conjunction with fixed capital and raw material, acts upon the rate of wages with a force *more than proportional* to the increase or diminution in the supply; for it tells at the same time upon both the factors on which the result depends, modifying them in opposite directions—the fund undergoing diminution as the number of those who are to share it is increased; or, on the other hand, expanding as the sharers become fewer. This occurs, I say, where labor is of a kind to be employed in conjunction with fixed capital and raw material; and, it may be added, that the effect would only assume sensible dimensions where those agencies constituted a substantial proportion of the whole capital invested. Indeed it would be a mistake to regard this particular condition—the supply of labor considered as a cause affecting, not the rate of wages, but the aggregate Wages-fund—as under any circumstances more than a subordinate and modifying influence in the case. The point is one of theoretic rather than of practical importance; and, in considering the variations of the Wages-fund, it will rarely be necessary to take account of more than the two main determining conditions of that phenomenon—the growth or decline of capital, and the nature of the prevailing industries.

§ 9. It appears, then, that the aggregate amount of wealth appropriated to the laboring population in any country varies.

not simply with the progress of the national wealth, nor yet with the progress of the national capital, but with this latter circumstance taken in connection with the character of the national industries, the result being also, within certain narrow limits, modified by the supply of labor. In other words, it appears that the same amount of capital will yield under different circumstances Wages-funds of different dimensions, and will consequently be capable of supporting populations of different magnitudes. This position finds its illustration and verification in the industrial phenomena of different countries. For example, it is obvious at a glance that a given amount of capital invested in the Western States of North America supports a larger laboring population than the same amount invested in the New England States; and the reason is plain: the former States are more extensively agricultural than the latter, and consequently employ fixed capital and raw material less extensively in their staple industries; it follows of course that the proportion of the total investment applicable to the payment of wages is correspondingly greater in those States. Again, a comparison of an average investment in the United States—it matters not in what part of them—and in Great Britain would reveal analogous differences. Fixed capital being more largely employed in the industries of Great Britain, a given amount of capital invested in those industries would yield a smaller Wages-fund than the same capital invested in the United States, and consequently would support—allowance made for the different rates of wages in the two countries—a smaller laboring population. Similarly, if, instead of comparing different countries, the comparison were made between different epochs, we should still find the power of capital to support labor varying with the changes in the character of the industries in which it is employed. And, in connection with this, we may notice what amounts to an economic derivative law in the industrial development of progressive communities.

The modifications which occur in the distribution of capital among its several departments as nations advance are by no means fortuitous, but follow on the whole a well-defined course, and move toward a determined goal. In effect, what we find is, a constant growth of the national capital, accompanied with a nearly equally constant decline in the proportion of this capital which goes to support productive labor. This is the inevitable consequence of the progress of the industrial arts, the effect of which is to cause a steady substitution of the agencies of inanimate nature for the labor of man. In making this remark it is perhaps superfluous to add that it is not to be inferred from the circumstance stated that the progress of those arts is unfavorable to the interests of labor. Even on the lowest and most materialistic view of the interests of labor the reverse is the fact; for what industrial progress under the influence of the advancing arts and sciences effects is a diminution, not in the absolute amount of the Wages-fund, but only in the *proportion* which it bears to the total capital of a country — a diminution which is perfectly compatible with a steadily progressive increase of the fund. One has only indeed to consider what the Wages-fund of such a country as Great Britain has grown to under a *régime* of advancing industrial art, and reflect on what it would probably now have been had that progress been arrested a century ago, to perceive the utter groundlessness of the notion that industrial art can, in the long run, be antagonistic to labor. Not the less, however, is it indispensable, if we would understand the most salient facts of modern industrial life, to keep constantly in view the tendency of the Wages-fund, with the progress of wealth and art, to lag behind the advances of the other factors of the national capital.* The fact is one of very great significance, and highly de-

---

* These remarks receive a practical illustration from the important and suggestive article by Professor Fawcett in the *Fortnightly Review* (January, 1874), in

serving the consideration of those who speculate on social subjects. For it involves this double consequence bearing on the laws of social growth—a tendency toward a relative increase of the classes not living by hired labor as compared with those who do: and again, a tendency toward increased inequality in the distribution of wealth.* I say it involves these consequences as tendencies; and I may add, that up to the present time those tendencies have in general been very fully realized in the actual experience of the world, and in an eminent degree in the experience of Great Britain. They exist, however, as tendencies only, and may, like other tendencies or laws of nature, be counteracted through the influence of tendencies of an opposite kind; in a word, the balance may be redressed by suitable expedients. Though the fund for the remuneration of mere labor, whether skilled or unskilled, must, so long as industry is progressive, ever bear a constantly diminishing proportion alike to the growing wealth and growing capital, there is nothing in the nature of things which restricts the laboring population to this fund for their support. In return, indeed, for their mere labor, it is to this that they must look for their sole reward; but they may help production otherwise than by their labor: they may save, and thus become themselves the owners of capital, and profits may thus be brought to aid the

---

which he calls attention to the slight increase which has occurred in the rate of wages in Great Britain contemporaneously with the large additions recently made to our national wealth.

* This latter result can not indeed be said to be necessary; since it is conceivable that laborers by limiting their numbers might keep the rate of their remuneration on a level with the growing incomes of other classes. To do this, however, two conditions would have to be fulfilled: the productiveness of industry would have to increase in a degree sufficient to permit of this high rate of remuneration consistently with yielding also a rate of profit high enough to attract capital toward investment; and secondly, the result would imply such a degree of self-control on the part of the laboring population as, I fear, experience gives us no warrant for expecting.

Wages-fund. I merely note this point at present as bearing upon the controversy respecting the future of the laboring classes, reserving the full consideration of the latter question for another place. There are those who regard it as a law of industrial development that capital should ever become more and more aggregated in a few hands, and that, as a consequence of this, the position of the laborer in the future must remain substantially what it is at present in the more advanced industrial countries—that of a recipient of wages merely. I do not pretend here to pronounce upon this question—the economic data for its determination have not yet been fully worked out; but I am justified even here in asserting this much, that the permanent maintenance of a *régime* such as is contemplated, co-existing with a progressive industry, can only issue in one result—a constant exaggeration of those features already beginning to mark so unpleasantly the aspect of our social state—namely, a harsh separation of classes, combined with those glaring inequalities in the distribution of wealth which most people will agree are among the chief elements of our social instability.

§ 10. I remarked just now, that under a progressive state of industry, though the proportion of the Wages-fund to the whole capital of a country diminishes, the positive amount of the fund for the most part undergoes increase. It must be confessed, however, that while this represents the ordinary rule, there is nothing strictly necessary in the relation of the phenomena thus presented; and that instances do occur, and sometimes on a large scale, in which the progress of wealth and industry is accompanied with a positive contraction of the Wages-fund. Such a result happens whenever that process takes place which is described by economists as a conversion of circulating capital into fixed.

As Mr. Mill has remarked, the proceeding in question is not

one which in practice is frequently resorted to; the introduction and extension of fixed capital being, as a general rule, effected through the agency of fresh savings rather than by withdrawal from the support of labor of funds already thus employed. But it is beyond question that such conversions of circulating into fixed capital do sometimes occur; and, in this event, it is not less certain that the Wages-fund must, at all events for a time, be curtailed. For the most part, however, it happens that movements of this kind are on a limited scale, and, the resulting arrangements always issuing in increased efficiency of production (for this is the motive for adopting them), the gaps made in the Wages-fund are quickly filled up; so that the consequences which ensue, though perhaps serious enough, are rarely of large dimensions. I say this is what usually happens when circulating capital is converted into fixed; but there are times when the process is conducted on something like a national scale, and then it may be productive of even disastrous results. An occasion of this kind, for example, occurred in the industrial history of England during the sixteenth century, when the exchange of a very rude and primitive agriculture for one that might by comparison be called scientific, and more particularly an extensive conversion of tillage-lands to pasture, under the influence of causes then affecting her general trade, issued in the remarkable phenomenon of a rapidly growing national capital, with improved industrial processes and extending trade, accompanied by a sudden and portentous development of pauperism. No doubt the recuperative power of progressive industry told in the long run; and perhaps before the century was over, or the new Poor Law had well come into operation, the encroachment made on the laborers' division of the national wealth had been more than repaid: but it is nevertheless true that the event amounted to a crisis in the national industry, and was, for a large portion of the people, fraught with disaster and ruin. Something of the same kind has been in progress in our own day in Ireland. A protective Corn Law, combined with the demoralization of the people from political and social causes, had generated an industrial system which could not be permanently sustained. Under the combined influence of free trade and the potato disease this system suddenly collapsed, and it became necessary to pass from a crude *régime* of tillage to one in which capital was extensively converted into fixed and permanent forms. The result has been the introduction of an agriculture suited to the country, and largely carried on by improved modern processes, and a rapid increase in general wealth; but simultaneously with this a sudden contraction of the Wages-fund, of which the unequivocal evidence is found in a population reduced in a few years from eight to five and a half millions. Occurrences of this kind place it beyond doubt that extensive changes in the character of the industry of a country, even though they be all in the direction of scientific progress, improved processes, and ultimately and even immediately augmented wealth, may nevertheless effect a reduction in the means for supporting productive labor, and may for a time act disastrously on its interests.

§ 11. I have now stated the doctrine of the Wages-fund as I understand it, in connection with the general problem of the rate of wages; but before proceeding to trace its bearing upon the relations of capital and labor, and the various practical questions arising therefrom, it will be convenient to pause here for a short time in our development of the general theory, in order to consider the objections which have been urged against the doctrine by Mr. Thornton—objections which, as I have already informed the reader, have been powerful enough to effect the conversion of Mr. Mill. Mr. Thornton's argument ranges over a considerable portion of his volume, but the gist of it will be found in the following passage:

"If there really were a national fund, the whole of which must necessarily be applied to the payment of wages, that fund could be no other than an aggregate of smaller similar funds possessed by the several individuals who composed the employing part of the nation. Does, then, any individual employer possess any such fund? Is there any specific portion of any individual's capital which the owner must necessarily expend upon labor? Of course every employer possesses a certain amount of money, whether his own or borrowed, out of which all his expenses must be met, if met at all. With so much of this amount as remains after deduction of what he takes for family and personal expenses, he carries on his business—with one portion of that balance providing or keeping in repair buildings and machinery, with a second portion procuring materials, with a third hiring labor. But is there any law fixing the amount of his domestic expenditure, and thereby fixing likewise the balance available for his industrial operations? May he not spend more or less on his family and himself, according to his fancy—in the one case having more, in the other less, left for the conduct of his business? And of what is left, does he or can he determine beforehand how much shall be laid out on buildings, how much on materials, how much on labor? May not his outlay on repairs be unexpectedly increased by fire or other accident? will not his outlay on materials vary with their dearness or cheapness, or with the varying demand for the finished article? and must not the amount available for wages vary accordingly? And even though the latter amount were exactly ascertained beforehand, even though he did know to a farthing how much he would be able to spend on labor, would he be bound so to spend the utmost he could afford to spend? If he could get as much labor as he wanted at a cheap rate, would he voluntarily pay as much for it as he would be compelled to pay if it were dearer? It sounds like mockery or childishness to ask these questions, so obvious are the only answers that can possibly be given to them; yet it is only on the assumption that directly opposite answers must be given that the Wages-fund can for one moment stand. For if in the case of individual employers there be no Wages-funds—no definite or definable portions of their capitals which, and neither more nor less than which, they must severally apply to the hiring of labor—clearly there can be no aggregate of such funds, clearly there can be no national Wages-fund. And be it observed, fixity or definiteness is the very essence of the supposed Wages-fund. No one denies that some amount or other must within any given period be disbursed in the form of wages. The only question is, whether that amount be determinate or indeterminate. If indeterminate, it can not of course be divided, and might as well not exist for any power it possesses of performing the sole function of a Wages-fund, that, viz., of yielding a quotient that would indicate the average rate of wages."*

Mr. Thornton, the reader will perceive from this passage, does not deny the existence of a Wages-fund: he admits the legitimacy of contemplating in the aggregate those funds—the wages of individual workmen—of which we know the existence in detail; but he contends that neither the particular sums in detail, nor therefore the aggregate which they compose, are "determinate"—an expression under which he includes at once their "predetermination" toward the destination they afterward receive, and their "limitation" within their actual bounds. It must at once be conceded that, in the sense in which (as appears from this passage as well as from the whole tenor of his argument) Mr. Thornton understands the "predetermination" and "limitation" of the Wages-fund, his position is unassailable. Undoubtedly "there is no specific portion of any individual's capital which the owner must necessarily expend upon wages." "There is no law fixing the amount" of any man's "domestic expenditure, and thereby fixing likewise the balance available for industrial operations." Nor is any man "bound to spend," in the payment of labor, "the utmost he can afford to spend." I should have confidently asserted, I will not say that no economist, but that no reasonable being had ever advanced the theory of a Wages-fund in this sense, if it had not been that Mr. Mill had accepted the reasoning I have quoted as a refutation of that theory.† As it is, I can only say that

---

* "Labor, etc.," pp. 84, 85.

† Mr. Mill's acceptance of Mr. Thornton's argument on this point is the more perplexing as he has himself, in more than one passage of his work, strenuously disclaimed that notion of an economic law against which Mr. Thornton's reasoning is directed, and, on the other hand, asserted the view for which I contend in

this is not the sense in which I have myself understood the doctrine (and I first learned it from Mr. Mill's pages); and further, I must add, that if economic doctrines in general are to be understood in the sense here assigned to the Wages-fund doctrine—namely, as expressing principles which compel human beings to the adoption of certain courses of conduct in despite of their own inclination and will, there is not a single one within the range of economic science that could endure ten minutes' criticism. The doctrine, for example, that the supply of a commodity tends to conform to the quantity demanded at the normal price, is as well established as any principle of Political Economy. How is it proved? By showing that, if the supply of the commodity falls short of this quantity, the market price will rise above the normal price, profits on the production will be exceptionally high, and, as a consequence, a larger amount of capital and labor will be "determined" toward the production; while in the contrary case the "determination" of capital and labor would be in the opposite direction. But if by "determination" of capital is to be understood some force which compels the capitalist irrespective of his own wishes and views of his own interest, the reasoning is manifestly groundless. Mr. Thornton might say here, quite as truly as in his argument against the Wages-fund, there is no law, physical or legal, there is no moral principle, which compels any capitalist to employ his capital in a branch of production simply because profits in that branch are rising. Again, take the law of rent: how is that law established? By some such reasoning as this, namely, by showing that the competition of farmers for land

---

the text: for example, in the following: "Demand and supply are not physical agencies, which thrust a given amount of wages into a laborer's hand *without the participation of his own will and actions.* The market rate is not fixed for him by some self-acting instrument, but is the result of bargaining between human beings—of what Adam Smith calls 'the higgling of the market.'" (Book v., chap. x., § 5.)

will "determine" to the possession of landlords all that profit upon land which is in excess of the ordinary profits upon industry; while the competition of other occupations with agriculture will prevent the amount so determined from rising beyond the limits of the exceptional profit. But what is to prevent Mr. Thornton from interposing here the same series of objections he has urged against the Wages-fund? "Rent," he might exclaim, "determined by the law of exceptional profit! Is there any specific portion of a farmer's capital which the owner *must* necessarily expend upon rent? And who can tell beforehand what the amount of his exceptional profit will be? May not his outlay on repairs be unexpectedly increased by flood or other accident? Will not his outlay on materials vary with their dearness or cheapness, or with the varying demand for the produce? and must not the amount available for rent vary accordingly? And even though the amount of exceptional profit were exactly ascertained beforehand, even though the farmer did know to a farthing how much he would be able to pay to the landlord, while reserving average profit to himself, would he be bound so to spend the utmost he could so afford to spend?" And so the theory of rent would collapse, and Mr. Thornton might enjoy an easy triumph over Ricardo and all who have since followed in his wake. In short, it is evident that, if this style of reasoning be legitimate, the whole structure of economic doctrine must inevitably go down.

What then is the answer to Mr. Thornton? Why, I take it, this: that his reasoning from beginning to end proceeds upon a radically erroneous conception of the nature of an economic law—of what is meant by "predetermination" and "limitation" in the sphere of economic action. A "law" in Political Economy does not mean either legal coercion or physical compulsion, or yet moral obligation; nor does the "determination" expressed in an economic law mean the necessary realization of certain results independently of the human will. What an economic law asserts is, not that men must do so and so whether they like it or not, but that in given circumstances they will like to do so and so; that their self-interest or other feelings will lead them to this result. The predetermination in question is of that sort which leads a hungry man to eat his dinner, or an honest man to pay his debts, and depends for its fulfillment, not upon external compulsion of any sort, but upon the influence of certain inducements on the will, our knowledge of which enables us to say how in given circumstances a man will act. It is in this sense that, speaking for myself, I understand the "predetermination" of a certain portion of the wealth of a country to the payment of wages. I believe that, in the existing state of the national wealth, the character of Englishmen being what it is, a certain prospect of profit will "determine" a certain proportion of this wealth to productive investment; that the amount thus "determined" will increase as the field for investment is extended, and that it will not increase beyond what this field can find employment for at that rate of profit which satisfies English commercial expectation. Further, I believe that, investment thus taking place, the form which it shall assume will be "determined" by the nature of the national industries — "determined," not under acts of Parliament, or in virtue of any physical law, but through the influence of the investor's interests; while this, the form of the investment, will again "determine" the proportion of the whole capital which shall be paid as wages to laborers. It is in this sense I say that I understand the "predetermination" implied in the Wages-fund doctrine; and against the doctrine so understood I can not find that there is any thing very formidable in Mr. Thornton's criticisms. They are simply beside the mark — at all events, beside my mark. "Capitalists put aside a portion of their means with a determination that, whatever happens, they shall be spent in wages!" — The doctrine, as I understand it, makes no such assumption; nor am I, in holding it, bound to maintain any such absurdity. "Employers are anxious to buy their labor as cheap as they can, to spend as little as possible in wages." —No doubt they are; but while they are anxious to get their labor cheap, they are also anxious to place certain amounts of their wealth at profitable investment; and, to do this in the most advantageous way, a certain proportion of the sums so invested *must* go to the payment of wages.

I say deliberately "*must*" go to the payment of wages, for this is the consequence involved in the doctrine I have endeavored to expound. Assuming a certain field for investment, and the prospect of profit in this such as to attract a certain aggregate capital, and assuming the national industries to be of a certain kind, the proportion of this aggregate capital which shall be invested in wages is not a matter within the discretion of capitalists, always supposing they desire to obtain the largest practical return upon their outlay. To accomplish this, the instruments of production, labor, fixed capital, and raw material must be brought together in certain proportions—a condition which requires, as I have shown—the supply of labor being given—a distribution of the aggregate capital in certain proportions among those instruments. Supposing, now, capitalists to succeed in forcing down the rate of wages below the point at which, having regard to the number of the laboring population, the amount, which the fulfillment of this condition would assign to the payment of wages, was absorbed—either the capital thus withdrawn from the Wages-fund must remain uninvested and therefore unproductive, or if invested, and not invested in wages, it would take the form of fixed capital or raw material. But by hypothesis the fixed capital and raw material were already in due proportion to the labor force, and they would consequently now be in excess of it. A competition among capitalists for labor would consequently ensue; and what could this end in but a restoration to the

Wages-fund of the amount withdrawn from it? Mr. Thornton probably would tell me that the amount saved from the payment of wages might, and probably would, be turned to swell the private expenditure of capitalists, who, taking out the results in this form, would simply continue to receive larger profits at the expense of their workmen. No doubt this is a possible contingency in particular cases, but, the character of the wealthy classes remaining on the whole what it is, increased accumulations in other quarters would neutralize exceptional extravagance in some; and larger profits would not be less powerful than before to attract increased investment. In a word, my argument brings me back to the position from which I started, that, the aggregate investment being determined by certain mental and physical conditions, and the national industries being such as they are, there is but one distribution of the capital invested which is consistent with the greatest advantage to the investors. That distribution involves a certain proportion spent in the payment of wages, and it is to this result that capitalists, if true to their own interest, *must* conform their conduct.*

---

* The notion that any portion of the wealth of the country should be "determined" to the payment of wages would seem also to shock Mr. Longe's sense of economic propriety; which is strange, seeing that his own doctrine that it is "the demand for commodities which determines the quantity of wealth spent in the payment of wages" plainly involves this consequence. He puts the case of a capitalist who, by taking advantage of the necessities of his workmen, effects a reduction in their wages, and succeeds in withdrawing so much, call it £1000, from the Wages-fund; and asks how is the sum, thus withdrawn, to be restored to the fund? On Mr. Longe's principles the answer is simple—"by being spent on commodities;" for it may be assumed that the sum so withdrawn will, in any case, not be hoarded. "But," urges Mr. Longe, "it might be spent on foreign wines, or on a trip to Switzerland;" the suggestion of course being that in this case the expenditure could do no good to English labor. If so, then we seem to have made a mistake in repealing our protective laws; nor were protectionists, after all, so very wrong in seeking to encourage native industry by compelling expenditure toward domestic productions. May I venture to remind Mr. Longe that expendi-

So far as to one leading objection urged against the Wages-fund doctrine. It is further contended that the doctrine assumes the existence of a limitation to the amount of that fund for which there is no warrant in facts. As Mr. Thornton puts it, "may not the capitalist spend more or less on his family and himself according to his fancy—in the one case having more, in the other less, left for the conduct of his business?" The aspect of the question here brought into view involves considerations of so much importance that it will be best discussed in a separate chapter.

---

ture on foreign wines and in Swiss travel must and can only be paid for by an export of British productions, and that it therefore creates a demand for such productions, though more circuitously, quite as certainly as if it took a more direct form. The answer, therefore, to the case put by Mr. Longe is easy on his own principles; and I am disposed to flatter myself that the reader who has gone with me in the foregoing discussion will not have much difficulty in replying to it upon mine.

CHAPTER II.

DEMAND FOR COMMODITIES.—WAGES AND PRICES.

§ 1. I MUST here depart for a space from the main line of my argument in order to work out a side issue already partially dealt with, over which I think it must be confessed, notwithstanding some considerable discussion already bestowed upon it, no small amount of obscurity still hangs. I mean the question as to the relation existing between the demand for commodities and the interests of those who live by labor. We have already seen that this relation is not what it is commonly supposed to be: the demand for commodities does not determine the quantity of wealth spent in the wages of labor. Still, it is not to be denied that the agency in question stands in intimate relation with the wealth thus expended, or, as I call it, the Wages-fund; and my purpose now is to attempt some more precise determination of the character and the extent of the connection than has yet been given by writers on economic science.

With a view to this it will be convenient to distinguish two conditions of demand for commodities: (1) Where, the aggregate expenditure on commodities remaining the same, a change takes place in its direction, as, for example, when a country passes from a state of peace to one of war, or when any considerable change occurs in the tastes or habits of the people leading to a diversion of expenditure from certain classes of objects to others; and (2) where, as the consequence of a positive growth of purchasing power in a community, the aggregate demand for commodities undergoes increase.

§ 2. I. That a change in the mode in which the general income of a country is spent, if occurring on a considerable scale, is capable of affecting the condition of labor in different branches of industry, is extremely obvious; nor can there be much difficulty as to the manner in which the results are brought about. A change of fashion, for example, taking place, certain commodities are brought into increased demand, while the demand for others declines. The productive and distributive arrangements of the country having been made with a view to a different state of the public requirements, the supply of the former articles will be insufficient, and they will therefore rise in price; while the supply of the latter will be in excess, and they will fall. But, as I have pointed out, the price of the product is the fund from which the remuneration of capital and labor —viewing production as a continuous act—is derived; and this fund has now been increased in certain branches of industry and curtailed in others. It follows that capital or labor, or both, will receive in the former employments more, and in the latter less, than average rewards; and this state of remuneration will continue until, by increasing the supply of the one sort of products and reducing that of the other, prices are restored to their former level—a consummation which will only be accomplished when capital and labor in the industries affected have been re-adjusted to meet the altered conditions of the public demand. The immediate result will thus be, as regards such industries, a change in relative wages or profits, or in both. In point of fact, as we shall hereafter see, the effect is generally divided between both branches of remuneration, and for the present I shall assume that this is the case. Where, however, competition among workmen is effective, such a change can not be permanent: it will only last until the labor force of the country has adapted itself to the altered conditions of the market. So soon as this is accomplished, prices, profits, and wages will return to their former condition.

This is what will happen where competition is really effective. But we have seen that competition in the article of labor is not effective throughout the entire field of industry in a country like this. Certain industrial circles or groups exist, the workmen composing each of which, while competing among themselves, are, from social circumstances, excluded from effective competition with the workmen of different groups; with this result, that the relative value of the products of such non-competing groups are determined, not by cost of production, but by reciprocal demand. Now, where this is the case, a change in the mode of expending the general income of a community may, under certain circumstances, be attended with more than temporary consequences. For, supposing the change in expenditure to involve a transfer of demand from the products of one of those non-competing industrial groups to those of another, the result in the first instance would be the same as in other cases; namely, an advance in the rates of remuneration for laborers and capitalists within the group profiting by the enlarged demand, accompanied by a corresponding fall in the other group. But this would not be followed in the present instance by the same consequences as in the case in which effective competition prevailed. Capital, indeed, would still move freely to the more lucrative occupations; but labor would not follow, or would follow in inadequate proportions; and the equalization of profits would be effected, not by a reduction of prices, but by an advance of wages. To restore the prices of the commodities affected by the change in demand to their former relative level, it would be necessary to adjust the supply of these commodities to the altered conditions of demand; and to do this it would be necessary to distribute the labor force of the country in conformity with the altered requirements. But this is just what, under the circumstances we are supposing, it is not possible to do. The occurrence, therefore, would issue in an advance at once in the price of the products falling under the enlarged demand, and in the wages of the workmen engaged in their production, while profits, after some fluctuation, would return to their former state; and, on the other hand, there would be an equivalent decline in prices and wages in the branches of industry from which the demand had been withdrawn, and these results would be definitive—that is to say, they would continue until social progress had removed the barriers which interfered with industrial competition, or until the altered condition of the workmen in the different industrial groups should have acted on the growth of population within the groups. In this way, then, a mere change in the direction of national expenditure may issue in permanent effects in the relative remuneration of laborers.

It need scarcely be remarked that in occurrences of this nature, whether the results are temporary or permanent, no addition would be made to the aggregate Wages-fund, nor therefore to the well-being of the laboring population as a whole.* The effects would be limited to a mere transference of wealth from certain groups of workmen to others, so that the gains would always be compensated by corresponding losses. The former might indeed be sometimes concentrated and the latter diffused, and the gains might in consequence be seen and the losses not seen; or the contrary result might happen. But, from the nature of the case, there could be no clear gain: if Peter were enriched, there would always be some Paul at whose expense it was done.†

---

* The tendency indeed is the other way; since a portion of the products of industry having, in consequence of the change in the public tastes or requirements, been deprived of their power of satisfying human wants, a certain amount of productive effort would have been wasted, and consequently the aggregate wealth must for a time have suffered diminution. The loss, however, would not necessarily be shown in the average rates of wages or profits (measured in money, which I suppose constant in value), but would be realized by the public at large, including capitalists and laborers, in their capacity of consumers.

† In theoretical strictness, this position needs qualification. It would only be

And what may happen to a particular industrial group in its relation to other industrial groups in the community of which they form parts, may happen equally, and through the action of precisely the same causes, to an entire community in its relation to other communities in the larger society of commercial nations. For, as has been already pointed out, independent nations occupy, as regards the circumstance of industrial competition, a position entirely analogous to that of the industrial groups which we have been contemplating. Labor passes from country to country, indeed, with even greater difficulty than from the less to the more highly skilled industries within the same country; and the consequence is that changes in the international demand for commodities are even more likely to issue in permanent effects on the rates of wages in different countries than similar changes in the domestic demand to produce permanent consequences in the internal rates. Thus any circumstance which should turn any considerable portion of the general purchasing power of commercial nations from English toward French productions, or *vicè versa*, would have the effect of enhancing in France and depreciating in England, or *vicè versa*, the general value of products. The

---

strictly true, if the Wages-fund bore always the same proportion to the capital employed in production, which is not the fact. Supposing, *e. g.*, expenditure were largely directed from clothing to food, and that in consequence capital were transferred from manufactures to agriculture, inasmuch as a given amount of capital employed in agriculture will in general contain a larger element of Wages-fund than the same amount of capital employed in manufactures (owing to the larger use of fixed capital in the latter case), it follows that a substitution of a demand for food for a demand for clothes would in this case issue in an increase of the aggregate Wages-fund; as a substitution in the contrary sense would have the opposite effect. A change of this kind, however, occurring in Great Britain, would not probably be attended with any such consequences, because it is not probable that it would lead to any transference of capital to agriculture. The additional food would be obtained from foreign countries through an extension of our exports.

wealth of one country would be increased, that of the other diminished, and the results just traced would be realized on an international scale. Here, however, as in the former case, although the laboring classes of an entire community might be benefited, yet, taking an international or cosmopolitan view, there would be no clear gain for the interests of labor. It would be merely so much withdrawn from industrial well-being in one country in order to be added to the same cause in another.

§ 3. II. Such changes in the demand for commodities are in the nature of mere diversions of purchasing power, where the aggregate amount remains the same. But the aggregate purchasing power of a community, or of the world, may experience increase, and, in fact, is pretty constantly increasing; and we have now to consider what may be the effect on the Wages-fund of an increased demand for commodities arising under this state of things. Now here it is most important to observe that the increased demand for commodities is a mere incident in the general conditions which the assumed case supposes. An increase in the aggregate demand for commodities, resting on a larger aggregate of purchasing power—putting aside the case of a mere inflation of credit unsustained by any basis of real wealth—means an increased production of wealth; and implies, therefore, a corresponding increase in the aggregate supply of commodities. Supply and Demand, in short, *considered as aggregates*, are, as I have already more than once observed, the reciprocals of each other, and in effect the opposite faces of the same facts. An article is produced and is offered in the market: it is now supply, but the possession of that article confers upon the owner a purchasing power, and that power being exercised, the article becomes a source of demand; nor is there any other source from which demand can spring. Demand, as an aggregate,

can not increase without supply, nor supply without demand.
This is fundamental, the direct consequence of industry carried
on upon the principle of division of labor. But, this being so,
we are led to ask, what is the significance of the question
which has been proposed? Suppose the Wages-fund to increase under the circumstances imagined; and suppose further,
that, in every instance, the increase is found to be connected
with a demand for commodities—what then? Have we sounded the problem when we attribute the result to the demand for
commodities? Or rather, is it not very evident that, in offering this as a solution, we are confounding the mechanism by
which certain results are brought about with the motive forces
which work through this mechanism. The upward and downward movements of the piston of a steam-engine are invariably
preceded by certain movements of the valves which admit the
steam alternately above and below it. As the action of the
valves becomes more rapid, the movements of the piston become more rapid, and if the former ceases, the engine stops.
Yet it will scarcely be maintained that the motion of the
steam-engine is explained by referring it to the action of the
steam-valves. This, however, is precisely the sort of explanation that satisfies those persons who undertake to explain an
increase of wealth by reference to the demand for commodities.
They observe, for example, a sudden increase of prosperity in
some branch of industry, and they perceive that this has been
preceded by an increased demand for the products of that industry. They perceive also, that the increased prosperity of
this industry will extend itself to others through the medium
of a demand for products; and from these again to others, in a
still widening circle. Further they perceive, or at least, if they
carry their study of the problem so far, they may perceive,
that, when the supply of each commodity has been brought up
to the enlarged demand for it, the returns on the industry decline to their normal level; and again, that, where the exten-

sion of supply is carried beyond this point, and demand falls short, the gains are converted into losses. Trading gains are thus found in every instance to be associated with a demand for commodities, and trading losses with a failure of demand; and our philosophers, struck with the coincidence, exclaim "εὔρηκα!" and exultingly produce "the demand for commodities" as the key to the industrial problem. It never occurs to them to inquire what set the economic valves in motion, or to reflect that the increased demand for commodities is itself a phenomenon requiring explanation; but having traced the industrial movements up to the valves of supply and demand, they consider their task accomplished, and all searching after remoter causes as supererogatory, if not profane.

The real nature of the connection between the demand for commodities and the progress of industrial well-being is, after, all, not mysterious—at least for any one who bears in mind the elementary truth that our industrial system is founded upon division of labor. It results from this, that every increase of wealth implies an increase of products to be exchanged—an increase, therefore, at once of demand and of supply; and it results also from this—seeing that the satisfaction of reciprocal needs is the end and purpose of the system—that a demand for a producer's or a dealer's commodities must always be a condition precedent to the realization of his gains. This is the real nature of the connection; which, though it implies a constant correspondence between the aggregate income of a country and the aggregate demand for commodities within that country, does not imply that the latter phenomenon is the cause of the former; nor that any particular branch of the aggregate income, such as that which supports the laboring population, must increase *pari passu* with the increase of the whole, or with that of the aggregate demand for commodities. If this were so, as the same argument would apply equally to all other branches of the aggregate income, it would follow that the several constituent parts, into which the income of every community resolves itself, should always bear the same proportion to each other, and that, for example, wages, profits, and rent should always preserve the same relative magnitude. This ought to be a sufficient *reductio ad absurdum* of the doctrine. But I have already given direct proof of its fallacy.

Of the well-being which results from a growth of national wealth, there is, however, one element which, though not properly attributable to the increased demand for commodities, yet connects itself with this agency in a somewhat special and peculiar way. Adam Smith, in a well-known passage, has remarked that the division of labor is limited by the extent of the market, and it is obvious that, not merely division of labor, but the use of machinery, is limited by this condition. Production, universally in manufacturing industry, and to some extent in agriculture, must be carried on upon a certain scale of magnitude before labor can be duly organized, and the most efficient appliances be brought into operation; but production on this scale will not be profitable unless the demand for the commodity at the normal price be sufficiently great to take off the whole supply. Where, therefore, the scale of production has not already attained the maximum of efficiency, an enlarged demand for commodities, by permitting its extension, may lead to a more efficient organization of productive forces, and thus accelerate the growth of wealth. This consequence, indeed, has no special connection with the remuneration of laborers, any more than with that of any other industrial class. But it at least favors, as every thing that tends to increase wealth and render industry more productive must favor, the growth of the Wages-fund. Even here, however, the attribution of the result to the demand for commodities fails to set the phenomenon in its true light; while this mode of stating the case is open to the objection of countenancing the notion that the demand for commodities may increase independently of the supply—a notion, as I have said, at the bottom of nearly all the confusion of thought that prevails on this subject. The fact only receives its adequate explanation when it is referred, neither to demand nor to supply, but to that extension of the field for the interchange of products incident to an increasing production of wealth, which leads to an augmentation at once of demand and of supply.

In the remarks just made I have had in view the effect of an increase in the demand for commodities upon the condition of the laboring population as a whole. I have not considered its effect upon relative wages. But it is evident that what has been already said upon this aspect of the case in connection with diversions of demand will apply here, with this difference, that the changes in relative wages which may result from an increase in aggregate demand will in general be in the nature of different degrees of advance, and will not necessarily, or in fact generally, issue in the positive depression of wages in any department of trade. According as the new demand takes one direction or another, certain industries will gain more or less largely than others; and the capital of the country will be distributed to meet this state of things; but as, in the case we are now supposing, the aggregate capital of the country would almost certainly increase—whether in proportion to the increase in the aggregate demand for commodities or not would depend upon the general conditions affecting investment—the larger application of it to particular industries would not necessarily imply any withdrawal of it from others. Such changes, therefore, in relative wages as might occur would generally be in the nature of different degrees of advance; and these relative results would, as in the case of diversions of demand, be temporary merely or permanent, according as there was or was not an effective competition among the workmen in the industries concerned.

§ 4. Summing up the results of this discussion, we may lay down the following propositions:

I. Where the influence exerted by the demand for commodities arises, not from an increase in its aggregate amount, but from a change in its direction, the effect is limited to a change in the distribution of the Wages-fund, without affecting the aggregate amount of wealth placed at the disposal of labor.

II. Such changes in the distribution of the Wages-fund are attended with changes in the relative rates of remuneration in different branches of industry, leading to a rise in some and a fall in others; and those changes may or may not be permanent, according as labor is free or not to move between the occupations affected. Where competition among workmen is effective, the relative rates will after a little time be restored to their former level; but, where competition is not effective, the changes which take place become definitive—that is to say, will continue so long as social circumstances remain the same and the altered conditions of remuneration in the several industrial groups do not operate to disturb the relation of population to capital within those groups.

III. The influence thus exerted by changes in the demand for commodities may be operative on an international scale, and may thus affect the average level of wages throughout an entire community; the gain, however, to the country profiting by the movement being always compensated by a corresponding loss incurred by some other country or countries.

IV. When the change in the demand for commodities is in the nature of an increase in its aggregate amount, arising from a growth of general wealth, the increase of demand is here an accompaniment of conditions which are favorable to the growth of the Wages-fund; but its connection with the consequences that ensue is not that of a causal kind: it is merely an incident of the industrial mechanism by which, under a system of division of labor, the results of increased production are realized by individuals and classes.

V. Such an increase in the aggregate demand for commodities may, however, produce changes in the relative remuneration of labor, analogous to those produced by changes in the direction of demand—changes which, as in the former case, will be temporary or permanent according as the competition among the workmen concerned is effective or not.

§ 5. The point of view which we have now reached will enable us, I think, to set in a somewhat clearer light than has hitherto been done a problem of some intricacy—the nature of the relation between wages and prices. The doctrine laid down upon this subject in the best treatises of Political Economy is contained in two propositions to the effect, first, that general wages (understanding by this general *real* wages, the real remuneration received by the workmen) and general prices have no necessary connection. High wages, we are told, do not make high prices, any more than high prices make high wages. And, secondly, that when the wages of any class of workmen are exceptionally high or low—that is to say, either above or below the rate prevailing in other occupations, allowance being made for the special circumstances of each case—then they do affect prices. Apparently it is not considered that in any case prices may affect wages.

The first of these propositions I hold to be indisputably sound and quite fundamental. It is scarcely possible indeed that any one reflecting on the elementary conditions of human well-being should hesitate to admit its truth. For to suppose that the real wages of labor—the food, clothing, lodging, and other comforts and conveniences which go to form the remuneration of industry—have any necessary connection with the general range of prices, is to suppose that the well-being of the mass of mankind is linked to the abundance or scarcity of the particular substance which happens to form the material of money; nay, if the position taken be that money, wages, and prices must, as *general* facts, fluctuate together, it is to suppose, not only that the condition of the immense majority of human beings is determined by this purely artificial circumstance, but also that it is fixed and unchangeable; since there could manifestly be no improvement in the laborer's condition if every augmentation of the money paid him was attended with a corresponding diminution of its purchasing power. The first of the propositions laid down, therefore, must be taken as incontrovertible; and yet perhaps there are few statements in economic science that are more apt to strike an outsider as paradoxical. It would, on the contrary, be held by those who only look at the phenomena from the practical stand-point that wages and prices are, as a general rule, strictly connected; that high wages make high prices, and high prices high wages; a view in support of which they would confidently appeal to experience, and might easily adduce facts which, at all events, the current theory, as it stands, wholly fails to explain. In short, there is here a conflict between the conclusions of theory and the generalizations of practical observers. Now where this happens, we may pretty confidently assume, even though, as in the case we are considering, the popular inductions can be shown to be erroneous and even absurd, that the theory also is in fault. It will in general at best be incomplete; and I think it will not be difficult to show that this is so in the present instance.

The economic doctrine as to the relation between wages and prices, as commonly set forth, seems to be defective in two points. First, it fails to recognize, or at all events to take due account of the fact, that changes in general wages or prices never take place *per saltum;* that the general result is always reached by a succession of partial movements, usually extending over a considerable period of time. And, secondly, the recognition given to the connection between prices and wages is quite inadequate. According to the current doctrine, prices may be effected by wages, where wages in particular trades are exceptionally high or low: this is the sole relation acknowledged to subsist between the phenomena; and the language suggests that the connection in this case is abnormal. Now, in the first place, it is not true that, where wages and prices vary together, wages are always the cause and prices the effect. In point of fact, the rise or fall of price more frequently precedes than follows that of wages. The most usual order of occurrence would probably be—a rise or fall of price; then a movement of capital toward or from the trade; and lastly an advance or fall of wages.* Instead of prices rising, in order to allow capital the current profit on a production *in which wages have already risen* (which is the usual way of putting the case),† the more common event is—wages for a time quiescent, until the exceptionally high profits of capitalists, *due to a previous rise of price*, attract new capital to the trade; then competition for labor, issuing in an advance of wages and a

---

* Nearly such has been the order of proceedings in the recent movements in the iron and coal trades. "It is clearly shown," says the Select Committee on Coal (p. xi. of their Report) "that the real order of events has been the rise in the price of iron, the rise in the price of coal, and the rise in the rate of wages." I say "nearly such," because in this case the movement of capital toward the affected trades did not precede the advance of wages; the two latter stages of the process having been accelerated, and made to synchronize, by the action of strikes.

† For example, Professor Fawcett writes: "It frequently happens that the wages of the laborers employed in the manufacture of a particular commodity advance as the demand for the commodity increases. If this occurs, these particular manufactured goods will rise in price, in order that the employer may be compensated for the higher wages he is now obliged to pay" ("Manual of Political Economy," p. 290). That is to say, the increased demand for the commodity will cause an advance in the wages of the laborers who produce it *before producing any effect upon its price*. I confess that appears to me to be a scarcely possible occurrence: at least, I can not but regard it as an inversion of the usual order of events.

fall of profits to the current level. Nor is the close correspondence and mutual interaction of the phenomena in any sense abnormal or exceptional: it may, on the contrary, be said to be the rule; while the case in which they diverge or move independently of each other is the exception. The actual state of this portion of economic theory, therefore, however irrefragable so far as it goes, is plainly inadequate; failing as it does to elucidate many familiar phenomena of wages and prices; and the purpose of the remaining portion of this chapter will be to supplement, as far as seems needful, existing deficiencies in this respect.

§ 6. And here I must premise by observing that the relation which it is proposed to examine is that between prices and wages *measured in money*, not that between prices and *real* wages; a remark which needs to be supplemented by another, viz., that it is *not* to be assumed on this account, that the real interest of the laborer is not involved in the discussion. A parallel movement between wages and prices is immaterial where it is general, where all wages and all prices are affected at the same time and in the same degree. But, as I have already observed, this is what never happens. The changes which occur in prices and wages are always confined, for a period longer or shorter, according to circumstances, to particular branches of trade; and where this is so, a change in money wages will generally* involve a change, though not necessarily a proportional change, in real wages too; since, owing to the circumstance that the movement is not general, it will place the recipients in a better or a worse position (as the case may be) in reference to all commodities of which the prices remain at their former level. Where in one or more

---

* Not necessarily always—*e. g.*, if the things which did *not* rise or fall were commodities only consumed by the rich, the laborer would be none the better or worse for the change.

trades wages and prices advance or fall equally, the workmen in the trades thus affected will neither gain nor lose so far as they consume their own productions; but they will gain or lose to the full extent of the advance or fall in their wages so far as they consume the productions of other trades. So much being premised, I proceed now to the consideration of our problem.

It has been already shown that a change in the demand for commodities, proceeding from a diversion of expenditure from its ordinary course, may produce a change in relative wages, raising the rate in some branches of industry and lowering it in others; and, further, that occurring on an international scale, the same circumstance may affect the rate of wages throughout an entire community. Now in all such cases—and they comprise a large proportion of all fluctuations in wages—the result, if not brought about through an action on prices, at least coincides with an action on prices: the two phenomena move always in the same direction, and generally in parallel lines. The reasons for this have been already partially set forth, and will be presently more fully stated. But, again, not in such cases only, but, with a single important exception to be presently noticed, in all considerable movements of prices and wages, if not a strict parallelism, at least a general correspondence between the phenomena of prices and wages will be found to obtain. An advance or fall of prices in any branch of production, if sustained for any considerable time, will, pretty certainly, be followed by an advance or fall of wages in the same industries; as an advance or fall of wages will with equal certainty be followed by an advance or fall of prices. In order to exhibit the grounds of this statement, it will be desirable to consider the several sets of conditions (irrespective of that already referred to which consists in a change in the demand for commodities) under which important alterations in the rate of wages may take place. In what I am about to say I shall confine my attention chiefly to the case of an advance of wages; but it will be obvious that precisely analogous considerations apply to that of a fall.

§ 7. We may take then, first, the case of a new country, in which the rate of profit is still considerably above the practical minimum; in which, consequently, wages may rise at the expense of profits, and therefore without any increase in the productiveness of industry; and we will suppose that the advance is occasioned by a growth of capital more rapid than that of population. The advance of wages which would occur under such circumstances would not be a mere relative movement— an advance in some industries balanced by an equivalent fall in others, such as occurs under the action of a demand for commodities, but an advance unaccompanied by any fall, and implying therefore a rise of the average rate. Even here, however, though the movement might be ultimately general, it would still proceed by partial and limited steps. The new capital would not be distributed indifferently over all industries, but would be determined toward the particular industries in which at the moment there was the best prospect of an enlarged sale for products; and it would be in those industries that wages would first rise. But these would be the industries in which the products were selling above the normal rates. In other words, high wages, if not produced by high prices, would at least attend on high prices. And this coincidence would not be confined to the first steps, but would be maintained throughout the whole course of the ascending movement; which would be realized in the several industries in the order in which the prices of their products ranged above the normal level. It is true, indeed, the advance in wages and prices would not necessarily be a proportional advance. Wages might advance more than prices, or prices more than wages. And it is also true that the correspondence, such as it was, might not be of long continuance; since the increased production would sooner or later bring down the abnormally raised prices, while (profits not being at the minimum) the advance in wages might be maintained. But, conceding all this, the correspondence would still be generally maintained at all events while the movement was in progress; while it is further to be considered that, as the case is that of a normal growth of capital, unaccelerated by any important improvements in production, it is probable that population, under the stimulus of its bettered condition, would speedily overtake the increase of capital, in which event wages would subside to their former level; and, in subsiding, would again follow the course indicated by prices, falling first in those industries in which prices were lowest. On the whole, then, in this case, though I do not pretend to say that the parallelism would be exact, and though it is possible the ultimate result might be a definitive divergence of the two phenomena; still, speaking broadly, we may say that a general correspondence between prices and wages would be maintained, a correspondence quite sufficient to account for the popular impression.

§ 8. Let us now consider another case: an advance in wages arising under a growth of wealth due either to improved industrial processes, or to an extension of foreign trade. The latter cause, as I have already pointed out, would operate always through a demand for commodities, and the advance of wages would therefore in this case be always preceded or attended by an advance of prices—not indeed, it must always be remembered, a general advance of prices, but an advance in the particular industries affected by the extension of foreign trade. But, where the growth of capital proceeded from improved industrial processes, the course of things would be somewhat different. This is the case which offers the most striking exception to the general correspondence between wages and prices: for here, while wages would rise, prices in the industries profiting by the improved processes would fall. Nevertheless, though the rule would fail in the instance of those industries, it would receive abundant illustration from the accompanying phenomena. For one result of the cheapness effected in certain products would be to leave a larger amount of purchasing power available for expenditure in other directions. Hence would arise an increased demand for the commodities of other industries, which would be followed by an advance in their prices, by a larger application of capital to their production, and finally by a rise in the wages of the producers. The advance in prices would not indeed in this case (assuming the value of money to remain constant) be permanently maintained, at least where the competition among workmen was effective; but no more—profits being at the practical minimum—would the advance in money wages; and the improvement in the real wages of laborers, so far as it was permanently realized, would be only in proportion to the cheapening of products. On the other hand, where circumstances had given a virtual monopoly to any particular class of workmen, money wages and prices alike, as I have already shown, would remain permanently above the normal level; and such workmen would be enriched by a double process—they would receive larger money returns for their own labor, and would obtain the products of other industries at a reduced price. In this case also, then, though in certain branches of production there would be a marked divergence between wages and prices, in the great majority of industries the two phenomena would fluctuate together.

§ 9. One case still remains to be considered, and it deserves our attention the more, as the influence which it exhibits is one now in constant operation—I mean the effects produced on wages and prices by an increased supply of the precious metals, and a consequent depreciation of money. As the case is ordinarily represented, a depreciation of money takes effect in a uniform and simultaneous advance of all wages and prices; a state of things which would leave the real well-being of the several classes of society substantially unaffected; each person receiving a larger sum of money, and paying away a proportionally larger sum, in every transaction. But such a statement, though it expresses truly enough the final result of an increase of money, after the disturbances it creates have found their due correction—a result which it may take perhaps half a century to accomplish—yet, as an exposition of the actual phenomena which it purports to describe, must be pronounced to be absolutely erroneous. The supposition that wages and prices advanced *pari passu* over the whole area of productive industry is no more true where an increase of money is concerned than in any other case. The new money can only produce its effects by being made the instrument of demand; and the demand is not distributed indifferently over commodities in general, but is directed toward particular classes of commodities according to the needs and tastes of its possessors. What happens, therefore, in this case is what happens in all others. Certain commodities rise in price first; these are followed by others, and these again by others, the interval between the several steps being often of considerable duration; and the advance in prices is followed by an advance of wages. What chiefly distinguishes this case from those previously adverted to is, first, that the movement ultimately extends over the whole area of industry, embracing all occupations; and, secondly, that, though the prices of some commodities may temporarily drop from overproduction, and with them the wages of the producers, the normal level of both wages and prices is permanently raised.*

---

* I say the "normal," not the actual, level; for prices might be actually lower than formerly, yet if production had been cheapened by improved processes in a still greater degree, the lower actual price would indicate a higher normal price.

The result of our examination, then, has been to show a very intimate relation subsisting between wages and prices. The movements indeed are not always in the nature of strictly parallel movements; but they are always in the same direction, and are manifestly under the attraction of some common influence. Nor can there be much difficulty in determining what that influence is. As I have already frequently remarked, the real source of the remuneration of producers, looking at production as a continuous act, is the value of their products. Money wages and profits, therefore, as an aggregate, *must* vary in each branch of trade with the sum representing the aggregate products proceeding from the industry of the producers in that trade; or (assuming the efficiency of industry in the trade to remain constant)* with the prices of the specific commodities which constitute those products. If wages, therefore, do not rise or fall strictly in proportion to the money value of the aggregate products, or (in the absence of changes in productive power) to the prices of the specific commodities, it can only be because a larger share of the result has fallen to profits, whether in the form of loss or gain. But profits will not remain permanently in any branch of trade above or below the normal level; and the competition of capitalists will result either in lowering prices or raising wages, or, *mutatis mutandis*, in raising prices or lowering wages. In any case, wages and prices will gravitate toward each other. Where, indeed, prices have been reduced through improvements in production, the result will follow, not the variations in the price of the specific commodity, but those in the money

---

* The reader will note the reason for this qualification. The price of the commodity may rise or fall: but, if it only rises or falls in proportion to the cost of production, the money value of the product proceeding from a given exertion of industry will remain the same. It is only on the supposition that the productiveness of industry remains constant, that the price of the specific commodity will vary with the money value of the product.

value of the aggregate product. This latter will be larger in proportion as industry is more productive; but the specific price falling with the cost, the money returns divisible among the producers will be the same as before;* and the ultimate gain for them will be realized, not in an increase of either wages or profits (measured in money), but in the lowered price of the article they produce. There is thus a real and fundamental connection between money wages and prices. Yet I conceive it would be incorrect to describe either phenomenon as the cause or the effect of the other:† they are rather co-ordinate results of a common cause—that cause being the influence, whatever it may happen to be, which determines the products of a particular industry to exchange for those of others on more or less favorable terms than had previously obtained.

§ 10. One point in connection with the problem we are considering remains still to be cleared up. It has been strongly asserted that there is absolutely no necessary connection between the high or low range of general prices and the real well-being of workmen; that high general wages do not make

---

* I assume for convenience that the demand for the article would increase in proportion to the fall in the price. There is, of course, no necessity that this should happen; but on any other supposition, with regard to the effect of the fall of price upon demand, the argument, though a little more complicated, would be equally valid.

† In the cases which I have examined, the advance or fall in price would almost always precede the advance or fall in wages; but it is quite possible that the change in wages should occur first, as happens, for example, when laborers by a strike compel an advance in wages, for which capitalists are led afterward to indemnify themselves by putting an increased price upon their commodity—an expedient which, it must be carefully borne in mind, is only possible when the circumstances of the trade or the conditions of production are such as would in any case, after a time, lead to the same result, and probably by the more usual process in which the rise in prices precedes the rise in wages.

high general prices, nor high general prices high general wages (understanding wages here to mean the real remuneration of the laborer); and yet it has appeared from our investigation that money wages stand in intimate relation to prices, to a very great extent fluctuating with them; while it has been also pointed out that changes in money wages are scarcely ever merely nominal, but almost always entail a real improvement or deterioration of the workman's condition. These two positions, it is possible, may seem contradictory to some people; and it will therefore be desirable to look a little more closely than we have yet done into the reciprocal action of the several phenomena. For this purpose I will consider briefly the case in which the supposed discrepancy assumes its most prominent shape—that, namely, in which a rise of wages and prices results from an increase of money.

To put the supposed contradiction in its strongest form—what results in wages and prices as the final outcome, from an increase of money, is a *régime* of higher nominal values in which all wages and all prices have risen in an equal degree; in which, therefore, it is evident, no one's real position, as regards command over the necessaries and comforts of life, is substantially altered: and yet, in each step toward the higher nominal level, the particular advance will have brought to the workmen whose wages are affected a distinct gain in real wellbeing. The final outcome of a process, every step of which is productive of positive effects, will thus be purely negative. The thing to be shown is, the process by which these several partial but positive movements issue in this general negative result; and for this a simple illustration will suffice.

As I have already remarked, the advance in wages and prices under an increase of money will follow the direction of the demand for commodities. Now let us suppose the commodity first to feel the effect of the increased money demand to be shoes: shoes will then rise in price, and in due time the money wages of journeymen shoe-makers. But it is evident that this will be for the shoe-makers an advance of real wages: since, while receiving larger money wages than before, the only article of their consumption of which the price will have proportionally risen will be shoes. Next, we may suppose the enlarged demand to reach clothes, leading to a rise in the money wages of journeymen tailors; but this, again, will be for the tailors a rise of real wages; for the case will stand thus: shoes have already risen; and the only prices affected as the condition of the advance in *their* wages will be the price of clothes: on all commodities, therefore, except clothes, the tailors will gain in full proportion to the rise in their money wages. It is plain that the same considerations will apply to every step in the ascending process, until the entire cycle of the industries is completed; at which point shoe-makers, tailors, and producers of all kinds will find themselves in possession of incomes increased exactly in proportion as prices have risen—that is to say (excluding the gains and losses which may have been realized during the period of transition), neither better nor worse off than at starting. The solution of the enigma —if enigma it is to be considered—is of course to be found in the circumstance that the gain made by each class of workmen is in every instance obtained at the cost of other workmen, those namely whose wages do not share in that particular advance. The journeyman shoe-maker is, in the first instance, benefited, when, receiving a larger money remuneration, he pays the same sum for his clothes, hats, and bread; but the tailor, hatter, and baker, who, receiving the same money returns as before, have to pay more for their shoes, lose in the aggregate precisely what the shoe-maker gains. The subsequent advance in *their* wages and prices deprives the shoe-maker, for the future, of so much of the gain accruing from the advance in *his* case, and places them at an advantage as regards other workmen; whose wages and prices rising in their turn gradually restore them to their original position, though at the expense of those who, during the period of transition, profited by their depression. Thus each class of workmen gains by the advance of money wages in its own case; but as the circle extends, and the advance reaches other classes, those previously benefited part, item by item, with the advantage they had apparently secured, until in the end the real condition of each is restored to the original footing. It is like the gains and losses at a round game of cards. Every time the pool is won, the winner is richer precisely by the amount of the pool; but, if the pool were always of the same amount, and each player won in turn, it is plain that at the end of the evening every member of the company would rise from the table neither richer nor poorer than he had sat down.*

We may now resume the general argument interrupted by this incidental discussion.

---

* Analogies do not run on all fours, and the present analogy is not perfect. The card-players at the close of the game would not merely have regained the relative positions from which they started, but would each have recovered the losses he had incurred during the progress of the game; on the other hand, the gains and losses, incident to the period of transition from a low to a high *régime* of prices, would be definitive.

CHAPTER III.

TRADES-UNIONISM.—I.

§ 1. THE question whether in any given state of national wealth there can properly be said to be a limit to the amount of wealth available for the payment of wages, and if so, what the nature of that limit is, is one which brings us into immediate contact with Trades-Unionism in its most ambitious, if not its most important, aims. If there be no limit to the fund available for expenditure in wages, or if such limit as exists be of a kind which may easily be overpassed; if beyond the amount actually spent on wages at any given time there be an indefinite margin of wealth which workmen by judicious combination may conquer; then it is evident Trades-Unionism has a great field before it, and workmen will naturally and properly look to this agency as the principal means of improving their condition. But if, on the other hand, the amount of wealth spent in wages at any given time be confined within limits which, the conditions of industry and the character of the owners of wealth being what they are, can not be permanently extended by the action of workmen, then it follows that the scope for Trades-Union action is proportionally narrowed; and all attempts to accomplish a permanent increase of wages by such means, beyond what the unassisted action of supply and demand would ultimately bring about, are doomed beforehand to disappointment and failure. The question, therefore, of the limitation of the Wages-fund is evidently one of paramount importance in the present position of the controversy between labor and capital in this country: and we should approach the problem with all the care and circumspection which so momentous an issue demands.

§ 2. And, in the first place, I need scarcely point out that there are at all times certain limits to the possible Wages-fund which, if not strictly physical limits, come very close to that character. The Wages-fund of a country, at any given time, must, at all events, find a limit in the total wealth of the country at that time, and manifestly, under any circumstances, it must fall very much short of that total; for, in order to maintain the stock of commodities of all sorts which in any civilized community goes to support the laboring population, a certain large proportion of the general wealth must exist in the form of fixed capital and raw material. The wealth available, therefore, for the remuneration of labor can not at the utmost be more than the balance which remains after these indispensable requirements have been provided for, under pain of a complete failure of the fund. These are what we may describe as the physical limits of the Wages-fund, and they are obviously such as must be observed under all forms of industrial organization, even under a system of the most absolute communism. But the question I wish now to consider is whether, within these *quasi* physical limits, there are not, at least for societies organized as ours, and resting on the institution of private property and personal freedom, what may properly be called economic limits—that is to say, limits arising from the action of human interests operating under the actual circumstances of man's environment in the world. Now the principles already established in this work, taken in connection with other fundamental truths of economic science, will, I think, lead us to the conclusion that such limits do exist, and will also enable us to perceive the character of the obstacles which they oppose to the indefinite extension of the Wages-fund.

The reader has already seen the conditions on which depend

the investment of capital in productive industry, and the circumstances which determine its distribution, when invested, among the several instruments of production. He has seen that the motive to its investment is the prospect of profit, and that, the character of the owners of wealth being given, the strength of the inducement will vary as this prospect varies. Such being the fundamental facts on which the accumulation and investment of capital depend, there exists for every industrial society, as Mr. Mill has pointed out, a certain rate of profit which is the lowest that will suffice to call the accumulative principle leading to the investment of capital into action. This lowest rate of profit will be different for different communities and for different stages of civilization. It will be comparatively high where the accumulative principle among the owners of wealth is weak, since here the inducement will need to be proportionally strong, and low where that principle is strong. But under all circumstances there will be a minimum rate, below which, if the return on capital fall, accumulation, at least for the purpose of investment, will cease for want of adequate inducement. Mr. Mill has further shown that in all progressive societies, after a certain stage in their career is reached—that stage, namely, at which the best soils and the most productive natural agents of all kinds have been brought into requisition for the purposes of production—the tendency of profits is to fall, and ultimately to approach the minimum which exists for each society. This tendency is, indeed, constantly counteracted by the progress of invention and improvement in the industrial arts (including under this head the extension of the field for division of labor by the growth of trade), but nevertheless it continues to operate, and on the whole prevails against the opposing forces. With every increase of capital, this stage in the economic growth of a country once attained, a fall in the general rate of profit occurs, unless so far as the diminishing productiveness of industry is compensated by these incidents of progressive societies, until at length capital in its growth reaches the point at which the rate of profit is at, or, to borrow Mr. Mill's expression, within a hand-breadth of, the minimum. Lastly, Mr. Mill has shown that in countries in which capital has grown to this point, and among such countries, pre-eminently in Great Britain, the principle leading to accumulation is, as a rule, always strong enough, not merely to keep the aggregate capital of the country up to that amount at which profits approximate to the minimum, but even to cause it to exceed this amount; the proof of which lies in the large and continuous exportation of capital which occurs in such cases for investment in colonies or in foreign states. It results from these several positions that the amount of capital actually invested in Great Britain and in countries similarly circumstanced is, as a rule, at or close upon its maximum—that is to say, as great as, economically speaking, it can be in the actual state of the industrial arts and of general trade.

Such is the doctrine of the "tendency of profits to a minimum," for the proof of which I must refer the reader to Mr. Mill's chapter on that subject;[*] and I have now to ask him to consider the bearing of this doctrine upon the problem we have undertaken to discuss. As he has seen, it is of the essence of the doctrine, first, that, in any given state of the arts of industry and of trade, the quantity of capital which can be employed in a country is strictly limited, limited by those conditions which limit the inducement to save and invest—to perform those acts, that is to say, which constitute the source and spring from which capital is derived and fed; and, secondly, that, in countries which have attained that stage in their economical development which England has long ago reached and passed, the accumulation of capital under the influence of the ordinary motives, is, as a rule, constantly in excess of the amount which

---

[*] "Principles of Political Economy." book iv., chap. iv.

can be invested in the country consistently with obtaining the minimum rate of profit. These things being so, what can be the effect of an attempt on the part of Trades-Unions to compel, by pressure upon capitalists, an increase of the Wages-fund? Such an increase can only be accomplished in one or other of two ways—either by an increase of the total capital invested, or by a change in its distribution among the several agents of which it consists, in favor of labor, for example, by a conversion of what now goes to maintain machinery to the payment of wages. But either of these courses would inevitably result in a fall of profits, and profits are already at or within a hand-breadth of the minimum. It is true that the field for the investment of capital is being constantly extended in this and other progressive countries. Every step in the progress of industrial invention, every gain in the efficiency of labor, every new market opened to our trade, pushes farther back the limit set by the minimum of profit, and creates new room for the investment of capital. But the doctrine we have been considering shows us that the ordinary motives pressing upon capitalists are always sufficient, of their inherent strength, to fill up the room thus constantly created for fresh investment, and do in fact fill it up; and this being so, where is the scope for Trades-Union action in enlarging the Wages-fund? I confess I am unable to see how, in presence of these considerations, founded as they are on incontrovertible facts, the larger pretensions of Trades-Unionism can be sustained. The permanent elevation of the average rate of wages—or, what comes to the same thing, the permanent elevation of the rate of wages in any branch of industry not accompanied by an equivalent fall in some other branch or branches—beyond the level determined by the economic conditions prevailing in the country, is, as it seems to me, a feat beyond its power. Such is the broad general conclusion to which economic principles applied to the facts of the case appear to conduct us.

§ 3. We must be careful, however, not to strain this conclusion beyond the limits which its terms define. The reader will observe that it applies to the *average* rate of wages, as a *permanent* state of things, and further, that the question is left open as to the possibility of accelerating the operation of economic conditions, by action on the part of those whom they affect. Now it will be found that, these qualifications of the position just laid down duly considered, a certain scope still remains for Trades-Union action on the rate of wages—a certain scope, but of a range altogether more limited than that which the pretensions of those bodies to control the labor market commonly assume.

In the first place, it is not inconsistent with the general conclusion arrived at that an advance of wages in certain departments of industry should be effected by the action of Trades-Unions where this is accompanied by an equivalent fall in others; and, supposing the workmen in such departments of industry had it in their power to exclude the competition of outsiders, it is quite possible that an advance of wages so effected might be permanently maintained. Such a result is not only a perfectly possible achievement, but one which has occasionally been accomplished.* It amounts, however, merely

---

* According to Mr. Thornton, this has hitherto been the nature of all Trades-Union victories, and must be so until Unionism becomes universal. "In a country commercially stationary in which national wealth is not increasing—when a permanent advance of the rate of wages is obtained artificially by Unionist action, there must needs be a corresponding lowering of wages in other trades. Even in a country commercially progressive, it is impossible for Unionism to raise wages in any particular trade without causing the demand for the produce of other trades to be less than it would have been, or without equally checking the demand for labor in those other trades. Whether a country be stationary or progressive, an exceptionally high rate of wages can not be maintained in any particular trade, unless the workmen of all other trades are prevented from entering that particular trade, and endeavoring to get the same rate. *Unionism can not keep up the rate in one trade without keeping it down in others.* It can not benefit one portion of

to a change in the distribution of the Wages-fund, while its aggregate quantity is left unaltered; and for the present it will be more convenient to confine the discussion to the power of Trades-Unionism in relation to the general fund—its power, that is to say, to effect an advance of wages by a positive increase of capital, and not simply by drawing off capital from fields in which it was already invested, at the cost of the laborers in those fields.

Confining our view, then, for the present to this aspect of the case, we have now to consider—Trades-Unionism being, as we have seen, powerless to effect a permanent increase in the average rate of wages beyond what the economic conditions of the country permit—how far it is capable of modifying the rate for a time, or of accelerating an advance rendered possible by the state of trade and industry, but still pending and unrealized.

It is obvious at once, even apart from experience, that, where workmen have the power of combining, it will always be possible for them, by taking advantage of particular exigencies, to compel their employers to a temporary advance of wages. For example, where employers have bound them-

---

the laboring population without, during a period of stagnation, injuring the remainder, nor even in a season of prosperity, without at least shutting out the bulk of the laboring population from the advantages secured for a portion." ("On Labor," p. 310.)

I confess I am quite unable to reconcile the drift of this passage with Mr. Thornton's denial of the existence of a determinate Wages-fund; but, not to dwell upon this, it appears to me that the inference drawn from the state of things he describes, namely, that as Unionism is extended its advantages will be proportionally enlarged, until finally, becoming universal, they will represent pure gain unqualified by any set-off, is exactly the reverse of what the facts warrant. An advantage which depends upon the exclusion of others can not but be impaired by the admission of any of the excluded, and can not but be wholly lost by the admission of all. But I have dealt with this point more fully in a later chapter, post pp. 246–248.

selves under penalties to execute certain definite work within specified limits of time, it is evidently possible for workmen, by combination, to place their employers in the alternative of either complying with their demands or of incurring a greater loss; and under such circumstances a strike, it may be assumed, will be successful, so far as the immediate aims of the workmen are concerned. This, if an extreme case, is in actual life a very common one; and the principle on which the success of the workmen depends has a much wider range than that of time contracts. To a certain extent all persons who embark their means in business are at the mercy of those on whose co-operation they rely for carrying their plans into effect; and this liability to be injured by refusal on the part of others to co-operate will evidently become greater in proportion as the preliminary outlay incident to the undertaking is large. A capitalist, for example, who has committed himself to an industrial enterprise by making large purchases of building and plant, wherewith to carry it on, must find laborers to work for him, or suffer heavy loss; for either, his capital lying idle, he loses the interest it might bring him, or, if he attempts by sale or otherwise to convert it into other forms, it is pretty sure to be largely depreciated in the process. Under these circumstances, supposing the workmen on whom he relies to strike for higher wages, and that he has reason to believe that they possess the resolution and are in command of funds sufficient to enable them to maintain a prolonged strike, it may be his wisdom to concede their demands, even though the result should be not merely to bring his profits below the minimum, but to annihilate them altogether, or even convert them into loss; since the entire cessation of his business for so long a period might involve him in still greater loss. It is evident, therefore, that workmen have, by means of combination and by accumulating sufficient funds, very considerable power of acting upon the rate of wages. But the question remains as to the ultimate consequences of such action; as to its effect upon the workman's well-being, taking an extended view of his interest. To determine this point, we must consider two distinct states of industry and trade—one where the business of the country is in its normal or average condition, and where consequently, in old countries like Great Britain, the rate of profit is at or close upon the minimum; the other, where trade is exceptionally prosperous, and profits may be assumed to be considerably in advance of the minimum rate. Taking the former case first, what will be the definitive result under those circumstances of a successful strike for higher wages? The rate of profit having been previously at or near the lowest point at which there is an adequate inducement to invest capital, the action of the workmen has forced it below this point. As has already been intimated, capital can not, except at great loss, be withdrawn suddenly from industries in which it has once been embarked, and therefore workmen may for a time enjoy the fruits of their success. But though capital can not be withdrawn suddenly, it may be withdrawn by degrees—at the worst by the simple process of not renewing it as it is worn out. And this is what, in the case we are considering, we may confidently assume would happen. Employers whose capital is bringing them a rate of profit below what (allowance made for risk and other drawbacks) they might obtain from its investment in other industries or in other places, will seize every opportunity that offers for withdrawing it from an employment so unremunerative. After a little the successful workmen will find that their services are not required, and will be compelled for their support to throw themselves on the general labor market. The inevitable result must be a fall in the general rate of wages at least to its former level—to a level, that is to say, which is consistent with giving to capitalists what they conceive to be an adequate return upon their outlay. This is the least unfavorable consequence which could ensue from the success of a compulsory action on wages where the condition of trade is what we may describe as quiescent. Supposing, however, that proceedings of this kind were not merely isolated and exceptional, but became sufficiently frequent to be looked forward to by capitalists as a normal incident of productive investment, the consequences for workmen would be much more serious than a mere return to the former state of things. The constant liability to a sudden reduction of profits from such causes would become an element in the regular calculation of capitalists, and before embarking in an industrial undertaking they would look for compensation in a rate of profit high enough to cover such risks. In other words, the action of Trades-Unions in forcing up wages under the circumstances in question, however it might for the moment raise wages at the expense of profits, would have for permanent consequence precisely the opposite result; for, by increasing the risks of investment, it would tend to raise the minimum rate of profit, and, in proportion as it did so, to narrow the field for the employment of capital in the country. The aggregate capital being less, the Wages-fund, *cæteris paribus*, would be less, and unless laborers consented to reduce their numbers, the general rate of wages would fall.

Such, it seems to me, must be the inevitable consequence of frequent and systematic attempts to force up the rate of wages when the economic conditions of the country do not warrant a rise; and *a fortiori*, I may add, these disastrous results would be only more certainly realized, if this policy were attempted in a depressed condition of trade when profits barely reached the necessary level. But let us now consider how the case would stand supposing the demand for an advance to occur when trade is exceptionally prosperous. Mechanical inventions, we may suppose, or improved processes, have cheapened production; or the opening of new markets for trade has enabled our manufacturers to exchange their commodities on better terms with foreign countries. Under such circumstances profits may advance considerably above the minimum; and the question arises, what is the scope for Trades-Union action offered by a contingency of this kind. We have already seen that, even under the ordinary conditions of trade, it is frequently in the power of workmen, by skillfully taking advantage of the position of their employers, to force up wages above the actual rate. But a state of trade in which profits were sensibly above the minimum limit would obviously be highly favorable for such operations. For, by refusing to work, the men could now not merely inflict the same loss as before on their masters, but could compel them to forego the opportunities of reaping the unusual gains which the time offered. There can be no doubt at all, therefore, that under such circumstances well-concerted Trades-Union action would be capable of achieving success. This, however, does not in itself establish the wisdom of such policy; for the question would remain, whether the game were worth the candle; whether the results attainable by this course would compensate for the trouble and risk involved in the movement. For it must be remembered that, under the influence of the ordinary motives which, we have seen, govern the growth of capital, the state of things we are considering would act as a powerful incentive to accumulation and investment. An increased demand for labor would sooner or later spring up, and ultimately an advance of wages to as high a point as the actual state of things permitted. This being so, it may be asked whether the action of Trades-Unions, mischievous in the case we last considered, would not here be superfluous. Now the answer to this question must, I think, be in the negative. The workman, no doubt, is interested in the final result, but he is also interested in its speedy realization; and the process by which the fruits of exceptionally prosperous trade issue in an advance of wages is a circuitous one, and generally covers some considerable period of time.

Employers as a class, we may take for granted, will not propose an advance of wages except under the stress of competition, and before competition becomes actually operative the new capital may lie for some time upon the market, in the "floating" condition, seeking investment, but not at once finding it. Even after investment has been found, preliminary arrangements have to be made, and a considerable time may elapse before the new demand for labor is practically felt. Throughout this period wages, in the absence of external pressure, may remain absolutely unaffected, and laborers may be excluded from all share in the prosperity of which the entire fruits are appropriated by their employers. If, then, laborers have the power, as we have seen they have, of shortening or of annihilating altogether this interval, why may they not use it? It seems to me that there is here a perfectly legitimate field for Trades-Union action. The state of trade being such as to permit an advance of wages, Trades-Unionism, using its powers judiciously, may determine capital at once toward those issues which, under the influence of the ordinary motives governing industrial investment, it would indeed in any case ultimately reach. A distinct and substantial gain may thus be secured for labor without encroaching on the indispensable margin for the remuneration of capital, and without impairing any of those conditions on which its own permanent well-being depends.*

It results from the foregoing considerations that the action of Trades-Unions, directed toward raising the rate of wages by combination among workmen, may be hurtful or beneficial according to circumstances. The practical utility, therefore, of this mode of action will depend upon the ability of those who control the conduct of these bodies to discriminate the states of

---

* The history of the Newcastle engineering strike is instructive. It was in that case admitted, on the side of the masters, that the conditions of trade from the beginning permitted an advance of wages; yet no advance was proposed till the pressure of Trades-Unionism was brought to bear.

the market in which action may be taken with advantage from those in which it can only be productive of harm. It thus becomes matter of deep interest to know if the working-class leaders possess this ability or may be expected to acquire it.

And here I touch a point on which I should not be justified in speaking otherwise than with extreme diffidence. I fear it must be admitted that, up to the present, the competency of Trades-Union leaders to form a correct judgment on the state of trade, even in the particular departments with which they each happen to be practically conversant, and to decide upon the seasonableness of a demand for increased wages, must be considered as at least problematical. The temporary success of a strike does not necessarily prove its wisdom; but the failure of a strike, immediate or ultimate, is decisive evidence that it ought never to have been undertaken; and hitherto unsuccessful strikes have been extremely numerous.

"The most protracted strikes (says Mr. Brassey) in which the workingmen have been engaged have generally taken place, not for the purpose of securing an advance of wages, but for the purpose of resisting a fall. Resistance to a proposed reduction was the cause of the engineers' strike in 1852; of the strike at Preston in 1853; of the strike in the iron trade in 1865; and of the strike of the colliers at Wigan in 1868. In each of these cases the masters had found it necessary, in consequence of the depressed state of trade, to reduce the rate of wages; but the men, ignoring the circumstances of the trade, and looking only to what they believed to be a degradation of their position as workmen, refused to accept the reduction. They therefore went out on strike; but, after a protracted struggle, were compelled to accept the original proposal of their employers. . . . . The leaders in several protracted strikes have exhibited a melancholy ignorance of the state of their own trade, and even of the market value of the goods in the production of which they are engaged. How much suffering might have been spared to the working-classes, if they had but known, before they engaged in a hopeless struggle, the true merits of their case! I was once present at a meeting of employers during a large strike in the coal trade. I had the means of knowing that the wages which had been offered were the highest which the employers could afford to pay, and that the markets were so overstocked that it was a positive advantage to suspend the working of the pits for a time. But the facts which I had the means of knowing were apparently unknown to the miners; and it was indeed lamentable to see the hard-earned accumulations of many years exhausted in an obstinate resistance to a reduction of wage, which had not been proposed by the employers until it had been forced upon them by the unfavorable condition of their trade."*

Nevertheless, I think there is evidence to show that Unionists are gathering wisdom with experience, and this Mr. Brassey admits. The great majority of recent strikes have been successful. But it is not so much the success of recent strikes, as the manner in which the success has been achieved—the moderation and good sense with which for the most part the demands of the men have been put forward and supported, and the increasing indications in their various manifestoes of a growing comprehension of the true conditions of the problem —that constitutes the most solid ground of hope. I would point in particular to the Newcastle engineers' strike of the year 1871 as an occasion when these qualities were manifested in an eminent degree. Certainly, to my apprehension as a disinterested spectator, the conduct of the men in that struggle contrasted favorably with that of their employers. But in order to convert Trades-Unionism into an agency, not merely capable now and then of achieving an advance of wages by a *coup de main*, while on other occasions it leads its supporters into ruinous contests, from which they only emerge enfeebled and impoverished, to accept worse terms than they had previously refused—in order to convert it into an agency permanently and constantly beneficent, workmen must learn to recognize more distinctly than they have yet done the essential conditions of success; and not merely this, but also to adopt

---

* " Work and Wages," pp. 6, 7, and 10, 11.

the needful means for determining in each case as it arises how far these conditions are fulfilled. In other words, Trades-Unions must frankly recognize the impossibility of forcing profits permanently below that rate which capitalists regard, and show by their conduct that they regard, as only an adequate return upon their outlay; and they must organize the means for obtaining sufficient and trustworthy information respecting the actual state of trade, with a view to determine whether profits are or are not in advance of this minimum level. It has been said, indeed, that workmen can not know the state of profits in a trade so long as they are excluded from access to their employers' books, and that this is a privilege which will never be conceded them. But for the purposes of Trades-Unionism I can not see that any such detailed knowledge as might be obtained by inspection of the books of employers is necessary. The object in view is not to know the precise gains of particular employers, which may depend quite as much upon individual skill and management as upon the general circumstances of the trade, but whether the circumstances of the trade, as a whole, are such as, with average management, to admit of more than the usual gains. The data for this lie in a knowledge of the state of prices, at different periods, alike of the finished article and of the raw material, of the conditions of production as regards mechanical, chemical, or other facilities, and of the greater or less accessibility of markets. These are circumstances an adequate knowledge of which is quite within reach of Trades-Unions, if only the proper means be taken to obtain it; and Mr. Brassey in the following passage gives an example of what these means should be:

"It is not the less essential to keep a watchful eye on all that is taking place abroad. The organization of Trades-Unions might be utilized for this important purpose. The resources of a joint purse should afford the means of sending delegates abroad, for whom opportunities ought to be

provided of studying foreign languages, and whose duty it should be to
keep the artisans of England closely informed of the fluctuations in the
activity of trade and the reward of labor in the countries in which they
resided. Trades-Unions can not in the long run materially influence the
rate of wages, but there are many valuable services which they can render; and none would be more practically useful than the frequent publi-
cation of faithful reports on the state of the labor market from well-placed
observers on the Continent."*

I believe the influence of Trade-Unionism organized thus
with a deliberate purpose of collecting and diffusing sound information among its supporters would be in more ways than
one largely beneficial. The collection of the necessary facts,
their careful study and examination, and the discussions to
which these would lead, combined with the sense of responsibility attaching to the formation of opinions on which practical
issues of the gravest import depended, would in themselves be
for workmen a means of practical education of the highest value. But the more obvious advantages of this course of action
would lie in its direct consequences—in the immense saving
which would result both to men and masters in preventing
abortive strikes. Indeed the adoption of such a policy by
Trades-Unions would powerfully tend to the cessation of
strikes altogether—at least for the purpose of effecting an advance of wages—by rendering them unnecessary. It is not
probable that, when employers came to understand that workmen had mastered the real facts of the situation and knew the
strength and weakness of their reciprocal positions, the refusal
of reasonable demands would be long persisted in. Each side
would perceive that both alike were cognizant of what the circumstances of the case permitted, of what was feasible, and of
what was not so; and neither would probably seek to strain its
pretensions beyond the limit thus mutually recognized.

---

* "Work and Wages," pp. 14, 15.

§ 4. The foregoing conclusions as to the power of combinations of workmen to effect an advance in the rate of wages may seem to be applicable only to old countries, in which, like our own, the rate of profit is normally at or close upon the minimum point, and from which, consequently, capital is from time to time flowing off into foreign investment. In countries like the United States, in which the rate of profit is still far above the minimum, and which, instead of lending capital to foreign countries, are themselves habitual recipients of their redundant supplies, it will perhaps be thought that the arguments which have been used would cease to have any force. It can not be denied that the same obstacles which set limits to Trades-Union action in the Old World do not exist in the New. Nevertheless, I apprehend that though the obstacles may not be the same, the limitations on such action will be found in effect to be scarcely less real there than with us. If, indeed, capitalists could be reduced to the alternative of either conceding the demands of Trades-Unions, or being deprived altogether of the opportunity of investing their wealth, one can imagine that, rather than accept the latter course, they might consent to so great an advance of wages as would, under the actual conditions of productive industry, issue in a decline of the returns on capital considerably below the level at which profits in the United States now ordinarily stand; and it is possible that the change in distribution thus effected might be permanent. I say this would be a conceivable result, if capitalists could be reduced to the alternative just stated. But in a country of such vast magnitude as the United States, covering as it does the greater portion of a continent, what grounds are there for believing that Trades-Union organization can ever become at once so complete and so all-embracing as to be capable of prescribing terms such as these? For my part, I find it impossible to contemplate such a consummation as a condition of things to be taken into serious account. Within a limited area—within perhaps a single State—one can imagine Trades-Unionism absolute; but, limited to a single State, or even to half a dozen States, the attempt to enforce its decrees in the sense described would issue, not in raising the rate of wages generally over the American continent, or even in raising it permanently within the State or States in which the organization was dominant, but simply in driving capital from one State to another—in sending it from New England or New York to Illinois, Missouri, or California; and workmen would find their prize escaping them just as they fancied they had grasped it. In this way, in the New World no less than in the Old, the larger aims of Trades-Unionism must, as I apprehend, find defeat. Under all circumstances the facilities of escape open to capital are too great to make it possible to hem it in, and so to compel a surrender at discretion; and we shall have no need to modify the conclusions at which we have arrived even in applying them to a country in its economical circumstances and development so widely separated from our own as the United States.

§ 5. As the reader has seen, the utmost power which I am disposed to concede to Trades-Unions over wages, where they seek their ends by compelling a positive increase of investment, is that of accelerating an advance, already, so to speak, in the air, and which would come in the end without their intervention. Where strikes have been permanently successful, where they have not merely gained to-day what has been lost to-morrow, but have issued in a permanently improved condition of the workmen, I believe the explanation of their success will always be found in a state of trade exceptionally prosperous which would in any case before long have attracted an increase of capital, and resulted in an enlarged demand for labor. But this explanation of the success of strikes is, I find, strenuously repudiated by Mr. Thornton, who regards Trades-Unionism as an agency capable not merely of raising wages in anticipation of the ordinary commercial influences, but of permanently sustaining them at a level higher than they would without its action ever have attained, and in conformity with this view is disposed to attribute the advance of wages which within twenty years has occurred in most branches of industry to Trades-Union action as its proper cause. I confess Mr. Thornton's argument on this point is to me singularly unsatisfactory. He writes:

"Of course it is open to any one to question whether the enhancement of labor's remuneration which has thus been going on at both ends is due to the influence of Trades-Unions, and whether it would not have taken place equally if the price of labor had been left to find its own level without extraneous interference. The questioner here, however, may very properly be left to answer himself, as he may satisfactorily do, by proceeding to inquire how often any portion of the enhancement referred to has been volunteered by the masters, and how often it has been only yielded to solicitation with force in the background. He will find the instances of masters spontaneously raising wages to be about as numerous as those of workmen conscientiously believing themselves to be overpaid and coming forward to insist that their wages should be reduced."*

Mr. Thornton apparently is unable to conceive a middle term between "volunteering" an advance, and "yielding to solicitation with force in the background;" as if it were not the essence of his opponent's case that there is this middle term—to be found in those economic influences distinct alike from mere benevolence and from coercion from without, which issue in increased competition for labor, and as a consequence an advance in its price. I commend to Mr. Thornton the following facts supplied by Mr. Brassey:

"In the famous engine-building establishment at Creuzot, founded by the father of Mr. Charles Manby, 10,000 persons are now employed, and the annual expenditure in wages amounts to £400,000. Mechanics were

---

* "On Labor," pp. 257, 258.

paid, when the establishment was first created, at the rate of 2½ francs a day. At the present time none receive less than 5 francs a day. Between 1850 and 1866 the mean rate advanced from 2s. to 2s. 11d. per head, or thirty-eight per cent., and some men earned from 6s. 8d. to 8s. 4d. per day. . . . . Compare what has occurred in this country with what has taken place at MM. Schneider's at Creuzot. . . . . At MM. Schneider's, *without the assistance of a Trades-Union,* the working-people have obtained, during the last seventeen years, an augmentation of wage of thirty-eight per cent. In England, in the corresponding period, the most powerful of all the Trade Societies, with an accumulated fund of £149,000, has found it impossible to secure any increase in the earnings of its members."*

How will Mr. Thornton explain the advance of wages at Creuzot? Trades-Union pressure not being there, will he refer it to the spontaneous benevolence of the iron-masters? A little reflection will probably suggest to him a means of escape from his own dilemma.

§ 6. The power of workmen to compel by combination an advance of wages has generally been considered as more or less an open question; but that capitalists possess the corresponding power of keeping wages down by combination has, for the most part, been taken for granted. In a well-known passage Adam Smith observes that employers are in a permanent conspiracy to keep wages down, and the context certainly implies the writer's belief that they are generally successful in this object. Nevertheless I must venture to question the assumption, even though supported by Adam Smith's authority. I hold that, at least in countries in which the industrial and commercial spirit is strong, the power of capitalists by combination to depress wages or to keep them down is not a whit more real than that of workmen by similar means to force them up. Either may, no doubt, effect their object for a time,

---

* "Work and Wages," pp. 159–161.

but neither, as I believe, can be permanently successful. The grounds of this opinion will be apparent to those who have followed the argument by which in a former chapter I have endeavored to prove the "determination" toward the Wages-fund of a certain portion of the national wealth.* It is quite true, no doubt, that capitalists, as possessors of wealth, have both the physical and the legal power of employing it as they please. They may, if they choose, withdraw all their capital from investment and squander it in unproductive consumption, or, for that matter, sink it in the sea; and the effect of such proceeding on their part, if this course were extensively adopted, would undoubtedly be to depress wages in the country for a considerable period of time. But I apprehend the real question is, not whether capitalists have the physical or legal power of doing such things, but whether, their character being such as it is, it is morally possible for them to adopt these or any other effectual expedients for accomplishing the object they no doubt much desire. The whole issue, as I conceive it, turns upon the character of capitalists as a class, and more particularly on the balance within them of two qualities of mind—on the one hand, the strength of the accumulative propensity, and, on the other, the taste for luxurious enjoyment, by which the former is constantly counteracted. Supposing these two qualities to be so adjusted in the owners of wealth in this country that the prospect of a certain rate of profit, say ten per cent., suffices to cause a certain proportion of the whole national wealth to be turned toward productive investment, this proportion will be turned to this destination. It is true, indeed, that those who thus employ their wealth would be very glad to obtain from it a larger return than they are likely to receive, and not a few would be only too ready, if they had the power, to force down the rate of wages with this view. But this is pre-

---

Ante, pp. 181-187.

cisely what they can not do consistently with gratifying the dominant propensity which, under the temptation of a certain rate of profit, draws them toward productive investment. Thus, supposing a group of employers to have succeeded, as no doubt would be perfectly possible for them, in *temporarily* forcing down wages by combination in a particular trade, a portion of their wealth, previously invested, would now become free—how would it be employed? I have already traced the consequences of such an occurrence, and need not weary the reader by repeating the deduction here. Suffice it that, though it is impossible to say what might be the course adopted in particular instances—unless we are to suppose the character of a large section of a community to be suddenly changed in a leading attribute, the wealth so withdrawn from wages would, in the end, and before long, be restored to wages. The same motives which led to its investment would lead to its re-investment, and, once re-invested, the interests of those concerned would cause it to be distributed among the several elements of capital in the same proportions as before. In this way covetousness is held in check by covetousness, and the desire for aggrandizement sets limits to its own gratification. My conclusion is that, though combination, whether employed by capitalists or by laborers, may succeed in controlling for a time the price of labor, it is utterly powerless, in the hands of either, to effect a permanent alteration in the market rate of wages as determined by supply and demand.

§ 7. Throughout the foregoing discussion it has been constantly assumed that an advance of wages involves as a consequence, *cæteris paribus*, a fall of profits. I beg to call the reader's attention to the condition here presupposed; for I observe, in some recent publications in which the relation of profits to wages is discussed, that there is an entire omission on the part of the writers to say whether, in challenging the doctrine just stated, they understand it as subject to, or irrespective of, this qualification. Mr. Brassey, for example, devotes a chapter to prove that "the cost of labor can not be determined by the rate of wages;" and this enunciation is characterized by Mr. Harrison in the *Fortnightly Review* as a "striking law of industry, which the book before us boldly formulates and completely proves," and he proceeds to contrast it with the "professorial dicta of so-called economists, based on the assumption that high wages inevitably imply dear goods and low profits." That any one ever maintained that the cost of labor, prices, or profits were determined simply by the rate of wages *irrespective of the efficiency of the labor*, is what, I own, I find it hard to believe; and until Mr. Harrison tells us who the economists are that maintain this enlightened view—as I have never myself happened to meet with a specimen of the class either in the flesh or in print—I shall be disposed to regard them as mythical entities evolved from the moral consciousness of writers more anxious to refute than to understand Political Economy. On the other hand, I find it almost equally difficult to suppose that either Mr. Brassey or Mr. Harrison would advisedly maintain, *on the assumption that the efficiency of labor is a constant condition*, that the cost of labor, and, as depending on it, the rate of profit, are *not* determined by the rate of wages. In truth, it is pretty clear that the entire controversy on this subject has arisen from some people not taking the trouble to understand what other people say. Ricardo, for example, has laid it down that profits are inversely as wages, but any tolerably careful student of Ricardo would see that by wages he meant "proportional wages"— that is to say, the laborer's share of the product, or, if wages in the ordinary sense, then that the statement was to be received subject to the condition that the efficiency of labor remained the same. Ricardo, however, has not been fortunate in finding careful students; and scores of writers who have undertaken to refute his doctrine have in reality refuted merely their own misconception of it. And what in effect is this "striking law of industry," now for the first time, according to Mr. Harrison, "boldly formulated and completely proved," and which puts to shame "the professorial dicta of so-called economists?" Why simply this, that it often pays better to employ a good workman at high wages than an inferior one at low. The fact is indubitable, but why it should be called "a striking law of industry" rather than the most common of industrial commonplaces, still more why it should be represented as a conclusive refutation of all that economists have written on the relation of wages to profits, is what I must confess myself wholly at a loss to discover.

It is possible, indeed, that the language I have quoted may refer, not to the perfectly sound though somewhat trite maxim, that efficient labor is often worth more than inefficient, but to a doctrine suggested, rather than "boldly formulated," in the chapter under consideration. In a passage headed "Uniform Cost of Labor," Mr. Brassey writes as follows: "High wages do not necessarily imply dear labor, just as, on the other hand, low wages do not, of necessity, make labor cheap. On my father's extensive contracts, carried on in almost every country of the civilized world and in every quarter of the globe, the daily wage of the laborer was fixed at widely different rates; but it was found to be the almost invariable rule that the cost of labor was the same—that for the same sum of money the same amount of work was everywhere performed. Superior skill, extra diligence, and a larger development of physical power, will often compensate the employer who finds himself obliged to pay higher wages than his competitors."*

Let me here say that I have not the slightest disposition to

---

* "Work and Wages," pp. 74, 75.

question the fact of a real connection existing between good wages and efficient work, and still less would I dispute the probability (to refer here to a later position of Mr. Brassey's) that shortened hours of work may up to a certain point find their compensation in the increased energy of the workman. As corroborative of these assumptions, I regard the statement of Mr. Brassey's experience furnished in this work as extremely valuable. But the reader will observe that there is something more in the passage just quoted than a mere statement of specific fact. The words "it was found to be an almost invariable rule that the cost of labor was the same—that for the same sum of money the same amount of work was everywhere performed," coming under the heading " Uniform Cost of Labor," seem to point to the existence of an economic law according to which the efficiency of labor, all the world over, varies with its price. An economic law, indeed, there is which connects efficiency of work with payment, but, as I have elsewhere shown, this operates only within the limits of competition.* Within such limits the tendency very obviously will be to adjust wages in each occupation to efficiency in that occupation, and thus to bring out as the result a uniform cost of labor, or, as I prefer to call it, price of work. But Mr. Brassey goes far beyond this, and lays down the rule of uniform cost of labor as "almost invariable in every country of the civilized world and in every quarter of the globe." This, indeed, would have been a "striking law of industry," had our author made the position good; but it is singularly disappointing to discover, ere we read many pages on, that the so-called law can only be regarded as a rhetorical expression. At page 84 we find that it must be understood as referring to "railway work executed by unskilled labor," while, even as thus limited, it is far from being universally true, failing, as Mr. Bras-

---

* See *ante*, p. 77, note.

sey informs us it does, in the comparison of English labor with the labor of India and of Italy (pp. 87, 90), and, as statistics given elsewhere in the volume show (pp. 38 and 49), in other instances also. That the rule does not hold of the skilled labor of different countries is what is implied in nearly every other page of Mr. Brassey's book; the constant moral there enforced being the heavy detriment which Great Britain suffers from her dear labor—a detriment so heavy, an economical drawback so serious, that only her great resources in other respects enable her to bear up under it against the strain of continental competition.

What, then, is the net outcome from Mr. Brassey's facts in their bearing upon the question as to the connection between wages and the cost of labor or price of work? A large portion of those facts relate to the wages of laborers in Great Britain in free competition with each other; and so far his statements form a striking and useful illustration of a familiar principle—the tendency of competition, within any given department of industry, to adjust payment to efficiency, so as to render the price of a given piece of work pretty nearly the same whether it is performed by labor of superior or of only moderate and ordinary skill. But where his examples are of broader scope, and exhibit the relative rates of wages in different countries and in labor markets not in free competition with each other, their value in relation to the question in hand is of a different kind. What they amount to would seem to be this: in the comparison of different countries, a very low rate of remuneration for labor is generally found to be accompanied with a very low degree of industrial efficiency, while, as the condition of the laborer improves, his efficiency up to a certain point is found to increase in nearly the same degree. I say "up to a certain point;" for it does not appear that the correspondence between remuneration and efficiency holds good beyond the range of those employments which call for mere physical energy and endurance, such as railway work performed by unskilled labor; nor is it found to be universally true even within these limits. When we pass from the ranks of unskilled to those of skilled labor, and when in the latter we confine our attention to those cases in which the remuneration has risen above the point at which it still contributes to mere physical energy, we find no evidence in the facts adduced by Mr. Brassey of the existence of a uniform cost of labor in different countries. On the contrary, the main tenor of his work goes to establish the opposite position; since, as I have already remarked, the constant moral deduced from his reasonings is the heavy disadvantage which England undergoes from her dear labor in comparison with the cheap labor of the Continent—a disadvantage so great as only, according to Mr. Brassey, to be just compensated by her superior resources in machinery, raw material, and coal. It follows most clearly from this that, in Mr. Brassey's opinion, that portion of English work which is performed by labor is more highly paid for here than abroad. And in truth we have only to consider the habits of the great majority of our artisan population to perceive how very slight the connection can, in the nature of things, be between efficient labor in those classes and the rate of their remuneration. An increase of wages which merely results in an enlarged consumption of beer and spirits is not likely to add much either to the physical powers or to the intelligence and skill of the recipients; and notoriously this is the way in which an increase of wages is, for the most part, taken out in this country. I repeat once again, I have no desire to dispute the existence of a real connection between good pay and efficient work; only let us note well the nature of the connection. It exists so far, and only so far, as the larger pay is applied to sustain the industrial qualities, physical or mental, of the workman. At present it would seem that this is very generally the case while wages are no more than sufficient to supply the primary animal wants. But where they exceed this limit, the increased pecuniary means placed at the laborer's disposal are quite as often employed to impair as to improve his industrial qualities, and the connection between remuneration and efficiency is at an end, or at most is but a matter of accident. I am one of those, however, who live in hope that the rule may not always be thus limited. When artisans shall learn to use their increasing resources to help their intellectual and moral progress, instead of, as now, squandering them in brutalizing dissipation, and when improved education shall go hand in hand with a larger command over material well-being, we may hope to see an approximation toward that uniform cost of labor of which Mr. Brassey speaks, but of which, outside the lower grades of labor, the indications at present are, it is to be feared, somewhat partial and rare.

So much for Mr. Brassey's facts. I fail to discover in them any new "law of industrial life"—indeed it is but right to say that Mr. Brassey disclaims for them any pretensions to this character—still less any thing in the least at variance with the well understood doctrines of Political Economy; but I find evidence, not always, as it seems to me, very accurately interpreted, of which a good part is illustrative of a very familiar economic principle, and the rest supports the view of a connection pretty widely existing between wages and industrial efficiency in the lower ranks of labor.

CHAPTER IV.

TRADES-UNIONISM.—II.

§ 1. THE methods by which Trades-Unions seek to operate on the rate of wages are numerous; but they all find a place under one or other of the three following heads:

1. Directly—by calling on employers to raise the rate of wages, or, what comes to the same thing, to reduce the number of working hours, the rate of wages not being proportionally reduced—a demand which involves either increased investment of capital in the form of wages; or—unless so far as the reduction in working hours may be compensated by increased efficiency—a proportionally diminished production from the same investment.

2. Indirectly—by regulations directed toward restricting the supply of labor.

3. Indirectly — by regulations directed toward increasing the demand for labor by increasing the need for it; or, as it is otherwise expressed, by increasing the quantity of work to be done.

The first of these methods is that which has been considered in the last chapter; and the reader has seen how far we found it to be efficacious and legitimate. The two remaining methods have now to be considered.

§ 2. And first, as to that mode of action which seeks to attain its end by acting on the supply of labor. In order to form a sound judgment on this portion of Trades-Union policy, it is important to discriminate between two perfectly distinct methods by which the supply of labor may be controlled. It may, in the first place, be controlled at its source by diminishing the number of people born to the calling of labor; and this is a result which Trades-Unions might in many ways promote—for example, by cultivating among the laboring classes a sounder public opinion on the subject of population than at present prevails, by impressing on parents their responsibility toward their offspring, and generally by encouraging prudence and foresight, which, once established as habits, would affect conduct in relation to marriage and its consequences, as well as with regard to other aspects of life; and this influence might be brought to bear either upon the laboring population at large, or upon those sections of the population with which each Trades-Union happened to be immediately in contact. This is one method by which it may be attempted to operate on the labor market through the supply of labor. But the end in view may also be sought by another path, namely, by opposing artificial barriers to the admission of workmen to particular trades—for example, by regulations excluding from employment in the protected trades all who have not been regularly apprenticed to them, setting limits at the same time to the number of apprentices which each master-tradesman may receive; the multiplication of the laboring people as a whole and of each portion of it being left to the influences which at present determine it. Of these two methods of proceeding we may confidently pronounce the first to be both sound and legitimate—sound, because the means adopted are fitted to attain the end in view, and legitimate, because the course pursued would be free from all attempts at coercion, and would be addressed exclusively to the reason and conscience of those concerned. We have no occasion here, however, to enter into any further examination of this mode of restricting the supply of labor, since it is not the method which Trades-Unions have adopted. Their action in this direction has been confined exclusively to that other mode of proceeding which consists in hedging round certain favored trades with artificial obstacles; and this accordingly is the mode of action we are now called upon to consider.

And here it may at once be conceded that the policy in question is capable of being made effectual for accomplishing its immediate purpose—that of raising the rate of wages in the regulated occupations above the level which in an open labor market it would attain; but conceding this, the question still remains whether this mode of action is consistent with the best interests either of the laboring people as a whole, or even of that section of them in whose favor the restrictive regulations are imposed. To enable us to form a judgment upon this point, it is important to bear in mind the real nature of the monopoly created by the restrictive rule. That monopoly is not, as might at first be imagined, one in favor of certain natural groups of population—the collection of families, namely, who supply candidates to the highly-paid trades—as opposed to the laboring population at large. It is a monopoly of a much narrower and more artificial sort than this. The line drawn is, not between such natural groups and the rest of the laboring people, but between certain selected members of such groups and all who are not included in the selection. Now this is an important distinction; because if the purpose were to reserve certain occupations to certain groups of families, say to those who at present fill the occupations in question and their descendants—though such a course would amount to the creation of industrial castes, and would be open to all the objections that apply to a caste system—still it would have one important merit: the end in view—the permanent elevation of wages in the favored occupations above the level prevailing in the country—would need for its attainment something more than the mere exclusion of competitors from other employments: it would require, besides this, a control of population within the protected groups, and consequently could only be accomplished by the cultivation of feelings and habits socially so valuable that they might almost be thought to compensate for the serious evils inherent in every such plan. Such, however, is not the object or character of the policy we are now considering. The thing aimed at is not the permanent elevation of any natural groups of population, but simply the maintenance of certain individuals who happen to be exercising certain callings in the enjoyment of a state of well-being not permitted to their fellows. Those, therefore, who charge upon Trades-Unions the purpose of creating industrial castes do not seem to have hit the precise weakness leavening the conduct they condemn. The scheme has, in truth, nothing in it so large or liberal as the social idea on which a caste system rests. It is conceived in a far narrower spirit, and is wholly incapable of promoting any end that can properly be called social. Far from comprehending in its aims the general interests of labor, it is not even large enough to embrace those of a single laboring group, or even of the family in its narrowest sense; for, as Mr. Thornton tells us,* "a journeyman is not permitted to teach his own son his own trade, nor, if the lad managed to learn the trade by stealth, would he be permitted to practice it. A master, desiring out of charity to take as apprentice one of the eight destitute orphans of a widowed mother, has been told by his men that if he did they would strike. A brick-layer's assistant who by looking on has learned to lay bricks as well as his principal, is generally doomed, nevertheless, to continue a laborer for life. He will never rise to the rank of brick-layer, if those who have already attained that dignity can help it."

The rule is thus a purely mechanical one, and operates wholly irrespective of any of the conditions on which indus-

---

* "On Labor," p. 343.

trial progress or human well-being depends. No attempt is made to control population within the protected trades, any more than outside them. Nor are the privileges enjoyed connected with any qualification which might serve as an educating influence for the people at large. On the contrary, the system presents to them the unedifying spectacle of a portion of their number enjoying exceptional advantages which they have done nothing to deserve, and which they obtain at the expense of others whose natural or moral claim is quite as good as theirs. It thus at once creates privileged classes, and does so in a manner which precludes even such partial advantages as might accrue from a *régime* of privilege.

Mr. Thornton, indeed, has offered a plea for these restrictions which, if it could be made good, might go some way toward excusing them. He writes: "The only apology that can be offered to the many is, that without the sacrifices exacted from them the privileges enjoyed by the few could never be preserved; and that, moreover, the sacrifices may be only temporary, for that the best chance the whole laboring population have of advancing is by each of its separate sections advancing separately, and that therefore each Trades-Union is best consulting the general good by attending in the first instance exclusively to its own." It must of course be admitted that the privileges enjoyed by the few under this scheme can only be preserved by imposing sacrifices on the many; but Mr. Thornton can scarcely have intended this as its justification, since precisely the same can be said for every monopoly that ever existed. The second portion of his plea, that the plan in question, though confined at present to a favored few, may be made instrumental for gradually elevating the whole laboring population, would be more to the purpose if the fact were as he assumes. But this is precisely what I must deny to be the case. The essential nature of the plan absolutely precludes the possibility of its being applied to any such enlarged purpose. For on what does its efficacy depend? Let the reader observe that, as I have already pointed out, it makes no provision for the control of population either within or without the protected trades; and further, that, while it leaves population to proceed as the unchecked instincts of its members may determine, it fails equally to take any steps for making labor more productive: indeed, as I shall presently have occasion to point out, there are other portions of the Trades-Union regulations which tend directly to limit and even positively to reduce the productive powers of industry. On what, then, does the efficacy of the arrangement depend? Simply and exclusively on the circumstance of the monopoly it creates—on the fact that those within the protected trades are few as compared with those who are outside them. Increase the numbers within the protected trades in relation to the outsiders, or, on the other hand, diminish the number of outsiders in relation to those who are protected, and the virtue of the scheme evaporates, and wages inside and outside return to their natural level. The entire efficacy of the system thus depending upon the fact that it is partially applied, the extension of its privileges to the whole population would be equivalent to their complete abrogation. Such a system, from its very nature, is incapable of the development claimed for it. At the utmost it can only do what it actually accomplishes—secure, that is to say, exceptional advantages for a select few, the condition of their enjoyment being that the same advantages shall *not* be shared by the many. I grant it is not for the richer or more educated classes to throw stones here at Trades-Unionists; and I have certainly no desire to do so. There is no class that has not shown itself, when opportunity offered, quite capable of sacrificing the most important interests of the community to the aggrandizement, real or imaginary, of its own members; and the working-classes are in this respect neither better nor worse than others. But if every anti-social regulation is to be sanctioned and upheld among working-men which has ever obtained footing among those who are called their betters, the prospect of social advancement seems but small. Into these class questions, however, I have no wish to enter here. My purpose has been simply to ascertain the real character and bearing of this particular portion of Trades-Union rules; and this is the result to which I am led: I find it to be in its essential character a monopoly of the narrowest kind, capable indeed of accomplishing some small results in favor of a privileged few, but wholly destitute of efficacy as an expedient for helping social improvement; a monopoly, moreover, founded on no principle either of moral desert or of industrial efficiency, but simply on chance or arbitrary selection, and which therefore can not but exert a demoralizing influence on all who come within its scope; in all its aspects presenting an ungracious contrast to all that is best and most generous in the spirit of modern democracy.

"If," says Mr. Mill,* "no improvement were to be hoped for in the general circumstances of the working-classes, the success of a portion of them, however small, in keeping their wages by combination above the market rate, would be wholly a matter of satisfaction. But when the elevation of the character and condition of the entire body has at last become a thing not beyond the reach of rational effort, it is time that the better paid classes of skilled artisans should seek their own advantage in common with, and not by the exclusion of, their fellow-laborers. While they continue to fix their hopes on hedging themselves in against competition, and protecting their own wages by shutting out others from access to their employment, nothing better can be expected from them than that total absence of any large and generous aims, that almost open disregard of all other objects than high wages and little work for their own small body, which were so deplorably evident in the proceedings and manifestoes of the Amalgamated Society of Engineers during their quarrel with their employers. Success, even if attainable, in raising up a protected class of working-people, would now be a hinderance, instead of a help, to the emancipation of the working-classes at large."

---

* "Principles of Political Economy," vol. ii., pp. 554, 555.

§ 3. There is yet another line of conduct by which Trades-Unions may and do seek to act upon the rate of wages—a course which is directed neither to augmenting the sum total of wealth applied to the payment of wages, nor yet to restricting the supply of labor, but to enhancing the difficulties of production, and thereby increasing the quantity of work needed to be done—in a word, it seeks to raise wages by "making work."

Now this portion of Trades-Union policy rests upon a view of the wages problem at once so plausible and so fallacious, and withal so pregnant with practical mischief, that I think it will be worth our while, before entering into the particular rules by which it is sought to carry it into effect, to consider briefly the theoretic principle underlying it; and I am the more disposed to do so, because I find that those who favor this principle are by no means confined to the supporters of Trades-Unions. In point of fact, in the discussions which have lately taken place on the wages problem, the soundness of the view in question has been very generally taken for granted on both sides. In Mr. Thornton's work it is not merely taken for granted: the doctrine is deliberately put forward and formally defended as an indubitable principle of economic science. Mr. Thornton indeed, it is proper to say, while upholding the theory, strongly denounces its practical application in the rules of Trades-Unions; but this logical inconsistency will not deprive his advocacy of the weight which naturally attaches to it; and I shall therefore make no apology for examining the doctrine as I find it set forth and defended in his work. The character and scope of the principle to which I refer will appear from the following passages.

At page 87 Mr. Thornton writes:

"The quantity of labor which an employer needs depends upon the work he wants to have done. If there are certain jobs which it is essential to him to get finished within a certain time, he will, if labor be dear, consent to pay pretty high for the quantity needed to complete the jobs within the time. But he will not, merely because labor happens to be cheap instead of dear, hire more than that quantity. If, on Saturday morning, he wants his hay cut or carried before night, and if fewer than ten men would not suffice, he will, perhaps, consent to give ten men 5s. apiece, but he would not engage twenty men for the same service, even if he could get them for 1s. a head."

Again, at page 103:

"This happens [*i. e.*, the demand for labor is urgent] in new colonies, in which the extent of land to be tilled, and the number of sheep or oxen to be tended, and of meals to be cooked, and floors to be scrubbed, is generally out of all proportion to the number of available hinds and herds, cooks and house-maids."

And lastly, I find this more decisive passage at page 339:

"I am myself unable to understand how mere labor-saving machinery can possibly, if no counteracting cause intervene, fail to diminish the demand for labor. If, indeed, the machinery increased the productiveness of labor in a greater ratio than that in which it saved labor, its influence on employment would be different. If, by using improved implements, one man were enabled not merely to do the work of two, but to turn out more produce than the two together had formerly done, the demand for labor might remain unabated, or might increase. If with only half the previous expenditure of labor two ears of wheat were made to grow where but one grew before, or twice as much iron-stone were brought to the pit's mouth, or twice as many herrings were caught, those men for whom there was no longer place in the corn-field, or in the mine, or on the fishing-ground, might yet find full employment in making the additional wheat into bread, or in smelting the additional ore, or in curing and packing the additional fish. But if there be no more corn, and no more ore, and no more fish than usual, if the new machinery has created no new work, and has only enabled the old work to be done with fewer hands, thereby causing some old hands to be discharged, how can it be asserted that the field of employment is enlarged? how denied that it is diminished?"

The theory expressed or implied in these passages is that the *demand* for labor, in so far as it affects the *wages* of labor, depends upon and is measured by the quantity of industrial work to be done, which quantity of industrial work, Mr. Thornton tells us, is "at any given time a fixed quantity" (pp. 334, 335); a position from which the direct inference is—an inference partially drawn by Mr. Thornton himself—that the interests of labor are promoted by whatever tends to increase the quantity of work which society has to do; while those interests are proportionally prejudiced by whatever tends to curtail the quantity of needed work. Now there can be no question as to the very great plausibility of this doctrine. I suppose there are very few working-men, and perhaps not a great many outside their ranks, who would not accept it as thus stated. We all see at once that labor will only be employed where there is work to be done; and again, that the more work there is to do of a particular kind, the more laborers there will be employed in doing that particular work; while it is also true that, where the work required is of a very urgent kind, employers will be disposed to raise their offer of wages in order to attract labor. All this is indisputably sound and true; and the conclusion drawn from these unquestionable premises, that the interest of the laboring classes lies in the work needed by society being as great and as urgent as possible, certainly seems plausible enough. Nevertheless I must make bold to say that, within the range of economic reasoning, no more profound fallacy finds a place than is contained in this inference: nor, I must add, is there one more pregnant with practical consequences of a pernicious kind. Observe some of the consequences that flow from it. If the interests of labor require that the quantity of work to be done by labor be as large as possible, then it follows that all labor-saving machines are opposed to the laborer's interests. Mr. Thornton, as we have seen, admits that this is so whenever the new machinery does not, as in the instances which he adduces, create as much new work as it sets aside of old (p. 339). What proportion of all the machinery employed in helping industry in this country would, under this qualification, escape condemnation, as not injurious to the laborer's interests, I will not attempt to conjecture—I should expect an exceedingly minute fraction of it; but at least it is evident that so much of it as is used in the later stages of manufacture—certainly all connected with the finishing stages of the process—would fall under the description of machinery which created no new work to take the place of what it superseded; and would therefore, according to Mr. Thornton's view, be properly characterized as hostile to the interests of labor. Again, by parity of reasoning, separation of employments is opposed to the same interests; for what else is the purpose of thus organizing industry, but in order to make it more effective; in other words, to abridge the amount of society's work? If every man who took part in pin-making were compelled to make the entire pin—to draw out the wire, to straighten it, to cut it, to point it, to grind it at the top for receiving the head, to make and put on the head, etc. —the number of men required for the work of pin-making would be indefinitely greater than at present, and, no other work being superseded, the field for the employment of labor would, according to the view we are considering, be greatly extended. Division of labor, therefore, which narrows this field, is, according to this principle, plainly opposed to the interests of labor. Nor is free trade less clearly condemned by the same doctrine. The international exchange which it promotes is merely an example of division of labor on a great scale, and works toward precisely the same end as the more simple forms—the economy of labor in the production of commodities. But these examples only represent one side of the consequences which may be drawn and have been drawn from this notable principle; for if the laborer is damnified by whatever tends to abridge the "work to be done," we may also argue conversely that he must be proportionally benefited by whatever increases it, more particularly if the additional work be of an urgent kind. A hurricane, *e. g.*, which strips our roofs, and smashes our windows, and sweeps away our haggards, becomes in the light of this theory a beneficent influence, pregnant with riches for the sons of toil—*

> "The clouds we so much dread
> Are big with mercy, and shall break
> In blessings on *their* head."

It increases the quantity of work to be done, and so, as the saying goes, "is all for the good of trade." So also must it be for the good of trade, according to the same doctrine, that thieves and burglars should abound, since does it not create plenty of policeman's work? Does it not compel us to place bolts and bars upon our doors and windows, thus creating work for smiths and carpenters? Further, consider all the work that is rendered imperative by the aggressive instincts and ambitious designs of nations against each other: standing armies, arsenals and fortifications, arms and ammunition — what a vast amount of work to be done do not these things represent! And how would not merely the soldier's, but the productive laborer's occupation be gone, or at all events be seriously abridged, if ever the disastrous consummation should arrive of general disarmament and universal peace! We are accustomed to laugh at the celebrated petition of the chandlers

---

* That I have not exaggerated the argument will be seen from the following extract from an editorial article in the New York *Tribune* (October 24, 1871) *apropos* of the burning of Chicago, which I find in Mr. Wells's Essay in the Cobden Club volume: "The money to replace what has been burned will not be sent abroad to enrich foreign manufactures; but, thanks to the wise policy of protection which has built up American industries, *it will stimulate our own manufactures, set our mills running faster, and give employment to thousands of idle workmen.* Thus in a short time our abundant natural resources will restore what has been lost, and in converting the raw material our manufacturing interests will take on a new activity."

and lamp-manufacturers, recorded by M. Bastiat, for excluding the light of the sun. But the simple object of that petition was to increase the quantity of social work to be performed; and, for my part, I am unable to see how those who accept the theory I am now combating could consistently refuse their signatures.

Where, then, is the fallacy in the reasoning which leads to these conclusions? If labor will only be employed where work is to be done, and will be employed more largely in any given work in proportion as there is more of that work to do; and if again, as the work becomes more urgent, the laborer is more sought; why is it wrong to say that it is the interest of the laborer that the quantity of work to be done should be as large, and the need for it as urgent, as possible? The answer is twofold: in the first place, what laborers are interested in is not work, but remuneration. People, said Archbishop Whately, go about saying "they want work," when what they really want is wages. This sounds like a jest; but the confusion of thought it exposes is precisely the confusion embodied in the argument just stated. Work and wages are there assumed to be, if not strictly convertible terms, at least facts so closely bound together that an increase of the one may be taken as equivalent to an increase of the other. Now, before going further, it may be well to expose the utter groundlessness of this notion as a matter of fact; and a Blue Book recently issued by the Government* fortunately supplies me with what is necessary for this purpose.

I take the three countries, Germany, England, and California: I find that in the first the number of hours in a working day varies between fourteen, for some occupations, and, for the great majority, twelve. In England it is now mostly ten, but, in an increasing number of trades, nine only. In California

---

* "Condition of the Working-classes in Foreign Countries," 1871.

ten is the maximum, while in many trades the number is as low as eight. Now it would no doubt be unwarrantable to assume that the work to be done in different countries varied for a given quota of working-people with the number of hours in a working day, inasmuch as one man may put as much work into nine hours as another into fourteen; but the criterion would be correct unless so far as it was affected by the different efficiency of labor in different countries. Taking account of this, and assuming, what I imagine is quite in excess of the truth, that English labor is more efficient than German in the proportion of fourteen or twelve to ten or nine, it would follow that the work to be done in Germany would bear about the same proportion to her laboring population as the work to be done in England bears to the laboring population of this country. With regard to California, I do not suppose it would be contended that labor there is more efficient than in England, and we may, therefore, assume that the work to be done in the two countries, in its relation to the laboring population of each, is fairly represented by the respective lengths of their working-day. The result of our comparison then is, that the work to be done in the three countries, Germany, England, and California, bears about the same proportion in each to the number of the laboring population. This being so, if the connection between work and wages be such as the theory we are considering assumes, wages in the three countries should be about the same. In point of fact, I need scarcely say wages in California, even after making all due allowance for the difference in the range of local prices here and there, are at least double what they are in England, and at least four times what they are in Germany. So little connection is there in reality between the quantity of work which a given society has to perform and the rates of wages prevailing in that society.

This, however, is neither the only, nor the least fallacy involved in the doctrine we are considering. It is a necessary assumption in that doctrine—indeed the position is formally taken by Mr. Thornton—that "the quantity of work to be done" is at any given time a "fixed" quantity. Now this must at once be met by a direct denial. The work which society has to do is not a fixed quantity. On the contrary, it is absolutely indefinite and practically unlimited: indefinite, as varying with human wants and desires; and practically unlimited, because always far in excess of what human hands can accomplish. I am speaking now, not of society in its early stages, when human desires, and therefore the work of society, may, with some truth, be said to be confined within certain narrow and tolerably fixed bounds, but of society as we know it in Western Europe and the United States, after civilization has kindled those insatiable aspirations and created those innumerable needs which distinguish the civilized from the uncivilized man. In society, when it has reached this stage, there is no practical limit to the desires of human beings, nor therefore to the quantity of work which they would wish to have done; and even though the course of civilization should be, as I trust it may be, toward the adoption of simpler tastes and habits in all that concerns mere physical well-being, the introduction of more simple modes of life, while limiting the range of wants in one direction, would not fail, we may reasonably assume, to open the door to new paths of expenditure in others. Benevolence and public spirit, the interests of science and literature, would become powerful and exigent, as the tastes for mere physical luxury and personal indulgence or aggrandizement declined, and would rapidly create wants to take the place of those which would now be no longer felt. The social work to be done, therefore, though under such a *régime* as we are contemplating differing much from that which now occupies industry, would still be as indefinite and as practically unlimited as ever. There is thus no practical limit to the quantity of social work to be performed; and we may now see the true nature of the relation in which all the various contrivances—machinery, separation of employments, free trade—which tend to economize and abridge human labor, stand to the interests of those whose labor they supersede. Their effect is not to curtail the aggregate amount of social work—that, as I have said, is always far in excess of what human capacity can accomplish—but to alter the nature of that work. So much labor and capital are relieved from the tasks formerly required of them, and set free for the performance of new work, for the satisfaction of cravings hitherto unfelt. I quite admit that the change from one mode of production, or from one system of industry to another, even though that other be a better one, is almost always attended with more or less temporary inconvenience, and sometimes even with considerable suffering, for those whose occupations have been displaced; and this is a good reason for society doing all in its power to alleviate and repair these inevitable but transitory evils. But we have now to do, not with the incidental consequences of improvements, but with their essential character and permanent significance as regards the interests of labor: and I say that, regarding them in this light, their tendency is, not to leave society without occupation, but to alter from time to time the occupations with which society busies itself—to provide for the easier satisfaction of its primary and more pressing wants, and thereby to render possible the further satisfaction of numerous secondary wants of a less urgent kind. A limit indeed there is—a very real limit—to the employment of labor in a limited area of country; but that limit does not lie in the quantity of social work, but in the productive power of the agents employed in performing it—in other words, in the increasing cost of production. The work is there to do, but the efforts needed to accomplish the work are greater than the product is thought to be worth. Here is the true and only limit to the employment of labor; and its removal or extension is to be sought, not in multiplying the obstacles that oppose the satisfaction of human desires, and so "making work," but in precisely the opposite direction—in the removal, as far as may be, of such obstacles, and in freely availing ourselves of all arts and contrivances by which human effort may be rendered productive of larger result. Increase the productive powers of industry, extend the knowledge of the industrial arts which support and comfort mankind, and there is little danger that laborers will ever fail of employment for want of work to do.

So much, then, for that view of economic doctrine which identifies human well-being with the maintenance and multiplication of the obstacles to its attainment; in the words of Bastiat, confounding obstacle with cause, and effort with result.

§ 4. Let us now observe its practical development in the rules of Trades-Unions. The following examples I take from Mr. Thornton's work:

"Some Unions divide the country round them into districts, and will not permit the products of the trades controlled by them to be used, except within the district in which they have been fabricated. . . . . At Manchester this combination is particularly effective, preventing any bricks made beyond a radius of four miles from entering the city. To enforce the exclusion, paid agents are employed; every cart of bricks coming toward Manchester is watched, and if the contents be found to have come from without the prescribed boundary the brick-layers at once refuse to work. . . . . The vagaries of the Lancashire brick-makers are fairly paralleled by the masons of the same county. Stone, when freshly quarried, is softer, and can be more easily cut than later: men habitually employed about any particular quarry better understand the working of its particular stone than men from a distance; there is great economy, too, in transporting stone dressed instead of in rough blocks. The Yorkshire masons, however, will not allow Yorkshire stone to be brought into their district if worked on more than one side. All the rest of the working, the edging and jointing, they insist on doing themselves, though they thereby add thirty-five per cent. to its price. . . . . A Bradford contractor, requiring for a stair-case some steps of hard delf-stone, a material which Bradford masons so much dislike that they often refuse employment rather than undertake it, got the steps worked at the quarry. But when they arrived ready for setting, his masons insisted on their being worked over again, at an expense of from 5s. to 10s. per step. A master-mason at Ashton obtained some stone ready polished from a quarry near Macclesfield. His men, however, in obedience to the rules of their club, refused to fix it until the polished part had been defaced and they had polished it again by hand, though not so well as at first. . . . .

"In one or two of the northern counties, the associated plasterers and associated plasterers' laborers have come to an understanding, according to which the latter are to abstain from all plasterers' work except simple whitewashing; and the plasterers in return are to do nothing, except pure plasterers' work, that the laborers would like to do for them, insomuch that if a plasterer wants laths or plaster to go on with, he must not go and fetch them himself, but must send a laborer for them. In consequence of this agreement, a Mr. Booth, of Bolton, having sent one of his plasterers to bed and point a dozen windows, had to place a laborer with him during the whole of the four days he was engaged on the job, though any body could have brought him all he required in half a day. . . . . 'Not besting one's mates' has by several Unions been made the subject of special enactment. 'You are strictly cautioned,' says a by-law of the Bradford Brick-layers' Laborers, 'not to overstep good rules by doing double work, and causing others to do the same in order to gain a smile from the master. Such fool-hardy and deceitful actions leave a great portion of good members out of employment. Certain individuals have been guilty, who will be expelled if they do not refrain.' The Manchester Brick-layers' Association have a rule providing that 'any man found running, or working beyond a regular speed, shall be fined 2s. 6d. for the first offense, 5s. for the second, 10s. for the third, and if still persisting shall be dealt with as the committee think proper.' As also shall be 'any man working short-handed, without man for man.' . . . . At Liverpool, a brick-layer's laborer may legally carry as many as twelve bricks at a time. Elsewhere ten is the greatest number allowed. But at Leeds 'any brother in the Union professing to carry more than the common number, which is eight bricks, shall be fined 1s.;' and any brother 'knowing the same without giving the earliest information thereof to the committee of management, shall be fined the same.' . . . . During the building of the Manchester Law Courts, the brick-layers' laborers struck because they were desired to wheel bricks instead of carrying them on their shoulders."

The purpose and general tendency of these regulations can not be mistaken. Their object is, by enforcing uneconomical methods, and proscribing recourse to the facilities offered by nature and circumstances, to create a necessity for work which otherwise would not have existed. The code is, from first to last, an example of that view of Political Economy of which the culminating triumph would be the exclusion of the light of the sun. It must be admitted at once that the method is not devoid of a certain efficacy. It does tend to cause a larger capital to be invested in certain trades than would otherwise find entrance to them, and thus either to raise the rate of wages in them, or to increase the number of laborers employed at a given rate. So much must be admitted. But then this end is attained at the cost of diminishing the sum total of result from human industry, so that whatever gain it procures for the individuals or classes who benefit by it is necessarily purchased at the cost of inflicting *a more than equivalent loss* on society as a whole. I say a more than equivalent loss; for the total return upon industry being diminished by this preposterous policy, while the share of certain classes is increased, it is plain that what falls to the remainder will be less, not merely by what the former gain, but by this *plus* the loss upon the entire social fund. The sort of selfishness, therefore, embodied in these rules of Trades-Unions is not selfishness of the ordinary humdrum kind, which merely grasps for one's self what would fairly have gone to another, but that more extreme form of the propensity which is ready to inflict a great evil on another in order to secure a small good for one's self—to burn down our neighbor's house in order to roast our own egg. Nor is this the most serious objection to this portion of the Unionist code. It carries the deeper stigma of sinning against the interests of civilization itself; for its spirit is antagonistic to all progress and improvement, and, if it did not carry us back, as logically it ought, to a rejection of all the labor-saving contrivances and aids which art and science have won for industry, would, at the very least, tend to stereotype industrial operations in their existing forms. The very meaning of industrial progress is the increase of the productive result in proportion to the labor undergone; while the direct tendency of the rules in question is to increase the labor undergone in proportion to the productive result. I am far, indeed, from desiring to charge these consequences, as a deliberate purpose, on the Unionist leaders, and still less on the workmen who have accepted and acted on their legislation. On the contrary, I am persuaded that the true character of those regulations is either entirely misconceived, or, at the utmost, most inadequately appreciated, by those for whose benefit they are intended. The view which has suggested them, far from being confined to the working-classes, has, as we have seen, found for its champion so able and dispassionate a writer as Mr. Thornton, who, while denouncing in language which certainly leaves nothing to be desired in point of vigor and heartiness those elaborate contrivances for rendering man's position in the world worse than it might be, has himself furnished the theoretical premises which would be quite sufficient, if only they were well founded, to justify the most extravagant of the acts which he reprobates. It must also be frankly confessed, with reference to this as with reference to other parts of the Unionist policy, that the better-off classes of society are by no means entitled to plume themselves at the expense of the workmen. In the practice of the legal profession, *e. g.*, there would, I fancy, be no difficulty in finding usages, not yet perhaps quite obsolete, conceived in this same spirit of aggrandizing a calling by "making work" for its members. One has only to watch the progress of an ordinary Chancery suit, or to read through an ordinary deed, to find examples which would scarcely lose in lustre by being placed beside some of the brightest of those furnished by the Manchester Brick-layers' Association. What, indeed, is the opposition given to law reform by too large a section of the legal profession but a flagrant example of this very spirit—a readiness to sacrifice the interests of society at large to those of the legal profession, to arrest the progress of social improvement, in order that work may be found for a few lawyers the more? The notion of aggrandizing one's order by "making work" for it may assume in Trades-Union codes a somewhat more extravagant and grotesque form than elsewhere; but the principle itself is deeply embedded in the practical modes of thinking and acting of nearly all classes; and it therefore needs all the more to have its true character and tendencies laid bare without reserve, and to be duly stigmatized as the most intensely selfish and the most flagrantly anti-social of all the plans of conduct by which, at various times, different classes of society have attempted, in disregard of the general social weal, to advance their several interests.

CHAPTER V.

PRACTICAL DEDUCTIONS FROM THE FOREGOING PRINCIPLES.

§ 1. IN the foregoing chapters the theoretical conditions governing the position of the laborer and the rate of his remuneration, have, it is to be hoped, been pretty fully set forth. It remains now to consider the practical conclusions, in relation to his actual condition and future prospects, which may be drawn from the premises thus furnished.

But at this point an objection would probably be interposed by a certain class of thinkers on social subjects, and I may be challenged to say why, conceding the economic principles affecting the subject to be such as I have stated them, the distribution of the produce of industry should be left to be determined by those principles; why it should not rather be regulated by the laws of justice? In answer to which I must reply, in the first place, that I am unaware of any rule of justice applicable to the problem of distributing the produce of industry; and, secondly, that any attempt to give effect to what are considered the dictates of justice, which should involve as a means toward that end a disturbance of the fundamental assumptions on which economic reasoning is based—more especially those of the right of private property and the freedom of individual industry—would, in my opinion, putting all other than material considerations aside, be inevitably followed by the destruction or indefinite curtailment of the fund itself from which the remuneration of all classes is derived.

§ 2. If justice be the principle according to which the proceeds of industry ought to be distributed, those who advocate this mode of distribution are bound to produce some working rule according to which the principle they contend for is to be carried into effect. Several such rules have indeed been propounded, and others may easily be imagined, which would have quite as good a title to the claim of representing natural justice as any that have been advanced by social reformers. For example, it has been held by one social reformer that the rule of distribution required by justice is that indicated by the wants of human beings and the degree of their urgency, in accordance with which view the formula of distributive justice would be—"to each according to his wants." In the opinion of another, distribution ought to be regulated by the degree in which each has contributed by his efforts to the fund available for distribution; the formula of distributive justice becoming in this case—"to each according to his works." And perhaps as plausible a principle as either might be constructed by founding the rule of distribution on the proportional sacrifice undergone by those who take part in the work of productive industry; in which case we should have as our formula—"to each according to his sacrifice." As to the amount of truth or morality which these several maxims embody, I am not concerned here to inquire. My business with them has reference exclusively to their efficacy as rules for regulating the distribution of wealth. But in proceeding to examine them with this view, I am anxious to disclaim all desire to disparage the ideals of human life which they suggest, provided they be regarded simply as ideals—as a goal toward which one may work and strive, due consideration being had of the actual circumstances of the external world, and of the character, as hitherto actually developed, of human beings residing upon it: indeed, so far from this, I have no hesitation in admitting that the realization of any one of them would imply a condition of society incomparably superior to any that now exists, or is likely for a long time to exist. So far I am quite prepared to join in socialistic aspirations. Where I take issue with the Socialists is as to the present feasibility of their schemes, and as to the means by which the ends they desire are to be promoted. I altogether deny that in the actual circumstances of mankind the distribution of wealth on the principles they contend for is feasible; and I believe that the attempt to carry those principles into effect by invoking for this purpose the powers of the State—which I take to be the essential characteristic of Socialism, and that which broadly distinguishes it from other modes of social speculation*—could only issue in disaster and ruin.

---

* In this I venture to differ from the great man recently taken from among us, whom I am proud to call my friend and teacher. In a remarkable passage of the "Autobiography," Mr. Mill represents himself as properly classed "under the general designation of Socialists," because his ideal of ultimate improvement had more in common with that of Socialistic reformers than with the views of those who in contradistinction would be called orthodox. "While we repudiated with the greatest energy that tyranny of society over the individual which most socialistic systems are supposed to involve, we yet looked forward to a time when society will no longer be divided into the idle and the industrious; when the rule that they who do not work shall not eat will be applied, not to paupers only, but impartially to all; when the division of the produce of labor, instead of depending, as in so great a degree it now does, on the accident of birth, will be made by concert on an acknowledged principle of justice; and when it will no longer either be, or be thought to be, impossible for human beings to exert themselves strenuously in procuring benefits which are not to be exclusively their own, but to be shared with the society they belong to." ("Autobiography," pp. 231, 232.) If to look forward to such a state of things as an ideal to be striven for is Socialism, I at once acknowledge myself a Socialist; but it seems to me that the idea which "Socialism" conveys to most minds is not that of any particular form of society to be realized at a future time when the character of human beings and the conditions of human life are widely different from what they now are, but rather certain modes of action—more especially the employment of the powers of the State for the instant accomplishment of ideal schemes, which is the invariable attribute of all projects generally regarded as Socialistic. So entirely is this the case, that it is common to hear any proposal which is thought to involve an undue extension of the powers of the State branded as Socialistic, whatever be the object it may seek to accomplish. After all, the question is one of nomenclature merely; but people are so

§ 3. As regards the first of the formulas to which I have referred, which proposes to distribute the wealth of a community among its members in proportion to their wants, I must frankly acknowledge that I am wholly unable even to conjecture the method of its application. How are the wants of individuals to be ascertained? Is it to be left to each to describe his own wants? And if the funds are not adequate to meet the requirements of all, who is to decide as to which wants are the most urgent? A man with a large family has greater wants than a man with a small one. Does this constitute a title to a proportionally larger share of the proceeds of industry? And if so, what is to keep the population of a country within the necessary limits of the means of subsistence? Such are some of the questions which meet us on the threshold in seeking to apply this formula, every one of which, it seems to me, leads us straight into a *cul de sac*. I must therefore put aside this particular form of the law of distributive justice as for me utterly unmanageable. The two latter principles, however, of which one would assign wealth to each person in proportion to the work he has accomplished, and the other in proportion to the sacrifice he has undergone, are not at once and obviously impracticable; and in point of fact both one and the other do exert, under our existing system of industry, a certain influence in determining the distribution of wealth. For example, wherever the results of industry admit of being measured and compared, as in all work of the same kind, the remuneration of the workman, if only competition is effective, naturally adjusts itself to the results of his work. A workman who in a given time can perform twice as much of a given work as another will in an open market command twice as much wages. But where the results of industry are

greatly governed by words that I can not but regret that a philosophy of social life with which I so deeply sympathize should be prejudiced by verbal associations fitted, as it seems to me, only to mislead.

different in kind, how is the rule of distribution in proportion to results to be applied? One man in a day produces a coat, another a table, a third superintends a body of workmen—by what standard shall we measure these several results, and say that any of them is greater or less than any other? It is plain that the rule of distribution in proportion to results fails us utterly here. Similarly, the principle of distribution in proportion to sacrifice has also, under our present *régime* (as was seen in a former portion of this work), a certain operation in determining the distribution of wealth. It is indeed the ruling principle of distribution wherever competition among producers is really free. But, as was then pointed out, the field of competition, though large, is far from being co-extensive with the industry of any country, and, in the absence of competition, it is not easy to see how relative sacrifice is to be determined. More particularly does this difficulty become formidable when we come to deal with what may be regarded as the crucial problem of distribution—the distribution of the proceeds of industry between laborer and capitalist. Even could the claims of laborers as among themselves be adjusted, there would still remain this problem, which the least consideration of the facts involved will show to be wholly unamenable to *a priori* treatment, whatever be the form which the rule of justice may assume.

Let us suppose, for example, a benevolent despot desirous of applying to this case what we may describe as the principle of efficiency—"to each according to his works." He finds that a house has been built by the combined action of a master-builder and workmen: the former has supplied the materials for the building and the means of supporting the laborers during the performance of the work, the latter have furnished the labor: how is our despot to determine how much of the house or of its value is to be credited respectively to him who has supplied the capital, and to those who by their labor have converted this capital into a house? Again, a master-tailor supplies a sewing-machine and cloth; journeymen tailors go to work on these articles, and a suit of clothes is the result—what proportion of the clothes is to be credited respectively to the machine and to the workmen? It is only necessary to propound such questions to perceive that they are absolutely insoluble. As well might we seek to determine the proportions in which the oxygen, the hydrogen, and the electric flash have contributed to the drop of water which results from their combined action. Nor would the standard of relative sacrifice be any more to our purpose here. As I have already remarked, it is not easy to see how relative sacrifice is to be estimated in the absence of competition; and more particularly is this the case where the sacrifices to be compared take forms so widely different in character as those undergone by laborer and capitalist. What are those sacrifices? On the one hand, certain physical and mental efforts, involving weariness, exhaustion, and sometimes positive pain; on the other, a mere abstinence from enjoyment which might have been indulged in, accompanied with a certain sense of insecurity as to the issue of an undertaking. Who can compare and appraise two such sacrifices, and undertake to assign to each its due reward? Manifestly at this point, the principle of sacrifice, no less than that of efficiency, inevitably breaks down. Even could they have solved all other cases, we are forced to confess that, in presence of the most important and pressing of all — the relative claims of labor and capital—both principles are impotent alike. Right or wrong, therefore, they are inapplicable to the question in hand, and so will not serve our turn.

§ 4. I am thus unable to find in the maxims of abstract justice any key to the practical problems of the distribution of wealth; and I am bound to add, that just as little can I discover in the actual results flowing from the action of econom ical laws a realization of the principles of abstract justice. There is indeed a school of economists, of whom M. Bastiat may be taken as the prophet, who have persuaded themselves that such a realization is in fact accomplished, who hold that the distribution of wealth which results from the free play of economic forces is not merely that which the circumstances of the case render inevitable, but also that which justice and natural right prescribe. I must frankly own that I am wholly unable to concur in this view. For when I look into the nature of those economic forces on the play of which the actual distribution of wealth in this and other civilized countries depends, what do I find? Certain physical, physiological, and mental conditions—on the one hand, a productive capacity in the soil and other natural agents; on the other, certain elements in the character of the people, such as the desire to accumulate wealth and provide for the future, and constantly counteracting this, a love of present ease and indulgence: lastly, the animal propensities which continue and multiply the race. These are the forces which, coming into play under a *régime* of private property and freedom of individual industry and enterprise, determine the proportions in which wealth is divided among a people. But what is there in such circumstances to make it necessary that the distribution which results shall be in conformity with what our ideas of justice would require? What is there in the case to secure that the action shall always be in the lines of moral right? The agencies in operation are essentially out of the moral sphere; and if it should in fact happen that the results arising from their free action in any given case prove to be in strict accordance with the claims of moral justice, and with so-called "natural rights," I do not see that we should be justified in regarding the coincidence as other than a fortunate accident. In point of fact, the practical consequences accruing from the conditions of industry in this and other civilized countries are not such as, for my part, I should find it easy to reconcile with any standard of right generally accepted among men.*

§ 5. It seems to follow from these considerations that while, on the one hand, mere standards of abstract justice or natural right are inefficacious as means of solving the actual problems of the distribution of wealth, on the other the solution actually effected of those problems under our existing system of industry is not such as entitles us to claim for it, as a necessary consequence of the agencies through which it is worked out, the character of satisfying the requirements of moral justice. If our present system of industry is to be justified, it must, according to my view, find its justification in quite another order of ideas than those of abstract right or natural law—namely, in the considerations of practical utility; and more specifically in the fact that it secures for the mass of mankind a greater amount of material and moral well-being, and provides more effectually for their progress in civilization, than any other plan that has been yet, or apparently can be, devised.

By our present system of industry, let me here explain, I mean simply the industrial arrangements and the mode of distributing wealth which prevail in this and other civilized countries, so far, and so far only, as these result from the recognition of private property and freedom of individual industry and enterprise. These latter institutions, it is true, are far from representing fixed and absolute conditions; and the modifications with which they are affected in different countries lead to important differences in the practical outcome accruing from their maintenance. Into the question of such modifica-

---

* I may here at least claim Shakspeare as an authority on my side:

> "Take physic, Pomp,
> Expose thyself to feel what wretches feel;
> That thou may'st shake the superflux to them,
> And show *the heavens more just.*"

tions I do not enter here. The issue taken by those who advance socialistic objections, founded on allegations of inequality and injustice, against existing industrial arrangements, has regard to the principles themselves, not to their modifications; and, therefore, in defending these arrangements against such objections, it is with the principles alone that we need concern ourselves. Nor, indeed, have I any need here to enter at large into the controversy between Communism and private property. That question may now, I think, be said to be, so far as argument can carry it, sufficiently disposed of: at all events, I could hope to add nothing to what Mr. Mill has so admirably said in his examination of the subject—an examination not less remarkable for its thoroughness than for the candor, and even tenderness toward those whose opinions he opposes, which it displays. But, without entering into the general question, I may venture to point out one capital consideration of a purely economic kind which, apart from the reasons, chiefly moral and political, relied on by Mr. Mill, appears to me to justify the opinion in favor of our existing system of industry in its essential circumstances which I have ventured to express.

I take it to be a fundamental and indispensable condition of all progressive human society, that by some means or other a large aggregate capital available for its requirements should be provided. Without such a fund, accumulated from the products of past toil, division of labor and continuous industry are impossible; population can not attain the degree of density indispensable to civilized existence; nor can that amount of leisure from physical toil be secured for any considerable portion of the people, which is required for the cultivation of science and literature. The maintenance, therefore, of an aggregate capital capable of providing for these requirements must be regarded as an indispensable condition to be fulfilled by every industrial system which undertakes to promote the well-being and progress of mankind. Now our economic investigations have shown us that this end, the storing up of the products of past industry for the purpose of sustaining and assisting present industry, can only be attained at the cost of certain sacrifices—those sacrifices, namely, implied in foregoing the immediate use of what people have the power of using, and in incurring the risk which attaches in a greater or less degree to all industrial investment. These sacrifices may be regarded as trivial or severe; but, as a matter of fact, they will not be undergone without an adequate motive in the form of a compensating reward. Such a motive our present system of industry provides in the maintenance of private property and industrial freedom. The prospect of profit is the prospect of enjoying as property the results of industrial investment; and this prospect under a system of industrial freedom is thrown open to all who are in possession of wealth. The inducement thus offered to the acquisitive propensity in man constitutes, under the actual system of things, the great spring and support of productive capital, and, in the last resort, the ultimate security for all the results which go to form our material civilization. The feeling appealed to may, if you like, be a coarse one, but it is at any rate efficacious; it *does* lead to habitual and systematic saving, and furnishes society with the necessary material basis for civilized progress. But this motive every system which annuls private property and freedom of individual industry takes away; and the question is, What do such systems supply in its place? Two possible substitutes, so far as I know, and two only, have been or can be suggested—benevolence and public spirit. I should be very unwilling to disparage such principles of action, or to deny that they are at present extensively influential in human affairs; but I can not affect to believe that either, or that both together—taking human beings, not as in the progress of human improvement they may possibly become, but as we now actually find them—could be trusted to supply the place of that desire for individual advancement and well-being to which the institutions of private property and industrial freedom make appeal. I am, therefore, unable to see how any system, which relies upon no stronger or more universal elements of human character than these for its support, can fulfill that primary and indispensable condition of all progressive society—the providing of a material basis for civilization in the form of an accumulated capital.

§ 6. So much I have thought it well to say in justification of the fundamental bases of our present industrial system: it remains to consider what are the prospects offered by the system to the working-classes living under it, taking their condition to be governed by the economic laws developed in the previous portions of this work.

The remuneration of industry, as we there saw, is derived from, and therefore must be limited by, the products which result from its exercise. In this exercise two distinct functions are embraced — that performed by labor and that performed by capital, each implying a sacrifice and demanding a reward. To the share of the produce to be assigned to the laborer Nature has herself very obviously set a minimum limit in the requirements essential to his existence: it can never permanently be less than will suffice to support, in such physical and mental strength as the work performed calls for, those who carry it on. On the other hand, the capitalist's share also finds a minimum limit in his disposition and character: it must at least be such as shall seem to him a sufficient compensation for the sacrifices which he incurs in investment, and will, therefore, in a given community be high or low, according as that element of character designated by Mr. Mill "the effective desire of accumulation" is weak or strong. It follows from this that, in order to the systematic prosecution of industry, the produce resulting must at least be sufficiently great to cover both these requirements—to yield, that is to say, a minimum wage and a minimum profit; if it be not equal to this, either labor will fail for want of support, or capital will cease to be invested for want of adequate inducement. But the produce may be indefinitely greater than this; and hence arises a margin of return over and above what the satisfaction of the minima of wages and of profits demands. Now it is evident that by the extent of this fund the possibilities of the laborer's position must, under all circumstances, be bounded.

Two questions, accordingly, here at once arise; first, as to the possible increase of this margin of return as industry, with the progress of industrial art, becomes more productive; and, secondly, as to the degree in which the working-classes are likely to appropriate such augmentation as may accrue. As regards the latter point, we have seen that profits in advancing communities tend to a minimum, from which we are justified in concluding that, however the gain may for a time be divided between capitalist and laborer, the permanent tendency of things will be toward an absorption of the whole by wages. In whatever degree, therefore, the margin of the return on industry, beyond what is needed to satisfy the minima of wages and profits, may increase with the progress of society, we are warranted in regarding the fund thence arising as available for the improvement of the laborer's condition. The question as to the possibilities of his future—supposing him to remain as at present a mere receiver of wages---thus turns entirely and simply upon the prospects of increase in this fund.

And here I regret to say the outlook of the laborer is by no means so bright as a superficial view of the case might lead us to suppose. Understanding by the rate of wages the real remuneration of the laborer, and by the rate of profit the ratio of the return upon capital, and bearing in mind that wages and profits are derived from, and in fact represent, the products of industry, it might seem a safe position to assume that the fund available for the augmentation of the rates of wages and profits would increase *pari passu* with every extension of the power of man in the industrial sphere. Plausible, however, as this position seems, we may easily convince ourselves that it can not possibly be true. Let us consider this fact. Within the last century an enormous increase has taken place in the productiveness of industry in Great Britain. A given exertion of labor and capital will now produce in a great many directions five, ten, or twenty times, in some instances perhaps one hundred times, the result which an equal exertion would have produced a hundred years ago: it is not probable that industry is in any direction whatever less productive now than it was then; yet the rate of wages, understanding this in the sense defined, as measured by the real well-being of the laborer— though some improvement no doubt has taken place in his condition during this time—has certainly not advanced in any thing like a corresponding degree; while it may be doubted if the rate of profit has advanced at all. If we were to take the current rate of interest as a criterion, we should be inclined to say that it had even positively fallen. It is certain, at all events, that neither the rate of wages nor the rate of profits, nor both rates combined, have experienced any increase at all commensurate with that which has occurred in the general productiveness of industry. Some one, no doubt, has benefited by the enlarged power of man over material nature; the world is beyond question the richer for it; but what I wish to call attention to is that the gain, however realized, does not show itself, at least on the scale of its actual magnitude, either in the real remuneration of the laborer, or yet in the ratio of return upon the capitalist's outlay.

What, then, is the relation of the productiveness of industry to these phenomena? and how far can we count upon the progress of industrial invention and improvement for enlarging that margin of return out of which all additions to the minimum rates of wages and of profits must be made? The correct answer to this question may, I think, be thus stated: *the productiveness of industry only affects the rates of wages and profits in so far as it results in a cheapening of the commodities which enter into the consumption of the laborer.* This is a point not in general correctly apprehended, but it will not be difficult to establish its truth. Let us suppose an improvement to take place in the mode of producing an article consumed only by the rich, and leading to a cheapened cost of production— what happens? . Assuming that there is no monopoly, and allowing time for supply to adjust itself to demand, there will occur a fall in the value of the article in proportion to the fall in its cost of production. A given capital will yield in this particular commodity a larger return, but this increased return will only possess the same value as the smaller return previously obtained. The ratio, therefore, of the value produced to the value expended will remain undisturbed. It follows that an improvement in industry of this description, however it may temporarily profit individual producers pending the adjustment of supply to the altered conditions of demand, has no tendency to raise the rate of profit.* And it is sufficiently evident that it will not affect the remuneration of labor. Why should it? It has not increased either the capital of the country (for the cheapened article is by hypothesis an article of luxurious consumption) or the value of its products. The laborer's wages, measured in money (which we assume to remain constant in value) continue as before, and the only article cheapened is one which by hypothesis he does

---

* This position would require qualification if the article of luxurious consumption which I have supposed to be cheapened could be made the means, through an exchange with foreign countries, of obtaining on cheaper terms food or other laborer's commodities.

not consume. If I am asked, Who then are the persons who benefit by improvements of this class? I answer, those who consume the commodity. If capitalists are consumers, then they will benefit *as consumers*, but not in their quality of receivers of profits. They will receive the same rate of return on their investment as before, but the sum resulting from this rate of return will give them a larger command than before over the articles of their consumption. We thus find that improvements in productive industry, where they apply to commodities consumed only by the rich, however they may benefit the rich, have no tendency to raise the rate of profit; while they leave the remuneration of the laborer entirely unaffected. But now observe the consequence of improvements of another kind—those, namely, which affect commodities entering into the consumption of the laborer. Here, again, as in the case just considered, the article affected by the improvement would fall in price in proportion to the cheapening of its cost; but one or other of the following consequences would also happen: either the real remuneration of the laborer would increase in proportion to the cheapening of the commodity multiplied by the degree in which it entered into his expenditure; or, failing this, the rate of profit would rise. It is probable that, in the first instance at least, the former result is that which would occur. There is nothing in the cheapening of an article of the laborer's consumption to diminish the investment of capital or at once to increase the supply of labor. Money wages, therefore (the value of money being assumed to remain constant), would continue as before, and the laborer, in common with other consumers, would reap the benefit of the improvement in the diminished price of the commodity. If this did not happen—if money wages fell, let us suppose, so as just to neutralize the cheapened cost of the commodity, leaving the laborer's real remuneration unaffected—then the state of things would imply an advance in the rate of profit; for the price of

the commodity falling in proportion as its cost had diminished
—that is to say, as the product of a given exertion of industry
employed in making it had increased—the value of the aggregate return upon industry thus employed would be the same
as before; but the value of the outlay upon the same exertion
of industry would have declined in consequence of the fall in
money wages, and the ratio of the return to the outlay, that is
to say, the rate of profit, would therefore have increased. It
is thus through a limited class of commodities only that the
progress of industry affects either the rate of profit or the laborer's well-being; in other directions improvements may occur and commodities be indefinitely cheapened to the advantage of consumers, but without extending in the least that margin of return from which augmentations of wages and profits
are derived.

And now I am in a position to explain the phenomenon to
which I have called attention—the fact, namely, that so little
impression has been made on the rate of wages and profits by
the immense industrial progress of recent times. The explanation lies in the following circumstances: 1st, the improvements have to a very large extent affected commodities *not*
consumed by the laborer; and, so far as this has been the case,
there is, as we have seen, nothing in the circumstance of an
increase in industrial efficiency to cause an advance in either
wages or profits; and, 2dly, when the improvement *has* affected commodities consumed by the laborer, the industrial advantage gained has rarely been maintained to its full extent, and
frequently after a time has been entirely lost. What has happened has been a temporary improvement of the laborer's condition, followed by an increase of population and an enlarged
demand for the cheapened commodity. Laborers' commodities, however, are for the most part commodities of raw produce, or in which the raw material constitutes the chief element of the value (clothing is, in truth, the only important ex-

ception); and of all such commodities it is the well-known law that an augmentation of quantity can only be obtained, other things being the same, at an increasing proportional cost. Thus it has happened that the gain in productiveness obtained by improved processes has, after a generation, to a great extent been lost — lost, that is to say, for any benefit that can be derived from it in favor of wages or profits; and though our industry is conducted with greater skill than formerly, yet being employed on natural agents of inferior power or of greater remoteness, to which the needs of an increasing population have compelled us to resort, and the cost of the portion of the produce raised from those inferior natural agents being that which governs the price of the whole — it comes to pass that it now yields, capital for capital and effort for effort, no greater, or but a slightly greater, return. Not indeed that the introduction of improved processes into agriculture has been for naught: it has resulted in a large augmentation of the aggregate return obtained from the soil, but without permanently lowering its price, and, therefore, without permanent advantage to either capitalist, or laborer, or to other consumers. The large addition to the wealth of the country has gone neither to profits nor to wages, nor yet to the public at large, but to swell a fund ever growing even while its proprietors sleep — the rent-roll of the owners of the soil. Accordingly we find that, notwithstanding the vast progress of agricultural industry effected within a century, there is scarcely an important agricultural product that is not at least as dear now as it was a hundred years ago — as dear not merely in money price, but in real cost. The aggregate return from the land has immensely increased; but the cost of the costliest portion of the produce, which is that which determines the price of the whole, remains pretty nearly as it was. Profits, therefore, have not risen at all, and the real remuneration of the laborer, taking the whole field of labor, in but a slight degree — at all events in a degree very far from commensurate with the general progress of industry.*

The reader will not fail to perceive the intimate bearing of the conclusion just reached upon the question which I have proposed for discussion in this chapter—the prospect of improvement in the laborer's material condition. It is evident that this condition is by no means so linked to the general progress of industrial improvement that we can count upon an advance in it *pari passu* with that progress. A very considerable proportion of industrial inventions do not affect his well-being at all; while with regard to those which, by cheapening the commodities of his consumption, do affect his well-being, the condition of permanent advantage to him from this source is that his numbers shall be kept within such limits that the

---

* "How," asks Mr. (now Sir William) Harcourt, "is the laborer to get higher wages, and yet the farmer to receive a reasonable profit, without which his business can not be carried on? There is only one way in which it can be done, and that is by increasing the productive power of the land, which is the fund out of which both the wages and the profit must be realized. Well, how is the productive power of the land to be increased? The answer to that, too, is simple enough, and is universally recognized, by applying more capital to the soil" (*Times*, Jan. 2, 1873). It does not seem to have occurred to Mr. Harcourt that the process which he advocates has been in operation on a great scale for at least a century, and yet that the agricultural laborer remains pretty nearly where he was before it commenced. Had he turned to Belgium, he would have seen the same experiment in operation with precisely the same result. Nowhere has capital been more liberally applied to the cultivation of the soil than in Belgium, and nowhere is agricultural labor more wretchedly paid (see Laveleye's "L'Économie Rurale de la Belgique"). The following passage may be commended to Sir W. Harcourt's notice: "Malgré ces différences assez notables, le mal général et profond qu'on ne peut se dissimuler, c'est qu'à peu près partout le salaire des ouvriers agricoles est insuffisant pour faire face aux besoins de leurs familles dans un pays où les denrées atteignent le plus haut prix des marchés européens. La statistique officielle constate elle-même que la population rurale de la Belgique est l'une des plus mal nourries du continent. Les produits de l'agriculture, quelque abondants qu'ils soient, ne suffisant point, avec la répartition actuelle, pour donner à tous une alimentation convenable" (p. 240).

necessity of resorting to inferior instruments of production shall not neutralize the gain in industrial efficiency. This, then—the limitation of his numbers—is the circumstance on which, in the last resort, any improvement at all of a permanent kind in the laborer's condition turns. For my own part, I can not pretend to discern in the circumstances of the time any solid ground for feeling sanguine on this point, at least so long as laborers remain what they are mainly at present—mere laborers, hired *employés* depending for each day on the result of the day's work. But I desire to go further than this. I think the considerations which have been adduced show that even a very great change in the habits of the laboring classes as bearing upon the increase of population—a change far greater than there seems any solid ground for expecting—would be ineffectual, so long as the laborer remains a mere receiver of wages, to accomplish any great improvement in his state—any improvement at all commensurate with what has taken place, and may be expected hereafter to take place, in the lot of those who derive their livelihood from the profits of capital. This is a point which perhaps needs some clearing up. It might seem to result from one doctrine on which I have laid some stress in this work — the tendency of profits to a minimum, while no such tendency can happily be asserted of wages — that the prospects of the laborer in the future of industry, in comparison with his present condition, were actually brighter than those of the receiver of profit. But any such inference from the doctrine in question would imply a very gross misapprehension of the facts of the case. It is perhaps as well to point out that the expressions "rate of wages" and "rate of profit" do not denote analogous facts with reference to the recipients of those two kinds of income. The rate of real wages expresses, so far as the laborer derives his income from wages, his actual material condition; but the "rate of profit" gives no clue to the position, in this respect, of the capitalist.

A very low rate of profit is compatible, and in fact generally co-exists, with very great wealth among those who derive their income from this source. The explanation lies of course in the fact that the income of this class is measured, not by the rate of profit, but by this multiplied by the amount of their capital, and that this last factor may increase to any extent whatever. Nothing, therefore, can be inferred from the tendency of profits to a minimum as to any limitation on the growth in wealth of those who live upon profits; while, on the other hand, the limitations on the advance of wages imply limitations on the laborer's well-being.

The possibilities of the laborer's position, accordingly — so long as he remains a mere laborer — must be considered as bounded by the possibilities of an advance in real wages. We have already seen the conditions on which this depends. Profits being at the minimum, real wages will advance with the productiveness of industry in producing such real wages—in producing, that is to say, the commodities of the laborer's consumption. As I have already remarked, these commodities are mostly commodities of raw produce, of which an augmented production always implies a resort to inferior sources of supply. Unless, therefore, the laborer would lose in the resort to such sources of supply what he has gained from the increased productiveness of industry, he must be content to impose a steady restraint on the increase of his numbers. And now I will make an extreme supposition on this subject: let us suppose the providence and self-denial of the masses of the people to be strengthened to such a point that the demand for food and other articles of their consumption can be satisfied without requiring a resort to any natural agents inferior in point of productiveness to those employed in the United States, what would be the effect on real wages of such an extreme control placed upon the natural tendency of population to increase? Its effect would be to place laborers in this country on an equal footing with laborers in the United States; and this is the very utmost that, on the most extreme supposition with regard to the control of population, could be expected for the laboring classes, assuming them to continue mere laborers. The supposition, I need scarcely say, is absolutely Utopian. Nothing is more certain than that, taking the whole field of labor, real wages in Great Britain will never rise to the standard of remuneration now prevailing in new countries—a standard which after all would form but a sorry consummation as the final goal of improvement for the masses of mankind. We see, then, within what very narrow limits the possibilities of the laborer's lot are confined, so long as he depends for his well-being on the produce of his day's work. Against these barriers Trades-Unions must dash themselves in vain. They are not to be broken through or eluded by any combinations, however universal; for they are the barriers set by Nature herself. I commend the consideration to those patrons of the laboring classes who encourage an exclusive reliance on Trades-Unionism, and would advance their interests by confining them to their present *rôle*. It was the opinion of M. Comte, as it is that of his disciples, that the true ideal of industrial society—the goal toward which all reforming effort should be directed—is a more and more complete and definitive separation of the laboring and the capitalist classes. The proper model for our industrial organization according to them is an army in which the capitalists are as the captains, and the laborers as the rank and file. I do not know whether the apostles of this creed have ever seriously thought out the consequences as regards the distribution of wealth of a *régime* of this kind; but it would be worth their while to master at least so much Political Economy, before committing themselves to the discouragement of movements which, so far as appears, offer to the laboring class the sole means of escape from a harsh and hopeless destiny.

§ 7. The conclusion to which I have been led by the line of argument developed above is precisely the opposite of that which the Positivists maintain. It appears to me that the condition of any substantial improvement of a permanent kind in the laborer's lot is that the separation of industrial classes into laborers and capitalists which now prevails shall *not* be maintained; that the laborer shall cease to be a mere laborer—in a word, that profits shall be brought to re-enforce the Wages-fund. I have shown that, in order to any improvement at all of a permanent kind, a restraint must be enforced on population which shall prevent the increased demands for subsistence from neutralizing the gains arising from industrial progress; and that even a very great change in this respect in the habits of the people—a change far greater than there are any good reasons for anticipating—would still leave them, while they remain mere laborers, in a position not very materially better than at present. But the significance of these considerations becomes much enhanced when they are connected with another doctrine established in a former chapter of this work. It was there shown that, in the order of economic development, the Wages-fund of a country grows more slowly than its general capital.* Now the Wages-fund of a country represents the means of the laboring classes as a whole; the general capital the means of those who live upon profit—we may say broadly of the richer classes. It appears, therefore, that the fund available for those who live by labor tends, in the progress of society, while growing actually larger, to become a constantly smaller fraction of the entire national wealth. If, then, the means of any one class of society are to be permanently limited to this fund, it is evident, assuming that the progress of its numbers keeps pace with that of other classes, that its material condition in relation to theirs can not but decline.

---

* See *ante*, pp. 176, 177.

Now, as it would be futile to expect on the part of the poorest and most ignorant of the population self-denial and prudence greater than that actually practiced by the classes above them, the circumstances of whose life are so much more favorable than theirs for the cultivation of these virtues, the conclusion to which I am brought is this, that, unequal as is the distribution of wealth already in this country, the tendency of industrial progress—on the supposition that the present separation between industrial classes is maintained—is toward an inequality greater still. The rich will be growing richer; and the poor, at least relatively, poorer. It seems to me, apart altogether from the question of the laborer's interest, that these are not conditions which furnish a solid basis for a progressive social state; but, having regard to that interest, I think the considerations adduced show that the first and indispensable step toward any serious amendment of the laborer's lot is that he should be, in one way or other, lifted out of the groove in which he at present works, and placed in a position compatible with his becoming a sharer in equal proportion with others in the general advantages arising from industrial progress.

In the conclusion just expressed I believe I shall have the concurrence of many who would probably attach little value to the reasoning by which I have been led to it. In all socialistic schemes for the elevation of the working-man, the necessity of raising him from the position of a mere laborer is generally taken for granted. I am, therefore, on this point at one with the Socialists; but while I agree with them so far, I am wholly unable to accept the means which Socialism proposes for effecting the required elevation. The leading idea in most schemes of socialistic reform is the notion of raising laborers from dependence on the labor market by throwing on society, in the person of the State, the duty of providing them with capital. Now by whatever means it is sought to give effect to this idea—whether through the mechanism of a State bank issuing loans in inconvertible legal-tender notes, or by special taxation directed against the rich, or by advances made to laborers without adequate security or on terms more favorable than can be obtained in the market*—one and all, they are open to the objection of doing violence to the principle of property, the weight and scope of which objection I have already sufficiently insisted on. But this is not all. Such schemes tend in the most direct way to the demoralization of the laborer himself, by relieving him from the obligation of sacrifices which, in the order of nature, all must undergo as the condition of the rewards which attend on industry, and so placing him in a position of privilege in relation to his fellowmen. If laborers can obtain command of capital by simply asking for it; or if, having failed in their undertakings, they are to be relieved from the consequences of failure, and to be started anew in fresh enterprises, it is idle to expect that they will exhibit the self-denial and providence through the exercise of which capital comes to exist and industrial enterprise

---

* It may be said that this principle has already been set aside in favor of other classes than laborers. This is true; and I am not concerned to defend such violations of the rule of justice and of sound policy. One recent example, however, of the practice of making advances for industrial purposes on terms more favorable than can be obtained in the market—I refer to what are known as "the Bright clauses" in the Irish Land Act of 1870—may, I think, be justified on special grounds. I need not enter into the general argument here; but it is scarcely likely that any set of workmen, unable from their own resources to start a co-operative enterprise, would be capable of furnishing the State with the same security for the money advanced, or with the same evidence of their industrial capacity, which must be furnished by every Irish tenant who is in a position to take advantage of the "Bright clauses." How little any such deviation from sound principle is called for in the present case is strikingly shown in the past history of co-operation. "It can not," says Professor Fawcett, "be too carefully borne in mind that those who have achieved the most striking success in co-operation have not been assisted by any extraneous aid. They have placed their chief reliance in union of effort, in prudence, and in self-denial" ("Manual of Political Economy," p. 279).

to succeed. The practice of those virtues would still, indeed, be the condition of attaining the industrial results; but the virtues, if practiced at all when the motives for practicing them had been taken away, would be practiced by one set of people, and the results reaped by another. Unsatisfactory as may be the actual state of things, I can not believe that this would be an improvement on it. As matters now stand, the progress of the laborer is at least connected with the exercise of industrial virtues; he only reaps where he has sown; but under a system in which he would find himself supplied at will with capital, the fruits of others' savings, what would there be to develop prudence or self-restraint? What motive for setting bounds to the most reckless self-indulgence.

§ 8. The problem, therefore, for those who accept the point of view here taken, is to combine the socialistic aim with means for giving it effect consistent with the maintenance of the fundamental bases of our present social state—to help the laborer to emerge from his actual position without doing violence to the principle of property, and without weakening in him those qualities of character on which industrial success depends. Keeping this object in view, I think it should at the outset be clearly laid down that there is no royal road to the possession of capital. Capital can only be created by saving, and, where people have not saved themselves, can only be honestly obtained by offering to those who have saved an adequate inducement in the form of security and interest to prevail on them to part with it. If, then, the laborer is to emerge from his present position and become a sharer in the gains of capital, he must in the first instance learn to save. To make saving practicable, it is true, there must be a margin of income beyond what is required for providing the necessaries and decencies of life; and I shall perhaps be told that this margin the laborer does not possess. But this is an assertion which can not for a moment be maintained in presence of the evidence furnished by our Excise returns. From these returns it has been calculated that a sum of no less than £120,000,000 sterling is now spent annually on alcoholic drinks. In what proportion the working-classes take part in this expenditure we have no means of accurately determining; but I imagine it will not be disputed that by much the largest proportion must be set down to their account; and I am certainly within the mark in assuming that of the money so spent the greater portion—I am sure I might say three-fourths of the whole—so far from conducing in any way to the well-being of those who spend it, is both physically and morally injurious to them. Here, then, is a sum of, let us say, some £60,000,000 sterling which might annually be saved without trenching upon any expenditure which really contributes to the laborer's well-being. The obstacles to this saving are not physical, but moral obstacles; and supposing laborers had the virtue to overcome them, the first step toward what might be fairly called their industrial emancipation would already have been accomplished. This indeed would be only the first step, and formidable difficulties would still remain. For, the capital being saved, it would need to be invested, and invested in undertakings which would yield at least the existing rate of profit, since we can not suppose that less than this would be regarded as sufficient compensation for sacrifices, in the case of the laboring classes, considerably greater than those which the present rate remunerates. To obtain, however, such a rate of return, mere monetary investment—advances, I mean, on loan to persons giving adequate security—manifestly would not suffice. The rate of interest on such loans at present rarely rises much beyond four or five per cent. With some £60,000,000 annually thrown upon the market as an addition to our present loan capital, it is probable the rate would fall to one or two per cent.—a return ridiculously inadequate as compensation for the sacrifices which saving would impose on the working-man. It would, therefore, be necessary that the new capital should be invested directly in industrial operations; and here a new difficulty presents itself. The savings of working-men would necessarily in the individual case be small: the capital arising from such savings, therefore, however large in the aggregate, would be held in small portions by a very numerous class. But we know that, for the great majority of industrial undertakings, a large scale of production is the condition of efficiency. How, then, is this condition of efficient industry to be reconciled with the existence of a capital diffused throughout the community in minute independent portions? Obviously there is but one way possible: those minute independent portions must be made to coalesce into masses large enough to furnish the means of efficient action. In other words, our reasoning brings us to this conclusion, that what is known as "co-operation"—the contribution by many workmen of their savings toward a common fund which they employ as capital and co-operate in turning to profit—constitutes the one and only solution of our present problem—the sole path by which the laboring classes as a whole, or even in any large number, can emerge from their condition of mere hand-to-mouth living, to share in the gains and honors of advancing civilization.

§ 9. To say this, however, is by no means to say that the laboring classes, as a whole, are now prepared to enter on this path, or that any very great change in our modes of carrying on industry can soon or easily be effected. I am far, indeed, from thinking so. But here again I desire to point out that the obstacles in the way are not physical, are not even economic, but moral or intellectual; or, if economic, only in so far as economic results depend on intellectual and moral conditions. What workmen have to overcome in order to engage effectively in co-operative industry is, first, the temptation to spend their means on indulgences generally pernicious, and which at all events may without detriment be dispensed with; and, secondly, the obstacles incident to their own ignorance and generally low moral condition. In using this language I have no desire to underrate the remarkable progress which a considerable section of our artisan population have already made toward fitting them for taking part in a system of co-operation; and in connection with this subject I may refer to the very satisfactory evidence adduced by Professor Fawcett, in the last edition of his "Manual of Political Economy," of the recent progress of the co-operative movement—evidence which fully justifies the opinion he expresses, that "any one who considers what it has already effected, and what it is capable of doing in the future, must, we think, come to the conclusion that we may look with more confidence to co-operation than to any other economic agency to improve the industrial condition of the country."* There can be no question, therefore, that even at the present moment there is a considerable section of the working population already ripe for co-operation; though I fear it must be acknowledged that among the best of them there is much still to be learned, more particularly as regards the qualities of mutual trust, forbearance, and submission to the guidance of those to whom they may assign the management of their joint concerns. With regard to the masses, however, it is but too obvious that every thing has yet to be done. In the first place, habits of saving have to be created, and, in the next, the intelligence, and still more the moral qualifications, required for effective co-operative action have to be developed. The difficulties, I admit, are great, but I can not see that they are insuperable; and this, as Professor Fawcett has shown, is assuredly not a time for the friends of co-operation to despair; for though it be true that such success as co-operation has

---

* "Manual of Political Economy," fourth edition, p. 279.

achieved in this country has been almost exclusively confined to the comparatively simple problems of distributive industry, the experience and training acquired in these tasks will help to qualify for more serious undertakings. Nor is it irrelevant to remark that we have just established, or at least, it is to be hoped, are on the eve of establishing, a system of universal compulsory education, from which it is surely not extravagant to expect that substantial improvement in the laborer's character will in due time accrue.

The all-important point, as it seems to me, is to recognize the direction in which the emancipation of labor from what is called (absurdly enough) the tyranny of capital lies. This I repeat is, and, so far as I see, can only be, that of co-operative industry. It is of course open to any one to question the feasibility of the plan; to such doubts the only effective answer, and it has already to some extent been given, will be actual performance; but what I think the foregoing argument establishes is that the alternative lies between this plan and none. If workmen do not rise from dependence upon capital by the path of co-operation, then they must remain in dependence upon capital; the margin for the possible improvement of their lot is confined within narrow barriers which can not be passed, and the problem of their elevation is hopeless. As a body, they will not rise at all. A few, more energetic or more fortunate than the rest, will from time to time escape, as they do now, from the ranks of their fellows to the higher walks of industrial life, but the great majority will remain substantially where they are. The remuneration of labor, as such, skilled or unskilled, can never rise much above its present level.

§ 10. Before quitting the subject of co-operation there is an aspect of the case on which I would offer a few concluding remarks. It may be asked, supposing a *régime* of co-operative industry established, does it follow that the future of the working-man is assured? Such a *régime* would indeed bring profits to the aid of wages, and thus largely increase the fund available for his support; but that fund, after all, would have limits; the means of subsistence could not be increased as fast as human beings' could multiply; and at bottom the great Malthusian difficulty would remain. Could workmen in their altered position be trusted to keep their numbers within the limits which the conditions of prosperous existence inevitably and under all circumstances prescribe?

Let me say that I am far from disposed to underrate the gravity of the consideration here adduced; but, while fully conceding the danger, it seems to me that we may yet find grounds for hopefulness in two circumstances: first, the fund for the laborers' support would, under a *régime* of co-operation, be derived, not as at present, exclusively from the Wages-capital of a country, but from the general capital in all its forms. Now we have seen that, in progressive communities, the general capital grows more rapidly than the Wages-capital; from which it follows that, under a *régime* of co-operation, the fund from which the laborer derives his support would not only be greatly larger than the corresponding fund under our present system, but would be a more rapidly increasing fund. Although, therefore, the necessity for restraining population would continue under co-operation as under all systems of industry, the restraint would not need to be as severe as it is when the laborer's resources are restricted to the most slowly growing portion of the whole national capital. The Malthusian difficulty, therefore, would not be removed by co-operation, but it would become, under that system, greatly less formidable. But, secondly, as we have seen, successful co-operation requires, and therefore presupposes, qualities of character which are not to be found at present in the masses of the laboring people—a capacity of self-denial, a tendency to look forward, and to attach increased importance to the future as compared with the present — in a word, self-control and prudence. Now these qualities once developed in a human being do not operate exclusively in any one direction: they affect his whole character, and will manifest their influence on his conduct in his matrimonial and domestic relations, as well as in every other part of his life. For this reason I am inclined to attach much more importance, as a means of controlling population, to the creation of modes of existence or habits of life in which the prudential faculties are called into energetic play, than to any amount of direct Malthusian teaching. No doubt the plain truth on this subject should always be spoken; but, unless accompanied with changes in the workman's condition which should at once make his obligations clearer to himself and also fortify him for their performance, I must own I should have little faith in its practical efficacy. As matters stand now — with the mass of the laboring population in absolute dependence on the labor market — is it any wonder that Malthusian prophets are as a voice crying in the wilderness? What do the majority of laborers know of the conditions determining the labor market? The demand for labor seems to come and go, like the wind blowing where it listeth, but those whose fortunes are governed by its changes know as little as they do of the wind, whence it cometh or whither it goeth. Why, they naturally ask in this state of ignorance, should they deny themselves for the sake of their children? Is it not all an affair of chance? and will not their children's chances be as good as theirs? Why, then, forego such enjoyment as the present offers for the sake of a future which is wrapped in clouds?

> "The present moment is their own:
> The next they never saw."

On the other hand, co-operation, while it appeals in the strongest way to those attributes of character which are concerned in the control of population, makes comparatively definite and clear the limits of the laborer's resources. He is now a payer as well as a receiver of wages, and, seeing the wages problem from both sides, is likely to acquire juster views; but, even though wages should still remain a mystery, at least it will be tolerably clear that profits will grow with the growth of capital, and that each man may count on receiving them precisely in proportion to the amount of capital he can command. Supposing a workman to have achieved comfortable independence, it will be clear to him that to maintain it he must maintain his capital unimpaired; and that to incur responsibilities which should compel him to encroach upon his capital to meet current expenses would be tantamount to a deliberate descent in the scale of well-being. The position of the co-operator would in this respect be analogous to that of the peasant proprietor, who, like him, draws his subsistence from a tolerably definite fund, and generally contrives to keep the expenses of his household within the limits which that fund will support. In these circumstances, it seems to me, there is good ground for hopefulness. Co-operation at once renders less formidable the obstacles to human improvement inevitably incident to our animal propensities, and tends to develop, in those who take part in it, a type of character fitted in a high degree for encountering them with success.

PART III.

INTERNATIONAL TRADE.

PART III.

INTERNATIONAL TRADE.

CHAPTER I.

DOCTRINE OF COMPARATIVE COST.

§ 1. It has been usual hitherto in treatises on Political Economy to consider the subject of international trade and international value, apart from the general theory of exchange and exchange value, as a distinct branch of economic doctrine; but the question has been lately raised whether this method of exposition is scientifically warrantable—whether, that is to say, it does not suggest a false view of the phenomena of commerce by implying a distinction in principle where in reality no such distinction exists. Assuming that the objection thus taken to the separate treatment of international trade is not a mere quibble on the use of the term "international," but intended to apply to the substance of economic theory as commonly expounded, the question raised by it is one as to the nature of the phenomena embraced by international trade, and what we have to decide is whether those phenomena are such as to find their solution in the same theory of exchange which furnishes the explanation of the facts of domestic commerce. In the event of their finding their solution in that theory, it is evident that the objection taken to the ordinary mode of exposition is well founded; while, in the opposite case, it is equally clear that the phenomena of international trade have need of a special theory for their satisfactory elucidation.

In order to determine this point, it will be well if we endeavor here to set before our minds in the most general way the fundamental circumstances on which trade, or the interchange of commodities, in all its forms, rests. These fundamental circumstances are to be found in the consequences arising from division of labor or separation of employments. In order that industry may be carried on upon this plan, and that advantage may be taken of the increased efficiency and economy thence resulting, the exchange of products among those carrying on the separated occupations becomes necessary, and in this fact we find the natural basis and explanation of trade. Trade, therefore, is the necessary means of giving effect to the separation of employments, and the advantages arising from it are the advantages incident to this scheme of things. The general nature of these advantages is familiar to all readers of economic works; but for our present purpose it will be convenient to consider them under two leading heads: first, we may consider those advantages which arise from the separation of employments, apart from any special circumstances which may give to this arrangement a peculiar importance; and, secondly, those which are due to the separation of employments, as furnishing the means of developing special faculties of production possessed by particular persons or places. As an example of the former class of advantages we may take the ordinary handicraft trades. There is an obvious advantage in having such employments as tailoring, boot-making, hat-making, and the various callings of blacksmith, locksmith, mason, joiner, etc., separated and carried on as distinct occupations; but, as most of them require the same, or nearly the same, sort of qualifications for their performance, it makes little difference to which of the group any particular member of the handicraft class devotes himself. A is a tailor, B a shoe-maker, and C a hatter; but if C had been a tailor, A a shoe-maker, and B a hatter, the arrangement would probably have answered equally well.

Nothing is here gained from the separation of employments beyond the increased dexterity incident to the increased familiarity of each workman with his work, together with the saving of so much time as would be wasted if the laborer had occasion frequently to change his occupation. This, then, is one description of advantage arising from the separation of employments to the realization of which trade ministers. But, as I have said, this advantage may be combined with advantages of another kind, and this happens where the separation of employments, while promoting the results just noticed, furnishes, at the same time, the means of developing the special capacities or resources possessed by particular individuals or localities.

In the examples given above the advantage obtained was derived from the mere fact of the separation of employments, altogether independently of the mode in which the separated employments were distributed among the persons carrying them on, as well as of the places in which they were conducted. But a further gain arises when the employments are of a kind which, in order to their effective performance, call for special capacities in the workman or special natural resources in the scene of operation. There would be a manifest waste of special power in compelling to a mere mechanical or routine pursuit a man who is fitted to excel in a professional career; and similarly, if a branch of industry were established on some site which offered greater facilities to an industry of another sort, a waste, analogous in character, would be incurred. In a word, while a great number of the occupations in which men engage are such as, with proper preparation for them, might equally well be carried on by any of those engaged in them, or in any of the localities in which they are respectively established, there are others which demand for their effective performance special personal qualifications and special local conditions; and the general effectiveness of productive industry will, other things being equal, be proportioned to the completeness with which the adaptation is accomplished between occupation on the one hand and individuals and localities on the other.

There are thus two distinct kinds of advantage derivable from the separation of employments; and I have called attention to this circumstance in order to say that it is one only of those sorts of advantage that international trade in the main tends to develop. The great trades of the world are carried on between countries pretty widely removed from each other either in the scale of civilization or in respect to their natural resources and productions, while in proportion as countries approximate to each other in natural resources or in the industrial qualities of their inhabitants, the scope for international trade is narrowed: it is even possible that it should fail altogether. The reason of this is by no means mysterious. The advantage to be derived from the separation of employments, where this separation is not connected with any special facilities of production, are, in countries in which industry has made any considerable progress, in general realized in their full extent by the separation which takes place within the limits of each of those countries. It is only when population is very sparse that the home market is not large enough to secure this result; and where this is so, it generally happens that any gain that might be obtained through a trade with foreign nations in articles in the production of which no special facilities, positive or comparative, are possessed by the trading countries, is more than counterbalanced by the loss incident to an increased cost of carriage. Accordingly in countries or districts which are very sparsely peopled, instead of the separation of employments in the simpler industries being carried out by an interchange with foreign nations, what usually happens is that no separation of employments, or a very imperfect one, takes place, and that things continue in a primitive state. International trade may thus be considered as practically restricted to giving effect to those examples of the separation of employment in which the more ordinary advantages flowing from that principle are combined with those which are due to the adaptation of industrial operations to the special circumstances of persons and places; while again it is tolerably obvious that, of these two sorts of adaptation, that which relates to places is, in the international sphere, by much the more important. The only case indeed in which personal aptitudes go for much in the commerce of nations is where the nations concerned occupy different grades in the scale of civilization. In the trade, for example, between England and India it is probable that the different characters of the two peoples, incident to the different stage of social growth to which each has attained, go a considerable way in determining the character and the amount of their commercial dealings. But perhaps the most striking example which the world has ever seen of a foreign trade determined by the peculiar personal qualities of those engaged in ministering to it is that which was furnished by the Southern States of the American Union previous to the abolition of slavery. The effect of that institution was to give a very distinct industrial character to the laboring population of those States, which unfitted them for all but a very limited number of occupations, but gave them a certain special fitness for these. Almost the entire industry of the country was consequently turned to the production of two or three crude commodities, in raising which the industry of slaves was found to be effective; and these were used. through an exchange with foreign countries, as the means of supplying the inhabitants with all other requisites. This is, perhaps, the most noteworthy instance on record of personal aptitudes extensively affecting the external trade of a country. In the main, however, it would seem that this cause does not go for very much in international commerce. The principal condition, to which all others are subordinate, in determining the existence and character of foreign trade must be looked for in that other form of adaptation founded on the special advantages, positive or comparative, offered by particular localities for the prosecution of particular industries.

Here, then, we have a well-defined characteristic which distinguishes international trade from domestic; but its presence alone would scarcely suffice to justify a special theory of the former. To satisfy ourselves on this point, we must advert to another circumstance to which I have now to call attention.

One of the principal conditions determining the relative profitableness of particular occupations and the terms on which their products are exchanged consists in the degree of facility which happens to exist for moving capital and labor from one to the other. Now this facility is very different in the case of occupations carried on within the limits of a single country, and those carried on in different countries; and in this difference is to be found the chief fact discriminating the phenomena of international from those of domestic trade. Let us endeavor to appreciate in a general way the range and the degree of this difference.

The assumption commonly made in treatises of Political Economy is that, as between occupations and localities within the same country, the freedom of movement for capital and labor is perfect, while, as between nations, capital and labor move with difficulty or not at all. In strictness neither member of this assumption can be maintained. Capital, indeed— so long at least as it exists in the form of purchasing power available for productive purposes — moves freely among all occupations and places within the same country; but labor, as we know, encounters impediments at certain points; the laborers belonging to the lower industrial grades being hindered by the circumstances of their position from entering into competition with those above them; while even for laborers occupying the same industrial stratum the obstacles to migration between distant localities are often very considerable, and such as sometimes to amount to practical prevention. Nor any more is it true, without large qualification, that labor and capital do not move from country to country. Capital, in a certain sense, is every day becoming less national and more cosmopolitan; and though labor is far from being equally mobile, still with the immense emigration taking place year after year from these islands and other countries of Western Europe, and with the fact before us that even Asiatic populations are now beginning to emigrate, it is impossible to deny that labor is capable, under the influence of economic causes, of international movement on a great scale. The assumption, therefore, in the unqualified form in which it is often laid down, can not be maintained either in its affirmative or in its negative part. But while so much must be freely admitted, it may still be affirmed that enough of truth remains in the assertion, after all due deductions have been made, to warrant the inferences that have been drawn from it, and to justify the distinction contended for. For it is by no means necessary to the truth of the doctrine, as it has been laid down, for example, by Ricardo and Mill, that there should be an absolute impossibility of moving capital and labor from country to country. What the doctrine requires is not this, but such a degree of difficulty in effecting their transference as shall interfere substantially and generally—that is to say, over the whole range of the commodities exchanged—with the action of industrial competition.* The one and sufficient test, as I have pointed

---

* The reader will here bear in mind the sense in which I use the phrase "*industrial* competition," as expressing the competition which takes place between *the producers of different commodities*—competition which tends to bring wages and profits into correspondence with the sacrifices undergone, in contradistinction to that which takes place between *dealers in the same commodity* and which operates toward equality of price. The latter might be called "*commercial* competition."

out, of the existence of an effective industrial competition, is the correspondence of remuneration with the sacrifices undergone—a substantial equality, that is to say, making allowance for the different circumstances of different industries, of profits and wages. Such a test, applied to domestic transactions, shows the existence of a very large amount of effective industrial competition operative throughout the various industries carried on within the limits of a single country. The competition of different capitals within such limits may be said to be universally effective; and that of labor, though interrupted at certain points, is effective over large industrial areas. Profits consequently within the same country, however great may be the fluctuations, gravitate steadily toward a common level, as likewise do wages within the limits of the industrial areas to which I have referred. The same test applied to international transactions shows an entirely different state of things. For, though capital migrates, it does not do so upon a scale large enough to establish an equality of profits in different countries, and profits consequently remain at a permanently higher level in some countries than in others. Indeed, in spite of all we hear of the international movements of capital, the amount of capital that can be truly called cosmopolitan—disposable for investment in countries other than that to which it properly belongs—is after all but a mere fraction of the national capital. It is in effect confined to a portion of what is called the "floating capital" of a country—that part of the capitalist's funds which he does not mean to superintend himself, and which he offers on loan. All that immensely larger part which the owners are not disposed to part with, but desire to superintend and work themselves—all this is practically confined to the capitalist's country. What passes off, though often considerable in its positive amount, is thus wholly unequal to producing a sensible impression on the general rate of profit in the country to which it goes; and so profits remain permanently at different levels in different countries. And just as little has an equilibrium in the rates of wages been brought about by the international movements of labor. Great as has been the emigration from Europe to the United States, it may be doubted if, outside the range of a few towns on the eastern coast, any appreciable effect has been produced on the rates of wages in the latter country. Throughout the Union wages remain in all occupations very considerably higher than in the corresponding occupations in this country. Nor do they show any sign of declining. It thus appears, alike with regard to labor and capital, that notwithstanding a certain amount of international mobility in these instruments of production, the impediments to their transference from country to country are yet sufficiently great to prevent effective competition from taking place between the industries of different countries, such as is really operative in each separate country over a very large proportion of its domestic industry. And this, and no more than this, is all that is assumed by economists—all at least that is essential to the validity of their arguments—when they contend for the necessity of separating the facts of international from those of domestic trade.

§ 2. It will aid us in giving the due circumscription to the facts with which we have to deal if, before developing the consequences involved in the state of things just described, we note briefly the nature of the obstacles which impede the movements of labor and capital in the international sphere. The most important of these are the following: 1. Geographical distance; 2. Difference in political institutions; 3. Difference in language, religion, and social customs—in a word, in forms of civilization. Each of these circumstances is capable of hindering, and does in fact, to a greater or less extent, hinder the free movement of labor and capital. As regards their relative importance, the social and political causes are probably, in the present state of the world, more powerful than the physical, more particularly when the former happened to be connected with differences of race; while geographical distance is apparently that which exerts the least obstructive force.

These being the principal obstacles to the movements of labor and capital from place to place, it will be at once apparent that the line of demarkation which would result from their interference, though largely coincident with that indicated by the words "international" and "domestic," is by no means strictly so. Australia and Canada, for example, are portions of a single political system, but the geographical obstacles offered to trade between those places, or between either of them and England, are far greater than those which exist in the trade of many independent nations; and the same may be said of the trade between the Atlantic and the Pacific States of the American Union. Similarly, we find within the same country differences of race, of language, and of religion, and to some extent of social tastes and habits. It is thus clear that no hard and fast line can be drawn between domestic and international trade founded on the character of the obstacles presented to the movements of labor and capital; and it must, therefore, be owned that the terms "international" and "domestic" do not accurately express the distinction which it is designed to mark. What we want is a term which would cover all that portion of the trade of mankind carried on between localities sufficiently separated from each other, whether by moral or physical obstacles, to prevent the action, as between producers in the trading localities, of effective industrial competition, and which would exclude the trade carried on under those more favorable conditions where industrial competition is effective. So far as I know, there is no one word that accurately meets this requirement. "International" is that which perhaps comes most nearly to what we want. In the intercourse of independent nations, all or most of the obstacles I have noted come into operation, and in their combination offer a substantial impediment to the free movement of capital and labor; while, as among different localities in the same country, they do not exist in the same number or in the same degree of intensity, and, where they do exist and operate, they are always counteracted and largely neutralized by the powerfully assimilating influence of a single central government. In the case of colonies, however, the political causes tending to facilitate the movements of capital and labor are, on the whole, overborne by the geographical, climatic, and physical circumstances which obstruct those movements; and therefore, for the purposes of economic theory, we must include colonial under "international" trade. Our economic nomenclature in this part of our subject is thus not free from objection; but, having noted its imperfection, we shall not be likely to be misled by it.

§ 3. We have now ascertained the grounds in the facts of the case for the distinction between "international" and "domestic" trade, and the sense in which these terms are to be understood. It remains that we endeavor to trace the consequences which result in the trade of nations from the circumstances, such as they have been shown to be, under which it takes place.

First among these consequences we may note the following: A trade may arise between two independent countries and be profitable for each under conditions in which it would not arise if the trading localities were within the range of a single country, that is to say, if they were so situated that labor and capital moved freely between them. To perceive the grounds of this statement, we may consider the following case. Suppose a trade between North Wales on the one side and Lancashire and Yorkshire on the other, the articles exchanged being slates on the part of North Wales against woolen and cotton manufactures on the side of the English counties. North

Wales has evidently a great and unquestionable advantage over Yorkshire and Lancashire in the production of slates; and it is probable that Yorkshire and Lancashire have an advantage, less decided, but still real, over North Wales in the production of their staple products. Of one thing at all events we may be sure: neither district is under a positive disadvantage, as compared with the other, in raising or manufacturing the product which forms the staple of its trade; for, were this so, the product in question would no longer be produced in that locality: the capital and labor employed in the business would migrate thence to the other locality, which offered greater advantage for the production of this article, and the trade between the places would cease. In a word, a migration of the instruments of production would take the place of a trade in the products. This is what would happen when the trading districts are situated within the same country, and labor and capital move freely between them. But now suppose the trading localities to be situated in different countries, between which labor and capital move with difficulty, or not at all. Under such circumstances either might have an advantage over the other in respect of all the staples of their trade—in the case supposed in respect to textile fabrics as well as to slates—and the trade might nevertheless go on; for, though it is true that here too, as in the case just considered, there would be a gain in productive efficiency if the people and capital of the less favored district were to transfer themselves bodily to the other, yet, as in point of fact this transference, for very sufficient reasons, does not take place, the question arises what, under these circumstances, will be most for the interests of the two countries in supplying their needs by means of industry? A very little consideration is needed to show that, under the circumstances supposed—the superiority in productive power lying in the case of every branch of industry on the side of one country—it may yet be for the interest of both to satisfy their wants by engaging in trade, *provided only that the advantage enjoyed by the country possessing the superior industrial resources be not equally great in each instance;* in other words, provided that each country possesses, in respect to the other, a greater advantage or a less disadvantage in the production of some than in that of other commodities. If, for example, it happened that North Wales and the manufacturing districts of England were situated in independent countries between which labor and capital refused to pass, under these circumstances North Wales might have an advantage over the English counties both in the production of slates and also in the production of textile fabrics; but if her superiority was not the same in both—if it were greater in the case of one than in that of the other class of commodity—greater, say, in the case of slates than in that of cloths, it would still be for the interest of the two districts to trade in those articles; for Wales, by devoting her industry to the production of slates, in which her superiority was greater than in the production of cloths, and using her slates as the means through trade of procuring cloths, would get them cheaper—with less real cost of labor and abstinence—than if she produced them; while, on the other hand, Yorkshire and Lancashire would get their slates cheaper by employing their industry in the production of fabrics in which their disadvantage was less, and using these as the means of obtaining their slates from Wales, than by attempting to produce slates or any substitute for them directly for themselves. It thus appears that a trade may take place between two districts, as independent countries, under circumstances in which no trade would occur, were those districts situated within the limits of a single country, and capital and labor free to move between them. This, I say, is a possible case, and, as will presently appear, in actual experience, a very common one; indeed, it may be said to be typical of a large proportion of the entire trade carried on between independent countries. We are thus brought, in the domain of international trade, into contact with a phenomenon of which the theory of trade in its simpler cases furnishes no explanation, for which therefore a special theory is needed. The writer who first detected the fact, and supplied the theory, was Ricardo; and the theory involved in the foregoing exposition is in effect that which he gave. It may be thus stated: In order to the existence of a trade between different countries, the essential and also the sufficient condition is, that there should be in those countries a difference in the comparative cost of producing the commodities which are the subject of the trade. The commodity forming the staple of a trading country may be, and frequently is, more cheaply produced in that country than in the country which imports it, but this is not necessary to the existence of the trade; and a trade between nations may be carried on where the superiority in point of productive power with respect to all articles which form the subject of the trade is upon the side of one of them. On the other hand, a difference in the absolute cost of producing commodities in different countries does not necessarily render a trade between them possible, since, if the difference were the same in the case of each article, there would be no motive for an exchange. The one condition, therefore, at once essential to, and also sufficient for, the existence of international trade, is a difference in the comparative, as contradistinguished from the absolute, cost of producing the commodities exchanged.*

Such is the theory of international trade as it was left by Ricardo, and expounded, but not substantially altered, by Mill.† It can not be doubted that it sounds the depths of the

---

* Ricardo's Works (M'Culloch's edition), chap. vii.; Mill's "Principles of Political Economy," book iii., chap. xvii.

† I say, the theory of international *trade* was not substantially altered by Mill: the theory of international *values* was; Mill having here supplied an important condition overlooked by Ricardo.

problem, and embraces in its scope all the most important—certainly all the most conspicuous—facts in the sphere of international dealings. Nevertheless, as I shall presently attempt to show, the doctrine as it stands is not absolutely complete, and in fact fails to take account of certain international exchanges, not perhaps very extensive in their range, but still of considerable importance. Such criticisms, however, as I have to make upon this point will be more conveniently reserved for another chapter. For the present I shall confine myself to a few further remarks in elucidation of the doctrine as it has been stated above.

And, first, it must be observed that by "cost of production," as employed in the foregoing context, the reader is to understand the actual difficulties of production as measured by the sacrifices which production requires, not the amount of wages and profits, whether measured in money or produce, comprised in the capitalist's outlay and return. It was in the former sense that Ricardo, who first discovered the truth in question, understood the words, and, notwithstanding that Mr. Mill has in his chapters on Value adopted the latter conception of cost of production, it is in the same sense that he has employed it in his exposition of the doctrine of international trade.* Indeed, it may be doubted if the theory of comparative cost of production as the ruling principle of international trade could ever have been worked out from the point of view which regards cost as consisting in wages and profits; and, however this may be, it is at least quite certain, as I shall hereafter demonstrate, that the theory of international values, adopted

---

* The only sacrifice taken account of by either Ricardo or Mill in working out the theory of international trade is that of labor, the cost being always reckoned in so many days' labor of so many men. Abstinence is entirely overlooked. The omission, however, does not seriously affect the reasoning, since labor and abstinence being each alike a sacrifice, the considerations applicable to the one are, so far as the argument is concerned, for the most part applicable also to the other.

alike by Mill and Ricardo, is absolutely irreconcilable with that view.

Secondly, when it is said that international trade depends on a difference in the comparative, not in the absolute, cost of producing commodities, the costs compared, it must be carefully noted, are the costs in each country of the commodities which are the subjects of exchange, not the different costs of the same commodity in the exchanging countries. Thus, if coal and wine be the subjects of a trade between England and France, the comparative costs on which the trade depends are the comparative costs of coal and wine in France as compared with the comparative costs of the same articles in England. England might be able to raise coal at one-half the amount of labor and abstinence needed in France; but this alone would not render it profitable for France to obtain her coal from England. If her disadvantage in producing other commodities was as great as in producing coal, she would gain nothing by an exchange of products, and the conditions for a trade between the two countries would not exist. But supposing she was, in the case of some other commodity, under a less disadvantage than in that of coal, still more if she had with regard to that other—as in wine—a positive advantage, it would at once become her interest to employ this commodity as a means of obtaining through trade her coal from England, instead of producing coal directly from her own mines.

So much in the way of explanation of terms. Let me now endeavor to set before the reader a few examples of the practical working of the principle of comparative cost in the actual commerce of the world. For this purpose I shall take, in the first place, a case to which I have both in this and in former publications frequently referred—the external trade of the principal Australian colonies before and since the discovery of the gold-fields. Previous to that discovery, which occurred in 1851, no gold being produced in the country, the cost to the colony of such gold as circulated there would consist in the cost—by which the reader will bear in mind I mean the labor and abstinence—incident to the production of those articles by the exchange of which with foreign countries Australia obtained her gold. Certain quantities of wool, tallow, and hides were exported, and sold in foreign countries for certain sums of the precious metals, and these, or their equivalents in value, came back to the Australian producers, to whom they became wages and profits. These wages and profits, therefore, measured in the precious metals, or, let us say, in gold, which was the standard of value in the colony, would be the return upon the labor and abstinence employed in producing the commodities through the sale of which they were obtained. In proportion as they were great, the cost of obtaining gold would be small; in proportion as they were small, the cost of obtaining gold would be great; in a word, the cost of obtaining gold would vary inversely with the money rates of wages and profits prevailing in the colony. Supposing, for example, that 4s. a day was the wages of unskilled labor in the colony in 1850, and ten per cent. per annum the ordinary return upon capital, then the cost of gold, so far as it consisted of labor, would be a day's unskilled labor for 4s. worth of gold, and, so far as it consisted of abstinence, a year's abstinence from the enjoyment obtainable by means of £100 for £10. For simplicity of illustration, as labor is so much the principal element in the case, we may confine our attention to it exclusively, and say briefly that the cost of gold in Australia previous to the gold discoveries was represented by a day's labor for as much gold as could be purchased with 4s. Under these circumstances the gold discoveries took place; and now mark what happened. At once the same workman who previously by a day's labor could earn but 4s. worth of gold could now by washing the auriferous sands earn from 15s. to 20s. worth. The same exertion could now procure for him four or five times as much gold as formerly; in other words, the cost of gold had fallen in the proportion of from four or five to one. But while the cost of gold in the colony was thus reduced, no change had taken place there in the cost of producing other things. A given exertion of labor and abstinence would still procure the same quantity as before of corn, of meat, of wool, of tallow. It followed that the comparative cost of producing gold and other things had been altered in the immense proportion indicated by the reduction in the positive cost of producing gold; in other words, the conditions were realized under which, according to the theory of Ricardo, an immense change ought to take place in the external trade of the colony; and this was precisely what happened. From that time until the conditions of trade were again modified, partly through the gradual exhaustion of the richer gold deposits, and partly through the advance of prices in foreign markets, a period of some four or five years, Australia became an importer of every thing that from its nature admitted of being imported; and, what is especially to be noted, among the things thus imported were many which she could have produced herself at far less cost, with far less labor and abstinence, than they were produced at in the countries from which they were brought. For example, timber was imported from the Baltic, although there were forests in Australia capable of yielding timber quite good enough at least for the mining purposes for which timber was mostly required. Butter was largely imported from Ireland, and I believe also from England and Holland, though the advantages possessed by Australia for dairy farming in her unrivaled pastures and abundant cattle were exceptionally great. Similarly, with unlimited areas of fine agricultural land, she imported nearly all her food; and with the materials of leather cheaper than in any other part of the world, she imported all her shoes. What was the explanation of these facts? In all cases one and the same: it was to be found in the principle of comparative cost. Australia had considerable advantages over other countries in respect to timber, butter, food, and shoes; but she had a greater advantage still in respect to gold; and so it became her interest to obtain the former things by means of the latter. I have always regarded the commercial results of the Australian and Californian discoveries (for things in California followed a very similar course) as one of the most striking experimental verifications which a purely abstract doctrine has ever received. Ricardo was considered, and is still considered by some people, a dreamer of dreams, a spinner of abstract fancies; but his dreams and abstractions, when brought to the test of experiment, as commonly happens with the dreams and abstractions of men of genius, have proved to be far more practical, far more closely in accordance with actual occurrences, than the prognostics of so-called "practical men," based though these may have been upon one knows not what collections of carefully tabulated statistics. Compare the facts which I have stated in connection with the Australian trade, as illustrating his doctrine of "comparative cost," with the speculations of some of our leading bankers and actuaries at the time of the occurrence of the gold discoveries, as to the probable effects of those events on the course of the money market—speculations in which one writer confidently predicts that the increased abundance of gold must lead to a fall in its price; another, that it would lead to a fall in the rate of interest; a third, that the exportation of gold from Australia would cease to be profitable, and would therefore cease to be carried on, as soon as the price of gold in Sydney rose to the London level! All these, and many more absurdities no less glaring, are to be found in pamphlets, and even in pretentious volumes, published soon after the epoch of the gold discoveries, by commercial men who piqued themselves upon their knowledge of practical business and their contempt for abstract speculation.

The external trade of the gold countries presents, in a somewhat exaggerated shape, the action of the principle of comparative cost. The superiority of productive power was here, in almost every instance, on the side of one of the exchanging parties—the Australian colonies. The reader will not, however, suppose that, in order to the existence of a trade between nations, there is any necessity that this particular state of things should occur. In point of fact, it is probable that the more frequent case is that in which the superiority of productive power is divided between the trading countries, each having a positive as well as a comparative advantage over the other in respect of the commodities which form its own staples. Still it would be a mistake to suppose that the Australian example represents a purely exceptional case. So far from this, I am inclined to believe that in a large portion of the trade of the world—in most of the trade, for example, carried on between tropical and temperate regions, as well as in the trade between old and new countries—the condition which we found so prominent in the Australian commerce—a superiority of productive power in respect to the staples on both sides possessed by one of the exchanging parties—will also be found to obtain. One instance, which I find in the work of Mr. Bowen, an American economist, may here be given.* It occurs in the case of the trade between the State of New York and some adjoining districts and the Island of Barbados. The trade consists chiefly of an exchange of breadstuffs and meat on the side of the former country against various kinds of tropical produce furnished by the latter. As will be readily understood, Barbados has an immense advantage over the State of New York in the raising of tropical products, such as sugar, coffee, spices, etc.: but Mr. Bowen informs us that it has also a decided advantage over the same regions in the produc-

---

* Bowen's "Political Economy," p. 460.

tion of food—that a given exertion of industry employed for a given time in raising food in Barbados would be attended with a larger result than the same exertion employed for the same time in the United States. The advantage, therefore, in respect to both the staples of the trade is on the side of Barbados, and the phenomenon of the Australian trade is here repeated. The explanation, of course, lies once more in the law of comparative cost. Barbados and the United States find their account in developing those of their resources in which either possesses the greatest comparative superiority, or the least comparative inferiority, in respect of the other, employing the products thus obtained as the means of supplying themselves, through trade, with others in the production of which the advantage of either is relatively less pronounced, or its disadvantage greater. I have said that this is by no means an exceptional case, but rather the rule, in certain great departments of cosmopolitan trade. It is probable, for example, that in a large portion of the trade carried on between the United States and Europe the advantage of production in respect to the staples on both sides lies with the United States; but this fact is kept out of sight through the misty conception ordinarily prevailing as to the nature of cost of production. Thus, in comparing the costs of production of different commodities in, say this country and the United States, people allow their thoughts to run off on questions of comparative wages and profits; and finding wages and profits higher in the United States than here, they are apt to jump to the conclusion that this is evidence of higher cost of production in the former country. In truth, so far as wages and profits are indications of cost of production at all—a point to which I shall hereafter recur—high wages and profits are indications of a low cost of production, since they are indications—being in fact the direct results of—high industrial productiveness; and accordingly, if wages and profits are higher in the United States than here, it is because those things in which wages and profits consist are more easily obtained—that is to say, are obtained at less cost—there than here. The prevailing theory, which makes cost of production consist in wages and profits, has thus thrown a dense haze over the working of the principle on which the interchange of commodities between different nations is carried on. Indeed, as I shall hereafter show, the doctrine in question is answerable for some of the most plausible fallacies of the Protectionist school. For the moment, however, I am merely concerned to point out how this erroneous notion of cost tends to conceal the true nature of no small portion of the trade of the world.

CHAPTER II.

INTERNATIONAL TRADE IN ITS RELATION TO THE RATE OF WAGES.

§ 1. I HAVE endeavored in the foregoing chapter to set forth the theory of international trade, as it was first thought out by Ricardo, and subsequently expounded by Mill. In doing so, I remarked that the doctrine, though undoubtedly comprising the more fundamental conditions determining the interchange of nations, is, nevertheless, in certain respects defective. It remains for me now to point out wherein consists the shortcomings then referred to.

In the first place, I must observe that cost of production, though it may be, and generally is, the ultimate condition governing international exchange, is never in any case the proximate or immediate cause. That proximate or immediate cause is not cost, but price. The ordinary merchant whose business leads him into foreign trade knows nothing of "cost of production," as consisting of labor and abstinence, and still less does he know of "comparative cost of production." The considerations which determine his conduct are far more simple. He attends, not to the cost—the expenditure of labor and abstinence—at which commodities may be produced, but to the prices at which they may be bought and sold, and the only comparison he enters into is a comparison of the prices of the articles he deals in as they are in his own country and in the foreign market with which he trades. When the state of prices in these different localities is such as to render it profitable to transport commodities from one to the other for the purpose of sale, he engages in this operation and looks no farther: when the state of prices does not admit of this, he ceases to operate. Further, as Ricardo himself pertinently reminds us, "every transaction in commerce is an independent transaction;" and if there be a prospect of profit on the export or import of any single commodity, that commodity will be exported or imported wholly irrespective of what may be the state of the markets as regards other commodities. How are these facts to be reconciled with the theory expounded in the last chapter, that international trade is governed by comparative cost of production? Ricardo's answer would run in some such form as this: first, he would say, by virtue of the fact that relative prices within each country correspond to, and vary with, the relative costs of commodities produced within that country; so that a state of relative prices which would make it profitable to export certain commodities and import others would indicate a corresponding condition of the relative costs of production of the commodities thus exchanged. And, secondly, he would meet the difficulty as to the independent character of each commercial transaction by showing that, though independent, in the sense of being undertaken without reference to any transaction beyond itself, each commercial transaction nevertheless entails consequences which connect it with subsequent commercial transactions. The case may be illustrated by a hypothetical example. Suppose the price of some commodity suitable for international commerce to be lower in country A than in country B—I assume the difference in price to be sufficient to yield a profit on the investment during the period between purchase and sale, and I put aside, for simplicity of illustration, the element of cost of transport—nothing more than this is necessary in order that the commodity should be sent from the former to the latter country. It will accordingly be sent; and the merchant who undertakes the transaction will get his profit. But this is not the end. The commodity being sold, its value must be transmitted from country B. in which the sale took place, to country A. The question arises, in what form will it be sent? If it be sent in the form of some commodity produced in country B, the price of this commodity, to make the transaction profitable, will need to be lower in country B than in country A. The former commodity was lower in country A than in country B: the latter will be lower in country B than in country A. The comparative prices of the two commodities will therefore be different in the two countries, and, prices being ruled by costs, the transaction will only be profitable when the comparative costs are different. But country B might pay for its import, not by the export of a commodity of its own produce, but by remitting gold. Let us consider this case. There are two suppositions possible. Country B either produces gold or it does not. If, taking the former supposition, and assuming therefore that gold is for country B a staple of merchandise, the gold price of the imported commodity is higher in country B than in country A—this proves that the cost of obtaining gold is lower relatively to the cost of the commodity in the former than in the latter country. There is thus a difference in the comparative costs of gold and of the commodity in the two countries, and the trade would be carried on by an exchange of one for the other in strict conformity with Ricardo's doctrine. But now take the other supposition. Gold, we will suppose, is not a product of country B. Under these circumstances, and assuming further, for simplicity of illustration, that the two countries trade exclusively with one another, it is evident that the trade can not be carried on permanently upon the terms of an exchange of a commodity on the side of country A against gold on that of country B; for the continued transference of gold from the latter to the former country would sooner or later act upon prices in the two places, lowering them in B and raising them in A; and then one of two things would happen: either the commodity which formed the subject of the trade would rise in price in country A till it became no longer profitable to export it, and then the trade would come to an end; or before this occurred, the price of some commodity in country B would be brought below the level of its price in country A; and this commodity would become then for B the means of paying for its import. There would thus be established a difference in the comparative prices of the exchanged commodities in the two countries; and, prices within the limits of each country being governed by cost of production, this would imply a corresponding difference in their comparative costs. Under all circumstances, therefore, it would be concluded, notwithstanding that prices are the immediate consideration, and notwithstanding that each commercial transaction, so to speak, stands upon its own merits, the fundamental condition underlying the whole, supplying the motives and determining the result, is the comparative costs of producing commodities.

The logic of the foregoing argument, which is in substance the argument employed in Ricardo's exposition of the doctrine, appears to me to be without flaw. But to one of the premises involved in it I have already taken exception, and, unless my reasoning is fallacious, it can no longer be admitted. It is assumed throughout that the relative prices of commodities within the limits of each country are universally—or at least so generally that the exceptions are not worth noticing—governed by the relative costs of their production. Now I have endeavored to show in an early chapter of this work* that this assumption is not well founded. Cost of production, as a principle regulating value, is only operative within the limits of effective competition; and, though this condition is largely realized in this and most civilized countries, and still more exten-

---

* Part i., chap. iii.

sively in new communities like our Australian colonies and
some American States, it is yet far from being universal, and,
especially in countries in which, as in England, the social
structure is very complex and of long standing, suffers numerous and serious checks. The consequence is, that cost of production, though the principal influence in the case, is not the
only one. To a considerable extent in countries of old civilization, to a less extent in new communities, Reciprocal Demand
takes the place of Cost of Production as the regulator of domestic prices. In all those exchanges, for example, carried on
between what I have called non-competing industrial groups,
the law governing such exchanges, and therefore governing
the relative prices of the products proceeding from such groups,
is that furnished by the former, not that furnished by the latter
principle. But prices, as we have seen, are the proximate conditions determining international exchange. It follows, therefore, that international exchange is sometimes determined, not
merely proximately but ultimately by other conditions than
cost of production; and that the theory of that branch of trade,
as left us by Ricardo, is by no means as complete and exhaustive as he and his most distinguished successors have
regarded it.

§ 2. It remains, then, that we endeavor to bring the theory
into correspondence with the facts such as we have found them
to be; and in order to this it will be necessary to subject it to
some such modification as the following: The proximate condition determining international exchange is the state of comparative prices in the exchanging countries as regards the commodities which form the subject of the trade. But comparative prices within the limits of each country are determined
by two distinct principles—within the range of effective industrial competition, by Cost of Production; outside that range,
by Reciprocal Demand. The ultimate conditions, therefore,

on which international trade depends are, where the commodities are produced in each country under a *régime* of competition, a difference in the comparative costs of producing them; where effective competition does not obtain such a state of Reciprocal Demand among non-competing groups as shall issue in a difference, in the exchanging countries, in the comparative prices of the products proceeding from such groups.

§ 3. And now, in order to exhibit the practical consequences involved in the modification of the received doctrine just proposed, and to satisfy the reader that the point raised is something more than a mere formal and barren criticism, I will ask his attention to a question which has been of late a good deal discussed—the connection, namely, between the rate of wages prevailing in a country and the course and character of its external trade.

It is a very general opinion among commercial men in this country that, if not the most important, at least at the present time the most urgent, condition required for promoting the development of British commerce, is that the rate of wages should generally be reduced, or, at the least, should not be permitted to rise above its present level. "Dear labor," says Mr. Brassey, expressing an opinion which has since been echoed in many a leading column, "is the great obstacle to the extension of British trade." Nor is this opinion by any means confined to Great Britain. Ask a New England merchant why the United States are unable to compete with Great Britain in the manufacture of cotton fabrics, and it is one hundred to one he will tell you it is owing to the high price of labor in the Union as compared with the low rates prevailing on this side of the Atlantic. Ask, again, a Melbourne merchant why Victoria, notwithstanding her fine agricultural resources, still continues to import a portion of her food, and the answer will be similar: the higher price of labor in Victoria than in the other Australian colonies, or in the districts of South America from which corn may be obtained, will be considered as telling us all it is needful to know in order to a full comprehension of the fact.

Such is the nearly universal opinion on this subject among commercial men; and yet it needs but little consideration to show that it is in direct conflict with the received economic doctrine, as expounded by Ricardo, as to the causes governing foreign trade. For it must be remembered that by cost of production, at all events in connection with the theory of foreign trade, both Ricardo and Mill understood what I have maintained to be in all cases the proper signification of the phrase— namely, cost *as measured in number of days' labor and abstinence;* and it is by comparative cost as thus measured that, according to the theory, international trade is governed. But inasmuch as a rise or fall in the rate of wages has no effect on the comparative quantities of labor required for the production of different commodities, it is evident that if the received theory be true, this circumstance must be incapable of altering in any way the course of foreign trade; and this was undoubtedly Ricardo's opinion. Indeed it was a leading doctrine in his scheme of ideas, on which he insisted with reiterated emphasis, that high wages do not make high prices—a position which of itself involves the negative of the prevailing view. There can be no question, therefore, that the opinion so widely entertained as to the effect of wages on foreign trade finds no sanction whatever in the theory of Ricardo. I have already, however, shown reasons for regarding that theory as imperfect. As I view the case, external trade is governed proximately by relative prices, and relative prices are, in some instances, not indeed determined by wages, but so intimately connected with wages that the movements of the two phenomena are steadily coincident. The theory of international trade, therefore, as I hold it, does not exclude the possibility of its course being

affected by movements in the rate of wages: at the same time
I believe that what may be described as the commercial view
of this subject is almost wholly erroneous.

Let us consider the sort of argument by which it may be
supposed the opinion in question would be supported. It
would, I apprehend, run in some such form as the following:
taking, for example, the case of wheat imported into Victoria
from South Australia or from the nearest South American
ports, it would be argued that this was owing to the inability
of Victoria to compete with these latter countries, owing to
the high price of her labor. Let the price of labor in Victoria
only fall to the same level as in the countries from which it
imports its wheat, it would be plausibly urged, and it will at
once become profitable to raise wheat in Victoria from soils
from which it can not now be raised with profit. What would
be the reply of Ricardo to this argument? He would answer
that if wages fell in agriculture, they would also fall in gold-
mining, in sheep-farming, and in all the other industries of the
colony. The relative attractiveness of the several occupations,
as investments for capital, would not be altered, and there
would be no reason that capital should be distributed among
them in other proportions than at present. It is true indeed
that, with a reduced rate of wages, the cultivation of wheat
would yield a profit where it would not yield one now, but
that is not the question. The question is, would it yield *the
rate of profit current in the colony?* Now it must not be forgotten that the change which we suppose to have taken place
—a fall in general wages while the conditions of production
remain in other respects unaffected—would imply a rise in
general profits. Australian farmers, therefore, would not be
satisfied with the rate of profit which they now receive; they
would expect as high a return upon their capital as—allowance made for the special circumstances of different pursuits—
could be got in other occupations; and this they could only

obtain by confining their operations to lands of equal fertility with those which they now cultivate. In a word, the change in the rate of wages being general, and affecting all occupations alike,* there would be no more reason for extending the employment of capital in agriculture than for doing so in any other branch of production. The capital at the disposal of the colony, under a low, as under a high, rate of wages, would, therefore, continue to be distributed among the various industries pretty much as it now is; and Victoria would have precisely the same reasons as at present for importing a portion of her food.† It need scarcely be added that this reply, whatever its merit, would be not less valid against the same argument whether urged in Melbourne, New York, or London.

§ 4. It is evident that the reply which I have attributed to

---

* As has been pointed out by Ricardo and others, it is not strictly true that a fall or rise in general wages would affect all industries alike. Industries in which fixed capital was largely employed would be less affected by the change than those in which the outlay consisted mainly of wages, and the result would be made manifest by a change in the relative values of the products of the respective industries. These are details, however, into which it is scarcely necessary to enter in arguing the general question of the effect of wages on foreign trade. So far as they took effect, however, the course of foreign trade would no doubt undergo more or less modification, but by no means necessarily in the direction which the common opinion supposes. A fall in wages, for example, might easily have the effect of checking instead of promoting the exportation of an article if it happened to be one in the production of which fixed capital was largely employed; as, on the other hand, a rise in wages might lead to the exportation of a commodity which it had not previously been profitable to export. In the particular instance discussed in the text the circumstance in question would have scarcely any practical operation, the industries of a new country like Australia standing pretty much on the same footing as regards the use of fixed capital.

† I shall be told, perhaps, that for some time past Victoria has, as a matter of fact, year after year extended her agriculture and curtailed her importation of food from abroad; and that this has been synchronous with a fall of wages in the colony. The fact is so, and I shall presently have occasion to point out the real connection between the two phenomena.

Ricardo is valid on the assumption which he constantly makes, that industrial competition is effective over the entire range of a country's industry; but it is equally plain that it ceases to be cogent just in the degree in which this assumption ceases to be true in fact. In old countries like England, as I have pointed out, the *régime* of industrial monopoly covers a considerable area, but even in new communities like the Australian colonies competition is not quite universal. I shall now advert to an example of this failure of industrial competition furnished by the industry of Australia which will set the point at issue in a clear light.

As all the world knows, the colonies of Australia have been mainly peopled by immigrants from this country and their descendants. Among the population as thus constituted industrial competition would, I should apprehend, be nearly, if not quite universally, effective. No one would be excluded by law, by social circumstances, or, after he had been a short time in the colony, by want of means, from taking part as a laborer in any industrial occupation. If this be so, wages throughout the principal industries of the country would follow the law which apportions remuneration to sacrifice, as assumed by Ricardo; and a rise or fall of wages would consequently within this range have no effect upon the distribution of capital among the various industries, nor, therefore, upon its foreign trade. But into the ordinary population a small infusion of alien races has found entrance; in particular, the Chinese have found their way into Victoria and New South Wales, and for some years a considerable importation of Polynesian laborers into Queensland has been in progress. These people do not take part in the general industrial competition of the country; but partly through the prejudices existing against them, partly through physical or intellectual inability, are confined to a few of the simple and cruder industries. It results that the rate of remuneration in their case fails to follow the same rule which holds among the Anglo-Saxon population. A rise or fall of wages may occur among those alien races without affecting wages generally in the colony, and consequently may affect the relative attractiveness, as investments for capital, of the particular industries in which they are employed. In this way the course of foreign trade may come to depend upon the price at which a particular kind of labor may be obtained. The most decisive example in point is that of the Polynesian laborers in Queensland. Sugar cultivation has been started in that colony, and it is asserted—so far as I can gather, with good reason—that the prosperity and even the continuance of the industry depends upon the possibility of obtaining cheap labor from Polynesia. The immigrant from this country is but ill fitted to endure the exposure to the extreme heat of that region which labor in the sugar fields demands, and consequently can not be drawn to that work unless by the inducement of a proportionally high reward. But the Polynesian can expose himself without detriment to a tropical climate; the processes of sugar cultivation are of a simple mechanical sort such as the rudest laborer may perform; and, his expectation of reward not being pitched high, he is easily induced, for a rate of pay considerably under that prevailing in the colony, to hire himself for the work. On the other hand, the Polynesian is unfitted, from his habits, and to some extent from his inferior physique, for taking part, except in a quite subordinate way, in the ordinary mining, pastoral, and agricultural occupations. It results from all this that the possibility of cultivating sugar in Queensland with the ordinary profits of the place depends almost entirely on the presence there of these Polynesian laborers; and sugar being mainly used as an article of export, it comes to pass that the course of foreign trade in this article turns almost entirely upon a question of wages.

The case I have taken for illustration affords a somewhat

exaggerated example of the consequences which may arise in the foreign trade of a country from an interruption to the free play of industrial competition. But though the results may be less conspicuous, they are in character and principle the same, wherever a similar interruption, in whatever degree, is experienced. In Australia the obstacle to free competition lies in difference of race. In Great Britain the impediments are of a social and material kind; but the economic effects are identical. In each case alike partial and limited movements in the wages of labor are rendered possible; and, in the manner I have explained in a former chapter,* such partial and limited movements are always attended by corresponding changes in the relative prices of commodities. But, as we have seen, the relative prices of commodities are the proximate condition on which the course of foreign trade depends.

So far, therefore, the theory of foreign trade, modified in the manner I have proposed, finds room for the common notion, at least to the extent of admitting the existence of cases in which international trade may be affected by changes in the rate of wages—a view which the theory, as it came from the hands of Ricardo, absolutely excludes. The nature and extent, however, of the results which may accrue from occurrences of this kind are by no means of that simple and obvious character which is commonly supposed. It will serve to clear our ideas upon this point if we consider the possible consequences involved in the following hypothetical case.

Let us suppose a fall of wages to take place in some leading branch of English manufacture—say Sheffield cutlery—what would be the effect of this on the external trade of England? It has been already seen that, if the change supposed were accompanied by a corresponding change over the whole field of English industry, the effect would be *nil* upon the distribution

---

* Part ii., chap. ii.

of capital in the country, and therefore upon the course of our external trade; but the same conclusion may easily be reached by another path. For example, the common notion is that a general fall of wages would lead to a general fall of prices, and this again to an immense extension of the export trade of the country. Now, supposing this result to happen, it is at least evident that there would be nothing in the case to cause a corresponding extension of our import trade. Observe then what would ensue. Foreign nations would become heavily our debtors, and a great flow of gold would set in from all quarters toward England, which, becoming the basis of new creations of credit, would quickly reproduce the former state of wages and prices, when our export trade would at once return to its former limits. We are thus, though by a different route, conducted to the same conclusion as before, that a movement of wages, where it is general, can have no effect upon foreign trade. Let us now consider what the result would be, supposing the fall in wages not to extend beyond the group of trades in effective competition with the principal industries of Sheffield. It is evident that it is only in so far as the fall in wages is followed by a fall in prices that it can affect foreign trade at all. I will assume, then, that the prices of Sheffield manufactures fall in proportion to the fall in Sheffield wages; and on this assumption any of three possible consequences might ensue. The increased demand of foreign countries for Sheffield wares might be in proportion to their increased cheapness, or it might be in less proportion or in greater. In the first case, while sending a greater quantity of cutlery abroad, we should only send the same value: foreign nations would be in our debt as regards this item in the international account to no greater extent than now, and—no change having occurred in the price of foreign commodities—we should consequently receive from them the same quantity of the produce of their industry, neither more nor less, than they now send us. The net result, therefore, of what had happened would be a gain for all consumers of Sheffield wares, whether living in this country or abroad, obtained at the expense of the workmen of Sheffield. Sheffield employers might reap some temporary gains, but competition would quickly reduce their profits to the usual rate: as a permanent result, they would be no better off than before; while the foreign trade of England would not be extended. Take now the second case, and let us suppose that the increased demand from abroad is less than in proportion to the fall in price of Sheffield wares. In this case, also, the consumers of those wares would everywhere be benefited, but the foreign trade of the country, so far as Sheffield contributed to it, would, at least in the first instance, be positively curtailed. This, however, would be merely the initial effect. The reader must remember that, by hypothesis, the export of Sheffield manufactures, though greater in point of quantity, has, through the fall in price, become smaller in value than formerly. It follows that our exports—assuming the state of things previously in existence to have been one of commercial equilibrium, and that other things remain the same—would be insufficient to discharge our foreign liabilities. An efflux of gold from England to foreign countries would, therefore, set in, and would continue so long as prices here and in foreign countries remained at the same relative level which had rendered the drain necessary. This, however, could not be for long. The transfer of gold from England to foreign countries would, in the usual way, lead to a re-adjustment of relative prices, and, as a consequence of this, to a re-adjustment of reciprocal demand. What the exact character of this re-adjustment would be it is impossible *a priori* to say. English demand for foreign products might fall off, which would imply a contraction of English foreign trade, or foreign demand for English products might increase, which would imply an augmentation; or both consequences might in different degrees be realized, which would be consistent with either diminution or increase. All that is certain is that, in the definitive result, commercial equilibrium would be restored—the exports of England, that is to say, would be brought into due relation to her foreign liabilities.* The third possible case is that the foreign demand for Sheffield wares should increase in a proportion beyond that of their cheapness. In this event foreign nations would, in the first instance, become our debtors to a greater extent than the proceeds of their ordinary trade would cover. An efflux of gold would now set in from them to us; and the necessity would again arise of a change in the reciprocal demand of England and foreign nations. Commercial equilibrium would here, too, ultimately be re-established; but, as in the former case, the end might be reached by any of the same three methods, and the definitive result would be equally compatible with a contraction or an expansion of international trade.

In the foregoing example I have argued on the assumption of a fall in wages occurring in some leading branch of English industry. If instead of a fall we supposed a rise, and this rise to be confined to some particular departments of trade, we should find ourselves conducted, by a similar course of reasoning, to precisely the same conclusion. In the first instance the advance in price would check foreign demand for the English commodities which had risen, but this would lead to a re-distribution of the precious metals between England and the countries with which she traded, and this again to a change in relative prices, which would issue in a restoration of the equilibrium of trade—a result, in this case also, compatible alike with augmentation or decrease.

We may, then, sum up the results of this part of our investigation: Partial, as opposed to general, movements in the

---

* I am here obliged to anticipate a portion of the theory of international values to be set forth in the next chapter.

wages of labor affect the foreign trade of a country, but it is impossible to say *a priori* in what direction, whether of expansion or of contraction. To know this it would be necessary to know what the definitive result would be as regards relative prices in the country in which the change of wages had occurred, and those with which it trades. If this were, on the whole, to augment the difference in relative prices in the two places, an extension of international trade would be the consequence; but in the contrary event, which is equally possible and probable, the opposite effect—a contraction of trade—is that which would be realized.

§ 5. Let me now state the point to which the general argument has been carried. I have endeavored to show that a rise or fall of wages in a country, so far forth as it is general, has no tendency to affect the course of foreign trade: a fall in the general rate does not tend to an extension of foreign trade, any more than a rise in that rate necessitates a contraction. On the other hand, I have pointed out that, where, owing to the existence of impediments to the action of free industrial competition, partial movements in the rate of wages occur, inasmuch as these issue in a change of relative prices, the course of foreign trade is in this case affected, though it is impossible, previous to experience, to say in what direction the change may take place. So far the argument has been carried. I desire now to consider a problem which, except upon its negative side, has not yet, so far as I know, received the attention of economists—I mean the nature of the connection that exists between general wages and foreign trade. We have seen that that connection is *not* one of cause and effect; but we have yet to discover what its nature is. General wages do not determine foreign trade, but it by no means follows that the two phenomena are not intimately connected; and this we shall find to be, in point of fact, the case.

I recur once again to that rich repertory of economical experience, the recent history of our Australian colonies. As we have already seen, the discovery of gold in those colonies in 1851 was the signal for a sudden and extraordinary development of foreign trade, which was accompanied by an equally sudden and extraordinary advance in the wages of labor. This remarkable movement reached its culmination about the year 1852 or 1853, when the rate of wages in the rough work of gold mining was, for some time, maintained at the very high point of 20s. a day. We have unfortunately no exact commercial statistics previous to 1856; but in that year the total external trade of the principal gold colony, Victoria, amounted to over £30,000,000 sterling. From 1856 to the present time the history of the colony has been one of extraordinary prosperity; but coincidently with this prosperity we notice two remarkable facts—a pretty steady decline throughout the whole of the period at once in the wages of labor and in the dimensions of external trade. As I have just said, that trade in 1856 had attained the large aggregate of £30,000,000 sterling. In 1870, after fourteen years of such prosperity as I have referred to, it stood at less than £25,000,000. The fall in wages has not been less striking. It had risen to 20s. a day: it has now fallen for the same mining labor to about half that rate. Wages and foreign trade have thus declined *pari passu;* every step in the descent of wages having been accompanied by the dropping off of some former import, and, as a consequence of this, a corresponding extension of domestic industry in the colony. The facts, it will be observed, negative most decisively the prevalent commercial opinion on the subject under consideration. Dear labor in 1852 did not prevent the sudden and extraordinary expansion of Victorian trade, any more than comparatively cheap labor in 1870 has been able to prevent its contraction. On the other hand, it must be allowed that the power of Victoria to compete with foreign nations, evidenced as this has been by an extension of her domestic industry which has been coincident with a fall in the price of labor, seems to furnish corroboration of the popular notion at the root of the commercial doctrine. It is indeed very evident that all three facts—the decline of foreign trade, the fall in the rate of wages, and the extension of domestic production—are intimately connected; but the question is, what is the nature of the tie that binds them? The true answer is to be found in the fact that the several occurrences are co-ordinate effects of a common cause; that cause being the gradual exhaustion of the richer and more accessible gold deposits. As industry became less productive in raising gold, the amount to be divided between laborer and capitalist became less, and money wages *therefore* fell. As gold, with the increased difficulty of production, became more costly, it became, just in the same degree, a less profitable means of obtaining the various commodities which Victoria required: she ceased, *therefore*, to employ this means to the same extent as formerly, and began instead to produce commodities directly from her own resources: in other words, her foreign trade underwent contraction, and her domestic industry was extended. And as these results have been the consequence of a decline in the productiveness of the gold mines, so, it might be confidently predicted, a new discovery of auriferous deposits equal in abundance and richness to those of the earlier period would have the effect of reversing the present course of development, and by a single stroke send up money wages, give a fresh impulse to external trade, and arrest the extension of miscellaneous industries in the colony. Such is the nature of the connection between the rate of wages in a country and the course of its external trade and domestic industry. They are co-ordinate effects of a common cause, and are consequently symptoms and indications of each other.

In the illustration just given the condition on which the several results depended was the changing cost of gold; and—the change being great in point of degree, and gold being also the material of money—the results have been more palpable and striking than they would have been had the cheapened commodity been one of ordinary consumption. But the effect, though less palpable, would not really be different in this latter case—provided only the article affected were of a kind in tolerably extensive demand and suited for exportation to foreign countries. I am unfortunately unacquainted with any actual occurrence sufficiently simple and decisive to enable me to exhibit, in a perfectly unequivocal light, the operation of the principle in this more general form, and I must, therefore, have recourse for this purpose to hypothesis. I will then suppose that, as the result of some mechanical invention not known to other nations, a great improvement has been effected in the manufacture of woolen goods in England—an improvement which would reduce the cost of manufacturing this class of goods in as great a proportion as the cost of gold in Australia was reduced by the discovery of gold—what would be the effect of such an occurrence on the external trade of England and on the remuneration of labor in the country? In the first instance, it is evident, there would be an extensive diversion of English capital into the branch of manufacture thus beneficially affected; and the increased production of woolen goods would lead to a fall in their price, which would only stop when brought into the usual relation with their now diminished cost of production. With the fall in price a large increase would take place in the foreign demand for English woolens. As, however, there would be nothing in the case to cause a corresponding increase in the demand of England for the commodities of foreign countries, a transfer of gold from the latter to the former in payment of the enlarged exportations would be necessary, and this would continue until, through a rise of prices in England and a fall of prices abroad, the equilibrium of trade was re-established. At this point many articles which had formerly been produced in England, and perhaps produced for exportation, would now be selling at lower prices in foreign countries. Such articles would cease to be produced in England, or at all events to be produced on the same scale as formerly, and would in greater or less quantity begin to be imported from abroad. Ultimately we should arrive at this definitive result: a larger proportion than formerly of the aggregate capital of England would be devoted to the production of woolen goods, a smaller proportion to her other miscellaneous industries; while the things formerly produced by the displaced industries would now be obtained from abroad through an exchange for woolen goods. In other words, England would avail herself of her great comparative superiority in the production of woolens for the purpose of obtaining more cheaply than before all commodities in the production of which her superiority was relatively less. The result, so far as foreign trade was concerned, would thus be exactly analogous to what happened on the discovery of gold in Australia. But I shall be asked how as regards the wages of labor? The gold discoveries, as we saw, had the effect of raising the rate of money wages in Australia in proportion to the fall in the cost of money. Would a similar consequence follow on the hypothesis we are now considering? Beyond question, yes; that is to say, as wages in Australia rose, measured in the commodity of which the cost had been cheapened, so wages in England would, in the supposed case, rise, and in a corresponding proportion, measured in the commodity similarly affected. In the one case that commodity was gold, in the other woolen goods. English laborers, so far as they were consumers of woolen goods, would, in the supposed case, obtain that commodity more cheaply; so far as they were consumers of foreign goods, procured through an exchange for woolens, would also obtain those commodities more cheaply;

so far, again, as they were consumers of commodities produced in England other than woolen goods, would gain nothing by what had occurred. It may be added that those other commodities of English production, inasmuch as they were not affected by the same cause which had cheapened English woolens, would be represented in exchange by a larger quantity of the cheapened article than before, just as the products of Australia were represented by higher gold prices in proportion as the cost of gold fell. To state the result in a single phrase, the wages of English laborers, *measured in woolen goods*, would rise in proportion as the cost of those goods had fallen; in exact analogy with what happened in Australia. Here, then, we find, in the case of a commodity of general consumption, as we had before found in the case of gold, the course of foreign trade and the rate of wages intimately bound together through the link of a common cause in the state of productive industry. It is rare indeed that changes in the cost of production take place on so great a scale as that realized or assumed in our illustrations; but where such changes do occur, be the scale large or small, the results which follow, though different in point of magnitude, are in character such as I have described. Every new invention, every happy discovery, that cheapens the cost of producing particular commodities, and so alters their comparative cost, sets in action forces which operate in the directions I have indicated, however slight and even imperceptible may be the actual results which flow from each.

The real nature of the connection between the rate of wages prevailing in a country and the character and course of its external trade ought now, I think, to be tolerably clear. They are co-ordinate effects of a common cause, that cause being the degree and direction in which a nation's industry happens to be productive. Whatever be the articles with respect to which the industry of a nation is specially productive, these are the articles which will form the staple of its external trade, and, *measured in these*, the wages of labor will be high. If wages are high, measured in money, this will indicate either rich mines of gold or silver, or a high productiveness of industry in some commodities in large demand abroad with which gold or silver may be purchased on favorable terms. If they be high, measured in food, clothing, and other necessaries and comforts, we may infer similarly a high productiveness of industry, direct or indirect, with regard to those commodities. Thus the commodities, whatever they are, measured in which wages are high, will either form the staples of her foreign trade, or will be such as may be obtained at small cost through those staples. The notion, therefore, which prevails both here and in the United States that the high rate of general wages obtaining in each country is a hinderance to the extension of its foreign trade must be pronounced to be absolutely without foundation. Supposing a fall in wages to occur in either country, the other conditions of production remaining as at present, and supposing the fall to be general, this circumstance would not, as I have shown, affect the relative attractiveness of the different branches of industry as investments for capital. Capital would, therefore, be distributed among them as at present, and nothing would occur to alter the course of its foreign trade. The sole result would be a general rise of profits: capitalists would gain what laborers had lost. A fall of general wages, on any other assumption, would inevitably imply diminished productiveness in some of the great departments of productive industry; and such diminished productiveness involving, as it would, changes in the comparative cost of commodities, would no doubt entail changes in external commerce. But the point to be borne in mind is that the latter result, though coincident with, would not be the effect of the fall in general wages, but that both would be co-ordinate effects of the decline in the productiveness of industry; and further, that the changes in external commerce, occurring under the circumstances supposed, would not necessarily be in the direction of extended trade. Quite as probably in either case, in the case of the United States much more probably, the movement would involve a contraction of dealings with foreign countries. Thus, supposing a general fall of wages in the United States, measured, let us say, in gold and provisions, or, what comes to the same thing, supposing money wages to fall, the prices of provisions remaining as at present, let us consider what this would imply. Would it not imply that industry in the United States was less productive than it now is in procuring the commodities in question; and, therefore, more nearly on a par than at present, in the case of such products, with industry in other countries? Would it not, in a word, imply that the comparative cost of producing commodities there and elsewhere had been brought into closer approximation, and that consequently the possible field for international exchange had been narrowed? The rate of wages and the course of foreign trade are thus intimately connected; but that connection (except within the limited range within which reciprocal demand governs domestic values) is not one of cause and effect, but of co-ordinate phenomena depending upon identical conditions.

CHAPTER III.

INTERNATIONAL VALUES.

§ 1. WE have now ascertained the circumstances under which international trade arises, and the nature of the advantages that flow from it. These advantages, as we have seen, are such as result from a more effective distribution of the productive forces of the world. Supposing a universal freedom of trade, it would not indeed follow that every product of industry would be raised precisely in that part of the world in which it could be raised with greatest advantage; for this would require that population and capital should be distributed with no other view than to economical gain. The course of population and capital, however, it is needless to say, is influenced by many other considerations as well; and what international trade, so far as it is allowed free scope, accomplishes for mankind is, that the industry of the world is carried on, not indeed with the utmost possible advantage, but with the utmost advantage practicable, regard being had to the manner in which the world is peopled and to the condition of its inhabitants.

Such is the nature of the gain; but here another question arises: On what principle is the increase of wealth which results shared among the nations which co-operate in producing it? To put the same point in a different form—What causes determine the proportions in which trading nations exchange their products? These proportions may conceivably be such as to give all the advantage to one only of the exchanging parties, or such as to share it among a few to the exclusion of the rest, or such, again, as to distribute it in any ratio whatever among them all. According as one result or the other is attained, will be the quantum of advantage which each nation derives from its commercial dealings with others. We are thus conducted by the course of our investigation from the doctrine of international trade to the special problem of international values.

§ 2. It may be well, perhaps, to remind the reader that the subject of our present inquiry is normal, not market, values—the proportions in which nations exchange their products as a rule, or when trade is in a state of equilibrium, not those in which the exchange may take place on a particular occasion, or under the influence of exceptional conditions. Now we have already seen that normal values depend on one or other of two principles: where industrial competition prevails, on cost of production; and in the absence of effective industrial competition, on reciprocal demand. Inasmuch, however, as the condition of effective industrial competition (in the sense defined) is not satisfied in the intercourse of independent nations, it is at once evident that the ruling principle of international values is not cost of production, and can only be that other influence which prevails in the absence of effective competition. So much is recognized in the received text-books of Political Economy. But here I must call attention to an inconsistency in which those text-books are involved, to which, indeed, incidental reference has been already made. It will be remembered that in a former portion of this work I criticised at some length the received doctrine of Cost of Production, which, as expounded by Mr. Mill and others, is represented as consisting in, and varying with, the wages and profits of producers. I stated then that this conception of cost was not reconcilable with the doctrine of international values upheld by the same authorities, which refers these phenomena, not to cost of production, but to the reciprocal demand of exchanging nations. I now propose to justify that criticism by showing that, regarding cost of production in the sense assigned to it, international values do, in point of fact, in all cases correspond with this principle; in other words, that, while they are said *not* to be governed by cost, they nevertheless invariably conform to it. A simple illustration will enable me to make good this position.

Let us suppose two commodities, one the product of English industry, the other produced in the United States, and selling for the same sum of money, say £1000 each. These commodities will (cost of carriage being omitted on both sides) exchange for each other, and will, therefore, represent equal values in international trade. This being so, how stands the case as to their respective costs of production? Assuming these to consist in wages and profits, the answer must be that their costs of production are equal also; for, as I have elsewhere shown, the wages and profits of producers are, where industry is continuous, in effect the outcome of the values they produce. The former, therefore, must be constantly proportional to the latter; and accordingly, where the values of commodities are equal, as these values resolve themselves into wages and profits, the wages and profits of their producers— that is to say, according to the view we are now considering, their costs of production—must be equal. Now it is obvious that this argument admits of being applied to every instance whatever of international exchange;* and we are thus confronted with this singular result, that, while cost of production, according to our text-books, has no place in determining international values, international values, nevertheless, according to principles supplied by the same authorities, invariably corre-

---

* It will be seen that the case would not be altered if, instead of money, we take any other article, the subject of international exchange, for example food, as the measure of cost and value.

spond to it. I must leave those who accept both doctrines of the received Political Economy to reconcile the two positions as they best can.

On the other hand, if we take as our conception of cost that view of it for which I have contended, according to which it consists in labor and abstinence, the truth of the accepted doctrine on its negative side follows as a matter of course. To establish this we need not go beyond the illustration just given. Two commodities respectively of English and American production, each worth £1000, exchange for each other, and therefore represent equal values in international trade. Further, as I have just pointed out, their values being equal, they constitute equal aggregates of wages and profits for the producers on each side. The American scale of remuneration, however, is much more liberal than the English, and the proceeds of those equal values will therefore be distributed in higher wages and larger profits on one side than on the other. ·It follows that they will *not* be distributed in proportion to the labor and abstinence remunerated : in other words, the costs, to which they correspond, will not be equal. The sacrifice will be less on the American than on the English side. English and American commodities, therefore, do not exchange for each other in proportion to their costs of production, as consisting in the real sacrifices undergone by the producers. The negative side of the received doctrine respecting international values is thus found to be true, but only on the condition of understanding cost of production in the sense for which I have contended.

§ 3. The argument just stated brings into view a principle already more than once referred to in these pages, which, as it will be found to have important bearings on some problems of international value, may conveniently be set forth with some distinctness here. The principle to which I refer is, that the relative rates of wages and profits in the different branches of industry afford an indication, *in an inverse sense*, of the relation in which the exchange values of the commodities, proceeding from such branches of industry, stand to their costs of production. It will of course be understood that I use the term "cost of production" here in the sense which I hold to be the right one. Thus, to revert to a former illustration, supposing that in the manufacture of scientific instruments wages and profits ranged considerably higher than in ordinary handicraft trades, let us say, carpentry, the fact would show that, in the exchange of the products of the former for those of the latter industry, the sacrifices involved in the production of mathematical instruments bore a smaller proportion to the values of those instruments than the sacrifices involved in producing common tables and chairs, for example, bore to their values. The cost would be low relatively to the value in the trades in which wages and profits were high, high in the trades in which they were low, while the relation would be one of equality where the rates of wages and profits were equal on each side. We are thus furnished with an easy means of determining the relation in which the exchange values of any two compared commodities stand to their costs of production. If the rates of wages and profits obtained by the respective producers of the two commodities be equal—that is to say, in proportion to the sacrifices undergone—it is matter of demonstration that the commodities in question exchange in proportion to their costs. If they are unequal, the contrary conclusion not less certainly follows; and further, the difference in the relative rates of remuneration will indicate the degree in which the exchange values of the commodities deviate from the proportion existing between their costs of production. But this simple criterion may be made simpler still. For practical purposes, we shall not lose appreciably in point of accuracy if, instead of making it consist in wages and profits, we confine our attention to wages alone. Profits form but a small element in the value of most commodities, and the divergence of the rates of profit in different occupations and in different countries is (owing to the greater mobility of capital than labor) much less considerable than that of the rates of wages. We may, therefore, without danger of serious error, substitute "wages" for "wages and profits," and we are at once provided with an easy means of determining the relation of exchange value to cost of production in all cases whatever.

To give now some examples of the application of our criterion to the transactions of international trade, I find that, according to investigations made by Mr. Wells,* the United States Commissioner, which on the whole have been confirmed by the Reports lately received from our agents in foreign countries, the relative rates of wages for similar kinds of labor in the leading manufacturing industries in the United States, England, Belgium, France, and Germany range nearly as follows: As compared with England, wages in the United States are from 25 to 50 per cent. higher; as compared with Belgium, from 48 to 70 per cent. higher; while, as compared with France and Germany, the difference rises to nearly 100 per cent.† I need hardly say that if the comparison were extended so as to include Oriental states, for example, India and

---

* See his Report for 1868, pp. 67–69.

† It is true that the returns quoted represent the rates of wages per day; and a day's labor, even in the same occupations, does not always represent equal exertion undergone, since men work harder and longer in some countries than in others. This consideration, however, if taken account of, as no doubt it should be, would only have the effect of strengthening the grounds of the argument in the text—at all events so long as the comparison is confined to the United States and Europe: for from the parliamentary reports recently published upon this subject it appears to be almost a rule that, comparing different countries, the laboring day is long nearly in proportion as the rate of wages is low. Thus it is generally shorter in the United States than in England, in England than in Belgium and France, and in Belgium and France than in Germany: the rates of wages in these several countries, as we have seen, declining in a corresponding order.

China, the differences in the scales of remuneration would become still more striking, the remuneration of a day's labor in the United States being probably equivalent to that of four or five in the latter countries. Now what, according to our criterion, do these differences indicate as regards the terms of international exchange? They indicate this—in the first place, that the several nations named do not exchange their products with the United States in proportion to their costs of production; and, secondly, that the proportion in which the exchange takes place deviates from the principle of cost in the degree marked by the differences between the rates of wages in each country and in the United States; in other words, our criterion shows us this—that, in the commercial dealings of those several nations, the product of a day's labor in the United States enables the workman to command the product, in round numbers, of a day and a third's labor in Great Britain, the product of a day and a half's labor in Belgium, the product of from one and three-quarters to nearly two days' labor in France and Germany; while it probably would command the product of four or five days' labor in China and India. Such, or nearly such, are the proportions, measured by the standard of cost, in which the leading commercial nations of the world, at the present time, exchange their productions; and so very far is it from being true that international values, in the actual dealings of commerce, correspond with that standard.*

§ 4. So far as to the negative side of our argument. The

---

* The position here contended for is very clearly, though incidentally, established in Mr. Senior's essay on the "Cost of obtaining Money," and by the application of the same criterion. Mr. Senior, nevertheless, held the current doctrine as to cost of production; for though defining it in his treatise as consisting of "labor and abstinence," he at once abandons this definition, and substitutes for it "wages and profits," as equivalent and more convenient expressions! In the essay just referred to he speaks of the question as one of nomenclature.

products of trading nations do not exchange for each other in proportion to their costs of production. There is no reason that they should do so, inasmuch as industrial competition is not effective in the intercourse of nations; and the evidence just adduced proves that they do not do so in point of fact. The principle, therefore, which determines international values must be that one which operates in the absence of effective industrial competition, namely, Reciprocal Demand ; and this, as I have already said, is the received doctrine of Political Economy. But though Cost of Production is not in this case the determining cause, it does, nevertheless, exercise an important influence in international trade by controlling the aberrations of value which are possible under a *régime* where monopoly is the presiding principle. This, indeed, is implied in the ordinary expositions of the doctrine; but I do not think the fact has hitherto been brought out with as much distinctness and prominence as it deserves.

To aid toward this result, it may be observed that industrial monopoly may exist under various conditions involving a corresponding variety in the results which flow from it. It may exist, in the first place, in an absolute form, as where an individual or a nation possesses the exclusive power of producing certain commodities: or, secondly, it may be qualified, springing from the possession of certain special facilities of production not shared by others, as in the case of those peculiarities of soil and climate which give an advantage to some districts and countries over others in the production of certain articles, which it is still possible for the latter to produce, though under less favorable conditions; while again, in commercial dealings, monopoly may be either one-sided or reciprocal—confined to one of the trading parties, or extending to both with regard to their respective staples. Examples of monopoly in all these forms will be found in international trade, and the power of reciprocal demand over value will be greater or less, according to the form which the monopoly in any given case may assume.

For example, where the monopoly is at once strict and reciprocal—a case not frequent in international trade, but which sometimes does occur, as in the traffic which takes place between the tropical and the frozen zones, in the exchange, suppose, of spices for ice—in this case the influence of reciprocal demand on value is unqualified and absolute, since under such circumstances there is nothing but the desires on each side, supported by such means as are available to give them effect, to determine the bargain.

A more frequent and important case is that in which the monopoly is strict, but one-sided, or, if existing on both sides, only strict on one side, while it is qualified on the other. This species of monopoly is largely exemplified in the trade between tropical and temperate countries, and again in that between the gold-producing districts of the earth and the countries which trade with them. Reciprocal demand here operates, but subject to a limit on the side of the country which has the power of producing both the commodities, or classes of commodities, forming the subject of exchange. To give an example: in the trade between England and Australia (for simplicity of illustration, I suppose all other gold countries to be excluded from the commerce) there is no limit to the possible rise which might take place in the value of gold—to the possible quantity, that is, of her products which England might give in exchange for gold—save in the desire of England for gold and her ability to pay for it; but, on the other hand, the fall in the value of gold—the price in gold which Australia will consent to pay us for our goods—has a very definite limit short of Australian needs for what we produce—the limit, namely, set by the cost at which Australia can produce those articles for herself. So soon as prices in gold have reached the point at which Australia can satisfy her requirements more easily by the direct production of the commodity than by producing gold to be exchanged for it, the fall of gold, in relation to that commodity, has reached its limit, and no increasing requirements on the Australian side will have any further effect on its international value.

But again, there is a third case, the most frequent and important of all in international trade—that, namely, in which monopoly exists on both sides, but is qualified on both. This occurs when each of the trading nations is in the possession, not of an exclusive power of production, but of a comparative superiority (in the sense in which this phrase has been explained) with reference to the articles which constitute its staples in the trade. Here reciprocal demand still determines international values, but the range of its influence finds a limit on both sides. This, I say, is the most frequent and important case of all in international commerce. It is largely exemplified in the trade between the various countries of Europe, and still more strikingly in that between Europe and North America. In the exchange, for example, of wheat for cotton yarn, or of timber for iron, each of the exchanging countries has a comparative advantage in its own staple; and any terms of international exchange which are within the limits of that advantage will imply a gain, though not necessarily an equal gain, for both countries. Within these limits, therefore, reciprocal demand will operate to determine what the precise terms of the exchange shall be; but beyond those limits on either side international values can not permanently remain, since the moment the limits thus set are transcended the resources of the country so placed at disadvantage can be brought into requisition, and the motive for the trade ceases.

These limitations on the action of reciprocal demand in international exchange are such as would exist if each country only traded with one other. But when we take into account the actual state of things, and consider that the external trade of each country comprises dealings with many others, we find that the limits to the deviations of value under the action of demand are considerably narrower than we might at first have supposed. For example, reverting to the illustration already given of the trade between certain parts of the United States and Barbados, it is probable that the difference in the comparative costs of sugar and flour in those two countries is very considerable; and that consequently a very considerable latitude would exist for possible variations in the terms on which the staples are exchanged under the influence of American demand for sugar and Barbadian demand for flour. But before the extreme limit could be reached on either side, the resources of other countries would come into requisition. Any considerable advance of sugar in relation to flour, or of flour in relation to sugar, or, let us say (since money is the medium through which the transactions would be effected), any considerable advance of United States prices in relation to prices in Barbados, or the reverse, would bring other countries into the field, and make their resources available for controlling the advancing price, on whichever side it might happen to be. The cereal capacities of Canada and South America would control the aberrations on the side favorable to the United States; while those on the side favorable to Barbados would be kept in check by the competition of the sugar producers of Jamaica and Cuba. It thus appears that it is not the difference in the comparative costs of production in each pair of trading countries that fixes the limits to the possible variations of international values under the influence of reciprocal demand, but, among all countries mutually accessible for commercial intercourse, the difference of comparative costs, as it exists in the particular countries in which that difference is least. The limits of variation are thus set by the minimum, not by the maximum, difference in comparative cost among the various exchanging and competing countries.

Such is the nature of the influence exercised respectively by reciprocal demand and by cost of production in international exchange. The former *determines;* the latter only *controls.* The distinction between these two functions will be made clear by comparing the action of cost, as just described, with its action in domestic trade. In domestic trade cost of production, within the limits of effective competition, not merely controls, but determines normal value—not merely sets.limits to the variations, but establishes a point toward which they converge. It has accordingly been aptly represented by Adam Smith as a central point about which market values move, and toward which they gravitate. In the instance of international trade, the correct figure by which to describe its action would be, not a point about which values move, but a circle within which they move. Accordingly, it must be carefully remarked that, even in those cases in which its influence is operative, there is no correspondence—at all events no necessary correspondence—between values and costs. The examples I have already given of the relative rates of remuneration prevailing in different countries sufficiently establish this point.)

§ 5. As regards the mode of operation by which international values are determined under the action of international demand. I do not propose to attempt any detailed illustration here. The subject will be found very fully treated in text-books in every one's hands. There is one point, however, on which it seems to me the correct doctrine has not been quite clearly laid down, and on this it may be well here to attempt a few remarks.

The transactions of international trade are of course carried on through the medium of money—that is to say, of gold and silver; and Ricardo has shown that the effect of the play of international demand is to produce such a distribution of the precious metals, and such a relative scale of prices in commercial countries, as on the whole to cause the trade of each country with all others to be carried on upon the same terms as it would be if conducted by barter. When this state of things is realized, the precious metals (so far as they are employed as a medium of exchange, and not as a staple of commerce) cease to pass from country to country; and international trade is in a condition of equilibrium.* The point I desire now to call attention to is the condition of international demand which issues in this result.

The solution commonly given of this problem is that commercial equilibrium is attained when the value of the imports into a country, measured in gold or silver, the universal money of commerce, is equal to the value of the exports from that country. In the language of Mr. Mill, "the produce of a country exchanges for the produce of other countries at such values as are required in order that the whole of her exports may exactly pay for the whole of her imports."† Now, as a matter of fact, it very rarely happens that the whole exports of a country, even if we take an average of many years, exactly pay for the whole of its imports; nor can it be truly said that there is any tendency in the dealings of nations toward this result. The evidence of this is to be found in any statistical

---

* The equilibrium of commerce may, accordingly, be defined for all countries, *not being themselves producers of the precious metals*, as that state of trade which results in maintaining the *real* exchanges, one year with another, at par. Where it happens, however, that a country produces gold or silver for export, a premium on the exchange is, in this case, the normal state of things. During the last twenty years the commercial equilibrium has been extensively disturbed in most countries—the necessary consequence of the large additions now being made to our stock of money.

† In a later passage at the end of the chapter on the "Distribution of the Precious Metals," Mr. Mill recognizes that there are other causes than commercial which affect the relation of imports and exports, and the equilibrium of commerce. But the recognition, only introduced at the end of the discussion, and in quite a summary way, seems scarcely adequate to the requirements of the case.

table showing the exports and imports of different countries. An examination of such a table will show that there are countries which constantly, and as a normal state of things, import largely in excess of their exportations, while there are others of which the exports as regularly exceed the imports. In other cases, again, the imports will be found for a time to have exceeded the exports, after which the relation is inverted, and the exports begin to outstrip the imports. With such facts before us we can not easily admit that an equalization of imports and exports is the necessary condition of a staple trade; and this being so, we have to consider what that condition is.

To elucidate this, a better example can not be found than the external trade of the United Kingdom. I take it as set forth in the Statistical Abstract for the years between 1856 and 1870 inclusive. During the whole of this time the imports remained constantly and largely in excess of the exports. At the commencement of the period the exports stood at, in round numbers, £115,000,000, the imports at £172,000,000; the imports thus exceeding the exports by the amount of £57,000,000 sterling. At the end, that is to say in the year 1870, the exports were £199,000,000, while the imports reached £303,000,000, showing a difference in favor of imports of £104,000,000; and the returns of the intervening years exhibit a constant predominance on the same side, and nearly in the same proportion. The question arises, How has this large excess of imports been paid for? The answer is, to a small extent it has been paid for in services, principally in the services of our mercantile marine, performing as it does a large proportion of the carrying trade of the world, but, in the main, it has not been paid for at all. It came to us from foreign nations, as all our imports have come, in the ordinary course of trade, but the proceeds on sale have never been returned in any form to those from whom the goods came: they were applied instead to the discharge of debts owing to us—debts, however, incurred on account of transactions wholly apart from our export trade. In point of fact, what has happened has been this: Great Britain has for a long time occupied the position of a lender of capital to other nations; she has invested her capital freely in her own colonies; she has lent money to many countries for industrial undertakings, and has been a large purchaser of foreign stocks. On all these accounts foreign nations, including under this term our own colonies, have become her debtors, and, in discharge of their obligations accruing in the form of profits, interest, and dividends on stock, are compelled to send her, year by year, value to a large extent for which no payment in return is required. Here we find the explanation of the large normal excess of our imports over our exports. But an examination of the facts will further evince that this excess is, in the case of Great Britain, the indispensable condition of commercial equilibrium; that under any other circumstances the present relation of prices between her and foreign countries, or, what amounts to the same thing, the present proportion in which they exchange their products, could not be maintained. This will be evident if we consider what would be the consequence of an equality of value being established between British imports and exports, the financial relations of the country with the rest of the world being such as they are. Foreign nations would have to pay us, as now, for what we export, and for this, bills drawn against the goods they send us, that is, our imports, would exactly suffice. But they owe us besides, say a hundred millions, on account of dividends, interest, and other obligations. How are they to discharge this latter liability? It is evident they could do so only in one way, namely, by sending us gold to the value of the amount in question. An extensive influx of gold from foreign countries to Great Britain would thus set in, and—so long as the state of international prices, and therefore of international demand, remained at the point which had produced the equality of imports and exports — would continue. It is plain, however, that international prices and demand could not long remain steady under the circumstances supposed. The large and continued influx of gold into England would necessarily be attended by a rise of prices here, and a fall in foreign countries; and this would quickly lead to a change in the demand of England and of foreign countries for their respective products. England, in possession of enlarged monetary resources, and finding prices falling abroad, would extend her demand for foreign commodities; while, for precisely opposite reasons, foreign countries would curtail their demand for the commodities of England. English imports would thus increase, and English exports diminish; and this would go on, year by year, so long as gold continued to flow. But the question arises at what point would the process terminate, and trade find its equilibrium? The answer is: precisely when the excess of imports over exports had attained its present dimensions—when the former, that is to say, had exceeded the latter by a hundred millions sterling; for it would only be then that foreign countries could discharge all their liabilities to us without remitting gold. Gold would, therefore, at this point cease to flow, and prices would remain at the level they had reached. In a word, the trade between England and the world would once more have attained equilibrium.

And now we are enabled to answer the question propounded a few pages back. The answer may be formulated thus: The state of international demand which results in commercial equilibrium is realized when the reciprocal demand of trading countries produces such a relation of imports and exports among them as enables each country by means of her exports to discharge all her foreign liabilities—a position from which the following corollary may be deduced, that all payments, due from one country to another or to other countries on other accounts than that of imports, of a permanent character—for example, an annual tribute, interest on borrowed capital, dividends on stock, and so forth — and in excess of similar payments due from these latter to the former, will be represented in the foreign trade of that country by an excess of exports over imports; while, conversely, an excess of payments of this character to be received over payments due will find its commercial expression in an excess of imports over exports. This is, in truth, merely to say that the foreign trade of each country will adapt itself to the pecuniary requirements of that country in relation to the countries with which it trades. If a country has been a large borrower of foreign capital, and so is indebted to foreign nations in annual interest, or if, again, her people are much given to traveling in foreign countries, and so have occasion to remit annually large sums abroad for which no return is required, under such circumstances her exports will tend to exceed her imports; while, under an opposite state of things, that is to say, if a country has been a large foreign lender, or if it be the scene of travel for the inhabitants of other countries—the imports will tend to exceed the exports. With many, indeed with most countries, it will happen that they are debtors to foreign countries upon one score and creditors upon another; and the state of the import and export trade will be such as the state of the balance in each case may prescribe. For example, Great Britain makes large remittances abroad every year to meet the expenses of Englishmen residing or traveling in foreign countries. This would tend to make her exports exceed her imports, and would actually produce this effect, if it were not that the debts due on this account to foreign nations are more than balanced by larger debts due on other accounts by them to us. The balance of such non-commercial payments being, on the whole, largely in favor of Great Britain, it results, as we have seen, that her imports are, as a rule, largely in excess of her exports. An illustration of the same principle in an opposite sense is afforded by the foreign trade of the United States previous to 1860. As all the world knows, the people of the United States had long been, as they are still, much addicted to foreign travel: they had also for a long time been extensive borrowers in European money markets. Both these practices combined to place them under the necessity of remitting annually large sums to Europe over and above what they owed on commercial account; and this obligation was discharged in the only way, in the long run, possible, namely, through the medium of United States products exported. Accordingly, if we turn to the Reports on the external trade of the United States for the period previous to 1860, we find, as the normal state of things in that trade, a pretty steady excess of exports over imports—an excess which in her dealings with Europe assumes very large proportions.*

§ 6. The foregoing examples show the effects of international lending and borrowing on the external trade of nations *after* these practices have issued in monetary relations of a definitive kind. At the commencement, however, and for so long as the process of incurring debt is still in actual operation, the effect of such practices on the foreign trade of a country is exactly the reverse of that which is subsequently realized. The nations which have engaged to lend are, during this period, those which have pecuniary obligations to discharge; the na-

---

* The total excess of exports over imports on the aggregate external trade of the United States in the ten years from 1851 to 1860 (inclusive) was 60,200,000 dollars, that is to say, an annual average of about 6,020,000 dollars; but the excess of that portion of it which was carried on with Europe was immensely greater. The excess of exports over imports, for example, in the trade with Great Britain for the single year 1860, amounted to 57,600,000 dollars. This large excess, however, was compensated by an excess the other way in her trade with several countries, chiefly American, in reference to which she holds much the same position financially which Great Britain holds toward her. (See "Wells's Essay:"' "Cobden Club Essays," pp. 513 and 515.)

tions which borrow, those which are entitled to receive payments in excess of what is due to them on their ordinary trade; and for a time the external trade of both tends to adapt itself to this state of things. The subject is perhaps of sufficient importance to deserve some detailed illustration.

Let us, then, suppose an industrial colony, starting on its career, to become a borrower of capital from its mother-country; and, for simplicity of illustration, we will assume that neither is a producer of the precious metals, which, therefore, would only pass between them in discharge of pecuniary debts. The amount which the mother-country undertakes to lend, and the colony to receive, we will set down at one million sterling annually. This being the position of affairs, it becomes necessary that the sum to be lent should be remitted each year from the mother-country to the colony, and this, it is manifest, can only be done, either by a remittance of gold to the amount required, or by an exportation, in addition to that ordinarily taking place, of commodities to the same value, or by a combination of both these methods. If the colony is content to take the entire amount, or any portion of it, in commodities, this would imply a corresponding increase in colonial imports over colonial exports; for it would only be in the event of the increased importation being unbalanced by exports from the colony to the mother-country that the proceeds arising from it would be available for the mother-country in discharge of the loan, and there would obviously be nothing in what had occurred to lead the latter to increase her demand for colonial products. But it is probable that at least a portion of the loan would be sent in gold; and this would operate indirectly toward the same result. For the flow of gold into the colony year by year would necessarily raise colonial prices, while it would tend in the opposite direction in the mother-country; and this, through a play of forces I have already more than once described, would be followed by an increase of colonial importations, and a corresponding decline in the exportation of colonial products—a process which would manifestly continue, until at length the excess of commodities sent from the mother-country to the colony over those received from thence would enable the former to pay the whole annual loan by means of her commodities alone. At this point the trade between them would be *in equilibrio;* the exportations from the mother-country having become sufficient to enable her to discharge by this means all her liabilities to the colony. Up to this stage, then, the effect of foreign borrowing on the colony would, so far as we have yet traced it, tend toward an excess in her importations from the mother-country over her exportations thither. This would be the initial effect.* But during the continuance of the process just described, the grounds of an opposite state of things would be steadily developed. With every million sterling annually remitted, the colony would become indebted to the mother-country for the interest on the amount. Supposing the rate of interest to be five per cent. per annum, at the end of the first year the debt of the colony to the mother-country would be £50,000: consequently, in making her next remittance on account of capital, the mother-country would only need to send value to the amount, whether in commodities or gold, of £950,000. In the following year, the colony would owe on account of interest £100,000, which, still supposing the same amount of capital to be lent, would reduce the liabilities of the mother-country on this score to £900,000, and this process of gradual diminution of the mother-country's extra commercial liabilities to the colony would, at the end of twenty years, issue in this result, that the sum due by the colony on account of interest would equal the

---

* If the reader desires to verify the soundness of the position thus far, he has only to turn to the statistics of the external trade of some of the leading colonies of Great Britain, in which the imports will be found steadily and systematically to exceed the exports.

entire amount of the annual loan. What would be the effect on the external trade of the colony of this growing indebtedness to the mother-country? Manifestly to neutralize that produced by the operation of the influences developed in the early stages of these transactions. The obligation of the mother-country to remit value to the colony, in addition to what she owed on account of goods imported thence, gave an impulse to her export trade, and caused the importations of the colony to exceed her exportations. The obligation of the colony to discharge its growing liability to the mother-country would now, year by year, operate to reduce the excess, until at length the liabilities incident to the loans on each side balancing each other, the equilibrium of trade would be found in such a relation of exports and imports as would balance their remaining obligations—on the supposition that these latter should consist exclusively of commercial debts, then in an equality of imports and exports. This state of things, however, would be but momentary.

We have supposed the colony to have continued borrowing at the rate of £1,000,000 sterling annually for twenty years. At this stage, let us make the supposition that she suddenly ceases to borrow, and observe what, on this hypothesis, would be her financial position in relation to the mother-country. In the first place, she would be bound to pay £1,000,000 sterling annually on account of interest; but, no longer receiving the proceeds of the loan as formerly, she could not set off one obligation against the other. It would, therefore, be necessary for her to remit value to the amount required—in other words, her position relatively to the mother-country at this stage of affairs would be financially identical with that of the mother-country toward her at the outset, with this difference, that no new indebtedness would be growing up on the side of the mother-country to neutralize the permanent obligations incurred by the colony. The financial conditions of the case being thus changed, the external commerce of the two countries would adapt itself to the altered state of their reciprocal liabilities. Gold would once again begin to flow, but the tide would this time be directed from the colony to the mother-country, and it would be followed by a series of effects similar in character, though opposite in direction, to what we have already traced. Year by year the exports from the colony to the mother-country would exceed its imports thence, until at length the excess became sufficient to enable the former to discharge its financial liability in the products of its own industry. The efflux of gold would at this point cease, and the trade between the two countries would be *in equilibrio* once more.

We may make yet another supposition. The colony, instead of suddenly ceasing to borrow at the end of the twentieth year, might continue her borrowings on the former scale of £1,000,000 annually. On this supposition, her debt to the mother-country, on account of interest, at the end of the twenty-first year would be £1,050,000; but £1,000,000 of this could now be set off against the annual loan. In other words, the net balance due to the mother-country would be £50,000; but, on the supposition that the borrowing continued, this balance would grow year by year in arithmetical proportion, and would act upon her external trade, in proportion to its amount, in the manner already shown. In course of time we may assume that, as wealth increased in the colony, she would have less need of foreign capital, and would borrow less or not at all, but she would still be liable to send abroad value in excess of her commercial obligations to the amount of the interest due on all debts previously incurred. The normal state of the external trade of the colony would, therefore, under the circumstances supposed, be one in which her exports largely exceeded her imports; and such it would continue to be until either the original debt was paid off, or the colony herself had become a lender, and by this means imposed a similar tribute upon other countries

§ 7. Such is the nature of the influences, immediate and remote, exerted on the external trade of countries by the practice of foreign borrowing. In order to render the principle clear, it was necessary, in the first place, to exhibit its operation under very simple conditions; and I, therefore, had recourse to a hypothetical case. But so much, it is hoped, having now been accomplished, it may be well to turn from our imaginary mother-country and colony to an actual instance of international lending and borrowing on a vast scale. During the last thirteen years the financial transactions of the United States with Europe have far exceeded all former examples of the same kind, and the effects which they have produced, both on her external trade up to the present time, and still more on her commercial and financial position with reference to the future, have been of a magnitude correspondingly great. As furnishing, therefore, a striking practical illustration of the principles we have been considering, and in particular of the modes in which international settlements on a great scale are effected, it will, I think, be profitable to consider here in some detail the character and scope of those transactions.

It has been already seen that previous to 1860 the normal condition of the external trade of the United States was one in which the exports steadily exceeded the imports, this being the natural commercial outcome from the state of her financial relations with Europe. But the advent of the Civil War brought with it a series of events, each of potent influence, and which in their combination have sufficed to shake American trade to its centre, and to render the financial position of the Union in presence of Europe unprecedented and critical in the extreme. Of these events the most important were (1), the enactment of the Morrill tariff in 1861, by which the United States passed from what was substantially a free trade commercial *régime* to one of high protection; (2), the sudden cessation of cotton cultivation, and, as a consequence of this and of the Civil War, the temporary collapse of the cotton trade with Europe; (3), the creation of an enormous national debt, simultaneously with considerable additions made to State and other debts previously contracted, a large proportion of the funds in both cases being furnished by foreigners; and, lastly, the issue of an inconvertible paper currency to take the place of the mixed system of coin and convertible credit which formerly prevailed. The passing of the Morrill tariff and the present rigidly protective system of the United States will be the subject of special examination in a future chapter. For our present purpose it will be sufficient if we attend to the three last of the occurrences named, and mainly to the consequences involved in the sudden increase in foreign indebtedness, taken in connection with the collapse of the cotton trade.

Let us first observe the scale on which the new debt was created. It amounted—we may say in round numbers—to about five hundred millions sterling, of which some two hundred millions were taken by foreigners.* In addition to this, numerous other loans were effected on State, railway, mining, and other securities, reaching in the aggregate a very large sum, of which the amount that found its way to Europe was, according to Mr. Wells, not less than one hundred millions sterling. These transactions were spread over several years—we may say broadly, over the last three years of the war, and the two or three immediately succeeding. Regarding them as they affected the financial relations of Europe and the United States, the result may be thus stated: Europe undertook to send immediately, that is to say, as fast as the several obligations were incurred, some £300,000,000 sterling to the United States; while the United States on her side engaged to pay the interest on this sum to Europe for all time, or until the principal was discharged. The transactions, as I have said,

---

* See Wells's Report, 1869.

were spread over some five or six years, and, making allowance for the dividends which would be accruing on the investments from the time they were effected, and which might be used as a set-off against the principal sums still becoming due as new investments were made, the amount required to be sent from Europe to the United States during the period under review would not be less than some £40,000,000 sterling annually. Under ordinary circumstances—in such a state of external trade, for example, as had existed previous to 1860—so enormous and sudden an increase of payments from one continent to the other could only have been effected through the medium of bullion. The ordinary flow of gold from New York to Europe would have been suddenly checked, and a counter-current would have set in from Europe to New York —operations which could not fail to produce a profound ferment in the money markets of the two continents. As it was, however, the settlement of these vast transactions occasioned very little disturbance of any kind. The explanation is mainly to be found in another of the circumstances to which I have called attention, the collapse of the cotton crop; for the effect of this was suddenly to leave the United States without the means of paying Europe for her ordinary importations thence, swollen as these had recently been by large purchases of material of war. In the result the United States stood largely a debtor to Europe on commercial account; while on financial account the balance was not less decidedly against Europe; and, the amounts on both sides nearly corresponding, the settlement of the complex transactions became possible by the simple expedient of setting off one class of obligations against the other. This, in effect, is what was done. The reciprocal obligations of Europe and the United States were thus adjusted for the time, though by a sort of financial *coup de main* that could not well be repeated; and now I invite the reader to contemplate the state of things which has supervened.

§ 8. On the termination of the war the cultivation of cotton was, of course, resumed, and already that staple, as an article in the trade of the United States with Europe, has attained its former proportions, if not in quantity at least in value. On her other domestic exports (in which, be it remembered, specie is included) there has been an increase, though not a large one, and only during the last two years. But while this has been the case as regards exports, her imports have risen from 335,200,000 dollars, at which they stood in 1860, the year previous to the war, to 617,000,000 dollars, their amount according to the latest returns.* The reader will remember that previous to the war the exports of the United States had, as a normal state of things, exceeded the imports; the excess on this account during the ten years between 1851 and 1860 (inclusive) having amounted to an average sum of 6,000,000 dollars annually. Now, however, the balance is on the other side. It is the imports which are in excess of the exports. In the

---

* The following table shows the state of the external trade in the years immediately preceding the Civil War, and will enable the reader to compare the import and export trade of that time with the import and export trade of the five years ending 1872. The earlier figures I have taken from Mr. Wells's Essay in the Cobden Club volume: for the later, I am indebted to the kindness of my friend Mr. Horace White, of Chicago:

	Imports (less re-exports).	Domestic exports (including specie).
1858	$251,700,000	$293,700,000
1859	317,800,000	335,800,000
1860	335,200,000	373,100,000
1868	351,200,000	352,700,000
1869	412,200,000	318,000,000
1870	431,900,000	420,500,000
1871	513,100,000	513,000,000
1872	617,600,000	501,100,000
Annual average of last 5 years	$465,200,000	$421,060,000

Average annual excess of imports over exports during last 5 years, $44,140,000.

five years, 1868–1872 (inclusive), the excess amounted on an average to 44,000,000 dollars annually; while in the last year of the period (1872) it grew to no less a sum than 116,000,000 dollars. Now, from the explanations already given, the reader will understand that such a state of external trade, assuming it be sound and normal, would imply a state of financial relations between the United States and Europe in which the former country was largely a creditor of the latter; for it is only on this supposition that a large excess of imports over exports could continue consistently with national solvency. So far, however, from the facts being in accordance with this supposition, they are exactly the reverse of this. The United States is largely a debtor to Europe on financial account, while her exports are not even sufficient to cover her commercial liabilities. It will be worth while to consider this position of affairs somewhat more in detail.

As I learn from figures given by Mr. Wells in his Report for 1868, the dividends due to European holders of United States stocks of various kinds amounted in that year to 80,000,000 dollars. This, however, is but a portion of her extra commercial obligations to Europe. Her remittances to foreign countries to meet the expenses of her citizens residing or traveling abroad reached in the same year, according to the same authority, so large a sum as 25,000,000 dollars, and it does not appear that there was any thing exceptional in this expenditure. Lastly, we learn from Mr. Wells that an annual debt to foreign countries of 24,000,000 dollars more is incurred on account of freights carried in foreign bottoms. The aggregate of these various sums is 129,000,000 dollars, in round numbers we may say about £26,000,000 sterling; and this sum the United States has to pay annually to foreign countries, over and above what she owes on account of her importations. Now, as I have already explained, there is but one means by which a nation can in the last resort discharge her liabilities to other nations—namely, through the value of her products exported. We have seen, however, that the exports of the United States, as things now stand, far from being adequate to the liquidation of her annual aggregate liabilities, are insufficient to meet those incurred on commercial account alone; the deficiency, taking the average of the last five years, having, as I have just shown, reached the large sum of 44,000,000 dollars — let us say in round numbers about £9,000,000 sterling. We have thus a balance of £9,000,000 on commercial account, plus a further sum of £26,000,000 on extra-commercial account—in all £35,000,000 sterling—due, year by year, by the United States to foreign countries, in excess of what the value of her exported goods enables her to discharge. The question arises, How is this liability to be met? How it has been met up to the present time I have no means of accurately determining; but one expedient, we know, has been brought extensively into requisition. During the period since the war the sale of American securities in the markets of Great Britain and the Continent has been large and increasing. The United States has ceased, indeed, to add to her public debt, and has even made some progress in reducing it, but it is probable that the proportion of this debt in the hands of European holders has of late increased, and it is certain that the amount of European capital which now finds its way to private investment in America is immensely greater than it has ever been at any former period. Here, then, is a resource which, so far as it goes, and so long as it lasts, the United States may employ in liquidation of her uncovered liabilities; the sums payable by Europe in purchase of American securities being as much available in discharge of American debts as if they were obtained in payment of exports.* Whether those sums

---

* The mechanism through which these international transactions are carried into effect is the Foreign Exchanges. I have not, however, thought it necessary to enter into this part of the subject, as it has been already so fully and lucidly

have hitherto proved sufficient for the purpose required, must, for the moment, remain matter for conjecture, but it may be confidently asserted that, in any case, they can only be regarded as a temporary make-shift. No nation can continue to pay its foreign debts by the process of incurring new debts to meet a balance yearly accruing against it; yet this, in truth, is the nature of the financial operation by which of late years the United States has contrived to settle accounts with the rest of the world. Even on the supposition that European investment is to continue on its present scale, the interest upon it would, as I have shown, come in time to exceed the principal annually invested; while the balance uncovered by exports would still remain absolutely unprovided for. These considerations lead me to the conclusion that the present condition of the external trade of the United States is essentially abnormal and temporary. If that country is to continue to discharge her liabilities to foreigners, the relation which at present obtains between exports and imports in her external trade must be inverted. Her exports must once again, as previous to 1860, be made to exceed her imports, and this by an amount greater than the excess of that former time in proportion as her financial obligations to foreign countries have in the interval increased. This, it seems to me, is a result which may be predicted with the utmost confidence. The end may be reached either by an extension of exportation, or by a curtailment of importation, or by combining both these processes, but by one means or other reached it will need to be. It is simply the condition of her remaining a solvent nation. The people of that country may, therefore, if I am right in this speculation, look forward to witnessing a result for which the promoters of their present commercial policy have often sighed — they

---

expounded by Mr. Göschen in his work on the "Foreign Exchanges," to which the reader is referred.

may expect, before many years, to see United States commodities selling in foreign countries in vastly greater quantities than the commodities of foreign countries in the markets of the United States. How far their estimate of this condition of their trade will be affected by the circumstance that a large proportion of the proceeds from those augmented foreign sales will find its way into European pockets, is a point on which it would be scarcely becoming in the present writer to offer an opinion.*

The conclusion just stated suggests a further reflection. A change in the relation of exports and imports in the trade of a country can only be effected through a change in relative prices (measured in gold or silver) as they exist in that country and in those with which it trades. To establish, therefore, an excess of exports over imports in the trade of the United States, in lieu of the balance the other way which now exists, prices there must be lowered in relation to prices in Europe. This may be accomplished partly by an advance in prices here not shared by the United States, as in fact has already happened in the case of some important commodities; but it

---

* In the *Times's* Philadelphia Correspondent's letter of October 17, 1873, it is stated that the imports from the United States had at that time begun to decline, the diminution for the first nine months of 1873, as compared with the same period for 1872, having amounted to nearly $35,000,000. On the other hand, it is observed that the exports from New York during the same time have increased by $32,000,000. The writer goes on to remark: "This decrease in imports and increase in exports shows a balance of trade in our favor, and explains the decline in sterling exchange. The *New York Journal of Commerce* is jubilant at the prospect; declares that the tide of gold must flow toward America, and announces that the balance of trade being in our favor the 'sovereigns of Great Britain must melt their pride in the crucibles of the American mint.'" The *New York Journal of Commerce* is overhasty in its conclusions. In its exultation it overlooks the circumstance that the favorable balance will be all too small to discharge the liabilities of the United States to Europe on account of interest and dividends on American securities held on this side. The sovereigns of Great Britain, therefore, will have no need to melt their pride in American crucibles for the present.

is probable that the end will be reached mainly through a decline of prices on the other side. A considerable fall of general prices, however, is a remedy to which manufacturers and merchants will only submit when pushed to extremity. It will, therefore, only come when credit has been strained to the utmost, and a catastrophe is seen to be inevitable; and then it will probably come with a crash. For these reasons I should be disposed to look forward to the immediate future of American trade as a period of much disturbance and fluctuation, culminating, it is possible, from time to time in commercial crises.*

In offering these remarks on the prospective character of the external commerce of the United States, I have deliberately abstained from adverting to some contingencies, and in particular to two, which can not fail, more or less seriously, to affect it—I mean the course that country may adopt with regard to Protection, as well as with regard to the redemption of her paper money. I have thus far avoided these topics, because I do not conceive that any decision she may come to with reference to either—powerfully operative as no doubt it will be on her future commercial fortunes in various directions—can possibly affect the particular issue to which the preceding remarks have been addressed. A persistent policy of Protection will, no doubt, have the effect of preventing the due expansion of her external trade in the future as it has done in the past, if it does not lead to its positive curtailment; while the adoption of free trade would as certainly tend to its rapid development, and thus greatly relieve the extreme tension of the situation. But, under all circumstances, if the United States is to remain a

---

* As I write, the news of the commercial crisis in New York (19th September, 1873) has reached me. From the accounts we have yet received it would seem to have had its immediate origin in railway speculation: how far the collapse may be connected with the causes to which I have been calling attention, the sequel will probably show.

solvent nation, she must contrive to send a larger value out of the country than is received into it, and this larger value can take no other form than the products of her industry. Free-trader or protectionist, therefore, an excess of exports over imports in her foreign trade, sufficient in amount to discharge her international liabilities, is a condition she can not evade.

I may venture on a further remark. It appears to me that the influence, attributed by many able writers in the United States to the depreciation of the paper currency as regards its effects on the foreign trade of the country, is, in a great degree, purely imaginary, founded, as I conceive it to be, upon an erroneous view of the circumstances which determine international demand. An advance in the scale of prices, *measured in gold*, in a country, if not shared by other countries, will at once affect its foreign trade, giving an impulse to importations, and checking the exportation of all commodities other than gold. A similar effect is very generally attributed by American writers to the action on prices of the greenback inconvertible currency. But it may be easily shown that this is a complete illusion. Foreigners do not send their products to the United States to take back greenbacks in exchange. The return which they look for is either gold or the commodities of the country; and if these have risen in price in proportion as the paper money has been depreciated, how should the advance in paper prices constitute an inducement for them to send their goods thither? The nominal gain in greenbacks on the importation is exactly balanced by the nominal loss when those greenbacks come to be converted into gold or commodities. To put the argument in a still more practical shape: Whatever the importing merchant gains in the increased price at which he sells his goods, precisely the same amount he looses when he comes to purchase a bill by which to remit the proceeds of the sale to the country whence the goods came. The nominal premium on the bill will just neutralize what he had appeared to gain on the sale through the depreciation of the paper money. It is true the gain may, in particular cases, exceed the loss, but if it does, the loss will also, in other cases, exceed the gain. On the whole, and on an average, they can not but be the equivalents of each other. In making these remarks the reader will not understand me as contending that a depreciated currency is absolutely without influence on the foreign trade of a country. So far as it introduces uncertainty and risk into commercial transactions it no doubt affects foreign as well as domestic trade, and affects both injuriously; but this is an entirely different thing from acting as an encouragement to importation, and a check upon exportation—the effect attributed to a depreciated currency by the writers to whose views I have referred.

CHAPTER IV.

FREE TRADE AND PROTECTION.

§ 1. The foregoing discussions have exhibited the conditions under which international trade arises, and the nature of the advantages that flow from it. It has been seen that nations only trade with one another when by doing so they can satisfy their desires at smaller sacrifice or cost than by direct production of the commodities which minister to them. The establishment of this position is the justification of the doctrine of free trade; since it is manifest that, if nations only engage in trade when an advantage arises from their doing so, any interference with their free action in trading can only have the effect of debarring them from an advantage. For those, therefore, who accept the economic theory of international trade, no further proof of the essential soundness of this fundamental principle of commercial policy is needed. Nevertheless, I am unwilling to leave the subject of these chapters without some fuller consideration than has yet been given to it of the great controversy, not yet, unfortunately, extinct, of Free Trade *versus* Protection. I have said, "not yet extinct: perhaps I should rather have said, even now active and glowing with something of its pristine fervor; for we have only to turn our eyes to France, or to the United States, not to speak of our own colonies, to see with what vigor, and I regret to say with what success, the venerable sophism still maintains itself, alike in the public press and in national legislatures. Under such circumstances an examination of the specific doctrine of Protection will even yet, perhaps, not seem altogether out of date; and, thanks to Mr. Wells, the United States Commissioner, we are not without abundant illustrations of the recent working of the principle, which have only to be duly pondered in the light of economic theory, to teach a lesson such that he who runs may read.

§ 2. The system of Protection naturally grew out of the system of the Balance of Trade. They were not, indeed, so much distinct systems as different aspects of the same system. As the Balance of Trade doctrine began to give way, that of Protection was gradually inserted in its place, as it were to underpin the tottering edifice. The aim of the former was to enrich the country by drawing to it the precious metals; that of the latter to do so by encouraging native industry; but the means adopted were identical, as was also the point of view from which the supporters of the two theories regarded commercial problems.* Consistently carried out, the Balance of Trade

---

* And I may add the criterion by which they tested results. This has been quite unequivocally evinced by the recent controversies in France. In a statement made before a commission of inquiry, appointed just before the war, M. Pouyer-Quertier maintained that French agriculture in a period of twelve years, from 1858 to 1869, had suffered a loss of 300,000,000 francs. And what was the process of reasoning by which he arrived at this conclusion? Simply this. It appeared that during the period in question French imports had exceeded French exports by the amount stated, and from this fact M. Pouyer-Quertier drew the inference that France was a loser to this amount on her foreign trade. Why he supposes the loss to have fallen exclusively on agriculture I do not quite perceive. A reply to this statement was made by M. De Kergolay in a speech delivered by him a few months since as President of the French Central Agricultural Society. That reply is perhaps sufficiently conclusive as against M. Pouyer-Quertier, but coming as it does from a free-trader certainly does not give one a high idea of the present state of economic science in France. M. De Kergolay first objects to the period selected by the protectionist advocate for comparison; he next challenges the correctness of the calculations on which the result is based; lastly, he asks what does the fact prove. "The importation of products foreign to the soil can not be regarded as a loss to the country. Coffee and cocoa, tea and spices, woods for dye-

system must have extinguished foreign trade, since it is demonstrable that the permanently favorable balance which it aimed at producing is not capable of realization; and consistently carried out, Protectionism would put an end, if not to all foreign trade, at least to all such as furnished us with commodities capable of being produced in the protected country; for the essence of the doctrine is, to encourage native industry by excluding the products of foreign industry, wherever these come into competition with commodities which native industry can produce. Protectionists, however, rarely now attempt to carry out their doctrine in its rigor, and, instead of requiring an absolute exclusion of foreign products, are commonly content to demand such a measure of protection as, to borrow their language, shall put the home producer on a footing of equality with his foreign rival. If the latter possesses no advantage over the former, then the trade, as the phrase goes, "can stand alone," and no protective duty is asked for; but if the foreigner possesses an advantage, this must be neutralized by a countervailing duty. The reader who has followed the foregoing exposition of the grounds of international trade will perceive that this more modest form of the doctrine would, in its practical issue, be entirely tantamount to the former, since, as was there shown, the existence of international trade rests on the different productive capacities with respect to particular commodities of different countries: if, therefore, each nation is to

---

ing or working purposes, are not indigenous to the soil of France. They must be imported, but how can the necessary cost be set down as a national loss?" Apparently, if the imported articles were indigenous, the validity of the protectionist's conclusion would be admitted by this champion of free trade. As I have shown in the last chapter, the relation of imports to exports is determined by causes quite independent of the character of the tariff. Protection will indeed diminish the *aggregate amount* of exports and imports taken together, but, whatever be the commercial *régime*, the *relation* between them will be such as the position of the country, taking all her international credits and obligations into account, shall require.—See *Times*, September 18, 1873.

set itself to neutralize this difference, wherever it appears, by means of countervailing duties, it is plain that the triumph of the system would be the annihilation of foreign trade. If indeed equality in productive conditions could be attained by what might be described as a process of "leveling up;" if Protection could contrive that every commodity should be produced in every country with the same facility with which it is produced on the spot of the globe most suitable to its production — *though even so it would annihilate foreign trade* — there would yet be something to be said for this mode of attaining equality. It may, however, be doubted if the gain which might accrue in material comforts from the increased productiveness of the earth would not be more than counterbalanced by the intellectual and moral loss which would result from the withdrawal of the principal motive to the intercourse of mankind. Protectionists, however, not being able to "level up," propose to "level down," and aim at reaching equality by, so to speak, handicapping commercial countries against each other, making each carry weight in the markets of the others exactly sufficient to counterpoise its special advantages. Such is the theory of trade which now, it seems, finds favor on the other side of the Atlantic.* In the proposal, however, to sacrifice the very ends of industry and commerce in order to promote equality, we may, perhaps, detect the savor rather of a French than of an American origin. A theory essentially the same was propounded a few years ago by M. Alby, in the *Revue des Deux Mondes*, in an essay written with much elaboration and parade of scientific precision, and, it must be presumed, with skill and effect, since the exposition was accepted by protectionists in the United States as a triumphant statement of their argument, and met with consideration from even free-trade journals in that country. Under these circumstances I shall

---

* See Mr. Wells's Reports and Essays *passim*.

make no apology for devoting a brief space to the consideration of the protectionist case as stated by M. Alby.

§ 3. The position taken by M. Alby in his article in the *Revue des Deux Mondes** is, that the doctrine of Protection is in theory sound, though he admits that in old countries like France it is not possible fairly to carry it into effect. For this reason he is in favor of a modified free trade for France in her actual circumstances. But, while taking this line as a practical politician, he strenuously contends for the theoretic soundness of the protectionist's view. According to M. Alby, the apparent triumph which free-traders commonly gain over their opponents arises from the imperfect way in which the protectionist case is put. Free-traders attack the system in detail, joining issue on each particular duty; whereas the strength of the protectionist case lies in its *ensemble*, in its completeness as a whole.

"Let us take, for instance," says M. Alby, "the case of mining industry. Every one needs iron, and iron is produced in France by a very restricted number of furnaces; and here is the way free-traders put the case. 'The price of iron,' say they, 'is raised by the customs' duty on foreign iron. Is it just that thirty-eight millions of Frenchmen should pay more for iron than, in the absence of duty, it is worth, in order to enrich a few iron-masters?' If we go no further than this—if the case remains isolated, only one answer is possible. With the exception of the iron-masters, every one will exclaim, 'No, it is not just, it is an odious monopoly!' Very good; but let us put a similar case for another industry, the manufacture of cloth. The answer will be the same. Only this time the cloth manufacturer will turn round on the iron-master and say, 'Where is your grievance? I pay more for your iron than I should have to pay for foreign iron if it entered free. Is it not just that you pay me a higher price for my cloth than it might be purchased at abroad?' The argument is unanswerable. The iron-master will be forced to acknowledge this. As we run successively the entire circle of industrial

---

* See the number for 15th October, 1869.

and agricultural production, with each new industry that we take account of, the area of the apparent injustice will be continually narrowing till we end by finding ourselves in presence of a series of people paying dearer for what they purchase, but making others pay dearer for what they sell. They have no ground for mutual reproach. Well, such," continues M. Alby, " is the system of Protection in its *ensemble*. It is a sort of mutual assurance against foreign competition, an associative pact which embraces the entire country. Each consents to pay for all the products he requires a price augmented by the customs' tariff, on the condition of obtaining for his own products in the home market a price equally augmented by the same means, so that they shall return him a profit."

M. Alby apparently overlooks the fact that it is only those industries which are carried on under a relative disadvantage that stand in need of protection; and that consequently—since in no country are all industries equally favored by nature—the consummation he contemplates with so much satisfaction is incapable of realization in any part of the world, during any stage of commercial progress. How, for example, could the wine-growers or silk-weavers of France, or again, how could the Western farmers or Southern cotton-planters of the United States, be compensated, under M. Alby's system, for the price they pay for foreign imports in consequence of a protective tariff? By obtaining in return, forsooth, a protective duty, in France on wine and silk, and in the United States on wheat and cotton! But passing by this "little rift within the lute," let us, in order to exhibit the radical absurdity of this pretty theory, assume that all branches of production in France stand equally in need of protection. The argument is, that, provided each person receives in his capacity of producer a price for his commodity as much higher than its price under free trade as that which he pays in his capacity of consumer for what he requires, no harm will be done. Accepting this view, a perfect system of Protection might seem to be tantamount simply to a general depreciation of money. All persons would receive higher money remuneration than under free trade, and would pay this away in higher prices—a consummation, the advantage of which to native industry is not apparent. This mode of conceiving the case, however, implies a most inadequate appreciation of the consequences involved in M. Alby's scheme. M. Alby fails to perceive that the high price which Protection secures is rendered necessary in consequence of the more onerous conditions under which native industry, tempted by its inducements, is encouraged to work. Frenchmen are encouraged to produce iron from ores of inferior quality by the high price secured to them through their protective tariff. In the absence of Protection they would obtain their iron on more favorable terms—at a smaller sacrifice of labor and abstinence—by exchanging for it their wines and silks with England. A similar remark applies to every protective duty that is really effective for its purpose. It necessarily implies production carried on under more onerous conditions. On the supposition, therefore, that M. Alby's system were feasible, the practical result would be, not simply a general rise of prices, but an increase in the cost—cost, be it remembered, in the sense not of mere money outlay, but of actual difficulty, of real sacrifice—of producing every article the creation of French industry. All Frenchmen would be compelled to labor half as hard again, and to save half as much again, in order to procure every necessary and comfort they enjoy. But then equality and justice would be realized. No doubt, just as they might be realized by compelling every one to move about with a weight attached to his leg. The weight would, indeed, be an impediment to locomotion, but provided it were in each case exactly proportioned to the strength of the limb which drew it, no one, according to M. Alby's way of looking at things, would have any reason to complain. No one would walk as fast as if his limbs were free, but then his neighbor would be equally fettered, and if it took him twice as long to reach his destination as before, he would at least have company on his journey. Strange that such speculation should find acceptance in the country of Say and Bastiat!

§ 4. Such is the theory of Protection in its most general form, as set forth by one of its latest expositors, and accepted in the country in which its influence is at present supreme, almost to the degree of absolutely controlling legislation. But it will be instructive to enter into the argument in somewhat more of detail. As I have said, the position taken in the United States is, that Protection is only needed and only asked for where American industry is placed under a disadvantage as compared with the industry of foreign countries. What, then, we have to ask, in the first place, is the criterion by which the alleged disadvantage attaching to American industry is established? As we learn from Mr. Wells,* the criterion taken is the cost of production of the articles claiming protection, which again, he informs us, is estimated almost exclusively by reference to the money price of labor. The rates of wages measured in money are higher in the United States than in Europe, and therefore, it is argued, the cost of producing commodities is higher there than here. It is strange that those who employ this argument should not have perceived that it proves too much. The high rates of wages in the United States are not peculiar to any branch of industry, but are universal throughout its whole range. If, therefore, a high rate of wages

---

* "In most of the tariff discussions that have taken place of late in the United States, the question of the necessity and extent of Protection is made to turn almost wholly upon the difference in the cost [price] of labor employed in domestic as compared with foreign industry—which differences, as already shown, are certainly very considerable. And it is also very generally taken for granted in such discussions that the nominal rate paid for wages, of itself alone, or at least in a very great degree, determines both the cost of production and the social condition and prosperity of the laborer." (Wells's Report for 1868, pp. 69, 70.)

proves a high cost of production, and a high cost of production proves a need for Protection, it follows that the farmers of Illinois and the cotton-planters of the Southern States stand in as much need of fostering legislation as the cotton-spinners of New England or the iron-masters of Pennsylvania! A criterion which leads to such results must, I think, be regarded as sufficiently condemned. The fallacy is, in truth, the same as that which so awkwardly marred the pretty theory of M. Alby, who, as we saw, in carrying the boon of Protection with impartial hand round the whole circle of the industries, unfortunately overlooked the trifling circumstance that all industries are not in each country equally favored or disfavored by nature, and have not, therefore, equal need of his protecting care. If American protectionists are not prepared to demand protective duties in favor of the Illinois farmer against the competition of his English rival, they are bound to admit either that a high cost of production is not incompatible with effective competition, or else that a high rate of wages does not prove a high cost of production; and if this is not so in Illinois, then I wish to know why the case should be different in Pennsylvania or in New England. If a high rate of wages in the first of these States be consistent with a low cost of producing corn, why may not a high rate of wages in Pennsylvania be consistent with a low cost of producing coal and iron? or a high rate of wages in New England be consistent with a low cost of producing calico? I must own that Mr. Wells's treatment of this branch of the argument is, to my mind, eminently unsatisfactory. It is true he objects to the protectionist criterion of cost of production—money wages, but only on the ground that it fails to take account of the varying efficiency of labor, and of the varying purchasing power of money in relation to the laborer's requirements.* The fallacy, however,

---

* See his Report for 1868, page 70. I must acknowledge, too, that his reply

involved in that criterion goes far deeper than this, and is only fully exposed when exhibited as inverting the real relation of facts. As I have already proved,* the rate of wages, whether measured in money or in the real remuneration of the laborer, affords an approximate criterion of the cost of production, either of money or of the commodities that enter into the laborer's real remuneration, *but in a sense the inverse of that in which it is understood in the argument under consideration:* in other words, a high rate of wages indicates not a high but a low cost of production for all commodities, measured in which the rate of wages is high; as, on the other hand, a low rate of wages indicates a high cost for all, measured in which the rate is low. Thus in the United States the rate of wages is high, whether measured in gold or in the most important articles of the laborer's consumption—a fact which proves that the cost of producing gold, as well as that of producing those other commodities, is low in the United States. On the other hand, the rates of wages in Europe measured by the same standards are —at least as compared with rates in the United States—low,

---

founded on these exceptions wholly fails, in my judgment, to meet the protectionist argument. What he shows is that labor in England, though much higher priced than in most European countries, and in particular than in Russia, is still so much more efficient here than there, that the high English rates are practically cheaper for the English capitalist than the lower Continental rates for the capitalist of the Continent. What is the bearing of this upon the American demand for protection against *England?* Will Mr. Wells maintain that, as the efficiency of English labor is to that of Russian, so is the efficiency of American labor to that of English? If not, how does his objection to the protectionist criterion of cost, founded on the different degrees of industrial efficiency, affect the argument? And as little does he seem to me to make good the pertinency of his objection on the other ground taken. It is possible that in a few manufacturing districts in the United States the rent of an artisan's dwelling is higher than in some manufacturing districts in England, but in the most important articles of the laborer's consumption, in the whole list of "provisions," for example, the advantage in respect to price is unquestionably with the American consumer.

* See *ante*, p. 336, *et seq.*, and pp. 345-347.

which again merely proves that the cost of producing the commodities constituting those standards is high in Europe, as compared with their cost in the United States. This elementary truth is so far from being generally appreciated that I should not be surprised if its simple statement should appear to some persons, and possibly even to some economists, as paradoxical.* I would ask such to consider what are the true causes of the high remuneration of American industry. It will surely be admitted that, in the last resort, these resolve-themselves into the one great fact of its high productive power. Capitalists and laborers receive large remuneration in America because their industry produces largely. That is the simple and patent fact which all must acknowledge. But what is the meaning of a highly productive industry, if it be not a liberal industrial return as compared with the sacrifice undergone? And what, again, does this mean if not a low cost in relation to the thing produced? I must, therefore, contend that the high scale of industrial remuneration in America, instead of being evidence of a high cost of production in that country, is distinctly evidence of a low cost of production—of a low cost of production, that is to say, in the first place, of gold, and, in the next, of the commodities which mainly constitute the real wages of labor—a description which embraces at once the most important raw materials of industry and the most important articles of general consumption. As regards commodities not included in this description, the criterion of wages stands in no constant relation of any kind to their cost, and is, therefore, simply irrelevant to the point at issue. And now we may see what this claim for protection to American industry, founded on the high scale of American remuneration, really comes to: it is a demand for special legislative aid in consideration of the pos-

---

* And yet it ought not to do so. The doctrine was very clearly enunciated nearly half a century ago in Mr. Senior's Essay, already frequently referred to, on the "Cost of obtaining Money."

session of special industrial facilities—a complaint, in short, against the exceptional bounty of nature.

§ 5. Perhaps I shall here be asked how, if the case be so—if the high rate of industrial remuneration in America be only evidence of a low cost of production—the fact is to be explained, since fact it undoubtedly is, that the people of the United States are unable to compete in neutral markets, in the sale of certain important wares, with England and other European countries. No one will say that the people of New England, New York, and Pennsylvania are deficient in any industrial qualities possessed by the workmen of any country in the world. How happens it, then, that, enjoying industrial advantages superior to other countries, they are yet unable to hold their own against them in the general markets of commerce? I shall endeavor to meet this objection fairly, and, in the first place, let me state what my contention is with regard to cost of production in America. I do not contend that it is low in the case of all commodities capable of being produced in the country, but only in that of a large, very important, but still limited group. With regard to commodities lying outside this group, I hold that the rate of wages is simply no evidence as to the cost of their production, one way or the other. But, secondly, I beg the reader to consider what is meant by the alleged "inability" of New England and Pennsylvania to compete, let us say, with Manchester and Sheffield in the manufacture of calico and cutlery. What it means, and what it only can mean, is that they are unable to do so *consistently with obtaining that rate of remuneration on their industry which is current in the United States.* If only American laborers and capitalists would be content with the wages and profits current in Great Britain, there is nothing that I know of to prevent them from holding their own in any markets to which Manchester and Sheffield send their wares. And this brings us to the heart of the question. Over a large portion of the great field of industry the people of the United States enjoy, as compared with those of Europe, advantages of a very exceptional kind; over the rest the advantage is less decided, or they stand on a par with Europeans, or possibly they are, in some instances, at a disadvantage. Engaging in the branches of industry in which their advantage over Europe is great, they reap industrial returns proportionately great; and, so long as they confine themselves to these occupations, they can compete in neutral markets against all the world, and still secure the high rewards accruing from their exceptionally rich resources. But the people of the Union decline to confine themselves within these liberal bounds. They would cover the whole domain of industrial activity, and think it hard that they should not reap the same rich harvests from every part of the field. They must descend into the arena with Sheffield and Manchester, and yet secure the rewards of Chicago and St. Louis. They must employ European conditions of production, and obtain American results. What is this but to quarrel with the laws of nature? These laws have assigned to an extensive range of industries carried on in the United States a high scale of return, far in excess of what Europe can command, to a few others a return on a scale not exceeding the European proportion. American enterprise would engage in all departments alike, and obtain upon all the high rewards which nature has assigned only to some. Here we find the real meaning of the "inability" of Americans to compete with the "pauper labor" of Europe. They can not do so, and at the same time secure the American rate of return on their work. The inability no doubt exists, but it is one created, not by the drawbacks, but by the exceptional advantages of their position. It is as if a skilled artisan should complain that he could not compete with the hedger and ditcher. Let him only be content with the hedger and ditcher's rate of pay, and there will be nothing to prevent him from entering the lists even against this rival.

The end here proposed by American enterprise is, it must be owned, unattainable under free trade; for free trade is content to turn natural laws to the best account: it does not seek to transcend them. But, though unattainable under free trade, protectionists assure us that the thing may be done by means of their system. It is only necessary, say these authorities, to exclude foreign competition by laying high import duties on the products in which American superiority over Europe is not assured, and the same high returns which attend on American industry in its most productive fields will—the laws of nature notwithstanding—be realized throughout its entire range. And this is, in fact, the undertaking in which those who guide the commercial policy of the Union have been engaged since 1861. Let us for a moment pause and consider how this bold attempt to override the laws of nature has fared.

§ 6. And here we are confronted at once with the difficulty of interpreting an industrial experiment. The system of American Protection, in its present exaggerated form, may be regarded as dating from 1861, when the Morrill tariff became law. If all the other conditions of the case had remained substantially the same since that time, we might now, by a mere inspection of results, pronounce without hesitation on the effect of the policy then inaugurated; but instead of this observe how the facts stand. In the same year the great Civil War commenced, in the course of which the destruction of human life and of wealth in every form probably exceeded any thing which had before occurred within the same time in the history of human affairs. This was soon followed by the creation of an immense national debt, entailing a large permanent increase of taxation, and by the issue of an inconvertible paper currency, circulating throughout the Union, and affecting alike prices and wages in every branch of trade. On the other hand, occurrences of a very different kind marked the course of the period under review. Mineral resources were discovered which are now yielding vast wealth, and oil springs which have become the source of an entirely new and rapidly increasing trade. Railway enterprise, again, during the same time appears to have taken on a new activity, while the progress of invention in the mechanical arts has never for a moment flagged. In presence of influences so numerous, so novel, and so vast, each affecting industry in its own fashion so powerfully, who shall say what portion of what we now find existing can properly be attributed to any one of them? The problem, in its mere statement, brings into striking relief the utter futility of that so-called "inductive method" which some writers hold to be the proper one in social and economic inquiries— the method, that is to say, which would proceed by drawing general conclusions as to the operation of particular causes from the summarized results of statistical tables. For, assuming that we have taken accurate stock of the present industrial condition of the United States, as well as of that which was in existence previous to 1861, so long as we confine our view to the mere statistical aspect of the case, what warrant have we for attributing any portion of the change that has taken place to one cause rather than to another? Manifestly we have none; nor can we advance a single step toward the solution of any problem involved in the facts, till we pass from the mere tabulation of results to an examination of the nature and tendencies of the causes in operation. When we have ascertained these, and shown by deductive reasoning from them the effects they are fitted to produce, we are then for the first time in a position to attempt an interpretation of the varied and complex phenomena.

Now this is the vantage ground on which a student of Political Economy in dealing with such a problem stands. He has ascertained the direction in which the various industrial forces, operating in the field of the experiment, work; he knows, for example, that in the present instance the destruction caused by the Civil War must have left a large gap in the then existing wealth of the United States;* but he knows also, what is not so obvious, the extraordinary rapidity with which countries devastated by war, but in which the industrial habits of the people have not been broken through, so soon as peace and security are restored, recover from the havoc which war has made. He knows, again, that the meaning of a national debt is the necessity of submitting, so long as it remains unpaid, to a known amount of taxation, tantamount in its effects to an equivalent deduction from the general earnings of the community. He knows, further, the consequences likely to flow from the issue of an inconvertible currency; that, once depreciated below the par of gold, it results in a scale of nominal prices, having for its effect to derange the monetary relations of the community, to relieve debtors from their obligations at the expense of their creditors, and to introduce much risk and uncertainty into general business, but not, as is commonly supposed, to affect in any serious manner the external trade of a country.† At the same time, the economist can take account of the immense addition made to the material resources of the United States, by those mineral and other discoveries to which reference has been made, as well as by the progress of mechanical invention, the extension of the

---

* This, one would think, would be sufficiently obvious, but in arguing with protectionists it is difficult to know what to take for granted. According to the extreme zealots of the protectionist school the Civil War, it seems, is to be regarded as among the most potent causes of the recent prosperity of the Union. "The conclusion," says Mr. Wells, "was pointed at by some, and even soberly maintained on the floor of Congress by the advocates of the system of high Protection, that the war, regarded from a merely material point of view, was in reality a blessing." ("Cobden Club Essays," Second Series, p. 487.)

† This point has been dealt with *ante*, p. 373.

railway system, and the other industrial improvements which have marked recent years. Now these—putting aside for a moment the protectionist tariff—are the main and capital occurrences affecting the economic career of the United States since 1861; and, in order to judge experimentally of the action of Protectionism on the interests of the country since that date, it becomes necessary to effect some rough elimination of so much of the general result as may properly be attributed to those other causes. In other words, we must endeavor to determine in what direction, on the whole, has been the net bearing of their influence; whether in the direction of an abridgment of the productive power and commercial resources of the United States, or in that of their enlargement. For my part, I have no hesitation in accepting upon this point what appears to be the nearly universal opinion of Americans, that, the period of actual warfare once passed, the influences favoring industrial progress have, on the whole, largely preponderated over those tending to retard it; and that consequently, *if there were nothing else in the matter*, we should be justified in expecting, at all events since 1866, a more rapid expansion of American commerce, and a more liberal return on American industry, than prevailed in the period previous to 1861.

Well, how do the facts tally with this reasonable expectation? I will allow Mr. Wells to answer this question. In his two Reports to Congress, and in his Cobden Club Essay, he has gone very fully and in great detail into the whole subject, and those who desire particulars must be referred to those writings. It suffices here to state in summary the results of his investigations; and these are to the effect that, comparing the decade 1860–'70 with the previous decade, the commercial progress of the United States has, in the later period, suffered a serious check; that the commercial tonnage has during the same period positively declined; that the business of ship-building has undergone an almost complete collapse; that the rate of increase in the external trade which during the decade 1850–'60 had been represented by eighty-one per cent. on the trade of the preceding decade, has fallen to one represented by nineteen per cent.; and, lastly, and on this point I am content to rest the entire case, that—having regard, on the one hand, to the nominal rise in wages reckoned in a depreciated currency, and, on the other, to the nominal rise of prices measured in the same medium—the real remuneration of the United States laborer in all the leading departments of industry has during the nine years ending 1868 positively fallen in a proportion not less than twenty per cent. on his previous earnings.* These are singular results to have accrued from a still unlimited command of rich virgin soil, from enlarged mineral resources, ever progressing mechanical invention, and an industrial energy and enterprise which have certainly suffered no abatement. To what cause are they to be ascribed, and more particularly how are we to account for this lowered rate of return upon American industry? It is possible the ravages of the war may not even yet have been wholly repaired; the gap made in the national capital may not be even now quite filled up. The increased taxation certainly remains, and constitutes a deduction, let us say of some five or six per cent.† from American earnings. The depreciated cur-

---

* On this point Mr. Wells's conclusion is as follows: while "the average increase of all the elements which constitute the food, clothing, and shelter of a family has been about seventy-eight per cent., as compared with the standard prices of '60–'61," the increase which took place during the same time in wages was only in the proportion, "for unskilled labor of fifty per cent., for skilled mechanical labor of sixty per cent." . . . . (Report for 1868, pp. 14, 15.) Without knowing the proportions in which the several enhanced articles enter into the laborer's consumption, accurate deductions as to the effect of this change on his well-being can not of course be made; but it is at least certain that the facts stated imply a deterioration and a considerable one in his condition. In stating it at about twenty per cent. it seems to me that I am well within the mark.

† The revenue of the United States before the war stood at about £12,000,000:

rency has, no doubt, caused much individual hardship, and introduced more or less derangement into commercial affairs. But who will say that any of these occurrences, or all of them taken together, suffice to account for the facts which Mr. Wells has brought to light—the slackened rate of progress, the arrested commercial growth, and, above all, the diminished reward for the workman? The problem, I must own, is for me insoluble, until I take account of that one influence which, for the moment, I had put aside. I turn to the Morrill tariff, and to the aggravations of that code which have since been enacted. I find there duties amounting, on an average, to forty-seven per cent. *ad valorem*, imposed on nearly all articles* of any importance imported into the United States; on such raw products as coal, timber, iron, hides, and sugar; on such manufactures as clothing in every form, cottons, woolens, and every kind of textile fabric, on manufactured iron—in a word, on nearly all the raw materials of industry, and many of the most important articles of general consumption. And with these facts before me, the slackened rate of progress, the arrested commercial growth, and the workman's diminished reward become at once intelligible; for these are the precise results which such a system of protection is fitted to engender. With such a barrier as duties amounting to forty-seven per cent. *ad valorem* erected against foreign importation, what else could hap-

---

its amount since the war has fluctuated between £65,000,000 and £70,000,000: the increase, therefore, has been, we may say in round numbers, some £55,000,000, representing so much of the produce of the land and labor of the country, formerly left with the producers, now taken for the purposes of the State. According to Mr. Wells's estimate (Report for 1869, p. xiii.), the value of the total annual production of the United States in 1868 amounted to £1,365,000,000, from which a deduction of £55,000,000 would represent a proportion of about four per cent. To this there would have to be added the increase of the local taxation of the several States, of which I have no statistics.

* So nearly so, that if we substitute for "articles paying duty" the entire imports, the proportion is only reduced to forty-four per cent.

pen than a retardation of the growth of external trade? While coal, timber, iron are loaded with heavy duties, can ship-building be expected to prosper? and, as with ship-building, so with some scores of other trades, the details of whose decline will be found in Mr. Wells's repertory. But I prefer to rest the case upon the simple fact of the reduced real wages of the workmen; for here the symptom may be regarded as specific. As I have already had occasion to explain, the direct effect of a protective duty, when it is really operative, is to compel, on the part of the community employing this expedient, a resort to more onerous conditions of production for the protected article. Every article, therefore, produced in the United States, which would not have been produced there but for the protective tariff, represents an expenditure of labor and capital greater than would have been necessary to obtain the same article had it been obtained under free trade. In a word, American labor and capital, as a whole, have, effort for effort and outlay for outlay, been producing smaller results since 1861 than formerly; and this being so, what other explanation do we need of the actual facts which we encounter—of diminished returns on American industry, of a fall in the real wages of labor?

But, say the protectionists, though measured in products the returns on the protected industries may be less, we, by excluding foreign competition, secure for the producers a proportionally higher price; the effect of which is that, though working at a disadvantage, they nevertheless obtain the rate of profit current in the country. Let us observe the precise significance of this reply. It may be conceded that a small return upon industry in the form of products may be compensated to the producers by a proportional increase in the price; but then it is at the expense of those who pay the increased price; and the question remains, by whom are the higher prices paid in the present instance? There is only one possible answer—by the citizens of the United States. In effect these higher prices are the machinery through which the real rewards of American industry have been reduced. Consider, for example, the case of an Illinois farmer: it is tolerably plain that if, producing corn under the same conditions as previous to 1861, and getting for it the same price in foreign markets, he has to pay a higher price for every article of his clothing, and for every article into the composition of which coal, timber, iron, or hides enter, his real remuneration can not but be considerably less than if all these things could be obtained at free-trade prices. And the case of the farmer is not isolated: it is that of the workers in every department of industry, and exhibits unequivocally the net outcome of the protectionist experiment which commenced with the passing of the Morrill tariff. Protectionists then undertook to secure for the protected interests of their country as high industrial rewards as are reaped in the most flourishing branches of United States production—and, it may be allowed, they have succeeded in their venturous enterprise. But how? Simply by lowering universally the level of those rewards; by enforcing, through the medium of artificially enhanced prices, a huge deduction from the income of the community at large, and handing over the proceeds to the protected trades. Such is the upshot of this notable attempt to transcend physical laws, and to secure by legislation what nature has denied.

§ 7. In the foregoing examination of the working of Protection in the United States, the argument has been confined to what may be considered its purely economic side. It is not uncommon, however, to hear the system defended on social and political grounds; and it may, therefore, be well, before taking leave of the subject, to make some brief reference to this other aspect of the case. For example, the position is sometimes taken that, admitting all that can be urged economically in favor of free trade, a nation has yet other interests to take account of than the production and distribution of wealth; it has to consider its moral, social, and political advancement—ends to which the working of free trade, it is alleged, is not always favorable. For the tendency of free trade, even on the showing of its supporters, it is argued, is to turn the industry of a nation mainly into a few channels—those channels, namely, in which it happens to enjoy, in relation to competing nations, exceptional advantages, so that, in the practical result, the nation adopting it is compelled to confine its industry within comparatively narrow bounds. Free trade thus tends to circumscribe industrial experience; and, by doing so, to interfere with that practical education which a nation derives from the prosecution of industry. Far better, it is urged, deliberately to sacrifice some of the results of material prosperity, if by this means we can secure scope for a wider and more diversified cultivation, such as is furnished by an industry branching in numerous directions and offering to enterprise a varied field.

I can not deny that there is a certain basis of truth in the considerations just stated; and that circumstances may even be imagined in which they would possess real cogency. Indeed, the United States themselves at one time presented the world with a remarkable example in point. Free trade, as I had once occasion to point out, constituted undoubtedly one of the main supports of slavery in the South; for by its means Southern slave-masters were enabled, while employing their thralls in the few crude industries in which alone their labor was efficient, to command all the comforts and luxuries of civilized existence. Free trade thus undoubtedly favored, and rendered possible, the low state of civilization which up to 1860 was characteristic of the southern portion of the United States. Had that part of the country been dependent exclusively or mainly on its own industry for the direct supply of its material wants, a greater variety of industrial occupations would have been necessary. At the least a considerable portion of the negro population must have been educated and trained to mechanical pursuits, and a foundation would thus have been laid for social progress. It must be owned, therefore, that the line of argument we are considering is not without a certain support in the facts of past experience; an admission, however, which amounts to no more than this, that barbarism and tyranny have sometimes gained in strength by availing themselves of the expedients of civilization. But the practical question is, not whether under extraordinary and exceptional circumstances free trade may be made to serve the purposes of despotism, but whether in a country, such as the United States, of great and varied resources, peopled by free men in possession of all the most advanced industrial knowledge and trained in the usages of civilization—whether in such a country, artificial restraint upon the freedom of trade is needed, in order to secure for the people that variety of occupations which, it may be freely conceded, is favorable to national development.

And here, in the first place, it must be remembered that the capacity possessed by a country of yielding particular elements of wealth is never of a uniform character, but exists in general in very great variety, according to the fertility, accessibility, or other incidents of the natural agents from which such elements are derived. As a consequence of this, commodities obtained directly from natural agents, that is to say, raw products, are raised in all countries at various costs, and as, in conformity with the well-known economic principle, it is the cost of the most costly portion raised that governs the price of the whole, it follows that the actual price at which a commodity of this description sells, depends not simply on the inherent fertility of the sources of supply, but on this taken in connection with the total quantity of the commodity produced in the country. As the richest and most accessible natural agents are those which are first resorted to, the supply, up to a certain point, is obtained at the lowest cost at which the country, in the actual state of its industry, can yield it; but as the requirements of the community increase, recourse is had to natural agents of inferior capacity, and, as population progresses, to agents of capacity inferior still; the cost of production rising with each extension of the area of cultivation, and the price with the cost of production. Now, from this law governing the cost of raw products, it results that, however superior one country may be to others in its natural capacity of yielding particular elements of wealth, it yet rarely happens that these latter are not able to encounter its competition in raising even those products in respect to which its capacity is greatest, and this under the most perfect freedom of trade. Great Britain, for example, would be said to have a natural superiority over the United States in the production of coal and iron, just as the United States would be said to have a natural superiority over Great Britain in producing corn; but in neither case is the superiority of a kind to cause the United States, under a perfectly free trade, to give up producing iron and coal, any more than to cause Great Britain to give up producing corn. The effect of free trade would not be to extinguish any of those branches of production in either country, but merely to alter the proportions in which they are carried on. Great Britain would continue, as she does now, to produce corn so far as it was profitable for her to do so, and would satisfy her remaining requirements by importation, while the United States would follow a like course in the case of iron and coal. And so also it would be with such products as lumber and leather. It may be that Canada has in these products greater resources than the United States; and it is probable that the abolition of the high import duties now imposed by the latter country would lead to some more or less considerable re-adjustment of the proportions in which the industries they occasion are now carried on; but this is a very different thing from the extinction of those industries. Probably the utmost that under the freest tariff would occur is the abandonment in the United States of some of the least productive sources of supply, combined with a corresponding extension of the area of production in Canada, while the capital now employed in the United States in developing resources which would be better reserved for another day would not be slow in finding employment in more profitable channels. It is unnecessary to pursue further this line of illustration. The same argument, it is evident, may be applied in turn to every branch of production employed in extracting commodities directly from the store-house of nature. Within this circle of industries, at all events, it may be confidently asserted that Protection does not maintain in the United States a single one which would not exist equally under free trade. It is only when her people, not content with cultivating their magnificent resources in the degree in which nature has endowed them, seek to disturb the natural proportion and to push enterprise in certain directions beyond the profitable point, that the need arises for artificial support. The tendency of Protection, therefore, at least within this particular department of industrial activity, is not to create new industries, not to diversify industrial pursuits, but to disturb the natural development of the country, and to turn capital from profitable to unprofitable fields.

So far, however, the argument applies only to the industries of raw produce—as they are called, the "extractive industries;" and, it will be urged, that it is especially in manufactures that scope would be sought for the cultivation of industrial intelligence and skill. Carried, however, even thus far, I may observe, the argument at least suffices to destroy the *raison d'être*, so far as it rests on the ground we are now considering, of a large portion of the present tariff of the United States, which makes no distinction between raw and manufactured products, but loads alike both classes with heavy duties. But though the particular considerations that are applicable to the industries of raw produce do not apply to those of manufacture, it will not be difficult to show that here also the policy of Protection is wholly unnecessary as a means of securing for a nation that help to its general progress which is furnished by variety in its industry.

At the utmost, it must be remembered, all that Protection can do for producers is to secure for them a monopoly of the home market. But, in supplying the home market, manufacturers in a country like the United States, or in any new country rich in varieties of raw material, have, for a large circle of productions, very substantial advantages, even when matched against countries of long established and highly organized industry such as Great Britain. In the first place, most kinds of raw material will in the former class of countries be cheap, much cheaper for the most part than in old countries—supposing, that is to say, that the price is not artificially raised by protective tariffs. In the next, the manufacturer is close to the source of supply, and is thus saved the cost of transport on the raw material, always a considerable item; and, lastly, he is also saved the cost of transport, which falls on his foreign competitor, in sending to market the manufactured article. On all these accounts, manufacturers in old countries like those of Western Europe lie under heavy disadvantages in competing in the home markets of countries like the United States—disadvantages which constitute for the latter countries a sort of natural protection, which can not fail to secure for them under all circumstances a considerable field for the cultivation of manufacturing industry.

But it will be urged that, the disadvantages in question notwithstanding, experience has proved that, over a considerable area of manufacturing industry, European manufacturers are capable, under free trade, of underselling those of the United States even in their own home markets. The fact is undeniable; and I can only meet the objection founded on it by asking those who urge it, whether their object is to produce a state of things in which foreign nations shall be excluded from the markets of the United States *in the sale of all commodities whatever;* for if this be their object, its attainment must, let them well understand, be tantamount to the extinction of the foreign trade of their country. If foreign merchants can find a sale for no product whatever, raised in the countries from which they come, in United States markets, they are deprived of the means by which a trade with that country is permanently possible. It must be remembered that the point we are now considering is the utility of Protection as a means of helping the social and political progress of peoples, and supposing those who advocate this view are prepared to go the lengths just described, it comes to this, that their scheme for promoting civilization amounts to a plan for putting an end to international trade — putting an end to the chief occasion, and main and most enduring motive, for the intercourse of mankind! Now it must be freely admitted that this mode of advancing human interests is not compatible with the maintenance of free trade —nay, that it is precisely on the ground of its tendency to promote the interchange of commodities among nations that free trade claims for itself the credit of being one of the principal and most powerful of civilizing agencies. It can not, therefore, be denied that under free trade American manufacturers would not improbably have to undergo the patriotic anguish of finding themselves undersold in some kinds of goods by foreign merchants in their own markets. But there would be no need for them, therefore, to despair. It by no means follows that the range of their manufacturing industry would suffer contraction: it is even exceedingly probable—I am inclined to add, certain—that it would, on the whole, be largely extended. Particular branches of manufacture now carried on would probably be brought within narrower limits, or might altogether disappear; but on the other hand, others, now barely existing, would quite certainly take fresh root, and in all probability become the staples of a new export trade; for, be it well observed, Protection is not less efficacious—I would say, is far more efficacious—to circumscribe and crush, than to sustain and encourage. Once recognized as governing the policy of a country, every industry which can make out a plausible case becomes entitled to its supposed benefits, and industries engaged in raising raw material are as anxious to be protected as others. Accordingly, in the United States, as we have seen, coal, iron, lumber, and leather are all loaded with heavy import duties. But what is the consequence? Just this, that American manufacturers are thus deprived of the advantage they would naturally possess of obtaining their raw material cheap. They are placed at a disadvantage in relation to manufacturers in Europe precisely where under free trade their position would be strongest: a necessity for Protection is created which could never arise under natural conditions of trade: in this way Protection in the end becomes its own Nemesis, and the vicious circle is complete.

I have now, I trust, shown that, at all events in such countries as the United States, Protection is not needed to secure an extensive diversity in the national industries. And when we further take account of an influence to which I have not yet referred—an influence inseparable from the maintenance of a protective system—I think I may even venture to question whether a single industry of importance is kept alive by Protection in the United States which would not equally exist there in a healthier condition in its absence. I refer now to the effect of Protection on the *morale* of industry. When once the industrial classes of a country have been taught to look to the legislature to secure them against the competition of rivals, they are apt to trust more and more to this support, and less and less to their own skill. ingenuity, and economy in conducting their business. The inevitable result is that industry becomes unprogressive wherever it is highly protected.* It was so in France in the days previous to the commercial treaty, and it is so now in the United States, as may be learned from Mr. Wells's Reports. "The French manufacturers," says M. Chevalier, "if not all, at least a large number of them, had, anterior to the treaty of commerce, a serious disadvantage —that of old and defective machinery, which augmented the cost of production. This was due to prohibition, which prevented the manufacturers from feeling the spur of foreign competition, and dispensed them from the necessity of perfecting indefinitely, and without delay, their machinery and their processes. The treaty of commerce aroused them from this apathy as if an alarm-bell had sounded. There was a general

---

* This is the conclusive reply to the plea sometimes urged in favor of Protection in young communities as supplying a shelter to nascent industries until they have struck root and are able to endure foreign competition. We all know the passage in which Mr. Mill has given a sanction to Protection when employed under such circumstances, and the use that has been made of it in some of our colonies. It would have been well at least if those who had relied on this *obiter dictum* of a great writer had taken note of the strict limitations with which he accompanied its utterance. With or without such limitations, however, I can not but think that the position is untenable. If Protection tended to develop industrial virtues, and thus to qualify for independence, one could understand that it might be usefully employed for a time under the strict limitations laid down by Mr. Mill; but inasmuch as its tendency is exactly the reverse of this, inasmuch as Protection invariably begets a need for Protection, it is not easy to see how its adoption could under any circumstances forward the object in view. How little those in the United States who have once placed themselves in the leading-strings of Protection are inclined to dispense with these helps may be seen from the following remark of Mr. Wells: "There has never been an instance in the history of the country where the representatives of such [infant] industries, who have enjoyed Protection for a long series of years, have been willing to submit to a reduction of the tariff, or have proposed it. But, on the contrary, their demands for still higher and higher duties are insatiable and never intermitted." And he proceeds to illustrate his remark by some striking examples. ("Cobden Club Essays," Second Series, p. 533.)

renewing of machinery in the numerous factories which were badly or imperfectly furnished. Each wished to place himself in this respect on a level with England. The treaty of commerce encouraged this renovation by the lowering of duties upon every thing which enters into the composition of workshop machinery; and the Treasury even advanced to a certain number of establishments considerable sums, in all 40,000,000 of francs, or $8,000,000. French industry has drawn from this transformation of its machinery (*matériel*) a new force, of which it makes proof every day, and this is a reason why to-day, face to face with foreign competition, it has a confidence which it did not know before."*

To this statement of M. Chevalier's I will only add a single example, taken from Mr. Wells's Report: "In the summer of 1867, while studying the industries of Europe, the Commissioner visited a factory the products of which had for many years found an extensive market in the United States. The product being staple, and the industry one that it was exceedingly desirable should be extended in the United States, the Commissioner studied the process of manufacture with great care, from the selection of the raw material to the packing of the finished product; the rates of wages; the intelligence of the operatives, and the hours of labor. When his investigation was completed, the Commissioner said to the foreign manufacturer—a man whose name is a household word in his own country for integrity and philanthropy—'The duty on the import of these articles into the United States is, respectively, 35 per cent. *ad valorem*, and 30 per cent. *ad valorem* and 20 cents per pound; if you have given me your prices, products of machinery, and cost of labor correctly, I do not well see how you could export your fabrics to the United States, even if there was substantially no duty, as the advantage of raw material is

---

* Quoted from a letter in the *New York World*, November 28, 1873.

mainly upon our side.' 'I am sometimes at a loss myself to account for the course of trade,' was the reply; 'but perhaps it will help you to a conclusion if I tell you that some time ago, finding ourselves pressed with German competition, we threw out our old machinery, and replaced it with a new and improved pattern; and the machinery by us rejected was sold to go to the United States.' To complete the story, it is only necessary for the Commissioner to add that the owners of this second-hand machinery have since its importation demanded and received an increased protection on its products."*

I may now sum up the general result of this latter portion of my argument: (1) As regards the industries of raw produce, Protection does not call into existence a single branch of production which would not equally have existed under free trade; it merely alters the proportions in which such industries are carried on, hindering their natural and healthy development: (2) in the domain of manufacturing industry it is equally inefficacious as a means of creating variety in industrial pursuits; for if on the one hand it secures a precarious existence for certain kinds of manufactures, on the other, by artificially enhancing the price of raw material, it discourages other kinds which in its absence would grow and flourish: while (3) over and above all these injurious effects, it vitiates the industrial atmosphere by engendering lethargy, routine, and a reliance on legislative expedients, to the great discouragement of those qualities on which, above all, successful industry mainly depends—energy, economy, and enterprise.

To conclude, having regard to the geographical position, extent of territory, and extraordinary natural resources of the United States, as well as to the character of its people, trained in all the arts of civilization, and distinguished beyond others by their eminent mechanical and business talents, there seems

---

* Mr. Wells's Report for 1868, p. 74.

no reason that they should not take a position of commanding influence in the world of commerce—a position to which no other people on earth could aspire. But, to do this, they must eschew the miserable and childish jealousy of foreign competition which is now the animating principle of their commercial policy. If they desire to command a market for their products in all quarters of the world, they must be prepared to admit the products of other countries freely to their own markets, and must learn to seek the benefits of international trade, not in the vain ambition of underselling other countries, and so making them pay tribute in gold and silver to the United States, but in that which constitutes its proper end and only rational purpose—the greater cheapening of commodities and the increased abundance and comfort which result to the whole family of mankind.

CHAPTER V.

ON SOME MINOR TOPICS.

§ 1. I propose to devote this concluding chapter on International Trade to the consideration of some topics which seem to fall more easily under this than under other headings — topics more or less involved, and in general tacitly decided in one sense or another, in most commercial and monetary discussions, but the current ideas respecting which are by no means in accordance with the main principles of international trade as these have been developed in the foregoing pages.

The first of these questions to which I would ask the reader's attention is the following: What is the interest of a country in the scale of its general prices? Is it for the advantage of the people, as a whole, that the scale should be high or low? and, assuming that they have an interest in either alternative, what is the nature of the advantage, and what are its limits? A moment's reflection will enable us to take at least one step toward the solution of our problem: the interest involved, whatever be its character and extent, can only be real so far forth as the high or low scale of prices is *not universal*—so far forth, that is to say, as it is not shared in the same degree by all countries. A country can have no permanent interest in an advance, or in a fall of prices, which embraces the whole commercial world. Such a change leaves the purchasing power of each country in relation to every other precisely where it was before; reciprocal demand, therefore, would continue unaffected, and, by consequence, international values, and all interests that depend on that relation. But where the advance or fall is not general—where the high or low scale of prices is confined to one, or to a few countries — it is not at once apparent how it may affect the interest of those concerned.

I ought here, perhaps, to refer to a maxim advanced by some writers on monetary questions which, if well founded, would seem to preclude the existence of the phenomenon, the character of which I propose to discuss. It is held by the writers to whom I refer that the value of gold is, and must ever be, "the same all the world over."* Now if this be so, as the value of gold is merely another expression for the gold prices of commodities, it must follow that a high or a low scale of general prices existing in any country, and not shared by every other, is an impossible occurrence. As there is no local value of gold, so there can be no local scale of prices. I have no hesitation, however, in expressing my opinion that the doctrine in question, with whatever confidence advanced, is absolutely destitute of foundation.† The truth on the subject

---

* It is probable that by "the value of gold" the writers in question mean to designate its value *on loan* as well as its exchange value. But a reference to the rates of interest prevailing at any given time in the principal money markets of the world will suffice at once to refute this part of the doctrine.

† It has certainly no support from any writer of authority. Ricardo says broadly: "The value of money is never the same in any two countries, depending as it does on relative taxation, on manufacturing skill, on the advantages of climate, natural productions, and many other causes." He adds — and the remark may possibly help to clear up the confusion of thought in which the maxim I am combating has originated—"This higher value of money [in a country excelling in manufactures] will not be indicated by the exchange: bills may continue to be negotiated at par, although the prices of corn and labor should be 10, 20, or 30 per cent. higher in one country than in another. . . . . When each country has precisely the quantity of money which it ought to have, money will not, indeed, be of the same value in each, for with respect to many commodities it may differ 5, 10, or even 20 per cent., but the exchange will be at par. One hundred pounds in England, or the silver which is in £100, will purchase a bill of £100, or an equal quantity of silver in France, Spain, or Holland."—"Ricardo's Works," pp. 81-84.

seems to me to be as follows: among countries commercially connected there is a large class of commodities—all those, namely, which constitute the great staples of commerce, such as corn, flour, tea, sugar, metals, and most raw materials of industry—of which the prices can not vary much in different localities. As a rule the difference of prices will not be greater than the cost of carriage between the countries of production and consumption, always, of course, excepting the case where such articles come under the operation of local fiscal laws. In the exchange for commodities of this description, the value of gold, though not the same all the world over, does not greatly vary within the range of general commerce. But besides the commodities which form the staples of commerce, there are those which, through unsuitableness for distant traffic, or owing to some other obstacle, do not enter into international trade. With regard to these, there is nothing to prevent the widest divergence in their gold prices, or, therefore, in the value of gold in relation to them, not merely in remote quarters of the world, but sometimes even in localities within the same country; and the class of goods to which this description applies—it will vary in extent with the situation of each country and the means of communication at its command—far from being insignificant, must under all circumstances include some of the most important articles of general consumption. To perceive this, it is only necessary to remember that the group includes the items of house accommodation, meat, and a large proportion of those things which fall under the head of "provisions"—a list which would have to be greatly enlarged if we had to deal with countries lying aside from the leading thoroughfares of commerce, or in which the means of communication have been imperfectly developed.

It is not true, therefore, that gold is of the same value "all the world over." On the contrary, it varies in value in different countries, and sometimes in different localities within the same country, in some degree in relation to almost all commodities, but, in relation to a numerous and important class of commodities, in a very considerable degree, and this, not merely as a temporary fluctuation, but permanently, as a normal state of things; and the problem we have now to consider is, whether, the case being so, it is advantageous for the inhabitants of a country that the scale of its prices, within the possible limits of permanent divergence, should be high or low in relation to the cosmopolitan level.

The majority of those who write or speak on commercial questions would, I imagine, have little hesitation in pronouncing in favor of the former alternative; and plainly the most obvious appearances support this view. A high scale of prices and large accumulated wealth for the most part go together, while low prices are the incident of districts remote from the main current of civilization, and in general poor and barbarous. If we inquire, however, as to the nature of the connection between the phenomena in each case, the answer does not by any means lie upon the surface. Let it be remembered that a difference in local prices, if considerable and permanent, can only exist in the case of commodities which can not be made the subject of foreign commerce. High prices, therefore, can not serve us in our dealings with foreign nations, and it is not by any means clear how the people of a country can be profited by exchanging their goods among themselves on a high pecuniary scale. Moreover it is evident that, with regard to those commodities which do enter into foreign commerce, it is the interest of each competing nation that their prices should be relatively as low as possible; this being the condition of commanding a sale for them in neutral markets. Granting, therefore, that high prices and accumulated wealth on the one hand, and low prices and poverty on the other, are generally coincident phenomena, we have yet to discover wherein consists the bond that connects them.

The solution of the problem is contained in the following statement: What a nation is interested in is, not in having its prices high or low, but in having its gold cheap—understanding by cheapness* not low value, but *low cost*—a small sacrifice of ease and comfort; and it generally happens that cheap gold is accompanied by a high scale of prices. I say "generally happens," because it by no means follows as a necessary consequence that the two phenomena should go together. Gold may be cheap, and prices, at the same time, low, as a little reflection will easily convince us. The range of prices that actually prevails in a country is, speaking broadly, the resultant of two conditions—the cost at which that country produces or obtains its gold, and the cost at which it produces or obtains commodities. Fluctuations and disturbing causes apart, the gold and the commodities will exchange for each other in proportion to their costs; and cheap gold, therefore, will be the concomitant of high prices, only in so far as the cheapness incident to the gold is not shared by the other products of industry. The cheapness of gold, for example, in Australia does not occasion a high price of meat, of flour, of wool, of tallow, of hides, or of many other articles in that country, because the cost of producing those articles there is also very low. Any of them can be purchased in Australia at as low a price as in Europe: many of them, meat and wool, for example, at considerably lower prices. It is thus evident that cheap gold is no necessary concomitant of a high scale of prices. We must, therefore, distinguish between the two things; and, so distinguishing, I have now to show that the interest of a nation lies,

---

* This is, I admit, a departure from ordinary usage, "cheap" being more commonly applied to price or value than to cost of production. But we much need a word to express low cost as distinguished from low price or value, and it seems to me that "cheapness" may conveniently be appropriated to this purpose. At all events, having had notice of the sense in which I use the word, the reader will not be misled.

not in having its prices high, but in having its gold cheap; and that it is only in so far as high prices are an indication of cheap gold, and low prices an indication of dear gold, that either can be considered as furnishing any presumption whether in favor of or against the wealth or well-being of a community.

As I remarked just now, the problem we are considering can only arise with reference to *relative* prices. A rise or fall of prices shared by all nations equally can not affect the interest of any; and similarly the cheapness or dearness of gold—considered in the capacity in which we are now regarding it, as the instrument of general commerce, not as a commodity intended for consumption—is only of importance in so far as it is not universal. Gold cheapened everywhere and in the same degree, would mean, other things being the same, an equal and universal rise of prices, and there would obviously be no advantage in obtaining our gold at a lower cost if we were compelled to give proportionally more of it for all that we required. But assuming—what is simple matter of fact—that the cost at which different nations obtain their gold is different—that the cost may be reduced in some countries without undergoing a corresponding reduction in others—then a manifest advantage arises to a nation from the cheapness of its gold; for just in proportion as it obtains its gold at small cost—by a small expenditure of labor and abstinence—it will obtain at small cost all its imported commodities. The advantage would, indeed, be confined to its foreign trade. In domestic exchanges prices would adapt themselves to the cheapened cost of money, and in this field of its activity neither good nor evil would result for the nation as a whole; but in its dealings with foreign nations it would be otherwise. In relation to them, its position, as commanding gold on terms of exceptional cheapness, would be one of vantage, and would enable it through this cheapened medium to obtain from them, on terms correspondingly advantageous, all that they are capable of supplying.

Such is the nature of the advantage which a country derives from the relative cheapness of its gold; and, as I have already remarked, in old countries cheap gold is generally accompanied by a high scale of prices for all commodities not falling within the range of international trade. To exhibit the grounds of this connection we may take the case of Great Britain. The cost of gold is lower in Great Britain than in any country in Europe, or, we may say broadly, than in any in the world, America and Australia excepted. The evidence of this is to be found in the scale of our industrial remuneration measured in gold.* To what is the fact to be attributed? To this, that we possess in our coal, iron, and other mineral fields, combined with the skill and energy of our inhabitants, superior resources to those possessed by other countries for the production of certain manufactures in extensive demand throughout the world. Producing such manufactures at less cost than they can be produced at by other nations, and finding for them an extensive demand throughout the world, we are enabled at once to undersell other nations in neutral markets, and yet at the same time to obtain for our products a price which bears a larger proportion to their cost of production—to the labor and abstinence employed in producing them—than the price obtained by foreign nations for their products bears to the cost of such products. A given expenditure of labor and abstinence in this country thus enables us to command a larger result in gold than the same expenditure would enable foreign nations to command. In other words, we obtain our gold cheaper, while, as involved in this result, the scale of industrial remuneration, measured in gold, is higher

---

* This part of the problem has been ably worked out by Mr. Senior, in his well-known Essay, already referred to, "On the Cost of obtaining Money."

with us than with them. All this, I say, is the consequence of the great and exceptional advantages possessed by this country in certain departments of industry. We have here the explanation of our cheap gold, but not of our high scale of prices.* The explanation of the latter phenomenon lies in the fact that those industrial advantages are not general, but confined to a few departments of production. Supposing that they extended over the whole, or the greater portion, of our industrial field, our position would resemble that of some of the Australian colonies; and we should, along with cheap gold, have a low scale of general prices. In fact, however, the case is otherwise. We are in the position of an old country. Our land has all long since been appropriated, and, to supply us with food, even very inferior qualities of soil have been brought under the plow, and are cultivated at high cost. Food and provisions of all sorts, consequently, are dear; so also is house accommodation, and in general all those things which can not easily be made the subject of international commerce. In these respects we enjoy no special advantages over other nations: in obtaining gold, however, as has been shown, we do possess such advantages. Gold, therefore, with us exchanges in larger proportion against all this class of commodities than in other countries; but this is only in other words to say that the scale of prices over this area of exchange is higher here than in them. High prices, thus, in England are a consequence of cheap gold; and our cheap gold enables us to command, on terms proportionally favorable, the products of other countries. But we should equally enjoy this advantage, while we should also enjoy others in addition, if, having our gold as cheap as now, our scale of prices was at the same time as low as in other countries; for this would imply that our industry

---

* Points which Mr. Senior omitted to discriminate, as Mr. Mill has pointed out. See "Principles of Political Economy," vol. ii., p. 157.

was as productive in all its departments as in those through which we obtain our gold. It can not, therefore, be said that high prices are in themselves advantageous to a country: nevertheless, in so far as they are an indication of cheap gold, they are an evidence that the country in which they exist occupies a position of vantage in the world of commerce, and high prices will therefore, under such circumstances, generally be accompanied with commercial prosperity and large accumulated wealth. There is just one exception to this statement. It occurs where the scale of prices is raised through the operation of a protective tariff. Gold might, in this case, be cheap, and yet none of the advantages of cheap gold would follow; for, as I have explained, it is only through foreign trade that those advantages are realized, and just in so far as Protection is operative, the country maintaining it will be excluded from foreign trade. Countries, therefore, in which prices are kept high by Protection, are in the singular position of securing cheap gold, subject to the condition that it shall *not* be spent in the only market where advantage would arise from its cheapness.

§ 2. So much I have thought it worth while to say on the subject of high and low prices. I now turn to another topic, also much implicated in commercial discussions, and on which some strange notions would seem to be afloat. That a nation is enriched by its foreign trade is mostly taken for granted, and with good reason; but what is the nature of the gain? and by what standard are we to measure its amount? We are all familiar with the doctrine of the Balance of Trade, according to which celebrated theory the gain on foreign trade was measured by the excess of exports over imports, and consisted in the gold and silver which were supposed to come from foreign countries in liquidation of the balance. That view is now, I suppose, pretty generally abandoned. But I have observed of late, both in the press and among parliamentary speakers, a curious modern inversion of the ancient doctrine. I have seen it laid down, with much exultation over the ignorance of our ancestors, that the gain in our foreign commerce, instead of being measured, as was formerly thought, by the excess of exports over imports, is, on the contrary, measured by the excess of imports over exports. A contributor to an important provincial paper, writing some time since under the influence of this notion, calculated that the gain of England from her foreign trade amounted to about £100,000,000 sterling; this being about the amount by which her imports in that year exceeded her exports. If I mistake not, it was a part of the doctrine that this sum represented the profits of our merchants engaged in foreign trade. The reader who has followed the explanations given in a former chapter of the causes governing the relation of exports and imports in the external trade of countries will not need any further refutation of this extravagant notion. I may just add, as a sufficient *reductio ad absurdum*, that, inasmuch as the external trade of many prosperous communities exhibits a constant excess of exports over imports, it would follow from this view that all such communities are undergoing a steady course of impoverishment, and that those of their inhabitants who engage in foreign trade only incur losses on their investments. Such speculations show how little the Political Economy of some among us is in advance of the ideas of the seventeenth century.

Another method by which it is frequently attempted to estimate the gain on foreign trade proceeds on the assumption that such gain is identical with the mercantile profits accruing upon the capital thus invested. This view is only less absurd than the former in not identifying the amount of mercantile profit with the balance on the external trade. According to it, if we suppose the total capital embarked in the foreign trade of Great Britain to be £500,000,000, and the rate of profit £10 per cent., it would follow that the gain to the country upon her foreign trade would be represented by £50,000,000 sterling. This way of regarding the subject is, I imagine, sufficiently prevalent among our mercantile classes; but it only affords a proof the more how very little those classes have yet contrived to appropriate of the elementary truths of the science in whose name they so often speak. The notion betrays a fundamental misconception of the nature, not merely of foreign trade, but of all trade, and of the end and purpose for which it exists. "Consumption," says Adam Smith, "is the end and purpose of all production." .... "The maxim," he observes, "is so perfectly self-evident that it would be absurd to attempt to prove it." Not less self-evident is it that the end and purpose of all trade is to cheapen production, and so to minister more effectually to the ultimate end—the need of the consumer. But the gain upon trade must surely consist in the degree in which it fulfills its proper end—must, therefore, consist, not in the profits of traders, but in the advantage which it brings to those for whose behoof the trader exists. It is true the trader's motive when engaging in trade is to make a profit; but not the less is his *raison d'être* as a trader to minister to the wants of others. He must have his profit, or he will cease to trade; but his profit, though an incident of the good resulting from his office, is not the measure of it. The measure of the service which he renders—of the importance of his function—is not this, but the benefit he confers on the community whose servant he is; and this benefit is great in proportion to his success in serving the consumer; in other words, in cheapening commodities—in diminishing the obstacles which exist to the satisfaction of human wants. Nothing, therefore, can betray a more profound misconception of the true nature of trade and the purpose for which it exists than to represent the advantages derivable from it as measured by the profits of the agents who carry it on. It would be just as reasonable to represent the advantages of learning as measured by the salaries of teachers.

What, then, is the true criterion of the gain on foreign trade? I reply, the degree in which it cheapens* commodities, and renders them more abundant. Foreign trade not merely supplies us with commodities more cheaply than we could produce them from our own resources, but supplies us with many commodities which, without it, we could not obtain at all. The degree in which it does this is the true criterion and measure of the gain, but it is a measure which palpably does not admit of being applied in practice. To determine the amount or extent of the advantage derivable from foreign trade is, and, I venture to say, must ever be, an absolutely insoluble problem—a truth which will be sufficiently apparent if we advert to some of the data on which its solution depends.

As I have just said, one portion of the gain derived from foreign trade consists in the supply it yields us of commodities not capable of being produced in our own country. Great Britain, for example, obtains in this way her tea and sugar; and it will, perhaps, be thought that the satisfaction derived from the consumption of these articles constitutes the gain to the British consumer upon so much of our foreign trade. Even if this were so, it is pretty evident that the satisfaction in question is not capable of quantitative measurement. But, in point of fact, the problem is far more complicated than such a solution supposes; for it must not be forgotten that, in the event of our being excluded from the countries which furnish us with tea and sugar, we should have at our disposal all the capital now employed in producing the commodities in exchange for which tea and sugar are now obtained. This capital would then be available for the production of substitutes,

---

* The reader will bear in mind the sense in which I use "cheapen"—viz., as equivalent to lowering cost, to reducing the sacrifices involved in procuring a commodity.

or, in case none were forthcoming, for the production of other things; and the gain upon this portion of our foreign trade would be represented by the difference between the advantage conferred on the community by its present supply of tea and sugar, and that which it would receive from the substitutes, or other things, whatever these might be, which, in their absence, we might produce from our own resources. But, as we have no means of measuring accurately the satisfactions which we at present enjoy from the consumption of the articles in question, and still less of measuring those which we might derive from such things as in their absence we might provide ourselves with, it is evident that an accurate, or even an approximate, determination of the advantages accruing to us from our foreign commerce, so far at least as its function is to furnish us with articles we can not ourselves produce, is absolutely beyond our reach. All we can say with confidence is that the tastes and wants which are now satisfied through this service of foreign commerce are of a more imperious kind than any which our labor and capital, employed upon the materials furnished to us by our own country, are capable of satisfying: since, if it were not so, so much of our foreign trade as it represents would not exist. We are thus justified in concluding that there is a real gain, but beyond this our data do not carry us. We are absolutely without the means of estimating its amount.

So much for one portion of our foreign trade. With regard to that more important part of it, of which the function is not to supply us with commodities which we are incapable of producing, but to cheapen those which we might produce, the case might here seem to be more manageable. In order to ascertain the gain on this part of our trade, the data necessary would be, first, a determination of the cost at which we actually obtain our imported articles of the class under consideration; and, secondly, a determination of that at which we could produce them if thrown upon our own resources. The difference would represent what we gain by importation, and the data might seem to be not beyond our reach. When, however, we come to look closely at the problem, we find ourselves once more estopped by insuperable difficulties; for, to take a simple illustration—on the supposition that we import from foreign countries 10,000,000 quarters of wheat, how are we to estimate the gain which the nation derives from obtaining so much of its food in this way? We know, indeed, or we may ascertain, at least approximately, the cost in labor and abstinence of the 10,000,000 quarters of wheat which we import. It would be represented by the cost of the commodities which we export to pay for them. We know again, or we may ascertain, the cost at which wheat is now raised in this country, when grown under conditions which determine its average selling price. But what we do not know, and what we have no possible means of ascertaining, is the cost at which an addition of 10,000,000 quarters to our present home supply could be produced from the soil of Great Britain. Inasmuch as, in order to produce this quantity, it would be necessary to bring under cultivation for wheat soils far inferior to any now devoted to that purpose, we may be quite confident that the cost would be immensely greater than any portion of our home supply is now raised at; immensely greater, therefore,* than that at which we obtain the quantity now imported; but by how much greater we are absolutely without the means of determining—I might almost say, of conjecturing; and it is evident that the same argument applies with equal force to every article of raw produce that we import. It follows that, with regard to commodities capable of being produced in the coun-

---

* Home and imported wheat, quality for quality, selling in the same market at the same price, and the average price of home wheat being governed by the cost of producing the most costly portion, it follows that this cost will represent to us the cost of the imported portion of our wheat supply.

try, no less than with regard to those which can only be obtained from foreign sources, the data for ascertaining the quantum of gain accruing to us from foreign trade are absolutely wanting. We know the nature of the gain: it consists in extending the range of our satisfactions, and in cheapening the cost at which such as in its absence would not be beyond our reach are obtained; and we know that the amount which it brings to us under each of these categories can not but be very great; but beyond this indefinite and vague result our data do not enable us to pass.

THE END.

VALUABLE & INTERESTING WORKS

FOR PUBLIC AND PRIVATE LIBRARIES,

PUBLISHED BY HARPER & BROTHERS, NEW YORK.

☞ *For a full List of Books suitable for Libraries, see* HARPER & BROTHERS' TRADE-LIST *and* CATALOGUE, *which may be had gratuitously on application to the Publishers personally, or by letter enclosing* SIX CENTS *in Postage Stamps.*

☞ HARPER & BROTHERS *will send any of the following works by mail, postage prepaid, to any part of the United States, on receipt of the price.*

FLAMMARION'S ATMOSPHERE. The Atmosphere. Translated from the French of CAMILLE FLAMMARION. Edited by JAMES GLAISHER, F.R.S., Superintendent of the Magnetical and Meteorological Department of the Royal Observatory at Greenwich. With 10 Chromo-Lithographs and 86 Woodcuts. 8vo, Cloth, $6 00.

HUDSON'S HISTORY OF JOURNALISM. Journalism in the United States, from 1690 to 1872. By FREDERICK HUDSON. Crown 8vo, Cloth, $5 00.

PIKE'S SUB-TROPICAL RAMBLES. Sub-Tropical Rambles in the Land of the Aphanapteryx. By NICOLAS PIKE, U. S. Consul, Port Louis, Mauritius. Profusely Illustrated from the Author's own Sketches; containing also Maps and Valuable Meteorological Charts. Crown 8vo, Cloth, $3 50.

TYERMAN'S OXFORD METHODISTS. The Oxford Methodists: Memoirs of the Rev. Messrs. Clayton, Ingham, Gambold, Hervey, and Broughton, with Biographical Notices of others. By the Rev. L. TYERMAN, Author of "Life and Times of the Rev. John Wesley," &c. Crown 8vo, Cloth, $2 50.

TRISTRAM'S THE LAND OF MOAB. The Result of Travels and Discoveries on the East Side of the Dead Sea and the Jordan. By H.B. TRISTRAM, M.A., LL.D., F.R.S., Master of the Greatham Hospital, and Hon. Canon of Durham. With a Chapter on the Persian Palace of Mashita, by JAS. FERGUSON, F.R.S. With Map and Illustrations. Crown 8vo, Cloth, $2 50.

SANTO DOMINGO, Past and Present; with a Glance at Hayti. By SAMUEL HAZARD. Maps and Illustrations. Crown 8vo, Cloth, $3 50.

SMILES'S HUGUENOTS AFTER THE REVOCATION. The Huguenots in France after the Revocation of the Edict of Nantes; with a Visit to the Country of the Vaudois. By SAMUEL SMILES, Author of "The Huguenots: their Settlements, Churches, and Industries in England and Ireland," "Self-Help," "Character," "Life of the Stephensons," &c. Crown 8vo, Cloth, $2 00.

HERVEY'S CHRISTIAN RHETORIC. A System of Christian Rhetoric, for the Use of Preachers and Other Speakers. By GEORGE WINFRED HERVEY, M.A., Author of "Rhetoric of Conversation," &c. 8vo, Cloth, $3 50.

EVANGELICAL ALLIANCE CONFERENCE, 1873. History, Essays, Orations, and Other Documents of the Sixth General Conference of the Evangelical Alliance, held in New York, Oct. 2-12, 1873. Edited by Rev. PHILIP SCHAFF, D.D., and Rev. S. IRENÆUS PRIME, D.D. With Portraits of Rev. Messrs. Pronier, Carrasco, and Cook, recently deceased. 8vo, Cloth, nearly 800 pages, $6 00.

PRIME'S I GO A-FISHING. I Go a-Fishing. By W. C. PRIME. Crown 8vo, Cloth, $2 50.

ANNUAL RECORD OF SCIENCE AND INDUSTRY FOR 1873. Edited by Prof. SPENCER F. BAIRD, of the Smithsonian Institution, with the Assistance of Eminent Men of Science. 12mo, over 800 pp., Cloth, $2 00. (Uniform with the *Annual Record of Science and Industry for* 1871 *and* 1872. 12mo, Cloth, $2 00.)

VINCENT'S LAND OF THE WHITE ELEPHANT. The Land of the White Elephant: Sights and Scenes in Southeastern Asia. A Personal Narrative of Travel and Adventure in Farther India, embracing the Countries of Burma, Siam, Cambodia, and Cochin-China (1871-2). By FRANK VINCENT, Jr. Magnificently illustrated with Map, Plans, and numerous Woodcuts. Crown 8vo, Cloth, $3 50.

MOTLEY'S LIFE AND DEATH OF JOHN OF BARNEVELD. Life and Death of John of Barneveld, Advocate of Holland. With a View of the Primary Causes and Movements of "The Thirty Years' War." By JOHN LOTHROP MOTLEY, D.C.L., Author of "The Rise of the Dutch Republic," "History of the United Netherlands," &c. With Illustrations. In Two Volumes. 8vo, Cloth, $7 00.

TYNG ON A CHRISTIAN PASTOR. The Office and Duty of a Christian Pastor. By STEPHEN H. TYNG, D.D., Rector of St. George's Church in the City of New York. Published at the request of the Students and Faculty of the School of Theology in the Boston University. 12mo, Cloth, $1 25.

PLUMER'S PASTORAL THEOLOGY. Hints and Helps in Pastoral Theology. By WILLIAM S. PLUMER, D.D., LL.D. 12mo, Cloth, $2 00.

2 Harper & Brothers' Valuable and Interesting Works.

POETS OF THE NINETEENTH CENTURY. The Poets of the Nineteenth Century. Selected and Edited by the Rev. ROBERT ARIS WILLMOTT. With English and American Additions, arranged by EVERT A. DUYCKINCK, Editor of "Cyclopædia of American Literature." Comprising Selections from the Greatest Authors of the Age. Superbly Illustrated with 141 Engravings from Designs by the most Eminent Artists. In elegant small 4to form, printed on Superfine Tinted Paper, richly bound in extra Cloth, Beveled, Gilt Edges, $5 00; Half Calf, $5 50; Full Turkey Morocco, $9 00.

THE REVISION OF THE ENGLISH VERSION OF THE NEW TESTAMENT. With an Introduction by the Rev. P. SCHAFF, D.D. 618 pp., Crown 8vo, Cloth, $3 00.
This work embraces in one volume:
I. ON A FRESH REVISION OF THE ENGLISH NEW TESTAMENT. By J. B. LIGHTFOOT, D.D., Canon of St. Paul's, and Hulsean Professor of Divinity, Cambridge. Second Edition, Revised. 196 pp.
II. ON THE AUTHORIZED VERSION OF THE NEW TESTAMENT in Connection with some Recent Proposals for its Revision. By RICHARD CHENEVIX TRENCH, D.D., Archbishop of Dublin. 194 pp.
III. CONSIDERATIONS ON THE REVISION OF THE ENGLISH VERSION OF THE NEW TESTAMENT. By J. C. ELLICOTT, D.D., Bishop of Gloucester and Bristol. 178 pp.

NORDHOFF'S CALIFORNIA. California: For Health, Pleasure, and Residence. A Book for Travelers and Settlers. Illustrated. 8vo, Paper, $2 00; Cloth, $2 50.

MOTLEY'S DUTCH REPUBLIC. The Rise of the Dutch Republic. By JOHN LOTHROP MOTLEY, LL.D., D.C.L. With a Portrait of William of Orange. 3 vols., 8vo, Cloth, $10 50.

MOTLEY'S UNITED NETHERLAND'S. History of the United Netherlands: from the Death of William the Silent to the Twelve Years' Truce—1609. With a full View of the English-Dutch Struggle against Spain, and of the Origin and Destruction of the Spanish Armada. By JOHN LOTHROP MOTLEY, LL.D., D.C.L. Portraits. 4 vols., 8vo, Cloth, $14 00.

NAPOLEON'S LIFE OF CÆSAR. The History of Julius Cæsar. By His late Imperial Majesty NAPOLEON III. Two Volumes ready. Library Edition, 8vo, Cloth, $3 50 per vol.
Maps to Vols. I. and II. sold separately. Price $1 50 each, NET.

HAYDN'S DICTIONARY OF DATES, relating to all Ages and Nations. For Universal Reference. Edited by BENJAMIN VINCENT, Assistant Secretary and Keeper of the Library of the Royal Institution of Great Britain; and Revised for the Use of American Readers. 8vo, Cloth, $5 00; Sheep, $6 00.

MACGREGOR'S ROB ROY ON THE JORDAN. The Rob Roy on the Jordan, Nile, Red Sea, and Gennesareth, &c. A Canoe Cruise in Palestine and Egypt, and the Waters of Damascus. By J. MACGREGOR, M.A. With Maps and Illustrations. Crown 8vo, Cloth, $2 50.

WALLACE'S MALAY ARCHIPELAGO. The Malay Archipelago: the Land of the Orang-Utan and the Bird of Paradise. A Narrative of Travel, 1854-1862. With Studies of Man and Nature. By ALFRED RUSSEL WALLACE. With Ten Maps and Fifty-one Elegant Illustrations. Crown 8vo, Cloth, $2 50.

WHYMPER'S ALASKA. Travel and Adventure in the Territory of Alaska, formerly Russian America—now Ceded to the United States—and in various other parts of the North Pacific. By FREDERICK WHYMPER. With Map and Illustrations. Crown 8vo, Cloth, $2 50.

ORTON'S ANDES AND THE AMAZON. The Andes and the Amazon; or, Across the Continent of South America. By JAMES ORTON, M.A., Professor of Natural History in Vassar College, Poughkeepsie, N. Y., and Corresponding Member of the Academy of Natural Sciences, Philadelphia. With a New Map of Equatorial America and numerous Illustrations. Crown 8vo, Cloth, $2 00.

WINCHELL'S SKETCHES OF CREATION. Sketches of Creation: a Popular View of some of the Grand Conclusions of the Sciences in reference to the History of Matter and of Life. Together with a Statement of the Intimations of Science respecting the Primordial Condition and the Ultimate Destiny of the Earth and the Solar System. By ALEXANDER WINCHELL, LL.D., Professor of Geology, Zoology, and Botany in the University of Michigan, and Director of the State Geological Survey. With Illustrations. 12mo, Cloth, $2 00.

WHITE'S MASSACRE OF ST. BARTHOLOMEW. The Massacre of St. Bartholomew: Preceded by a History of the Religious Wars in the Reign of Charles IX. By HENRY WHITE, M.A. With Illustrations. 8vo, Cloth, $1 75.

RECLUS'S THE EARTH. The Earth: a Descriptive History of the Phenomena and Life of the Globe. By ÉLISÉE RECLUS. Translated by the late B. B. Woodward, and Edited by Henry Woodward. With 234 Maps and Illustrations, and 23 Page Maps printed in Colors. 8vo, Cloth, $5 00.

RECLUS'S OCEAN. The Ocean, Atmosphere, and Life. Being the Second Series of a Descriptive History of the Life of the Globe. By ÉLISÉE RECLUS. Profusely Illustrated with 250 Maps or Figures, and 27 Maps printed in Colors. 8vo, Cloth, $6 00.

Harper & Brothers' Valuable and Interesting Works. 3

LOSSING'S FIELD-BOOK OF THE REVOLUTION. Pictorial Field-Book of the Revolution; or, Illustrations, by Pen and Pencil, of the History, Biography, Scenery, Relics, and Traditions of the War for Independence. By BENSON J. LOSSING. 2 vols., 8vo, Cloth, $14 00; Sheep, $15 00; Half Calf, $18 00; Full Turkey Morocco, $22 00.

LOSSING'S FIELD-BOOK OF THE WAR OF 1812. Pictorial Field-Book of the War of 1812; or, Illustrations, by Pen and Pencil, of the History, Biography, Scenery, Relics, and Traditions of the Last War for American Independence. By BENSON J. LOSSING. With several hundred Engravings on Wood, by Lossing and Barritt, chiefly from Original Sketches by the Author. 1088 pages, 8vo, Cloth, $7 00; Sheep, $8 50; Half Calf, $10 00.

ALFORD'S GREEK TESTAMENT. The Greek Testament: with a critically revised Text; a Digest of Various Readings; Marginal References to Verbal and Idiomatic Usage; Prolegomena; and a Critical and Exegetical Commentary. For the Use of Theological Students and Ministers. By HENRY ALFORD, D.D., Dean of Canterbury. Vol. I., containing the Four Gospels. 944 pages, 8vo, Cloth, $6 00; Sheep, $6 50.

ABBOTT'S FREDERICK THE GREAT. The History of Frederick the Second, called Frederick the Great. By JOHN S. C. ABBOTT. Elegantly Illustrated. 8vo, Cloth, $5 00.

ABBOTT'S HISTORY OF THE FRENCH REVOLUTION. The French Revolution of 1789, as viewed in the Light of Republican Institutions. By JOHN S. C. ABBOTT. With 100 Engravings. 8vo, Cloth, $5 00.

ABBOTT'S NAPOLEON BONAPARTE. The History of Napoleon Bonaparte. By JOHN S. C. ABBOTT. With Maps, Woodcuts, and Portraits on Steel. 2 vols., 8vo, Cloth, $10 00.

ABBOTT'S NAPOLEON AT ST. HELENA; or, Interesting Anecdotes and Remarkable Conversations of the Emperor during the Five and a Half Years of his Captivity. Collected from the Memorials of Las Casas, O'Meara, Montholon, Antommarchi, and others. By JOHN S. C. ABBOTT. With Illustrations. 8vo, Cloth, $5 00.

ADDISON'S COMPLETE WORKS. The Works of Joseph Addison, embracing the whole of the "Spectator." Complete in 3 vols., 8vo, Cloth, $6 00.

ALCOCK'S JAPAN. The Capital of the Tycoon: a Narrative of a Three Years' Residence in Japan. By Sir RUTHERFORD ALCOCK, K.C.B., Her Majesty's Envoy Extraordinary and Minister Plenipotentiary in Japan. With Maps and Engravings. 2 vols., 12mo, Cloth, $3 50.

✓ ALISON'S HISTORY OF EUROPE. FIRST SERIES: From the Commencement of the French Revolution, in 1789, to the Restoration of the Bourbons, in 1815. [In addition to the Notes on Chapter LXXVI., which correct the errors of the original work concerning the United States, a copious Analytical Index has been appended to this American edition.] SECOND SERIES: From the Fall of Napoleon, in 1815, to the Accession of Louis Napoleon, in 1852. 8 vols., 8vo, Cloth, $16 00.

✓ BALDWIN'S PRE-HISTORIC NATIONS. Pre-Historic Nations; or, Inquiries concerning some of the Great Peoples and Civilizations of Antiquity, and their Probable Relation to a still Older Civilization of the Ethiopians or Cushites of Arabia. By JOHN D. BALDWIN, Member of the American Oriental Society. 12mo, Cloth, $1 75.

BARTH'S NORTH AND CENTRAL AFRICA. Travels and Discoveries in North and Central Africa: being a Journal of an Expedition undertaken under the Auspices of H. B. M.'s Government, in the Years 1849-1855. By HENRY BARTH, Ph.D., D.C.L. Illustrated. 3 vols., 8vo, Cloth, $12 00.

HENRY WARD BEECHER'S SERMONS. Sermons by HENRY WARD BEECHER, Plymouth Church, Brooklyn. Selected from Published and Unpublished Discourses, and Revised by their Author. With Steel Portrait. Complete in 2 vols., 8vo, Cloth, $5 00.

LYMAN BEECHER'S AUTOBIOGRAPHY, &c. Autobiography, Correspondence, &c., of Lyman Beecher, D.D. Edited by his Son, CHARLES BEECHER. With Three Steel Portraits, and Engravings on Wood. In 2 vols., 12mo, Cloth, $5 00.

BOSWELL'S JOHNSON. The Life of Samuel Johnson, LL.D. Including a Journey to the Hebrides. By JAMES BOSWELL, Esq. A New Edition, with numerous Additions and Notes. By JOHN WILSON CROKER, LL.D., F.R.S. Portrait of Boswell. 2 vols., 8vo, Cloth, $4 00.

SARA COLERIDGE'S MEMOIR AND LETTERS. Memoir and Letters of Sara Coleridge. Edited by her Daughter. With Two Portraits on Steel. Crown 8vo, Cloth, $2 50.

SHAKSPEARE. The Dramatic Works of William Shakspeare, with the Corrections and Illustrations of Dr. JOHNSON G. STEEVENS, and others. Revised by ISAAC REED. Engravings. 6 vols., Royal 12mo, Cloth, $9 00.

4   Harper & Brothers' Valuable and Interesting Works.

DRAPER'S CIVIL WAR. History of the American Civil War. By JOHN W. DRAPER, M.D., LL.D., Professor of Chemistry and Physiology in the University of New York. In Three Vols. 8vo, Cloth, $3 50 per vol.

DRAPER'S INTELLECTUAL DEVELOPMENT OF EUROPE. A History of the Intellectual Development of Europe. By JOHN W. DRAPER, M.D., LL.D., Professor of Chemistry and Physiology in the University of New York. 8vo, Cloth, $5 00

DRAPER'S AMERICAN CIVIL POLICY. Thoughts on the Future Civil Policy of America. By JOHN W. DRAPER, M.D., LL.D., Professor of Chemistry and Physiology in the University of New York. Crown 8vo, Cloth, $2 50.

DU CHAILLU'S AFRICA. Explorations and Adventures in Equatorial Africa with Accounts of the Manners and Customs of the People, and of the Chase of the Gorilla, the Crocodile, Leopard, Elephant, Hippopotamus, and other Animals. By PAUL B. DU CHAILLU. Numerous Illustrations. 8vo, Cloth, $5 00.

BELLOWS'S OLD WORLD. The Old World in its New Face: Impressions of Europe in 1867-1868. By HENRY W. BELLOWS. 2 vols., 12mo, Cloth, $3 50.

BRODHEAD'S HISTORY OF NEW YORK. History of the State of New York. By JOHN ROMEYN BRODHEAD. 1609-1691. 2 vols. 8vo, Cloth, $3 00 per vol.

BROUGHAM'S AUTOBIOGRAPHY. Life and Times of HENRY, LORD BROUGHAM. Written by Himself. In Three Volumes. 12mo, Cloth, $2 00 per vol.

BULWER'S PROSE WORKS. Miscellaneous Prose Works of Edward Bulwer, Lord Lytton. 2 vols., 12mo, Cloth, $3 50.

BULWER'S HORACE. The Odes and Epodes of Horace. A Metrical Translation into English. With Introduction and Commentaries. By LORD LYTTON. With Latin Text from the Editions of Orelli, Macleane, and Yonge. 12mo, Cloth, $1 75.

BULWER'S KING ARTHUR. A Poem. By EARL LYTTON. New Edition. 12mo, Cloth, $1 75.

BURNS'S LIFE AND WORKS. The Life and Works of Robert Burns. Edited by ROBERT CHAMBERS. 4 vols., 12mo, Cloth, $6 00.

REINDEER, DOGS, AND SNOW-SHOES. A Journal of Siberian Travel and Explorations made in the Years 1865-'67. By RICHARD J. BUSH, late of the Russo-American Telegraph Expedition. Illustrated. Crown 8vo, Cloth, $3 00.

CARLYLE'S FREDERICK THE GREAT. History of Friedrich II., called Frederick the Great. By THOMAS CARLYLE. Portraits, Maps, Plans, &c. 6 vols., 12mo, Cloth, $12 00.

CARLYLE'S FRENCH REVOLUTION. History of the French Revolution. Newly Revised by the Author, with Index, &c. 2 vols., 12mo, Cloth, $3 50.

CARLYLE'S OLIVER CROMWELL. Letters and Speeches of Oliver Cromwell. With Elucidations and Connecting Narrative. 2 vols., 12mo, Cloth, $3 50.

CHALMERS'S POSTHUMOUS WORKS. The Posthumous Works of Dr. Chalmers. Edited by his Son-in-Law, Rev. WILLIAM HANNA, LL.D. Complete in 9 vols., 12mo, Cloth, $13 50.

COLERIDGE'S COMPLETE WORKS. The Complete Works of Samuel Taylor Coleridge. With an Introductory Essay upon his Philosophical and Theological Opinions. Edited by Professor SHEDD. Complete in Seven Vols. With a fine Portrait. Small 8vo, Cloth, $10 50.

DOOLITTLE'S CHINA. Social Life of the Chinese: with some Account of their Religious, Governmental, Educational, and Business Customs and Opinions. With special but not exclusive Reference to Fuhchau. By Rev. JUSTUS DOOLITTLE, Fourteen Years Member of the Fuhchau Mission of the American Board. Illustrated with more than 150 characteristic Engravings on Wood. 2 vols., 12mo, Cloth, $5 00.

GIBBON'S ROME. History of the Decline and Fall of the Roman Empire. By EDWARD GIBBON. With Notes by Rev. H. H. MILMAN and M. GUIZOT. A new cheap Edition. To which is added a complete Index of the whole Work, and a Portrait of the Author. 6 vols., 12mo, Cloth, $9 00.

HAZEN'S SCHOOL AND ARMY IN GERMANY AND FRANCE. The School and the Army in Germany and France, with a Diary of Siege Life at Versailles. By Brevet Major-General W. B. HAZEN, U.S.A., Colonel Sixth Infantry. Crown 8vo, Cloth, $2 50.

TYERMAN'S WESLEY. The Life and Times of the Rev. John Wesley, M.A. Founder of the Methodists. By the Rev. LUKE TYERMAN, Author of "The Life of Rev. Samuel Wesley." Portraits. 3 vols., Crown 8vo, Cloth, $7 50.

VÁMBÉRY'S CENTRAL ASIA. Travels in Central Asia. Being the Account of a Journey from Teheran across the Turkoman Desert, on the Eastern Shore of the Caspian, to Khiva, Bokhara, and Samarcand, performed in the Year 1863. By ARMINIUS VÁMBÉRY, Member of the Hungarian Academy of Pesth, by whom he was sent on this Scientific Mission. With Map and Woodcuts. 8vo, Cloth, $4 50.

Harper & Brothers' Valuable and Interesting Works. 5

THOMSON'S LAND AND THE BOOK. The Land and the Book; or, Biblical Illustrations drawn from the Manners and Customs, the Scenes and the Scenery of the Holy Land. By W. M. Thomson, D.D., Twenty-five Years a Missionary of the A. B. C. F. M. in Syria and Palestine. With two elaborate Maps of Palestine, an accurate Plan of Jerusalem, and several hundred Engravings, representing the Scenery, Topography, and Productions of the Holy Land, and the Costumes, Manners, and Habits of the People. 2 large 12mo vols., Cloth, $5 00.

DAVIS'S CARTHAGE. Carthage and her Remains: being an Account of the Excavations and Researches on the Site of the Phœnician Metropolis in Africa and other adjacent Places. Conducted under the Auspices of Her Majesty's Government. By Dr. Davis, F.R.G.S. Profusely Illustrated with Maps, Woodcuts, Chromo-Lithographs, &c. 8vo, Cloth, $4 00.

EDGEWORTH'S (Miss) NOVELS. With Engravings. 10 vols., 12mo, Cloth, $15 00.

GROTE'S HISTORY OF GREECE. 12 vols., 12mo, Cloth, $18 00.

HELPS'S SPANISH CONQUEST. The Spanish Conquest in America, and its Relation to the History of Slavery and to the Government of Colonies. By Arthur Helps. 4 vols., 12mo, Cloth, $6 00.

HALE'S (Mrs.) WOMAN'S RECORD. Woman's Record; or, Biographical Sketches of all Distinguished Women, from the Creation to the Present Time. Arranged in Four Eras, with Selections from Female Writers of each Era. By Mrs. Sarah Josepha Hale. Illustrated with more than 200 Portraits. 8vo, Cloth, $5 00.

HALL'S ARCTIC RESEARCHES. Arctic Researches and Life among the Esquimaux: being the Narrative of an Expedition in Search of Sir John Franklin, in the Years 1860, 1861, and 1862. By Charles Francis Hall. With Maps and 100 Illustrations. The Illustrations are from Original Drawings by Charles Parsons, Henry L. Stephens, Solomon Eytinge, W. S. L. Jewett, and Granville Perkins, after Sketches by Captain Hall. 8vo, Cloth, $5 00.

HALLAM'S CONSTITUTIONAL HISTORY OF ENGLAND, from the Accession of Henry VII. to the Death of George II. 8vo, Cloth, $2 00.

HALLAM'S LITERATURE. Introduction to the Literature of Europe during the Fifteenth, Sixteenth, and Seventeenth Centuries. By Henry Hallam. 2 vols., 8vo, Cloth, $4 00.

HALLAM'S MIDDLE AGES. State of Europe during the Middle Ages. By Henry Hallam. 8vo, Cloth, $2 00.

✔ **HILDRETH'S HISTORY OF THE UNITED STATES.** First Series: From the First Settlement of the Country to the Adoption of the Federal Constitution. Second Series: From the Adoption of the Federal Constitution to the End of the Sixteenth Congress. 6 vols., 8vo, Cloth, $18 00.

✔ **HUME'S HISTORY OF ENGLAND.** History of England, from the Invasion of Julius Cæsar to the Abdication of James II., 1688. By David Hume. A new Edition, with the Author's last Corrections and Improvements. To which is Prefixed a short Account of his Life, written by Himself. With a Portrait of the Author. 6 vols., 12mo, Cloth, $9 00.

JAY'S WORKS. Complete Works of Rev. William Jay: comprising his Sermons, Family Discourses, Morning and Evening Exercises for every Day in the Year, Family Prayers, &c. Author's enlarged Edition, revised. 3 vols., 8vo, Cloth, $6 00.

✔ **JEFFERSON'S DOMESTIC LIFE.** The Domestic Life of Thomas Jefferson: compiled from Family Letters and Reminiscences by his Great-Granddaughter, Sarah N. Randolph. With Illustrations. Crown 8vo, Illuminated Cloth, Beveled Edges, $2 50.

JOHNSON'S COMPLETE WORKS. The Works of Samuel Johnson, LL.D. With an Essay on his Life and Genius, by Arthur Murphy, Esq. Portrait of Johnson. 2 vols., 8vo, Cloth, $4 00.

✓ **KINGLAKE'S CRIMEAN WAR.** The Invasion of the Crimea, and an Account of its Progress down to the Death of Lord Raglan. By Alexander William Kinglake. With Maps and Plans. Two Vols. ready. 12mo, Cloth, $2 00 per vol.

KINGSLEY'S WEST INDIES. At Last: A Christmas in the West Indies. By Charles Kingsley. Illustrated. 12mo, Cloth, $1 50.

SPEKE'S AFRICA. Journal of the Discovery of the Source of the Nile. By Captain John Hanning Speke, Captain H.M. Indian Army, Fellow and Gold Medalist of the Royal Geographical Society, Hon. Corresponding Member and Gold Medalist of the French Geographical Society, &c. With Maps and Portraits and numerous Illustrations, chiefly from Drawings by Captain Grant. 8vo, Cloth, uniform with Livingstone, Barth, Burton, &c., $4 00.

STRICKLAND'S (Miss) QUEENS OF SCOTLAND. Lives of the Queens of Scotland and English Princesses connected with the Regal Succession of Great Britain. By Agnes Strickland. 8 vols., 12mo, Cloth, $12 00.

6   *Harper & Brothers' Valuable and Interesting Works.*

KRUMMACHER'S DAVID, KING OF ISRAEL. David, the King of Israel; a Portrait drawn from Bible History and the Book of Psalms. By FREDERICK WILLIAM KRUMMACHER, D.D., Author of "Elijah the Tishbite," &c. Translated under the express Sanction of the Author by the Rev. M. G. EASTON, M.A. With a Letter from Dr. Krummacher to his American Readers, and a Portrait. 12mo, Cloth, $1 75.

LAMB'S COMPLETE WORKS. The Works of Charles Lamb. Comprising his Letters, Poems, Essays of Elia, Essays upon Shakspeare, Hogarth, &c., and a Sketch of his Life, with the Final Memorials, by T. NOON TALFOURD. Portrait. 2 vols., 12mo, Cloth, $3 00.

LIVINGSTONE'S SOUTH AFRICA. Missionary Travels and Researches in South Africa; including a Sketch of Sixteen Years' Residence in the Interior of Africa, and a Journey from the Cape of Good Hope to Loando on the West Coast; thence across the Continent, down the River Zambesi, to the Eastern Ocean. By DAVID LIVINGSTONE, LL.D., D.C.L. With Portrait, Maps by Arrowsmith, and numerous Illustrations. 8vo, Cloth, $4 50.

LIVINGSTONES' ZAMBESI. Narrative of an Expedition to the Zambesi and its Tributaries, and of the Discovery of the Lakes Shirwa and Nyassa. 1858-1864. By DAVID and CHARLES LIVINGSTONE. With Map and Illustrations. 8vo, Cloth, $5 00.

M'CLINTOCK & STRONG'S CYCLOPÆDIA. Cyclopædia of Biblical, Theological, and Ecclesiastical Literature. Prepared by the Rev. JOHN M'CLINTOCK, D.D., and JAMES STRONG, S.T.D. 5 vols. now ready. Royal 8vo. Price per vol., Cloth, $5 00; Sheep, $6 00; Half Morocco, $8 00.

MARCY'S ARMY LIFE ON THE BORDER. Thirty Years of Army Life on the Border. Comprising Descriptions of the Indian Nomads of the Plains; Explorations of New Territory; a Trip across the Rocky Mountains in the Winter; Descriptions of the Habits of Different Animals found in the West, and the Methods of Hunting them; with Incidents in the Life of Different Frontier Men, &c., &c. By Brevet Brigadier-General R. B. MARCY, U.S.A., Author of "The Prairie Traveller." With numerous Illustrations. 8vo, Cloth, Beveled Edges, $3 00.

MACAULAY'S HISTORY OF ENGLAND. The History of England from the Accession of James II. By THOMAS BABINGTON MACAULAY. With an Original Portrait of the Author. 5 vols., 8vo, Cloth, $10 00; 12mo, Cloth, $7 50.

MOSHEIM'S ECCLESIASTICAL HISTORY, Ancient and Modern; in which the Rise, Progress, and Variation of Church Power are considered in their Connection with the State of Learning and Philosophy, and the Political History of Europe during that Period. Translated, with Notes, &c., by A. MACLAINE, D.D. A new Edition, continued to 1826, by C. COOTE, LL.D. 2 vols., 8vo, Cloth, $4 00.

NEVIUS'S CHINA. China and the Chinese: a General Description of the Country and its Inhabitants; its Civilization and Form of Government; its Religious and Social Institutions; its Intercourse with other Nations; and its Present Condition and Prospects. By the Rev. JOHN L. NEVIUS, Ten Years a Missionary in China. With a Map and Illustrations. 12mo, Cloth, $1 75.

THE DESERT OF THE EXODUS. Journeys on Foot in the Wilderness of the Forty Years' Wanderings; undertaken in connection with the Ordnance Survey of Sinai and the Palestine Exploration Fund. By E. H. PALMER, M.A., Lord Almoner's Professor of Arabic, and Fellow of St. John's College, Cambridge. With Maps and numerous Illustrations from Photographs and Drawings taken on the spot by the Sinai Survey Expedition and C. F. Tyrwhitt Drake. Crown 8vo, Cloth, $3 00.

OLIPHANT'S CHINA AND JAPAN. Narrative of the Earl of Elgin's Mission to China and Japan, in the Years 1857, '58, '59. By LAURENCE OLIPHANT, Private Secretary to Lord Elgin. Illustrations. 8vo, Cloth, $3 50.

OLIPHANT'S (MRS.) LIFE OF EDWARD IRVING. The Life of Edward Irving, Minister of the National Scotch Church, London. Illustrated by his Journals and Correspondence. By Mrs. OLIPHANT. Portrait. 8vo, Cloth, $3 50.

RAWLINSON'S MANUAL OF ANCIENT HISTORY. A Manual of Ancient History, from the Earliest Times to the Fall of the Western Empire. Comprising the History of Chaldæa, Assyria, Media, Babylonia, Lydia, Phœnicia, Syria, Judæa, Egypt, Carthage, Persia, Greece, Macedonia, Parthia, and Rome. By GEORGE RAWLINSON, M.A., Camden Professor of Ancient History in the University of Oxford. 12mo, Cloth, $2 50.

SMILES'S LIFE OF THE STEPHENSONS. The Life of George Stephenson, and of his Son, Robert Stephenson; comprising, also, a History of the Invention and Introduction of the Railway Locomotive. By SAMUEL SMILES, Author of "Self-Help," &c. With Steel Portraits and numerous Illustrations. 8vo, Cloth, $3 00.

SMILES'S HISTORY OF THE HUGUENOTS. The Huguenots: their Settlements, Churches, and Industries in England and Ireland. By SAMUEL SMILES. With an Appendix relating to the Huguenots in America. Crown 8vo, Cloth, $2 00.

www.ingramcontent.com/pod-product-compliance
Lightning Source LLC
Chambersburg PA
CBHW051737300426
44115CB00007B/603